The Hard Disk Companion
Second Edition

Robert Jourdain
and
The Peter Norton Computing Group

Brady Publishing

New York   London   Toronto   Sydney   Tokyo   Singapore

Brady Publishing

Brady Publishing
A division of Simon & Schuster, Inc.
15 Columbus Circle
New York, NY 10023

Manufactured in the United States of America

10 9 8 7 6 5 4 3 2 1

Library of Congress Cataloging-in-Publication Data

Norton, Peter,   1943–
    The hard disk companion / Peter Norton, Robert Jourdain, 2nd ed.
        p.   cm.
        Includes index.
        1. Hard disk management.   I. Jourdain, Robert,   1950–
    II. Title.
QA76.9.H35N67   1991   91-4057
004.5'6—dc20   CIP
        ISBN 0-13-658782-8 :

Limits of Liability and Disclaimer of Warranty

Contents

Introduction   xiii

Chapter 1   Much More Than a Giant Diskette   1

Inside Hard Disk Technology   4
What, Where, and How to Buy   5
Installation and Setup   5
Navigating the Disk   5
Organizing Your Files   5
Optimizing Speed and Productivity   6
Backups Without Pain   6
Surviving Hard Disk Disasters   6

Chapter 2   Inside Hard Disk Technology   7

An Overview   7
The Disk Surface   11
Flux Changes   12
Magnetic Media   13
Head Crashes   15
Sectors   18
Sector Size   19

Cylinders **19**
Interleaving **21**
Read/Write Heads **24**
Head Actuators **26**
Bump Detection **29**
Head Parking **30**
Disk Geometries **33**
Disk Controllers **34**
Data Encoding **35**
Error Correction **37**
Interfaces **38**
Full Track Buffers **41**
Files **43**
Clusters **45**
Directories **46**
The File Allocation Table **50**
The Boot Record **51**
Partitioning **52**
Alternative Storage Technologies **55**
Diskette Drives **55**
Bernoulli Technology **57**
Optical Disks **58**
Solid State Storage **62**
Where Is Hard Disk Technology Going? **64**

Chapter 3 **What, Where, and How to Buy** **67**

How Much Disk Capacity Do You Need? **68**
Formatted versus Unformatted Capacity **70**
Nominal versus Actual Capacities **71**
Hidden Disk Capacity Requirements **72**
Emerging Requirements for More Disk Capacity **74**
Assessing Capacity Requirements **77**
Deciding How Many Diskette Drives You Need **78**
Choosing among Hard Disk Options **80**
Hard Disk Cards **81**
Removable Hard Disks **85**
Bernoulli Technology **87**
High-capacity Drives **90**
Planning for Adequate Power and Ventilation **92**

Assessing Performance, Quality, and Convenience   **94**
  How Important Is Disk Speed for You?   **94**
  Assessing a Drive's Quality   **96**
Where and How to Buy   **99**
  What You Need to Buy   **100**
A Shopping Checklist   **103**
  Hardware   **103**
  Original IBM PC Only   **103**
  IBM AT or Compatible Only   **103**
  High-capacity Drives   **104**
  Software   **104**
  Documentation   **104**
  Choosing a Vendor   **104**
  Payment   **106**

Chapter 4   **Installation and Setup**   **109**

Installing an Internal Hard Disk   **110**
  Inserting a Drive   **111**
  Cabling MFM, RLL, and ESDI Drives   **116**
  Installing External Drives   **121**
  Adding a Second Drive   **121**
  Replacing the Power Supply   **123**
  Replacing the ROM BIOS   **127**
  Reconfiguring the System   **127**
  Mopping Up   **129**
Formatting   **130**
  Low-level Formatting   **130**
  Partitioning   **135**
  High-level Formatting   **143**
Configuring the System   **145**
  Creating CONFIG.SYS and AUTOEXEC.BAT   **146**
  Configuration Commands   **147**

Chapter 5   **Navigating Around Directory Trees**   **151**

DOS Shells   **152**
  Command Stacks   **158**
Helping DOS Find Files Automatically   **160**
  The DOS PATH Command   **161**
  The DOS APPEND Command   **163**

Moving through the Directory Tree **164**
  Tracking the Current Directory **164**
  Changing Directories **167**
  Moving About Using Simple Menus **169**
  Moving About with Keyboard Macros **171**
DOS Commands That Temporarily Modify the Directory Tree **174**
  The ASSIGN Command **174**
  The SUBST Command **175**
  Dangers in ASSIGN, SUBST, and JOIN **177**
Copying and Moving Files **177**
  Shortcuts Using COPY **180**
  Moving Files **185**
Finding Files **190**
  Searching for Files by Name **190**
  Searching for Files by Content **193**
Running Programs **197**
Menu Programs **201**
  Limitations **203**
  Security Systems **204**

Chapter 6 **Organizing Your Files 209**

Designing the Directory Tree **211**
  Rule 1 **211**
  Rule 2 **213**
  Rule 3 **216**
  Rule 4 **217**
  Rule 5 **217**
  Rule 6 **218**
  Rule 7 **218**
  Rule 8 **219**
  Rule 9 **220**
  Rule 10 **220**
  Rule 11 **221**
Viewing and Cataloging the Directory Tree **222**
  The DOS TREE Command **223**
  Cataloging the Directory Tree **225**
Viewing, Sorting, and Printing Directory Listings **226**
  Sorting Directory Listings **229**
Viewing and Printing Files **231**
  Printing Files **236**

Cataloging Files   **239**
   Using DOS to Catalog Files   **239**
   Cataloging Files with Utility Software   **241**
   Archiving Files   **242**
Managing Disk Space   **244**
   Installing New Software   **244**
   Mass File Deletions   **247**
   Setting File Attributes   **253**
   Data Compression   **256**

Chapter 7   Optimizing Speed and Productivity   261

Fifteen Factors in Hard Disk Performance   **262**
Disk-Level Optimization   **264**
   Cylinder Density   **264**
   Reducing File Fragmentation   **265**
   Seek Times   **271**
   Optimizing the Interleave   **273**
Controller-Level Optimization   **277**
   Increasing the Data Transfer Rate   **278**
   Increasing Processor Speed   **278**
   Track Buffering   **280**
   RAM Disks   **282**
DOS-Level Optimization   **288**
   Optimizing the Number of DOS Buffers   **289**
   Applying Disk Cachers   **291**
   Optimizing Directory Tree Organization   **295**
   Optimizing Subdirectory Layout   **297**
   Optimizing File Layout   **298**
   Optimizing the PATH and APPEND Commands   **298**
   Using the FASTOPEN Command   **299**
Choosing Optimization Measures   **300**
   Tradeoffs   **300**
   Cost Effectiveness   **302**
   Recommendations   **304**

Chapter 8   Backups without Pain   305

Risks to Your Data   **305**
Some General Concerns   **309**
   Hardware versus Software   **309**

Speed versus Flexibility   **311**
Image versus File-by-file Backups   **313**
DOS versus Proprietary Formats   **314**
Backup versus Restore   **315**
Attended versus Unattended Backups   **316**
Error Checking   **317**
Backup Pitfalls   **318**
Varieties of Backups   **319**
Global Backups   **320**
Incremental and Differential Backups   **320**
Temporary Backups   **322**
Serial Backups   **322**
Diskette-based Backup   **323**
Backups Using COPY   **323**
Backups Using XCOPY   **325**
The DOS BACKUP and RESTORE Commands   **328**
Backup Utility Software   **332**
Tape Backup   **339**
Fundamentals of Tape Technology   **339**
Streaming   **340**
Misconceptions About Tape Backup   **341**
Tape Standards   **341**
Tape Backup Performance   **344**
Buying a Tape Drive   **346**
Installing a Tape Drive   **348**
The Future of Tape Backup   **351**
Instituting a Backup System   **351**
Deciding among Backup Options   **352**
Backup Frequency   **354**
Organizing Backup Media   **357**
Off-Site Data Storage   **358**

Chapter 9   Surviving Hard Disk Disasters   361

How Disks Fail   **362**
Recovering Erased Files   **365**
How DOS Erases Files   **365**
Unerasing a Deleted File   **366**
The Origins of File Fragmentation   **368**
Manual File Recovery   **369**
Unerase Utilities   **371**

Recovering from Accidental Reformatting   **376**
    The "Snap Shot" Approach   **377**
    The Recovery Approach   **378**
Recovering Damaged DOS Structures   **381**
File Recovery   **385**
    Orphaned Clusters   **386**
    Cross-linked Files   **387**
Guarding against Hard Disk Disasters   **390**
    Locating the Machine   **391**
    Power-Line Protection   **392**
    Guarding against Theft   **393**
    Vandalism   **394**
Repairs   **396**
    Dealing with Sporadic Failure   **396**
    Kinds of Repairs   **398**
    Deciding on a Repair Service   **399**
Afterword   **400**

Glossary   399
Index   439

Introduction

What? A *whole* book about hard disks? But hard disks are just big floppies, right? Wrong. A hard disk is the control center of your machine. If it is organized, *you* are organized. If it isn't, you are in big trouble. People who understand their hard disks make them the foundation for enhancing speed and productivity in all their work.

If you doubt the importance of hard disks, scan any computer magazine. You'll be overwhelmed by articles and advertisements on hard disk topics: unformat programs, disk caching, defragmenters, full track buffers, removable media, disk repair utilities, file archiving, image backups, tree design, system configuration, nonvolatile RAM disks, streaming tape backup units, super-high-density floppies, voice-coil actuators, cylinder densities, Bernoulli boxes, interleave optimization, transfer rates, backup utilities, DOS buffers, data compression, hardcards, unerase utilities, high-capacity drives, plated media, seek times, DOS partitions, low-level formatting, multiple drive installation, DOS shells, optical disks, security hardware, file searching, disk housekeeping, head crashes, Trojan horses, disk repairs, operating environments, PC/T, MTBF, ESDI, XCOPY, QIC, MFM, VD-I, SUBST, SCSI, WORM, RLL...and on it goes.

We cover all these topics in this book—and much more. You need only a basic understanding of DOS to follow our discussions; no technical knowledge is required. Newcomers to computers will be exposed to a wealth of new ideas. And more advanced readers will see how these all fit together. For example, we bring together every important disk optimization technique in one chapter and discuss the tradeoffs. We sort through myriad hardware features and explain how to choose among them. We also compare the ins and outs of various backup systems. Out goal is to give you a strong grasp of concepts that will serve you well for the years ahead amid constantly changing technology.

We've made every attempt to keep up with the latest IBM introductions. Throughout the book you'll find information on the PS/2 machines. We've also described important changes in DOS 5.0. In general, we've done all we can to help you make decisions for the future, particularly in view of the growing presence of Microsoft's Windows and IBM's new OS/2.

By the time you reach the back cover of this book, you'll be able to make effective, forward-looking purchase decisions; you'll handle routine hardware installation and configuration on your own; DOS and application software will be easier to use; you'll be able to monitor your work and that of others; your disk will run much faster than it does now; you'll have a nearly effortless backup system for your data; you'll be able to avert many dangers to your data, including some kinds of "crashes"; and when disasters occur, you'll be able to recover as much of your data as is physically possible.

Many of these benefits arise through utility software—often quite inexpensive. Because software is constantly changing, we've avoided recommending particular products. Indeed, we believe that any kind of comparative review would be inappropriate because products that performed best when this book was written may have long since been surpassed. Computer magazines are the best place to find up-to-date recommendations (*PC Magazine* gives especially detailed reviews).

We *do* mention many specific products in passing, however. Cited as examples, they often were chosen for a unique feature. Please don't construe every mention as a recommendation, and don't think that omitted products are under par. It's up to you to take the concepts you learn here and make your own decisions.

We hope you enjoy this book. If you absorb most of the information in it, you'll be well on your way to true *power user* status. And that's a good feeling. Not only can you strut your stuff at cocktail parties, but when you ask your computer to do something, it will actually obey. Nothing is quite like knowing what you're doing.

Peter Norton

Robert Jourdain

CHAPTER 1

Much More Than a Giant Diskette

Once upon a time, not long ago, a 10-megabyte hard disk carried as high a price as the computer in which it worked. When the exasperation of working with diskettes became too much to bear, people were willing to part with $2,000 and more for a small hard disk. Time is money, and it was clear that those fractions of a minute lost to swapping diskettes and waiting on diskette drives could add up to hours each week.

Then prices dropped. Tremendous excitement ensued when one company released a 10-megabyte drive for *only* $1,000. Soon the IBM PC AT was introduced, and suddenly a 20-megabyte drive was considered standard. Ten-megabyte drives plunged below the $1,000 mark, and the higher capacity drives soon followed. Today, nearly all new PCs have hard drives with capacities of 30 or more megabytes.

Hard disk prices fell just in time, because disks would soon have held less data than the systems' random-access memory (RAM). In a well-designed computer system, **secondary storage** (disk storage) should hold at least 20 times as much data as **primary storage** (random-access memory). This allows room for several programs that fill all of memory, plus their data files. The ratio was only five to one on the original IBM PC—320K diskettes served 64K of RAM. And, as memory chip prices dropped and many users installed the full 640K allowed

1

by DOS, system memory overtook disk capacity. The computer could generate files larger than it could store! A 20-megabyte disk restores a healthy balance of about 30 to 1. (Indeed, the problem today is that DOS's 640K limit to conventional memory has pushed the imbalance too far in the opposite direction.)

Considering the grief diskettes visited upon early computer users, it is no wonder that many people regard hard disks as a solution to the diskette's failings. Some users think of hard disks as *giant, speedy diskettes* that spare them the indignities of shuffling dozens of diskettes in and out of drives, losing data when a diskette fills, duplicating files repeatedly to keep them handy, and waiting and waiting and waiting as the diskette drives grind on and on.

But a hard disk is much more than a giant diskette. It can serve as the foundation for a system of software and procedures that greatly enhance organization and productivity. Consider these benefits:

- **Ease-of-use.** Because hard disks can make a lot of software available for use at any time, they can bring together a mixture of DOS features and software utilities that simplify work and shield the user from the intricacies of DOS. A network of menus, batch files, and keyboard macros can perform complicated tasks that would otherwise require hours of training. A few keystrokes can reconfigure the machine and quickly switch from one task to another.

- **Productivity.** Greater ease-of-use instantly increases productivity, in part because work proceeds more quickly, and in part because fewer time-consuming errors are made. Productivity also rises because software functions more quickly with a hard disk.

- **Manageability.** A large hard disk lets you keep all of your work in one place. Software can share and integrate large amounts of data. It's easy to catalog and archive your work. You can monitor and control access to files in machines shared by many people.

These benefits do not come without effort. You need to understand your computer and DOS well to be able to set up a high-productivity system. Just as important, you need to know how to avoid the dangers inherent in having all your work on one disk, managed by a complicated web of software. To avoid trouble, here's what you must learn:

Learn to buy the right equipment and software for your needs. The selections you make limit your options. Even if your hard disk purchase is already complete, you need to understand some technical issues so that you can identify and eliminate performance bottlenecks in your system. Without a clear understanding, you can easily squander hundreds, even thousands of dollars.

Learn to optimize hard disk performance. Without constant maintenance, a hard disk will run more and more slowly as the directory tree grows and more files are added. Some disks are crippled through mistakes made during installation. With a small amount of utility software, the speed of most poorly maintained disks can be tripled.

Learn to manage memory. The 640K limit on system memory will plague millions of people for years to come. PC and XT users, and some owners of AT clones, will not be able to use new, advanced operating systems that can access more memory. Unfortunately, many of the productivity gains made possible by hard disks rely upon memory-consuming utilities. Hard disk management and memory management go hand in hand.

Learn to lay out the directory tree and its files intelligently. Many hard disk owners set up inefficient directory trees. Work is hindered, vast amounts of disk space are wasted, and the disk is slowed. A well-ordered directory tree catalogs your work and speeds up DOS.

Learn to monitor the state of the disk. With time, it's easy to lose track of the contents of a hard disk. Periodic housecleaning, tree maintenance, and file cataloging see to it that work *stays* organized.

Learn to make backups effortlessly. A good backup system does its work quickly and reliably. A bad backup system may take *more* time and afford *less* protection. Backups should not be approached as an afterthought. You must devote time to planning an easy-to-use, largely automatic scheme. Once this investment is made, you'll be free of backup anxiety forever.

Learn to deter disasters. When you use a hard disk, you put all your eggs in one basket. *You must watch that basket!* There are ways to prolong the life of your disk drive and ways to detect when a drive is malfunctioning. Certain measures can protect you from various user errors, such as accidental erasures or reformatting. And special software can protect data from unauthorized access.

Learn to recover from disasters. Several disk "tool kits" let you recover damaged or erased files. There's much more available than just "unerase" programs. Utilities can repair disks whose formatting and directories (the information the system uses to keep track of your data) are damaged. In some cases they can bring a "crashed" (nonfunctional) disk back to life.

We aim to teach you all these skills in the eight chapters that follow. As with so much in computerdom, there's often a circularity in the explanations. You can't understand chickens until you understand eggs, which, of course, requires a thorough knowledge of chickens. We've begun the book with an indepth explanation of how hard disks work (Chapter 2). A knowledge of engineering or computer programming is not required. In fact, no science background at all is required. We strongly recommend you read it, or you may not be able to follow Chapter 7 (on optimization) or 9 (on data recovery).

Chapters 3 and 4, respectively, concern buying and installing hard disk drives. If you already own a drive, you can safely skip over them. But it's a good idea to read at least the beginning of Chapter 3, which discusses how much disk capacity you're likely to need. Many of today's application programs create very large files—and lots of them—leaving many hard disk owners in for a rude awakening when they realize the inadequacy of their current drives. There are also discussions of various hard disk options (removable media, hard disk cards, and so on) that will be of interest to many readers who may someday add a second hard drive to their machines.

Those who just want to use their machines, without worrying about how they work, will also find that Chapters 5 (Navigating Around Directory Trees), 6 (Organizing Your Files), and 8 (Backups) require little technical background.

Let's take a brief look at the contents of each chapter:

Inside Hard Disk Technology

Chapter 2 guides you through the bewildering array of hardware options on the market today. The sophisticated buyer does not march into a shop and ask for a "hard disk." There are too many choices in quality and performance to leave your purchase to the salesperson's discretion. Open any computer magazine and you'll find ads touting "RLL," "plated media," "track buffers," and "IDE." You'll also find a confusing (and sometimes dishonest) range of performance claims. We'll help you through this maze. We also take a glimpse at the future as we examine high-density diskettes, optical disks, and bubble memories. While our crystal ball is as cloudy as everyone else's, we try to show where the big changes in price and performance may take place during the 1990s.

What, Where, and How to Buy

Chapter 3 begins with a lengthy discussion of how to estimate disk capacity requirements. You may be surprised by how much disk space is required to support new operating systems and new software technologies, such as desktop publishing. We look at the many hard disk options available: ordinary internal and external drives, hard disk cards, removable media, and high-capacity drives. Finally, we go through the steps to making a carefree purchase, including choosing a vendor, negotiating terms for return and repair, interpreting warranties, and returning defective merchandise.

Installation and Setup

Chapter 4 deals with installing a drive, formatting it, and setting up the computer to accommodate it. You'll learn the intricacies of installing the various types of disk drives and related components. Then we explain every step of formatting a drive and configuring it to your machine, giving special attention to high-capacity drives that can be hard to set up.

Navigating the Disk

Having thousands of files on a single disk requires an elaborate directory tree that complicates all DOS operations. As you create ever more elaborate software configurations, maneuvering about the disk becomes complicated and tiresome. Chapter 5 shows you how to use DOS shells, menu systems, security systems, batch files, and keyboard macros to simplify DOS operations and automate complex software interactions. In evaluating the options, we place special emphasis on managing scarce memory.

Organizing Your Files

Most hard disk owners arrange their files and their directory tree in a haphazard way. As a result, files are lost or accidentally erased, software runs more slowly, and disk space is wasted. Chapter 6 shows how to design an efficient directory tree, and how to maintain it. Various file-maintenance utilities are covered, including file compressors, file searchers, and file catalogers.

Optimizing Speed and Productivity

Chapter 7 tackles the difficult topic of how to get a hard disk to run quickly and keep it that way. Hard disks seem incredibly quick to those who have only used diskettes, but heavy use slows them down. Many people believe that fast disk access requires expensive hardware. In fact, a well-optimized "slow" hard disk can outperform a neglected "fast" hard disk. There are many tricks of the trade, of which purchase decisions are only one part. We'll show you how to adjust the disk format and file layout to optimize DOS. And we'll examine an array of inexpensive utility programs that speed disk access. If your hard disk is currently poorly maintained, you may be able to *quintuple* its speed in some applications.

Backups Without Pain

The need for backups generates much more anxiety than action. Backups are widely neglected because, when done badly, they require a lot of time and result in confusion. Chapter 8 shows you how to organize and schedule a backup system that exactly fits your needs. We survey the myriad ways that you can lose data, and the several kinds of backup that guard against data loss. All backup media are covered, and we give special attention to selecting and using streaming tape units. We also discuss the full range of backup software offerings, and the many pitfalls you should look out for.

Surviving Hard Disk Disasters

Finally, Chapter 9 leads you through the Valley of Death. The dead in this case are files, which can be corrupted, scrambled, or annihilated in more ways than you can imagine. We look at what goes wrong with files and how to reclaim them. Our discussion takes us to file-recovery programs, disk editors and tool kits, unerase utilities, and programs that can resurrect an accidentally reformatted disk. We try to cultivate an appreciation of the *limitations* of these utilities. If you don't read our chapter on backups closely, you'll want to memorize this one.

If this looks like a lot to cover, it is. But mastering this information will take you far towards becoming a true *power user*. You'll be able to think through your options . . . solve problems . . . greatly increase your disk's performance . . . make backups in seconds . . . automate procedures . . . in a word, turn your machine into a roaring, well-ordered, organized tool.

Inside Hard Disk Technology

This chapter describes how hard disks work. While it is possible to live a happy and useful life without this knowledge, you'll find it invaluable when you try to sort through manufacturer's specifications, advertising claims, news reports, and unfriendly hardware documentation. You'll also need to know a bit about the technology to understand our discussions in Chapters 7 and 9 on optimizing your hard disk's performance. Besides, the technical stuff is kind of fun, and we promise not to journey too deep into the woods.

An Overview

Most computer users have never seen the inside of a hard disk drive. Unlike diskettes, which peek through their protective envelopes or shells, the recording surfaces must be permanently encased in a metal enclosure to shield them from dust and dirt. All that's visible is a hard disk *drive*—a metal box with some circuitry on it. There's no easy way to get inside the box to view the rotating disk—which is just as well, since to open a drive is to fatally contaminate it. Drives may be opened only in special **clean rooms** where workers wear surgical garb and all dust is filtered from the air. Some hard disks are enclosed in removable cartridges that are inserted into the drive, but most are non-removable. IBM invented small, non-removable drives and informally dubbed them **Winchester drives** (apparently because the drive's code number matched the model number of a popular Winchester rifle).

For all its impressive armor, a hard disk is not terribly different from the lowly diskette. Data is recorded as magnetic patterns written in circles around the hub of the disk. Each of the concentric circles comprises a **track**, and each track is divided into a number of equal segments called **sectors**. A **read/write head** moves from the outer edge of the disk toward the hub, stopping over the track that contains the information the computer needs. Once in position, the head waits for the correct sector of the track to revolve under it, and then it reads or writes data as the sector passes beneath. Figure 2-1 illustrates this scheme.

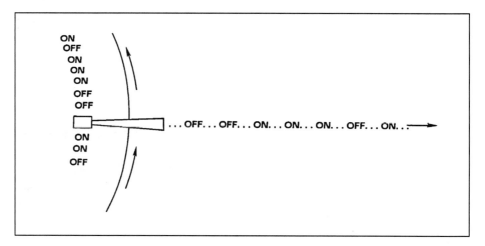

Figure 2-1. Data access

Differences Between Diskettes and Hard Disks

Hard disks are distinguished from diskettes by the high densities at which data is recorded on the disk surface and by the high speed at which these disks operate. While a 360K diskette has 40 tracks, hard disks of the same diameter may have well over 1,000. And they may pack several times as much data onto each track. While the read/write head of a diskette drive touches the surface, a hard disk drive's heads float less than a hair's breadth above the surface of the disk on a cushion of air. As the name implies, a hard disk platter is rigid, not flexible. Most are made of metals such as aluminum, though the light-weight drives in some portables have platters made of glass.

Hard disks are much quicker than diskettes. While a diskette turns at 300 or 360 revolutions per minute (five or six turns per second), most hard disks spin at 3,600 rpm (60 turns per second). This means that data flows to and from the hard disk more quickly. Also, hard disk drives move their read/write heads from track to track several times faster than diskette drives. Such high performance requires extremely precise machining and assembly.

Platters

To increase the drive's capacity, virtually all hard disk drives contain two or more actual disks. The disks, referred to as **platters**, are mounted around an axle called the **spindle**. All platters turn together. The motor that turns the platters may be built into the spindle, or it may reside below the spindle as a **pancake motor**.

Both sides of a platter hold data. Since it would be impractical for a single read/write head to serve all platter sides, each side has its own head. The heads are connected to a comb-like arm that moves all of them in tandem, as shown in Figure 2-2. The accuracy of this mechanism is astounding. The platters are kept spinning at a precise rate so that tiny magnetized areas of the disk, called domains pass by the read/write heads at exactly the rate the drive electronics expect. The platters and heads interleave, with each head positioned only 1/100,000 of an inch from the platter surface. This precise geometry is maintained as the lightweight heads rapidly shunt back and forth over the heavy gyrating platters. High-tech indeed!

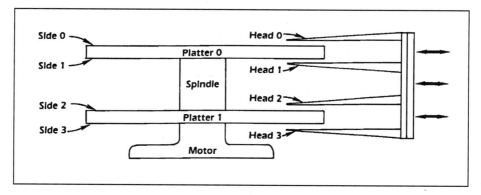

Figure 2-2. Heads and platters

The heads are able to stay so close to the platters without touching because they actually *fly* over the surface on a cushion of air created by the disk's rotation. The heads slowly lift off when the drive starts up, and they gently land when power is shut off and the platters grind to a halt. In most drives, the heads rest against the disk surface when power is off.

Disk Controllers

Most disk drives are connected to a **controller card** that plugs into one of the computer's slots. When data is read from the disk surface, it passes from the heads, through the disk-drive circuitry and into the controller card electronics. Data sent from the disk surface to the controller card arrives at a **buffer**—a small patch of memory that acts as a temporary holding area for data. When the buffer is full, the controller card sends a signal to the computer's **processor**—the chip at the heart of the computer, such as an 8088 chip or an 80386 chip. The signal tells the processor to begin moving the data onto the computer's own memory chips.

DMA

The data is moved from the controller card to the computer's memory by one of two techniques. In AT-style machines, the CPU does the job itself. But XTs and PS/2s use **direct memory access (DMA)**. DMA relies on a special chip that shifts the data directly from the controller to memory in a single step, rather than through the two-step process of moving it first to the CPU, and then to system memory. PCs and XTs use DMA because their 8088 CPUs cannot keep up with a hard disk's data transfer rate.

DOS Buffers

The data is sent to yet another temporary holding area, this time to one set aside in the computer's random access memory. These areas are called **DOS buffers**. Each buffer holds a single disk sector, which in DOS contains a 512-byte portion of a file. The number of buffers may be set by the user, as we'll see later. Typically, computers equipped with a hard disk run with 20–30 buffers. As a file is read, its sectors fill the buffers, one after another. Once all buffers are occupied, the next incoming sector is placed in the buffer that has been least-recently accessed by a program, overwriting that buffer's prior contents.

In the final step along the journey, DOS extracts data from the buffers and lays it down at particular memory locations requested by application software. Often, the data will be laid end-to-end in a long sequence, exactly as it appears in a file, such as a word processing document. Other times, the data will be distributed helter-skelter around memory, and the program loading the data will assemble it into the format appearing on screen. Figure 2-3 shows the path taken by data from disk to software.

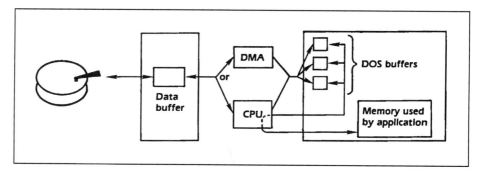

Figure 2-3. The path taken by data

This entire process is reversed when the computer *writes* data on a disk. A program tells DOS where to find data in memory. DOS moves the data to its buffers and then transfers it to the holding buffer on the hard disk controller. Then the disk controller begins writing. Following DOS's instructions, the controller specifies which sector on which track on which platter-side is to receive the data, sending commands to the disk drive that move the read/ write head into position. Then the drive electronics take over, carefully watching the disk surface for exactly the right moment to begin. When the required sector reaches the head, the head emits a stream of magnetic pulses that record the data in a line along the disk surface.

The Disk Surface

A disk is uniformly covered with a **magnetic medium**—a substance that retains patterns of magnetism that store the data. As it happens, DOS lays out the data in 512-byte arcs of a circle (sectors), but the surfaces of some disks can be organized differently if an operating system wished to do so. We'll only look at DOS in this section, but it's worth keeping in mind that the general principles we discuss apply to any microcomputer operating system, including OS/2, UNIX, or, for that matter, the Apple Macintosh.

Flux Changes

The surface of a hard disk contains magnetized particles of metal or a metal oxide. Each particle has a north and south pole, just like larger magnets. A hard drive's read/write head can apply a magnetic field to a tiny group of these particles, reversing their polarity, so that what was north becomes south, or vice versa. The smallest area of disk surface that can hold one of these **flux changes** constitutes a **magnetic domain**. Thousands of domains taken together make up a track. As the disk spins beneath the head, the head constantly changes the polarity of its magnetic field, creating a sequence of polarity changes along a track.

Data Encoding

All information in computers is stored as patterns of "1s" and "0s" that represent ONs and OFFs. For example, when you type the letter "A" in a word-processing document, the character is subsequently stored on disk in the pattern ON-OFF-OFF-OFF-OFF-OFF-ON-OFF. These are the eight **bits** that make up a byte of data. (The pattern, incidentally, is part of the **ASCII standard**, which means that "A" is an **ASCII character** ASCII stands for American Standard Code for Information Interchange.) When data is read, a read/write head examines each magnetic domain along a track, sensing whether the magnetic polarity is the opposite of that of the prior domain. A flux change in polarity indicates an ON (or binary 1) and a lack of a change indicates an OFF (or binary 0).

When a drive reads back the data, it essentially reverses the process. The head hovers passively over the disk surface, and, as the tiny magnets that comprise the magnetic domains pass beneath, they ever so slightly influence the head's magnetic field. Circuitry on the disk drive greatly amplifies these slight perturbations into patterns of ONs and OFFs that are fed into the computer's memory chips.

Even a diskette can pack an awful lot of these magnetic domains (ONs and OFFs) onto a single track—well over 30,000 domains, which is enough to hold two entire screens of text (25 rows of 80 characters, with eight domains per character). Hard disks write at least 10,000 domains *per inch* of track. If you consider that hard drives rotate at 3,600 revolutions per minute, you'll realize that the read/write head is working very quickly indeed. Several million domains pass under a read/write head in a second.

Magnetic Media

If you were to be so curious (and so unwise) as to take a screwdriver to your disk drive, inside you'd find either platters covered with the familiar reddish-brown iron oxide coating found on diskettes, or bright shiny platters reminiscent of chrome auto bumpers. The first would be an example of **coated media**, and the second an example of **plated media**. In either case, not far below the surface is a finely machined aluminum **blank** upon which the medium is applied. But it is the surface that matters.

Media Properties

Magnetic media vary in both their **coercivity**—the strength of the magnetic field they can hold—and their **retentivity**—the ability of the medium to retain a magnetic field. Media with *high coercivity* can store a detectable magnetic field in a smaller area than media with *low coercivity*—that is, the media can hold smaller magnetic domains. The smaller domains found on high-density media require a stronger magnetic field from the drive's read/write heads.

Media with *high retentivity* hold data more reliably. But all magnetic charges ultimately fade away. Several years, perhaps a decade, must pass before fading becomes a problem in most hard disks. Of course, much data is constantly rewritten to disk after it's been modified, and so its magnetic markings are renewed. Similarly, software updates tend to renew your program files. But archived data may gradually acquire errors.

The biggest problem in this regard is with the *low-level formatting*—a group of magnetic markings that tell the system where sectors begin and end. These are written only during the initial disk format and are never refreshed, ultimately posing a danger to any data on your disk, including directories and other DOS structures that manage your files. As we'll see in Chapter 9, utility software can renew format markings, and can discover fading data within sectors and restore it.

Media Density

Many diskette drives on PC compatibles can take two kinds of diskettes: **high-density diskettes** and **double-density diskettes**. A high-density 5¼" diskette can hold 1.2M versus 360K bytes for a double-density 5¼" diskette; a high-density 3.5" diskette can hold 1.44M versus 720K for a 3.5" double-density diskette. It's important to keep track of which is which, especially with 5¼" diskettes. High-density 5¼" diskettes have a higher coercivity and require a stronger magnetic field from the read/write heads than do their low-density counterparts; they also use tracks which are only half as far apart. A high-density 5¼" drive can read low-density disks, but (depending on the drive) may or not be able to write to them properly. 3.5" drives have fewer compatibility problems because the high- and low-density media have the same coercivity and the same number of tracks. High-density 3.5" drives can read or write either kind of 3.5" diskette with no problems.

Make sure you format disks to hold the amount of data they were designed to handle. If you try to format a 5¼" high-density diskette as a double-density diskette, DOS returns an *Invalid media* or *Track 0 bad* error message. This outcome might surprise you, thinking that there should be no problem fitting 720K or 360K onto media that can hold 1.44M or 1.2M. But the format fails because the read/write heads operate at half the intensity required by this kind of media.

Conversely, if you format a 720K (or 360K) diskette for 1.44M or (1.2M), DOS will complete the job, but the final message from the format program might tell you that many bad sectors were found where the media was not up to the job of holding data at this density. Still, the formatted capacity of the diskette may well exceed 720K (or 360K). Considering that double-density diskettes are cheaper than their high-density cousins, this seems like a good deal—but it's not. There's no such thing as a free lunch; data recorded on these disks may fade or prove unreadable. If you *do* accidentally format a double-density diskette as if it were a high-density diskette, throw it away—or pass it through a bulk eraser before reusing it. DOS will gladly reformat the diskette at 720K or 360K, but it does so using a relatively weak magnetic field. Low-level formatting left over from the higher-intensity, high-density format may not be fully obliterated, and these can lead to data errors.

Coated versus Plated Media

Until recently, nearly all hard disk drives built for PCs were of the coated oxide variety. The technology is well understood, being some 40 years old. The oxide coating is not much more than rust particles held in place by a binding agent. The coating is relatively easy to apply at the precise and regular thickness required. Plated media, on the other hand, are made by applying pure metal to the aluminum blank, either by vapor deposition or by a technique called **sputtering,** in which the metal is applied in a vacuum chamber. Working with vaporized metal is not easy, and it took the industry many years to arrive at techniques that produce near-perfect disk surfaces at a reasonable cost. Once reserved for drives that had high capacity, high speed, and high prices, plated media are increasingly common today.

An oxide coating is roughly 10 times thicker than a plated surface (which is but a few millionths of an inch) and it holds much larger magnetic particles. So much binding agent is required in oxide coatings that the magnetic particles are held relatively far apart. In plated media, on the other hand, the particles are packed against each other. The absence of a binding agent makes the coating much thinner, and often plated media are called **thin-film media**. Even though the oxide coating used on hard disks is denser than that used with standard diskettes, it still cannot pack as many magnetic domains on the disk surface as plated media can. A plated surface is also smoother than an oxide surface, and so the disk drive's read/write heads can fly closer to the disk surface. The closer the heads, the smaller the area they can affect, and hence the smaller the domains that may be created.

While coated media can hold up to 20,000 magnetic domains on an inch of track, plated media may exceed 50,000 domains. Higher densities may be achieved by **perpendicular recording**, where the magnetic domains extend from the disk surface inward, rather than end-to-end along the track. As disks move toward higher and higher data densities, there is an inexorable trend toward using plated media.

In the spring of 1990, IBM announced a breakthrough in magnetic recording technology, recording 158,000 bits per inch of track. The overall data density of this technique comes to one *giga*bit (one billion bits) per square inch, as compared to the 35 to 45 megabits per square inch found in most hard disks today. That's a 30-fold increase in storage density! It will take a while for this technology to come to PCs, but IBM claims that it should be possible to manufacture it at relatively low cost.

Head Crashes

Plated media have another advantage: They are extremely hard, making them resistant to **head crashes**. Most everyone has heard of a head crash, or at least knows that a disk can crash, but few people understand what a crash is. The origin of the term is unclear. The first experimental hard disk drives were giant contraptions with mammoth platters rotated by powerful motors. A mishap in the laboratory would cause the inside of a drive to literally tear itself to pieces. These calamitous events may have given rise to the term crash.

These days a disk crash is a much more genteel affair. Severe vibrations or a mechanical failure cause a read/write head to strike the surface of a platter and cut a tiny furrow in the medium. The momentum of the spinning platters adds considerable energy to the collision. Where a head cuts, data can no longer be held; if it is a place where data has been recorded, the data is lost. Worse, particles of magnetic material are loosened, freeing them to roam around inside the drive. These particles may be much larger than the gap that separates the heads and platter surfaces; when a head hits one, it may fly up, crash back down, and damage more data. Sometimes the particles adhere to the head and interfere with its magnetic field. Many drives have an internal air filter to trap particles lifted from the disk surface.

Sometimes DOS can write upon a lightly damaged point on the disk and the new data is successfully preserved. But when the damage is more severe, with a deep gouge made in the coating, data won't hold at all. The disk has developed a **bad sector**. DOS issues the message *Error reading Drive X:* or *Sector not found reading drive X:* when it encounters these gaps in the data. To repair the damage, the sectors must be placed off bounds to DOS's use. Some software utilities perform this service. Alternatively, you can back up all your files, reformat the disk, and then restore the files, including the backups you (presumably) made of the files that were damaged. The damaged area will be marked off-bounds during reformatting. We'll discuss these techniques in detail in Chapter 9, Surviving Hard Disk Disasters.

Severe Crashes

When a head crash occurs over the outermost tracks, the damage tends to be much more serious. These tracks contain special DOS files, the disk's main directory, and information about disk space allocation. If the heads dive into this data, DOS will not be able to read from the disk at all, and all data will effectively be "lost," even though every byte remains intact elsewhere on the platters. This is the most feared of all kinds of head crash. There *are* ways to get much of the data back from the disk, but often only through great effort or expense (we'll discuss these techniques in Chapter 9 also). Because the read/write heads spend a good deal of time hovering over these outer tracks, head crashes of this kind are relatively common.

For all but the saintly, a hard disk crash is cause for fury and vituperation. "The maker is incompetent." "The dealer is a cheat." "The consultant is a quack." One does well to remember that when the first IBM PC was released, small hard disk drives were barely a viable mass-market technology. The rate of

College Marketing Group
50 Cross Street
Winchester, MA 01890

ATT: **Cheryl Read**

technical progress has been remarkable, and quality rises year after year, even as prices fall. Besides, if the disk crashes and data is lost, the real cause for anger is clear: The owner has likely been negligent in making backups.

Crash-resistant Designs

Engineers are working on other kinds of disk media that are more resistant to head-crash damage. For example, 3M Company has developed **stretch-surface recording**, in which a special magnetic-coated film is applied to an aluminum blank with raised rims at the outer edge and center hole. The film is *stretched* between the rims so that the magnetic surface hangs slightly above the surface of the disk. As the head flies above the medium, the air cushion pushes a "dimple" into the surface. Should the head crash into the surface, the medium can much better absorb the force, and it imparts much less energy to the head. Laboratory prototypes show recording densities almost as high as those for plated media. Iomega's Bernoulli Box, while not really a hard drive, also uses flexible media and is less subject to damage if the head touches the disk surface.

Failures that are not Crashes

Although many people refer to any hard disk failure as a crash, many things can go wrong that have nothing to do with damage to the disk medium. Electronic components can fail, the motor that drives the platters can burn out, or the actuator that moves the read/write heads can go out of alignment. Or, an actual head crash may lead to a different kind of problem: The heads may become contaminated or damaged. Contamination usually occurs in drives with iron oxide coatings; the soft coating material adheres to the read/write heads, causing errors. Plated media, on the other hand, are so hard that they can smash the delicate heads. In either case, the drive must be replaced or repaired.

Hard and Soft Errors

Damage to a drive or to the data on its platters may or may not cause the drive to stop working. Instead, the drive may continue to function, but will intermittently have problems that result in data transmission errors. When these errors arise from hardware malfunctions, they are called **hard errors**. A hard error will occur again and again. For example, if a head crash has obliterated some of the drive's magnetic medium, every attempt to read data from that point on the medium will fail. Conversely, **soft errors** occur sporadically. These are errors where data is read or written unsuccessfully even though hardware works correctly. Soft errors are essentially freak accidents that tend not to recur regularly. For example, soft errors sometimes occur when a power surge passes through the circuitry. Soft errors also occur when hardware is on the verge of failure, as when worn-out bearings cause a platter to wobble slightly so that it occasionally pulls too far away from the head's magnetic field.

The hard disk controller can usually recover from a soft error simply by trying to read or write the data again. Most controllers automatically try 10 times before reporting an error to DOS. DOS, in turn, tries reading or writing data three times before it gives up and displays an error message. So a total of 30 tries may be made. In Chapter 9 we'll see how software can keep an eye on soft error rates and warn you about impending disk failure.

Sectors

Although it's possible to lay out a strip of data in one long sequence around the entire circumference of a track, it's not generally done this way. Instead, the track is divided into arcs called *sectors*. Because the word "sector" is used outside the computer world to mean a wedge of a disk that's the shape of a piece of pie, it encourages people to think of disk sectors as little wedges of data written at regular intervals along the disk surface. In computer parlance, however, a sector is defined as the portion of each track that would be cut out by that pie-shaped wedge.

On a *soft-sectored* disk, sectors are created when the disk is low-level formatted; the computer magnetically marks the disk to indicate where the sectors will be. On a *hard-sectored* disk, the positions of the sectors on each track are predefined at the factory and can't be changed. (As we'll see later in this chapter, formatting proceeds in two stages: low-level and high-level. It is low-level formatting that defines the sectors on soft-sectored disks, laying down a sequence of special codes that tell the controller where a sector begins. Then special identification numbers are written so that each sector has its own label to differentiate it from other sectors on the same track.)

Sector Density

360K diskettes are usually formatted with nine sectors per track. The AT's 1.2 megabyte diskette drives have 15. The 720K and 1.44M 3½-inch diskettes have 9 and 18 sectors, respectively. The hard disks used on the original IBM PC XT and PC AT have 17 sectors per track, but today's higher-capacity drives may have double that or more.

The number of sectors per track depends on a number of factors. The most obvious is the size of the disk drive platters, since a larger diameter leaves space for more tracks. Of course, the kind of magnetic medium used is also important because it sets the minimum length of track required for each sector.

High data densities require superior drive electronics. This is because disk platters turn at the same rate no matter the number of sectors per track. So, in drives with many sectors per track, sectors pass by the read/write heads more quickly. As we discuss a little later in this chapter, fast and accurate electronics allow the use of special codes (RLL recording) that also increase the number of sectors per track.

Sector Size

DOS fits 512 bytes of data into each sector; unless special software is installed, it uses this sector size for hard disks as well as diskettes. It's easy to see that tracks along the outer edge of a disk are a lot longer than inner tracks, and that they could hold a lot more data. However, to keep things simple, DOS expects every track to have the same number of sectors. The result is a good deal of wasted disk space. (Actually, some drive and controller makers put this space to use by "fooling" DOS. For example, one company puts 28 sectors on inner tracks and 34 sectors on outer tracks of its 40-megabyte disks. But the extra sectors are electronically represented as belonging to separate tracks, so that DOS sees a disk in which all tracks have the same number of sectors.)

We'll see later that some high-capacity hard disks use 1024- or 2048-byte sectors. But larger sectors do not in themselves lead to higher data densities. When sectors are large, there are fewer on a track.

Cylinders

When no more data can be crammed onto a disk, the only approach to higher disk-drive capacity is through adding more platters. Drives in the 10M to 30M range tend to have two platters; those with higher capacity may have three or more. The sides of the platters are numbered starting from 0, with the first platter holding sides 0 and 1, the second platter holding sides 2 and 3, and so on.

Because the drive's read/write heads move in tandem across the platter surfaces, all heads are positioned at a given track at any one time. Since individual files tend to become scattered around the disk surfaces, it would be preferable for the heads to move independently. As one head reads from one track, another head might be able to shift over to the track at which a file continues. But the mechanics would be prohibitively expensive.

How DOS Fills the Disk

To make the best of this situation, DOS tries to fit as much of a file as possible into all tracks at a given head position. For example, were DOS to record a new file starting from track 15, it might first fill all of track 15 on sides 0 and 1, then would continue at track 15 on the next platter with sides 2 and 3. Only when all tracks numbered 15 were filled would DOS initiate the time-consuming task of moving the read/write heads to track 16, where it would go on writing the file from side 0. (Of course, if there are parts of other files on some of these tracks, DOS might have to move the heads sooner.)

Taking all platter sides together, all tracks numbered 15 are called "cylinder 15." The concept is easy to grasp, since a cylinder would be formed if you joined the tracks from side to side, as Figure 2-4 shows. You will often see the term "cylinder" instead of "track" in hard disk documentation, and logically they are often interchangeable. A 40M hard disk might have 615 cylinders, while an 80M disk might have 1,024. This is precisely the same as saying that a side of one platter has 615 or 1,024 tracks.

Cylinder Density

An important concept is **cylinder density**. Unlike **track density**, which tells how many concentric tracks fit along an inch of a disk's radius, the cylinder density gives the *number of sectors* held in a cylinder. It equals the number of sectors per track multiplied by the number of platter sides. Disks with a high cylinder density are desirable, because they can fit a large file into fewer cylinders. By doing so, fewer head movements are needed to read the file, and the drive performs more quickly. Manufacturers increase cylinder density either by creating drives with more platters, or by using media and electronics that can achieve greater data densities, allowing more sectors on a track.

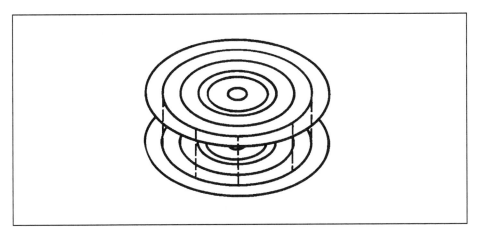

Figure 2-4. A cylinder

Interleaving

The rate at which data passes beneath a read/write head does not necessarily equal the rate at which the computer can read or write data. There are limits to how fast various circuits can move data. The disk controller transfers data between the disk surface and an internal holding buffer, and then either the processor or DMA (direct memory access) chips move the data between the controller's buffer and the computer's memory. The platters typically spin at 60 rotations per second (3,600 rpm), moving sectors under the read/write heads with each revolution. If a drive has 17 sectors per track and 512 bytes of data per sector, 522,240 bytes pass beneath the heads in a second. Since each byte is made up of eight bits (ONs or OFFs), roughly four million bits of data pass beneath a head during a second; other signals, including those which identify the sectors and help to correct errors in the data, bring the total to about five million.

The Data Transfer Rate

This calculation is the origin of the 5-megabit **data transfer rate** attributed to MFM drives—the slowest drives in common use today. (We'll explain what MFM means shortly.) This is the fastest possible rate data can move between the drive and the computer. Many people wrongly believe it is the electronics that set a drive's maximum transfer rate. Indeed, the electronics must be fast enough to read and write data at the rate it passes by the heads. But faster electronics could not transfer data more quickly, since the data could not be physically presented to the heads more rapidly without speeding up the drive motor. Later in this chapter we'll discuss RLL and ESDI drives, which have faster data transfer rates. They achieve this performance increase by packing more sectors onto each track so that more data passes under the read/write heads during each rotation of the disk.

Actual Data Transfer Rates

You may be doing a little arithmetic in your head and wondering why even a relatively slow disk drive with a 625,000-byte/second transfer rate may take an appreciable time to load a 100K file. Alas, the electronics can do their speedy work only when the read/write heads are in position. Even if the disk takes 18 milliseconds to position the head to a new track, every head move takes up 12,000 bytes worth of transfer time. And, at any given moment, the desired sector must be passing under the read/write heads. At 3600 rpm, 5,000 bytes of transfer time are taken up waiting for a sector on the opposite of the disk to swing around. Nor are the transfer electronics constantly active even under the best of conditions. The controller must wait for the processor to do its half of the job, including redistributing the data in memory. Application software may also be active, processing each incoming data item before requesting the next.

Think about what this means from the point of view of the spinning disk. A sector moves under the read/write heads and its data is transferred to the controller buffer. The next sector is coming up in a miniscule fraction of a second, and if the read/write head is to make use of it, the data from the prior sector must be moved out of the buffer and into memory in a big hurry. But 8088 and 80286 machines cannot make this transfer quickly enough. So the next disk sector flies by without being read. In fact, in a standard IBM XT, five sectors pass under the head before the controller is ready to read data again. Since ATs run faster, they're ready to read again after only one or two sectors pass by. It usually takes a 386 or 486 machine to read one sector after another.

The Rationale for Interleaving

If the second sector of a file's data is laid down on the disk surface right next to the first, the sectors are said to be "physically contiguous." Often, this is not the ideal condition. Because the controller is not ready to read the second sector when it physically follows the first, the disk must complete an entire revolution before the data passes under the head again. On a typical AT, the controller is ready to receive data in only a sixth as much time, wasting precious milliseconds. With the disk turning 60 times per second, waiting five-sixths of a revolution to read the next sector wastes 14 milliseconds. Reading 17 sectors in a row this way squanders 238 milliseconds—nearly a quarter of a second. A disk with four tracks to the cylinder would magnify this loss to a full second per cylinder. When a file spans many cylinders, you'd be strumming your fingertips waiting for the disk access to end.

Fortunately, there is no intrinsic need for disk drives to operate so ineffi-ciently. On a typical AT, a file's next sector of data is simply placed three sectors from the first. The read/write head reaches this sector just as the con-troller becomes ready to receive more data. Figure 2-5 diagrams the pattern taken when sectors are placed three apart. The sectors are no longer *physically* contiguous, but they are *logically* contiguous.

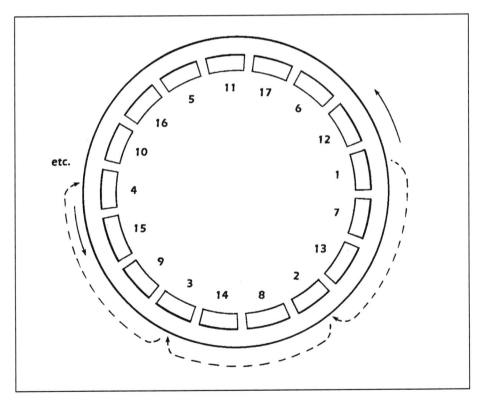

Figure 2-5. A 3:1 interleave

The Interleave Factor

The number of sectors between sectors with successive numbers is called the disk's **interleave factor**. Every disk has an interleave factor. On an IBM XT, the factor is 5:1. This means that a file continues at every fifth sector. Expressed differently, an "interleave factor of 5 to 1" means that it takes roughly five rotations of the disk to completely read all data from a track. Most ATs use a 3:1 or 2:1 interleave. A disk in which sectors are numbered in sequence has an interleave of 1:1. In this case, all data is read from a track in a single turn of the disk. This is the ideal interleave, and it usually takes a 386 or 486 computer to handle it.

A soft sectored disk's interleave factor is set when it undergoes **low-level for-matting** (the process that breaks up tracks into sectors). During low-level formatting, each sector is tagged with an identifying number. The numbers may be written in any order, setting the interleave. The interleave can be changed simply by redoing the format with a different interleave factor so that the sectors are numbered differently.

Cylinder Skewing

Interleave can be further optimized by altering the numbering from track to track. When a file spans several cylinders, the read/write heads must take time out to move between tracks. The added delay can cause the drive to miss the next sector. Time is wasted waiting for the sector to rotate around again. To overcome this inefficiency, the interleave numbering can be adjusted from track to track. The interleave factor is maintained, but, working inward from the outside of the disk, the numbering on each track is shifted forward by a sector or two to give the read/write heads time to move.

Read/Write Heads

The smaller a read/write head is, and the closer it flies over the disk surface, the smaller the magnetic domains it can write, and hence the more data it can pack onto the disk. Astonishingly, the read/write heads in most disk drives fly just 6 to 15 *millionths* of an inch above the disk surface. As of 1990, IBM has developed still-unreleased technology in which the distance is brought down to 2 millionths of an inch. A fleck of cigarette ash is huge by comparison.

A read/write head resembles a horseshoe magnet in that it is formed with opposite poles of the magnet facing each other across a narrow gap (Figure 2-6). This gap is made *extremely* narrow so that only very small areas of the disk surface are influenced at any moment as the disk swings by. Since the head must be large enough to manufacture and manipulate, the gap is much longer than it is wide. The result is that the magnetic domains are bar-shaped rather than dot-shaped, and magnetic "fringing" at the edges of the heads extend the domains quite some distance perpendicular to the tracks. Accordingly, data densities are much lower along the axis from the center of the disk outward than are data densities along the tracks.

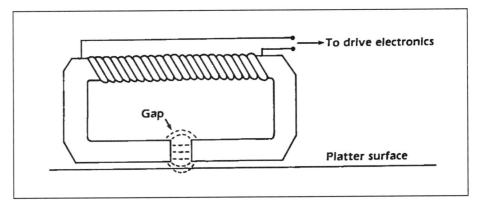

Figure 2-6. A read/write head

Although there may be several read/write heads, most drives use only one at a time because their controllers can handle data from only one head at once. Some more sophisticated drives can simultaneously access data on several sides, but this is only useful on very fast machines. Most computers can't move the data between the controller and system memory fast enough to take advantage of this feature.

Write Precompensation

Because a track is shorter at the interior of a disk than at its outer edge, magnetic domains are written closer together. To compensate for the smaller size of the domains, some drives boost the power delivered to the read/write heads when they write on these tracks. This feature is called **write precompensation**. Drives that use this feature begin write precompensation at a particular cylinder, and the number of that cylinder is part of the drive's specifications. For some hard disks, you may need to know this number when you first install and format the drive.

Head Designs

To increase data densities, engineers are working on the design of smaller and lighter heads. These improvements are also desirable because smaller and lighter heads are less likely to cause serious damage during head crashes. Manufacturers are increasingly using **Whitney** technology, a suspension system for very light heads. Such drives may use **mini-monolithic** heads to achieve densities of 1,000 tracks per inch, measuring from the center of a disk outward. (Compare this density to the 20,000 domains per inch written *along* tracks in an ordinary drive.)

Researchers are also working on *composite heads*, which achieve 1,500 tracks per inch, and *thin-film* heads that can exceed 2,000 tracks per inch. These high-tech heads are made with the same vapor-deposition techniques employed in integrated circuit manufacturing to mold extremely complex and fine head geometries. IBM has been using this technology for some years in mainframe hard disks. It is expected to be common in high-end PC hard disks by the mid-1990s.

Head Actuators

A **head actuator** moves the read/write heads back and forth over the platter surfaces. Two kinds of actuators are in common use, **stepper-motor actuators** and **voice-coil actuators**. The latter type is faster, sturdier, quieter—and more expensive. The hard disks sold with machines using 8088 and 80286 processors are usually of the stepper variety. Conversely, the fast disks found in 80386 and 80486 machines normally employ voice-coil technology. Let's look at stepper actuators first.

Stepper Motor Actuators

A stepper motor is a special kind of motor that rotates a few degrees at a time, in little *steps*. It can be made to rotate a precise number of steps in either direction. By converting these steps into linear motion by a **stepper band**, the motor can drive read/write heads back and forth. Diskette drives use stepper actuators. Each step of the mechanism moves the heads one track, creating a clicking sound; when many steps are made at once, you hear that all-too-familiar rasping noise. Hard disks that use stepper motors also make this sound, but it is muted by the drive casing.

Voice-coil Actuators

Voice-coil actuators work differently. They use a solenoid (a magnet that pulls at a metal rod) to draw the read/write heads toward the center of the disk. The heads are mounted on a hinge with a spring mechanism pulling the other way; when the magnetic field is relaxed, the heads move back toward the outer edge of the disk. Precise adjustments of the magnetic field move the heads to a particular track. The term "voice-coil" is used because the technology employs magnets like those found in loudspeakers. The drive shown in Figure 2-7 uses a voice-coil actuator.

Figure 2-7. A voice-coil actuator

When a stepper-motor actuator moves the read/write heads a long distance, it pushes the heads a track at a time to their destination. Twice the distance entails roughly twice the time. But voice-coil systems make only a single change in magnetic flux and the heads fly right to the desired position. This characteristic lets voice-coil drives function much more quickly than stepper-motor drives.

Differences between the Two Technologies

There is a price to be paid for the higher speed. Voice-coil drives are more complicated, and consequently, more expensive. Stepper-motor drives essentially "feel" their way to the right track by counting positions along the metal band that moves the heads. Although the metal bands are susceptible to going out of alignment if they overheat, accuracy comes naturally to the stepper mechanism. Voice coils, however, tend to over- or under-shoot their targets, and so constant secondary adjustments must be made. The stepper mechanism is an *open-loop* system: The disk controller commands the motor to move the heads and then proceeds as if the movement has been made accurately. Voice-coil mechanisms, on the other hand, are *closed-loop* systems: The controller repeatedly checks that the heads are locked on to the exact center of a track and adjustments are made when the heads wander.

Servo Data

A voice-coil system ensures that the heads are positioned correctly by reading **servo data** that is permanently encoded on the platters. Usually this information is "embedded" between the tracks. Special sensors on the .read/write heads monitor these **magnetic bursts**; when they sense a burst too strongly, the controller knows that the head is deviating from the center of the track, and it alters the voice-coil current accordingly. Some high-capacity disk drives use a **dedicated servo surface** (**DSS**), for which a whole side of one platter is given over to the servo data, instead of having the data embedded between data tracks. These drives use higher track densities that don't leave enough room for the servo data between the tracks. You may encounter a drive that has an odd number of read/write heads; this is because a platter surface is used for the servo data.

Actuator Performance

We'll discuss relative drive performance in Chapter 3. For now, suffice it to say that, on average, a stepper-motor drive takes from 40 to 60 milliseconds (40 to 60 thousandths of a second) to move from one track to another. Voice-coil drives typically work twice as fast, at 20 to 30 milliseconds. The best voice-coil drives work at double this speed. (It's worth noting that manufacturers have also been making ever faster stepper-motor drives, and a seek time in the 25 millisecond range no longer necessarily indicates a voice-coil drive.) We'll see later that these **average seek times** are only one determinant among many pertaining to drive performance.

Settling Time

There are a couple of other terms occasionally encountered in drive performance ratings. One is the **settling time**. When the heads are moved to a cylinder, they vibrate for a moment. The heads can't be used until they settle down, hence the "settling time." Settling times typically are about three milliseconds, so they can add significantly to the average seek time. To make their drives look better, manufacturers sometimes exclude the settling time from the average seek time rating.

Track-to-track Seek Times

Another measure of a drive's performance is its **track-to-track seek time**. This tells how long it takes the heads to move between adjacent tracks. The value ranges from a few milliseconds in a voice-coil drive to as many as 15 milliseconds in a stepper drive. As you can see, a head movement across many tracks is not merely the sum of the track-to-track seek times.

Average Latency

Another term you may encounter is **average latency**. It tells how long, on average, the drive must wait before a specified bit of data rotates under the heads. This is not the same as the drive's interleave factor. Rather, it indicates how much time will typically pass from the time a read/write head arrives at a track to the time it can begin reading or writing data. Since the figure is an *average*, the figure is exactly one-half rotation. Because most PC drives turn at 60 revolutions per second, the value is the same for almost all: 8.4 milliseconds.

It's worth noting that this figure—although a fraction of a typical seek time—is still quite large. Files that are dispersed around the disk surface incur the average latency period again and again. This also can happen when software processes data as it reads and writes it, so that pauses are introduced between sector accesses. In this way, inefficient software can undermine the performance of even a very "fast" drive.

Bump Detection

Bump detection is an error-avoidance feature first introduced in hard disk cards made by Plus Development Corporation. It provides a solution to the problem of read/write heads veering on to an adjacent track when a hard disk drive is jolted. This event is not terribly serious when data is being read. The controller electronics merely sense that a disruption has occurred, report the failure to the operating system, and the operating system orders a second try. So long as the heads do not touch the disk surface, no damage is done to the data. But when the heads are *writing* data, they continue to project a strong magnetic field as they swerve onto the adjacent track, damaging its data. The damaged data may belong to a different file, so repeating the write operation does not correct the error.

As we've seen, voice-coil head actuators provide constant feedback about the heads' position. In bump detection, the feedback mechanism is modified to include super-fast optical components that instantly sense that the heads have wandered off-track. Before the head reaches the adjacent track, a message is sent to the electronics to stop writing data. Since the data is kept in a buffer on the controller while it is written, the controller can try writing the data again after the heads have restabilized. Obviously, this feature is only possible in drives that use closed-loop head positioning—it can't be implemented on stepper-motor drives.

Head Parking

As we've seen, out-of-control read/write heads are the villain behind disk crashes. There's not much that can be done once a jolt starts the heads wobbling up and down. But keeping the heads away from data-bearing media at least avoids data destruction (although not the danger of head damage). Heads can crash as easily into disk surfaces when a computer is turned off. The damage tends not to be as great in this case, since no energy is added to the collision by the spinning platters, and media damage is kept to one spot rather than stretched along a track. Still, damage is damage, and a drive is particularly likely to be jarred when a computer is turned off and being moved.

The solution to this problem is called *head parking*, and it has a number of variants. In most cases, the drive's read/write heads are simply moved to a cylinder set aside for parking (a **landing strip**), often the innermost cylinder of the disk drive. While the parking track can absorb any amount of gouging, some manufacturers object to the resulting mistreatment and contamination of the read/write heads, and they have taken additional steps to protect the heads. Some have found ways of lifting the heads away from the platter surfaces. Others retract the heads into a "cage," in which the heads can do no harm to either the medium or themselves. Figure 2-8 shows how parking zones are laid out.

Automatic Parking

Nowadays, most quality disk drives perform **automatic head parking**. In automatic parking, the drive senses that the machine has been turned off and quickly moves the heads to their parking places. This action is not so trivial as it seems, particularly with stepper-motor drives, since there is precious little electricity available to drive the mechanics. One clever solution has been to use the drive motor as a generator, siphoning off the rotational energy held in the spinning platters, and using it to drive the head actuator. It is important that an automatic parking system locks the heads in place so that they cannot skip to other cylinders if the machine is moved around.

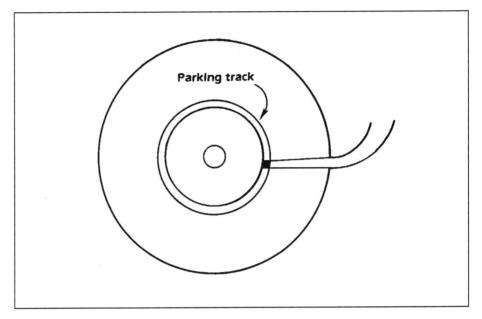

Figure 2-8. Head parking

Automatic head parking comes easily to drives that use voice-coil actuators. The magnetic field pulling the heads toward the center of the platters is countered by springs pulling the heads outward. At least in some designs, the heads naturally move to the outer edge of the disk when power is lost. But action still must be taken to stabilize the heads.

Manual Parking

Drives that do not have automatic head parking require **manual parking**. For a few very early drives, manual parking required that you actually reach into the machine and pull a lever. But these days the expression refers to the need to run a small utility program that moves the heads to the parking track. The utility is usually found on the diskette that accompanies the computer, although some manufacturers who distribute preformatted drives dispense the utility on the hard disk itself.

On IBM's XT and AT systems, this utility is called **SHIPDISK,** although you may encounter some other name, such as **PARK** or **PARKDISK.** It can be the simplest program in the whole world to use. Usually, the program is started up by typing its name at the DOS prompt:

```
SHIPDISK
```

A message appears on the screen informing you that the heads have been parked. That's all. The program is often found on a diskette shipped with the machine. In some clones, this program is built into the machine and called up by a keystroke when the computer boots. PS/2 users who need to park their drives can select option #6 ("Move the computer") from the *Reference Diskette* main menu. Head parking utilities also appear in disk utility collections. For instance, the *Disk Monitor* program in *The Norton Utilities* can park a hard disk drive. There is no such thing as "unparking" a drive. When the computer is turned on again, the disk-initialization code moves the heads away from their parking zone.

When Is Parking Necessary?

A hard disk can receive a jolt at any time, and its data is safer when the heads are parked. But it is not necessary to park the heads every time you finish using the machine. If your drive doesn't automatically park the heads when you shut the power off, it's probably not worth doing it manually. As its name indicates, **SHIPDISK** is meant for preparing the machine for rough treatment during moving, including moving between locations in the same office. If you're going to pick up the machine, be sure to park the heads. You'll find that virtually all portables and laptops that have hard disks park the heads automatically.

Parking during Disk Operation

There are many shareware and freeware utilities that keep a hard disk's heads parked if the drive is unused, even while the machine is turned on. This is done by sequestering a cylinder for use as a "safe zone," over which the heads hover when not in use. When a utility creates this zone, it relocates any data that currently resides there. Thereafter, the program is loaded as a *memory-resident program* every time the machine starts up (via the **AUTOEXEC.BAT** file), linking itself into the DOS disk control routines. When the disk is inactive for several seconds, the utility shunts the heads over to the safety zone, so that the effects of electrical surges or mechanical shocks are directed onto a part of the disk that holds no data. This simple measure greatly reduces the risk of catastrophic data loss through a head crash, because the heads are positioned over data only a small fraction of the time the machine is running.

Disk Geometries

We've seen that disk drives vary by their number of platters, the number of tracks on a platter, and the number of sectors on a track. Since both sides of a platter are recorded upon, it is clearer to refer to the number of *sides* in a drive, rather than the number of platters. A particular disk sector may be referred to as residing at "Side 2, Track 19, Sector 8." Sides are numbered from 0, so a typical two-platter drive has sides 0–3. Tracks are also numbered upward from 0; accordingly, *cylinder 0* consists of the outermost tracks on all sides. Oddly, sectors are counted from 1. A typical drive counts sectors from 1 to 17.

It's worth understanding this numbering system, because drives are usually delivered with a **bad track table** affixed to the drive casing. Some manufacturers print the table on a sticker attached to the drive; others ship the list of bad tracks with the disk on a separate sheet of paper. However, it always lists the tracks with imperfections, giving head and cylinder numbers for each. If you low-level format the disk, you may need to enter the locations of bad tracks, specifying a side and cylinder for each. We'll discuss this topic more in Chapter 4.

The BIOS

Although DOS is the disk operating system, the most fundamental control over the drive is made by the **Basic Input-Output System** (**BIOS**), which is a portion of the operating system that resides on read-only memory chips in the machine. The BIOS is not sophisticated enough to read files. It can perform only the most primitive of disk operations: reading individual sectors. Since the number of sides, tracks, and sectors varies by the drive's capacity and design, the BIOS needs to know the exact characteristics of the drive with which it is working. It needs to know the disk's **geometry**.

The BIOS is held in ROM (read-only memory) chips on the computer's main circuit board. Part of the BIOS is called the **fixed-disk BIOS**. It contains a table that lists the geometries used in a number of disk drives. The drives chosen are considered to be those most commonly used, with sizes ranging from 10M to well over 100M. Drive type 30, for example, represents a 42M hard disk that has two platters (four sides) with 611 cylinders. The fixed-disk BIOS varies between PC manufacturers, so drive type 30 may have different characteristics on a non-IBM-made machine.

New Drive Geometries

The BIOS constantly changes, and more and more drive geometries have been added with each version. The first AT BIOS, for example, which de-scribed 14 drive geometries, was then upgraded to 22, and so on. But dozens of new geometries have appeared, most of which are not supported by the IBM BIOS. Lower-capacity drives tend to follow the standard geometries. But high-capacity drives (those over 100M) usually require modification of the BIOS. There are a number of ways to do this, as we'll see in Chapter 4.

Sector Translation

One way that manufacturers deal with the problem of making unusual drive designs work with the existing BIOS is to make the drive "appear" to have a standard drive geometry when it does not. In sending and receiving data, these drives perform **sector translation**, telling DOS that a sector of data be-longs to a particular track and sector when, in fact, the data belongs to a differ-ent one. In this way, a drive with, say, 26 sectors on a track can pretend to follow a standard 17-sectors-per-track geometry. The drive electronics *translate* the phony sector and track numbers to and from the numbers actually used internally. Performance is in no way degraded. Because many EDSI drives have as many as 35 sectors per track, this scheme is common in ESDI drives (discussed below).

Disk Controllers

The controller card mediates the transfer of data between the disk and the computer's memory. It is called a "controller" because it contains a specially designed disk-controller chip that sends orders to the drive electronics to posi-tion the heads, read and write, and perform a host of other actions. These tasks are not trivial. The electronics precisely sequence the disk drive's activi-ties, translate the encoded bit patterns into actual data, and perform elaborate error checking so that the controller can tell when something has gone wrong. And all of this must be done at extremely high speeds—sometimes faster than the computer itself can process data. Controllers for both diskette drives and hard disk drives are usually combined. This is not true of XT-class machines, however, where a separate adaptor is required for the hard disk.

The disk controller may reside in different places on different systems. *IDE* (Integrated Drive Electronics) drives, for instance, have an **embedded controller**—that is, the controller is on a circuit board that's part of the drive itself. An IDE drive may plug directly into a computer's motherboard or connect to it via a small interface card called a **host adapter**, which merely serves to make a connection between the drive's onboard controller and the computer's bus. Drives that use an interface called *SCSI* (Small Computer Systems Interface) also contain embedded controllers; they connect to a computer either directly (if it has a SCSI interface built in, as does the Macintosh) or via an interface card called a *SCSI host adapter.*

Some motherboards have hard disk controllers built right in. These may be less expensive than a motherboard and a separate controller, but limit the user's choice of hard disk drives. The drive may plug into a socket at the back of the machine or into a socket that is specially positioned inside the machine. No cables are used in some cases; one edge of the drive presents a connector that plugs directly into the controller circuitry. PS/1 machines, some PS/2 computers, and most laptops follow this plan. **Hard disk cards** place everything—drive, controller, and circuitry to interface with the host—on one card. We'll discuss these in Chapter 3.

Data Encoding

One way in which controllers differ is in how they *encode* data. **Encoding** refers to the way raw data from the computer's memory is laid down on the disk surface. It is incorrect to think that the pattern of eight ONs and OFFs that comprise a single character of data is simply written in eight successive magnetic domains along a disk track, with a flux change for ON and no flux change for OFF. In reality, so much data is packed in so little an area that the disk controller would lose its way if extra information was not inserted within the data.

Consider what a difficult job the controller electronics must perform. Beneath the read/write head spins a track containing perhaps 60,000 flux changes. The track is but a few inches long, and its entire length passes under a head every 17 milliseconds—hardly a thousandth of a second per 512-byte (4096-bit) sector. How is the controller to know what part of the disk is under the heads? After all, it garbles the data completely if it misjudges the position by a single magnetic domain.

The answer to this question is that the controller finds the data by watching for patterns of magnetic pulses within the signal. These patterns, which are intermingled with the data, help the controller make sense of the signal it's receiving. Each of the several *encoding schemes* commonly used on hard disks uses a different set of patterns to perform this task. While they differ in their particulars, all the encoding schemes have one thing in common: They make sure that the controller never goes too long without seeing a flux change (a pulse of current) that helps it establish its position.

FM and MFM Encoding

Data must be encoded so that too many zeros (non-flux changes) do not occur in a row. In the **frequency modulation (FM) encoding** scheme, which was once used on floppies but never on PC hard drives, every other magnetic domain was given over as a **clock pulse**—an extra flux change. Half the disk space was wasted by this method. Then someone hit on a more clever scheme, in which the presence or absence of a pulse depended not only on the data but on whether or not there had been a pulse just before. The result was the **modified frequency modulation (MFM) encoding** scheme used on many disks today. By combining the data with the clock signal in a clever way, MFM encoding is able to pack twice as much data on a disk as FM encoding. In MFM encoding, each magnetic domain along a track corresponds to one bit of data.

RLL Encoding

In recent years, **run length limited (RLL) encoding** has gained in popularity. The technique is not new, but until now the electronics that performed it were complex and expensive. RLL translates data into a series of special codes, converting each 8-bit byte of data into a 16-bit code actually written on disk.

Here's how it works. The quality of a disk's magnetic coating determines how close two flux changes may be written without their blurring together. Recall that a flux change corresponds to a binary 1 (to a bit set to ON). Since a byte of data can be a sequence of eight 1s, it would seem that eight times the minimum distance between flux changes would set the minimum distance for storing a byte. Not so.

There are 256 possible patterns of 0s and 1s among the eight bits that form a byte of data. But 16 bits offers 65,536 patterns. So when RLL encoding converts data from 8-bit to 16-bit form, it uses only a small fraction of the patterns available, choosing patterns with special properties.

One desirable property is that at least two 0s be found between each 1. When this is the case, bits may be laid down on the disk at triple the normal density, yet flux changes will never occur closer than the allowable distance.

A second desirable property is that sequences of 0s do not go on too long. The controller attempts to calculate the position of the disk heads by watching a clock, that is constantly readjusted whenever a flux change is encountered (just as a musician in a symphony orchestra keeps an eye on the conductor's baton to synchronize his own counting).

These two criteria are combined to form **RLL 2,7 encoding** in which sequences of 0s always range from two to seven digits (that is, the "run length" of zeros is limited to seven digits). Of the 65,536 16-bit patterns available, 256 are chosen that follow these rules. Then the patterns are written on disk at triple the normal density. Twice the data at triple the density results in a 50 percent effective increase in storage capacity. Another code, **RLL 3,9 encoding**, can nearly double capacity.

Because data can be packed more tightly, RLL lets you increase the number of sectors per track and offers faster data transfer. In addition, having more data on a track means that files can be squeezed into fewer cylinders, so that head motion is reduced. When RLL controllers were first introduced for PCs, they cost 50 to 100 percent more than MFM controllers because they required extremely elaborate, fast, and precise circuitry. Now, however, the price gap has narrowed to the point where they're by far the most economical (though not the highest performance) choice. There's only one caveat of which users should be aware: Make sure that any drive you connect to an RLL controller is clearly marked as "RLL rated" or "RLL certified."

Error Correction

Hard disk controllers also perform error detection and error correction. The controller computes a **cyclic redundancy code (CRC)** from the data as it passes through. The block of data is put through a mathematical formula that yields a long number. This number is written just after the data in its sector. When the data is read back, the controller recalculates the number and compares it to the value recorded in the sector. If they do not match, the controller knows an error has occurred. This technique is sophisticated enough to catch multiple errors.

Depending on the severity of the errors, the controller may or may not be able to recover—either by rereading the disk or by using the information in the **error correction code (ECC)** that's written with every sector. On a typical drive, a **recoverable read error** occurs once in 10 billion bytes. **Non-recoverable read errors** occur once in one trillion bytes. And **seek errors** (where the read/write heads miss their mark) occur once in one million tries. Clearly, these levels of accuracy are more than adequate for most applications. Your data faces far greater dangers from electricial problems, mechanical failure, and human error.

Interfaces

Data transfer rates vary by the kind of **interface** the disk drive uses. An "interface" is the system by which one body of electronic circuitry connects to another, dissimilar body of circuitry, allowing them to communicate and cooperate. There are two interfaces between drive and computer. The disk drive circuitry must communicate with the controller circuitry, and the controller circuitry must communicate with the computer's main circuit board, that is, with the computer's expansion slots (its "bus").

These two kinds of interfaces are called **device-level interfaces** and **system-level interfaces**. As we just explained, data is stored on disk drives in an *encoded* form. On most drives, data leaves the drive in this encoded form and is *translated* into its original form by the controller card. Because, in computerese, the disk drive is a kind of "device," this arrangement is called a *device-level interface*, since the controller communicates with the drive in the drive's own language. Conversely, in a *system-level interface*, data is communicated in its original form—the form that the computer's processor can understand.

The ST506 Interface

Today, four device-level EDSI, SCSI, and IDE standard interfaces are used in IBM personal computers—the traditional **ST506/412 standard**, and the newer and faster **ESDI and SCSI standards**. The ST506/412 standard was designed around 1980 by Seagate Technologies. It was incorporated in a 5-megabyte drive called the ST-506 and, later, in a 10-megabyte drive called the ST-412. IBM chose these drives for use in the first PC XTs, and the rest is history. Other drive manufacturers adopted the standard, and the consumer soon could choose from a vast offering of drives and controllers, secure in the knowledge that they would work together.

You'll rarely see a drive with an ST506 interface with a capacity greater than about 140M. The standard also constrains data transmission speed. The ST506 standard usually runs at a 5-megabits-per-second transfer rate. This rate is well in excess of what an early XT could handle, because the machine could not move data between the transfer buffer as quickly as the disk controller could—the drive was faster than the computer. But this interface can't keep up with very fast 386 and 486 machines, which can easily send or receive data more quickly.

The ESDI Interface

The **ESDI interface** was introduced in response to the limitations of the ST506 standard. It was devised by Maxtor Corporation for use in both hard disks and tape drives (we'll discuss the latter in Chapter 8). Theoretically, this standard allows a 24-megabits-per-second transfer rate, although most ESDI controllers operate at 10 to 15 megabits. An ESDI controller requires an ESDI drive, which typically will have 34 sectors per track instead of the 17 usually found in an ST506 drive. IBM has opted to use the ESDI interface in its PS/2 line of computers for drives of 70M or more.

ESDI drives tend to be of higher quality than drives used with the ST506 interface, but *mechanically* they are much the same. Rather, it is in their electronics that the two kinds of drives differ. An ESDI drive automatically informs the controller of the number of platters, tracks, and sectors-per-track in the drive (it is said to be *autoconfiguring*). As we'll see in Chapter 4, drive configuration can be a problem with ST506 drives, and ESDI drives avoid these difficulties. ESDI drives also simplify disk formatting by automatically informing the controller of the presence of flawed media ("bad tracks") on platter surfaces. More on this is also found in Chapter 4.

An ESDI controller is much more "intelligent" than an ST506 controller. Properly designed, it can handle hard drives, diskette drives, and tape backup units, and it can itself manage file transfers between these devices, even when they use different sector sizes. In addition, the ESDI interface performs better data checking than the ST506 standard.

The SCSI Interface

A third standard has received considerable attention: the **SCSI interface** (pronounced "scuzzy"). The term stands for "Small Computer Systems Interface." SCSI drives are extremely "intelligent." All functions of the controller card are incorporated directly on the drive itself, including the translation of data to and from encoded form. Because no decoding is required on a controller card, these drives provide a *system-level* interface to the computer that can be connected directly to a computer equipped with a SCSI port (which, like an ordinary serial or parallel port, may exist as a socket at the back of the machine). The Apple Macintosh has such a SCSI port, enabling owners to connect hard disks, even though some models lack expansion slots.

IBM has made SCSI ports a standard feature in only a few high-end PS/2 models. For most other PS/2 machines, IBM offers a SCSI *host adapter*. This is a card that fits into one of the machine's slots and connects to one or more SCSI devices. It does little more than provide a pathway from drive to machine. Using only one expansion slot, the SCSI adapter can run up to seven peripherals simultaneously, including hard disks, high-capacity diskette drives, optical disk drives, scanners, and printers. One advantage is obvious: many peripherals can be accommodated without filling up the slots. SCSI is growing in importance in the PC world and (along with IDE) is expected to supplant ESDI because it is an ANSI standard (at this writing, ESDI was still in the final stages of the standardization process) and because it's easy to adapt to many different kinds of computers.

IDE Drives

In the late 1980s, Compaq introduced yet another drive interface for PCs. This one is called "IDE," for "intelligent drive electronics." IDE drives were developed to replace the ST506 interface in AT-style machines. The idea was to create advanced disk drives with built-in controllers (less expensive than a drive plus a separate controller card) and to make them "look" like an IBM PC AT's ST506 controller to the computer for compatibility purposes. Because of this charade, an IDE drive can be introduced into standard PCs without making any extensions to the machine's ROM BIOS (the built-in part of a PC's operating system). The drives are truly "standard," and compatibility problems are minimized.

IDE was designed so that the controller electronics reside within the drive itself. Only some simple circuitry is required to connect the drive with the computer. Like SCSI drives, an IDE drive can understand commands like "format a track" or "write a sector." By comparison, a controller must lead an ST506 or ESDI drive through every step of such a command.

Because the controller electronics are built into the drive, there's no need to fill one of the computer's slots with a controller card. Just a little circuitry and a connector on the computer's main board is all that's required. This feature makes IDE drives especially suitable for laptops. However, IDE adapter cards are available so that IDE drives may be used in machines that do not have a built-in IDE interface. The drives connect to the machine through a single, 40-lead cable.

IDE drives are built for moderate to high performance. Most run at a 1:1 interleave and have built-in data caching (a topic we'll look at in Chapter 7). Many IDE drives have extra sectors that are automatically used when other sectors fall. Yet, for all these advantages, IDE drives and their associated interface circuits are inexpensive. Many industry insiders believe that IDE will bring about the demise of the ST506 interface, and may well banish ESDI and SCSI to use in only the highest-capacity drives.

You should be aware of two disadvantages that accompany IDE drives. First, until recently, there has not been a single IDE standard that every maker has adhered to, and some drives have failed to behave exactly like a drive working through an ST506 interface. And second, some disk utility software won't work with IDE drives, particularly software that performs low-level formatting (many IDE drives are often hard-sectored and therefore can't be low-level formatted).

Full Track Buffers

An interesting feature has been added to some controller cards to allow faster data access. A buffer large enough to hold an entire track is built in. These are called **full-track buffers**. When a request is made to read any sector on a track, the controller reads the whole track, starting with the sector approaching the read/write head. With all sectors loaded into the controller's memory, requests for succeeding sectors are fulfilled instantly. Figure 2-9 diagrams this scheme.

In a sense, a track buffer gives any disk a 1:1 interleave, since data is mechanically read as quickly as possible. If the actual disk interleave is set to other than 1:1, a series of sectors is read from the controller's buffer in a different order than they were acquired. Even a disk operating with a 1:1 interleave may benefit from track buffering. This is because software often manages disk input-output very inefficiently if it processes data as it reads or writes it. The *optimum interleave* is really only optimal when files are moved to and from memory without processing. Processing breaks up the interleave timing, inserting many extra turns of the platters. A turn of the disk takes 17 milliseconds—as much time as a head seek on a fast disk. These delays quickly add up. But when the entire track is read during the first rotation, data can be sent to memory the moment the application software calls for it.

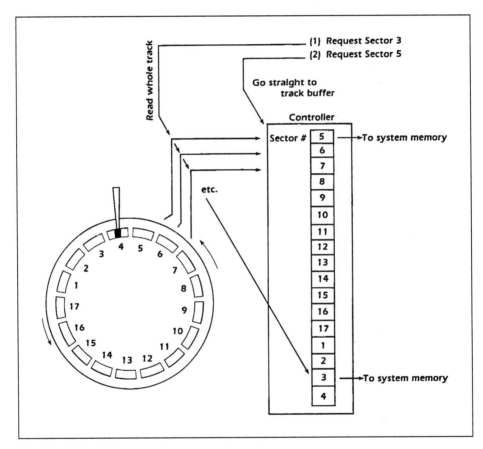

Figure 2-9. A full-track buffer

Writing Data through Track Buffers

So far, we've discussed *reading* data through track buffers. Similar efficiencies are possible when data is written. In principle, nothing is actually written to the disk until the entire buffer fills, whereupon the whole track is written during one rotation of the disk. But even if the buffer is not completely filled with new data, its contents are written out when DOS has the read/write heads move to another track. There's a problem in this approach. The last track "written" into the buffer would never actually be written on the disk. Sooner or later, the machine will be turned off and the data in the buffer will be lost. To avoid this pitfall, track buffers write out their data after a short period of disk inactivity.

Tracks without Sectors

One manufacturer's controller squeezes more capacity out of standard hard drives by not dividing tracks into sectors at all and using the space normally consumed by low-level formatting to store data. By so doing, it fits 26 megabytes on a nominally 20-megabyte drive. During a disk read, the controller copies the whole track into a track buffer, then splits the data into 512 byte chunks. DOS never knows the difference.

Caches versus Track Buffers

In Chapter 7, we'll talk about a genre of software called **disk caches**. These programs keep copies of frequently accessed disk sectors in memory to minimize the number of times the sectors are mechanically accessed on disk. Some caches can circumvent DOS and perform track buffering. When DOS asks for a particular sector, the cache fills memory with every sector it finds on the way to the requested sector.

A cache may be more efficient than a track buffer because it doesn't necessarily read every sector of every track. It may first determine if enough related data is on the track to warrant the trouble. It may also perform the reverse of track buffering and write only one changed sector when DOS would have it write several unchanged sectors as well.

Files

So far, we've looked at how the disk controller organizes data into sectors, tracks, and cylinders on the disk surface. But our applications programs store data as *files*. Most software is completely insulated from the intricacies of disk management. That is DOS's job.

There is a hidden side of DOS that only programmers know about. While most users think of DOS as a collection of commands like COPY and DIR, programmers can call on DOS to perform actions like opening and closing files, or moving the read/write heads to a particular point in a file. Although DOS gives programs access to particular disk sectors, most software is oblivious to the precise locations of files. A program simply asks for data and DOS delivers it, or it supplies data and DOS decides where to place it on the disk.

The Concept of a "File"

A "file" is the concept DOS uses to insulate programs, and people who use programs, from the complexities of data layout on the disk surface. It is really nothing more than a chain of sectors filled with data. Programmers make a distinction between **sequential files** and **random access** files. It's worth understanding the difference. All files consist of a series of data. If the pieces of data have different lengths, as would different length sentences in a word processing document, they are written one after another into the file with special "delimiting" characters placed between them. This is a *sequential file*. If a program wanted to find, say, the twentieth sentence, it would have to search for it starting from the beginning of the file. The software would need to read through the first 19 sentences, because it has no way of calculating the position of the twentieth sentence.

On the other hand, consider a database file consisting of many **records** (collections of data), each record requiring exactly the same number of bytes. Perhaps a record holds a person's name and age, with 20 characters set aside for the name and 2 for the age. These two values are referred to as **fields** in the record, and their length is unchanging. When a name is short, the 20-character field is "padded" to its end with blanks. Conversely, a very long name would be truncated to fit within 20 characters. In this way, all records are kept to 22 bytes, and individual records can be found by multiplying record numbers by 22.

This is a *random access file*. DOS sends the read/write heads directly to the particular sector or sectors from which it needs data, and fetches the data instantly. Random access files are rarely loaded entirely into memory. Sequential files almost always are.

It's important to understand that, from the point of view of the disk drive, and even from the point of view of DOS, sequential files and random access files are identical. A file is defined as being of one kind or the other only by the way that software structures it and accesses it. If required, DOS can read any part of a sequential file, or trace through all of a random-access file—it just seldom makes sense to do so.

File Access Methods

Because many files may be opened at once, DOS needs a way of keeping track of which is which. It does this by setting aside a few dozen bytes of memory to record information about the file. In the earliest DOS versions this area was called a **file control block** (**FCB**). Later DOS versions introduced a simpler approach using **file handles**—a mechanism in which DOS supplies a code number to identify each file. All recent software uses file handles, but DOS still supports FCBs just in case you run a very old program. In either case, the memory needed to track the files must be set aside when the machine starts up. DOS provides the FILES and FCBs configuration commands for this purpose (we'll discuss them in Chapter 4). These are merely means of organizing DOS's access to files. Any file can be read or written by either method.

Clusters

When a new file is recorded on disk, DOS does not usually allot the *exact* number of bytes required by the file. Because the disk controller cannot read *parts* of a sector, DOS must allocate disk space in whole sectors. If the file is anywhere from one to 512 bytes long, a full 512 bytes of space go to it. If it ranges from 513 to 1024 bytes, the 1024 bytes held by two sectors are allotted. Disk allocation is *chunky*.

In reality, only single-sided low-density diskettes and high-density 1.2M and 1.44M diskettes allocate space one sector at a time. Other diskettes and all hard disks allot space in 2-, 4-, or 8-sector chunks. While a 10-byte file takes up 512 bytes of disk space when single sectors are allotted, it consumes 1024, 2048, or 4096 bytes when the minimum allocation is 2, 4, or 8 sectors.

These minimum units of disk-space allocation are called **clusters** (also called **allocation units** in some DOS manuals). DOS numbers clusters from 0 upward, and uses the cluster number to calculate the locations of the sectors the cluster contains. 720K and 360K diskettes use 2-sector clusters; most hard disks use 4-sector clusters. It's important to understand that the cluster size is not an inherent property of the disk. Clusters are simply a unit of storage DOS uses to simplify decisions about disk storage.

Because of its name, it's tempting to conceive of a cluster as being made up of *physically* contiguous disk sectors—for example, that a 4-sector cluster is made up of four sectors in a row along a track. But the disk's interleave factor often prevents this state of affairs. In a disk with a 3:1 interleave, the first cluster might cover sectors 1, 4, 7, and 10. With 17 sectors on a track, some clusters will be spread over two tracks—even two cylinders—since 4 does not divide evenly into 17. And a cluster's sectors are *never* all contiguous unless the disk is formatted with a 1:1 interleave.

Large cluster sizes waste disk space. Whole sectors go unused in the last cluster given to a file, as shown in Figure 2-10. But there is a reason DOS groups sectors into clusters that will become clear when we explain how file allocation tables work. First, let's take a closer look at directories.

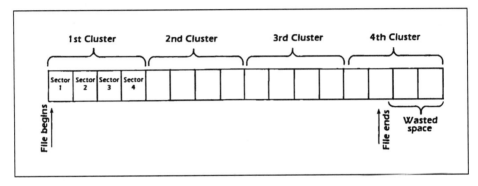

Figure 2-10. Unused space in final clusters

Directories

DOS keeps lists of files on the disk, calling these lists *directories*. A directory, like a file, is a sequence of sectors containing data. But in this case, the data is made by DOS for its own use. Thirty-two bytes is given over to each directory entry. Since sectors contain 512 bytes in DOS, each sector holds 16 directory entries or **slots**. Thirty-two bytes is more than enough space to hold some crucial information:

```
bytes 1-8    the file's name
      9-11   the file's extension (if any)
        12   the file's attribute
     13-22   (presently unused "reserved" space)
     23-24   the time the file was last accessed
     25-26   the date the file was last accessed
     27-28   the file's starting cluster
     29-32   the file's size (in bytes)
```

Most of this information appears in DOS's directory listings, including the file's name and extension, its time and date, and its size. Note that the period between the filename and extension is not recorded in the directory; DOS knows that it should be there, and prints it when it lists a file. When the file name is less than eight characters long, it is "left-justified" and spaces pad out the positions up to number eight. The same is done for the file extension.

The File's Date and Time

You may be surprised to see that the file's time and date are allotted only two bytes. After all, when written out, a date like **12-07-1987** ought to take eight bytes (omitting the dashes), and a time reading like **10:57:16** should take at least six bytes. But DOS does not store these readings as written numbers. Rather, the pair of bytes in a directory listing that hold a file's time or date are split into three parts (*fields*), each holding a month, day, or year, or an hour, minute, or second. A whole byte can hold a number from *0* to *255*, and parts of a byte can hold smaller ranges of numbers. The byte pairs are subdivided into fields just large enough to hold, say, *1* to *12* for months, or *0* to *23* for hours.

The File Size

Similarly, the four bytes allotted for the file size can hold a number from 1 to 4,294,967,296—more than adequate for the Great American Novel. In reality, DOS versions prior to 4.0 cannot create files larger than about 33 million bytes. We'll explain why in a moment.

The Starting Cluster

As you can see, each directory entry contains some information that is not listed by the DIR command. The **starting cluster** gives the number of the first (and possibly only) cluster allocated to the file. DOS takes this number, converts it to the equivalent sector numbers, and begins to access the file. The file allocation table (discussed below) points the way to the *next* cluster occupied by the file.

The Attribute Byte

The other concealed content of a directory entry is its **attribute byte**. An attribute byte holds a number indicating whether the file possesses certain special characteristics or **attributes**. For normal files, the attribute byte is 0. Adding 1 makes it "read-only," adding 2 makes it "hidden," and so on. Adding 1 *and* 2 makes it "read-only" *and* "hidden." There are six attributes in all.

Read-only, Hidden, and System Files

Only three of the attributes name special properties for an ordinary file. These are the "read-only," "hidden," and "system" attributes. When the **read-only attribute** is set, DOS knows that it must not write into the file, even if asked to do so by a program. DOS also stops the DEL and ERASE commands from deleting a file when this attribute is set. The **hidden attribute** tells DOS not to display the file in directory listings. And the **system attribute** informs DOS that the file is an operating system file. The system attribute has not been used consistently, and it generally occurs in combination with the hidden attribute. Note that files marked with these attributes are ordinary in all other respects. The attributes merely tell DOS how to handle the file.

The Volume Label

The remaining three attributes have special roles and do not categorize files. One is the **volume label attribute**. Recall that you can attach an electronic 11-character label—the **volume label**—to any diskette or hard disk. DOS begins directory listings with the volume label, as in:

Volume in drive A is SPELLCHK

The volume label is stored in a disk's root directory as a filename and extension. When DOS scans the directory, it knows from the attribute byte that a directory slot contains the disk's volume label and not a filename.

The Archive Attribute

The **archive attribute** is also special. We'll be talking about it a good deal in our discussion of backups in Chapter 8. DOS *sets* this attribute (changes it to ON) when it writes to an existing file or creates a new one. When backup utilities make copies of files, they scan directories for files with the archive attribute set, make the copy, then *reset* the attribute (turn it OFF). The next time backups are performed, the backup software can be made to copy only files that have been changed in the meantime and have had their archive attributes set once more. This feature makes *incremental backups* possible.

The Subdirectory Attribute

Finally, the **subdirectory attribute** marks a file as a subdirectory. To understand the function of this attribute, we need to look at how DOS constructs a directory tree. DOS places the root directory on the outer edge of the disk (on cylinder 0). The root directory size depends on the type of disk and its capacity. DOS typically allocates 32 sectors for the root directory on hard disks. Since each sector contains 16 slots, the root directory usually can hold no more than 512 entries (32 times 16). The root directory is a specially allocated area of the disk. DOS has no trouble accessing it because it is always found at the same place and never changes size. The root directory spans the full 32 sectors even when the disk contains one file.

Subdirectories, on the other hand, are constructed as ordinary files on the disk. Like the root directory, these files consist of a series of 32-byte listings. As with any file, space is allocated to a subdirectory one cluster at a time. When you use the DOS MKDIR command to add a subdirectory to the disk, DOS creates a file with the subdirectory's name, allocating a cluster to it. As files are added to the subdirectory, the first cluster fills and a second is added. There is no limit to the subdirectory's growth since there is no (realistic) limit to DOS file size. Hence, unlike the root directory, subdirectories can contain any number of files.

Consider the chain of subdirectories that form the path \MAMMALS\ PRIMATES\GIBBONS. The root directory holds an entry for the subdirectory file MAMMALS, MAMMALS holds an entry for the file PRIMATES, and PRIMATES holds an entry for GIBBONS. DOS knows that these files are subdirectory files, and not just ordinary data files, because the subdirectory attribute is set in the attribute bytes of each of these entries.

The Dot and Double-dot Entries

Listings of subdirectories begin with the peculiar "." (dot) and ".." (double-dot) entries. These represent the contents of the first two slots in the directory. The single dot refers to the file that holds the subdirectory itself. The double dot refers to the file holding the *parent* directory (the directory that lists the subdirectory). The root directory lacks the dot and double-dot listings because it requires neither of these references.

Erased Files

Finally, you should know how DOS tells whether a directory slot is occupied or not. When it creates a new directory, DOS sets the first byte of each slot to 0 to show that the entry is open. When a file is created, the first byte of the filename overwrites this 0, and DOS knows that the slot contains a file listing. To erase the file, DOS merely overwrites the first byte of the directory entry with the value 229. Thereafter, DOS can tell that the slot is available for another file. No other information in the directory slot is destroyed by the "erasure," and the file itself remains on disk until it is overwritten by another. Hence "erased" files and subdirectories are often recoverable—a topic we'll have a lot to say about in Chapter 7.

The File Allocation Table

Directories tell only the starting cluster for a file. Yet most files occupy more than one cluster. How does DOS find the remainder? While formatting the disk, DOS makes a **file allocation table** or **FAT**. The FAT is the most important entity on a disk. It's very difficult to recover data from the disk when the FAT has been destroyed by a head crash or by accidental formatting. When we discuss *unerase* and *unformat* utilities in Chapter 9, you'll see why the FAT is so important. DOS actually keeps two copies of the FAT on disk so that there is a standby when one is detectably damaged.

Structure of the FAT

The FAT is nothing more than a table of numbers, where every position in the table correlates with a cluster of disk space. The first position represents cluster 0, the next represents cluster 1, and so on. Each position holds a number telling where a file continues. Consider the file named LONGFILE. Its directory entry tells that the file begins at cluster 100. DOS reads the sectors in cluster 100 then consults *position 100* in the FAT for the number of the next cluster, say, 105. Then DOS reads the next portion of the file from cluster 105 and checks position 105 in the FAT to find the next cluster in the sequence. When DOS encounters a FAT position containing a special code number, it knows that it has reached the end of the file.

FAT Size

The size of a FAT varies by the size of a disk *and* by cluster size. Larger disks hold more clusters and, accordingly, require larger FATs. Similarly, when cluster size is reduced, more FAT entries are needed to point to the increased number of clusters. Another consideration is the size of the numbers used in the FAT to label the clusters. Diskette FATs use numbers a byte and a half long; these can range up to 4096, which is more clusters than a diskette can hold. But most hard disks have at least 10,000 clusters, so their FATs require two-byte numbers, which range to 65535. The larger numbers increase the FAT size by a third.

We saw earlier that single-sector clusters use disk space most economically. With single sectors, no more than a fraction of a sector is wasted at the end of each file. But small clusters make for many clusters, and that leads to a very large file allocation table. To use the FAT, DOS must move it into memory. But a 20M disk using single-sector clusters would have a 78K FAT!

When IBM first released the XT, memory chips were still very expensive, and few machines had more than 256K of RAM. To conserve memory, the DOS versions issued for the XT (DOS 2.x) used eight-sector clusters to minimize the size of the FAT. Later DOS versions (3.x) reverted to four-sector clusters as memory prices fell. Interestingly, 1.44M and 1.2M diskettes use a single-sector cluster. Because these disks have a relatively small capacity, the FAT is not unacceptably large. And the minimal cluster size helps pack as much data as possible onto a medium primarily intended for backups.

The Boot Record

As you no doubt know, when the computer is booted, DOS is loaded into memory and runs the show. But there's a paradox in this. "DOS" stands for "disk operating system," and "operating disk drives" is just what DOS does. So how can DOS be loaded from disk if it is not already in memory to do the work?

The solution to this conundrum lies in the expression "booting." It means that the machine "picks itself up by its bootstraps"—a similarly unlikely feat. A small part of the operating system—the **Basic Input-Output System** or **BIOS**—is built into the machine. It is kept on read-only memory chips on the main circuit board. When the computer is turned on, it is initially run by this tiny program. The program is just smart enough to find the disk drives, start them turning, and read a single sector on the outer edge of the disk.

This sector is called the **boot record**. It resides on side 0, track 0, sector 1; logically, it is the very first sector on the disk. The boot record contains all sorts of information about the disk that is essential for any operating system that will use it. It tells the sector size, the number of sectors per cluster and sectors per cylinder, the number of cylinders, and the FAT and directory sizes. It also contains a **media descriptor byte** that reports the kind of drive in use. The boot record records the DOS version that the disk was formatted under, and it holds some basic error messages it can throw on the screen if, for example, COMMAND.COM can't be found. Finally, the boot record contains the names of two special files that hold a bit more of the operating system.

System Files

With this information in hand, the machine is able to seek out a file called IBMBIO.COM (in PC DOS, or IO.SYS in MS-DOS). With IBMBIO.COM loaded, the operating system turns control over to it, and it in turn loads IBMDOS.COM (or MSDOS.SYS). (Incidentally, in their directory entries, these files are marked with both *hidden* and *system* attributes, so you won't see them in directory listings.) With IBMDOS.COM loaded, the machine is smart enough to load COMMAND.COM and start it running. The operating system has bootstrapped itself into control.

The SYS Command

Sometimes software manufacturers want their distribution diskettes to be bootable. But the system files are protected by copyright law, so the software vendors cannot include them. IBM has accommodated this need by providing the **/B** switch in the **FORMAT** command. It sets aside room for IBMBIO.COM and IBMDOS.COM in the root directory and on Cylinder 0. When the software buyer receives the diskette, he or she applies the DOS **SYS** command, which moves the system files from the DOS diskette to the reserved areas on the software distribution diskette, making it bootable. COMMAND.COM is not copied over by SYS; that must be done by the **COPY** command.

Partitioning

Our description of the boot record actually applies only to diskettes. Hard disks have two types of boot records. They are required because hard disks may be *partitioned* into two or more parts, each serving a different operating system, or acting as a different disk drive under DOS. Don't think of partitions as slices of a pie. Each partition is allotted a series of contiguous cylinders, so they're more like donuts.

Earlier, we mentioned **low-level formatting**, which maps out the sectors on the disk surface. A second type of formatting, **high-level formatting**, adds the root directory, file allocation tables, and other critical information to the disk. Partitioning is performed *between* low- and high-level formats. With the sectors in place, the partitioning program decides where each partition begins. It writes this information in the **partition table**, which is contained in the **master boot record**. After the partition is created, the root directory, FATs, and system files are placed at the beginning of the partition, at whatever cylinder it begins.

The Master Boot Record

Like an ordinary boot record on a diskette, the master boot record is located on side 0, track 0, sector 1. It contains just enough information to let the BIOS do some elementary disk operations. But unlike ordinary boot records, it contains no information pertaining to a specific operating system, such as the names of system files. Instead, it provides information in the partition table that gives the starting points on the disk for the various partitions. The computer reads it, learns from it which operating system is the one used for booting, and moves the read/write heads to the first sector of that operating system's partition. On that sector, it finds the ordinary boot record specific to the operating system, which it then reads, booting the machine. Figure 2-11 diagrams this scheme.

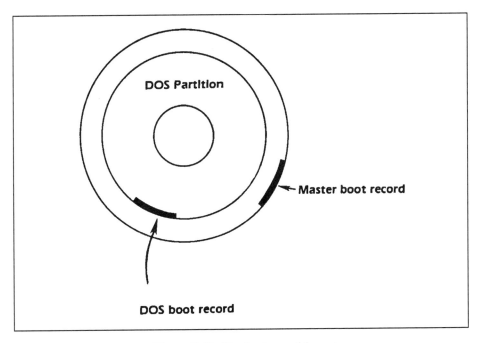

Figure 2-11. The boot record layout

The Rationale for Partitioning

It's easy to see why separate boot records are required for each partition, and why a master boot record is used to keep track of them. Each operating system has its own formats for directories, file allocation tables, or whatever. Given these irregularities, it would be impossible to give the operating systems equal access to all files. Generally, all operating systems share the same 512-byte sector size; but special utilities can change the sector size in a partition (as we'll see in Chapter 4).

Most PC users confine themselves to DOS, but they still must partition the disk, simply because every hard disk expects initially to find a master boot record—not an ordinary one. In such cases, the partitioning program (called **FDISK** in DOS) gives over the whole disk to DOS, and places the DOS boot record on the sector immediately following the master boot record.

The 32-megabyte Limit

You may have heard that DOS versions earlier than 4.0 cannot handle partitions larger than 32M and may wonder how computers can use drives larger than 32M. There *is* such a limit, but it is not related to the sizes of clusters or file allocation tables. Rather, it is the underlying nature of **16-bit architecture** that is the culprit.

The earliest processors—the ones DOS was designed around—work with 16-bit numbers. A number of this size can hold a value from 0 to 65,535. The machines can handle larger numbers, but they find them unwieldy. To keep matters simple, the designers of DOS limited the numbering of disk sectors to the 0 to 65,535 range. DOS refers to the first sector on the first track of the first platter side as "Sector 0." The next sector on that track is "Sector 1," and so on. The number system extends inward from cylinder to cylinder, all the way to "Sector 65535," if the disk is large enough. Since DOS always uses 512-byte sectors, simple multiplication gives the 32M limit: 512 x 65,536 = 33,554,432 (programmers define a "megabyte as 1024 bytes, so they call this number "32" megabytes in spite of its being more than 33). DOS cannot access data from sectors numbered 36,656 and beyond because it cannot count that high!

How can DOS work on high-capacity disks that contain far more than 65,536 sectors? In a moment, we'll see how a disk may be *partitioned* so that disk space is divided in a way that it works as multiple disk drives, one partition acting as drive C, one as drive D, and so on. A partition can begin at any point on the disk, even if it is at the 100,000th sector. But starting from that point, DOS (prior to Version 4.0) can count only 65,536 sectors. That is, the range of 65,536 sector numbers used by DOS is an *offset* from the start of the DOS partition.

Advanced Partitioning Schemes

Following the introduction of 40M (and larger) drives, DOS 3.3 was modified to allow DOS to use the entire disk capacity. This was done by permitting *multiple* DOS 32-megabyte partitions, not by making a single huge DOS partition possible (although utility software had been available to do this job for earlier DOS versions). With Version 4.0, DOS crossed the Rubicon and allowed single partitions to exceed 32 megabytes. This advance was achieved by introducing 32-bit sector numbers to allow huge partitions (*over four trillion bytes*). Of course, DOS can still handle disks that use the earlier 16-bit sector numbers. Before accessing a disk, it checks to see which system is used. This system continues unchanged in DOS 5.0. We'll discuss the details of partitioning in Chapter 4.

Alternative Storage Technologies

So far, we've described nonremovable hard disk drives. There are variants on this basic technology, including removable cartridge drives, high-capacity drives, and hard disk cards, which we'll look at in detail in Chapter 3. In addition to these variants, alternate forms of data storage technology have appeared, some of which may someday become as prevalent as hard disks. Even the lowly diskette has been making an impressive show. Laser disks have entered the market in earnest. And solid-state storage devices (banks of permanently-powered RAM chips) are now taken seriously. We'll take a quick tour of these technologies to help you understand them as they develop.

Diskette Drives

We tend to think of diskettes as "low-tech." But exciting developments are occurring in diskette technology. Diskettes are based on the same principles as hard disks, but the design differs slightly. The read/write heads press lightly against the disk surface when you close the drive door. The coating on the disk is made thick to withstand the abrasion of the heads and disk jacket.

Because diskettes are *floppy*—even those in hard plastic casings—they are given to deformation. The dimensions of a disk constantly change with temperature and humidity. And because diskettes are mounted in the drive by a flimsy hub, they tend to sway off-center. For these reasons, the positions of the tracks are not as precisely defined as on a hard disk. Diskette drives use stepper-motor head actuators which, you will recall, do not monitor a track's position, but simply move the read/write heads to its expected location.

To counter these deficiencies, far fewer tracks are placed on the disk, and the tracks are wider. A 360K diskette records tracks at 48 tracks-per-inch (tpi), compared to over 1,000 tpi on some hard disks. The "high-density" 1.2M drives double this track density to 96 tpi, and the 3½-inch drives extend it to 135 tpi.

Why Diskettes Don't Crash

You may have wondered why diskettes don't crash. In fact, diskettes would seem to be in a perpetual state of crash, given that the read/write heads always rest against the surface of the disks as they turn. But a crash requires the exertion of much energy upon a small point on the disk surface, and a diskette drive is not designed that way. The disk turns slowly, the heads are large, and the disk itself is flexible. When a force is exerted on the diskette drive, the energy imparted to the head is not amplified so much by the disk's own energy, the energy is distributed over a broader surface, and the diskette gives as the head punches it. Very little wear and tear results. But while diskettes do not crash, they are gradually worn down by the constant abrasion of the heads and the envelope in which diskettes reside. This is why DOS does not keep diskettes constantly turning.

3½-inch Diskettes

Diskettes make capacity gains mostly by packing more tracks on a disk, rather than more data on a track. Paradoxically, the smaller the diskettes, the higher the track density. A smaller diameter means that disk deformations are smaller, too. The hub in the rigid plastic packages can more precisely center the disk. And the package keeps the disk flatter as it turns, so that it doesn't bounce away from the drive's read/write heads.

High Data Densities

Manufacturers have started releasing diskette drives with extremely high data densities. They may fit up to 20M on a 3½-inch diskette. This density is achieved in part by writing five times as many tracks as on an ordinary high-density disk. The read/write heads use a closed-loop system (like voice-coil hard drives), and special circuitry is included to compensate for disk centering misalignment and disk deformation. Embedded servo data is written on the disks when they are manufactured (the disks are more expensive than ordinary ones). Although they use diskettes, such drives hook up to a standard hard-disk interface. These drives are still expensive compared to ordinary diskette drives.

Applications

The manufacturers of some high-capacity diskette drives offer them as alternatives to hard drives. However, while their seek times approach those of some hard drives, high-capacity diskettes have slower rotational speeds, which means slower data transfer rates and more time waiting for the right sector to come around. And, because there are only two tracks to a cylinder in diskette drives, files tend to be more widely dispersed, and more head seeks are needed to access them.

Still, super-high-capacity diskettes may be the ideal backup or archiving medium since they save the trouble of swapping numerous diskettes in and out of drives and they offer immediate random access to any file when data is read back. As larger markets for these drives develop, they promise to become cheaper than removable hard disks, optical disks, or streaming tape. Another advantage is that even huge programs can fit on a single diskette, reducing software distribution costs.

Bernoulli Technology

One approach to high-capacity diskettes deserves special mention. This is **Bernoulli technology**, in which diskettes are enclosed in a special casing in a way that makes them semi-rigid when they spin. The disks become as stable as hard disk platters, allowing much higher data densities. They are halfway between diskettes and hard disks.

The technology was introduced as the *Bernoulli Box* in 1982 by Iomega Corp. Bernoulli technology is based on a well-known principle discovered by the Swiss mathematician Daniel Bernoulli in the eighteenth century. It states that the pressure in a stream of fluid diminishes as the speed of its flow increases. The principle is the same one that accounts for lift on aircraft wings. In fact, it may be said that in Bernoulli technology the disk is made to *fly* over the read/write head, rather than vice-versa.

Cartridge Design

In Iomega's rendition of the principle, two 5¼-inch, single-sided disks are enclosed in a thick, hard-plastic cartridge that has openings for read/write heads. The two disks are single-sided, with their data-bearing sides facing outward. The openings on either side of the cartridge remain closed until the cartridge is inserted into a drive. At the openings, between the read/write heads and the disks, is a *Bernoulli plate,* a specially-formed metal sheet that facilitates the Bernoulli effect. As the disks spin, pressure drops, and they are drawn to within a few thousandths of an inch of the plates. The read/write heads project through the plate, and slightly beyond it. Secondary effects draw the rotating disks extremely close to the head.

Crash-proof Design

A wonderful benefit follows from this design. Since the heads are stationary and the disks are flying, when a disturbance occurs the Bernoulli effect is broken, the disk reverts to its floppy state, and it pulls *away* from the head. The drives are virtually crash-proof! This is just the opposite of an ordinary hard disk, where the heads plunge into the disk surface when the air cushion that supports them is broken. We'll talk more about Bernoulli technology in Chapter 3, where we'll go over some other advantages and disadvantages.

Optical Disks

One of the most interesting new areas of disk storage technology is **optical disks**. These come in several varieties: CD-ROMs, WORM disks, and read/write magneto-optical disks. CDs, or 5¼-inch "compact discs," are most often used for audio recording. But the same digital techniques that record an hour of music on one side of a compact disc can store as much as 550 megabytes of data. That's the equivalent of a dozen 40M hard disks, 380 1.44M diskettes, or 250,000 pages of text. Compact discs that store data are called **CD ROMs,** meaning "compact disc read-only memories." They are like ROM memory chips in that they come from the factory with information permanently written on them. They cannot be erased and reused.

Data Densities

Optical disks store data as tiny pits, dimples, or marks on a reflective layer that's sealed within the transparent disk. A laser shines on a track, and a sensor measures the light that's reflected. On CD ROMs and WORM drives, a bright or dark spot may indicate a binary 1 or a binary 0; on magneto-optical drives, the angle at which the reflected light is polarized determines the value of a bit. The markings are only a third of a micron (one millionth of a meter) across, allowing densities of about 15,000 bits per inch. Although this density is on par with magnetic recording, laser disks can achieve much higher *track densities* than hard disks. While a hard disk's magnetic domains form long bars in which the edges may interfere with adjacent tracks, the pits in an optical disk are circular and compact. Sixteen thousand tracks per inch are possible—more than 10 times as many as on a hard disk. There are signs that doubled, even quadrupled, data densities may evolve, leading to the one or two billion-byte CD ROM.

Read/Write Technology

The greatest drawback of CD ROM drives is that one cannot write new data to a disk or erase old data. But two kinds of **read/write drives** are now available. The first kind to be developed was **WORM** drives, meaning "write-once, read-many" (that is, each track may be written upon only once, but can be read any number of times). Write-once technology is simpler than erasable technology, but it's limitations are obvious. Everytime a changed file is written to disk, it must be written on previously unused tracks; space occupied by the prior version of the file is abandoned. Blank WORM disks—which can be quite expensive—fill quickly. For this reason, write-once drives are often closely coupled with hard disks. Rather than repeatedly writing to the optical disk, most users store intermediate versions of a file that is stored on the hard disk, and save copies on the WORM drive every now and then.

WORM drives are most popular as a backup and archiving medium. Because every version of a file remains intact on the disk, this technology is valued for leaving an "auditable" record of various kinds of business transactions. The data is not actually tamper-proof, however, since a drive can be made to write a second time on data, scrambling it. Some companies have used WORM technology for storing massive amounts of unchanging data. There are even giant jukebox-like contraptions that manage scores of 12-inch optical platters.

The second kind of read/write drive—called a **magneto-optical** drive—first appeared as a mass-market product in the NeXT computer. Unlike WORMs, magneto-optical drives allow data to be erased and rewritten; for this reason, some of NeXT's first machines contained a magneto-optical drive instead of either a diskette or hard drive. Unfortunately, users were dissatisfied with this arrangement. A magneto-optical drive wasn't a good replacement for a conventional hard disk because it was several times slower. Nor was it a good replacement for diskettes. The blank disks cost $50 or more each, which made them impractical for distributing software or data. As a result, NeXT's subsequent products contained ordinary diskette and hard drives.

Read/Write Techniques

Data is recorded on an optical disk using one of several techniques. CD ROMs are mechanically stamped. WORM drives write data by focusing a laser on the reflective layer inside the disk and melting a small spot. In magneto-optical drives, a magnet works in tandem with a laser to write the disk. A magneto-optical disk contains a layer of a special material that polarizes the light it reflects; the angle of polarization at each spot depends on the way that spot is magnetized. (This effect is known to scientists as the Kerr Effect.) The coating also has another important property: It can only be magnetized when heated. A magnetic field doesn't affect the disk at normal temperatures, but, when a high-energy pulse from the laser is focused on a spot on the disk's surface, the material at that one spot is heated past a temperature called the Curie Point. Above that temperature, data can be written or erased by a magnetic write head. Because only the spot that's heated can be changed, the magnetic field doesn't have to be aimed precisely, and the head doesn't need to be as close to the media as it would be in a hard disk. To read the disk, the drive simply focuses a much weaker beam of laser light on the same spot—not intense enough to heat the medium above the Curie Point, but bright enough to let a sensor measure the polarity of the reflected light.

Advantages

The advantages of optical disks are many. There can be no head crashes because only a beam of light touches the disk. The disks are not easily damaged, and they have a lifetime of at least 20 years. The high capacity makes space for elaborate error-checking codes. And CD-ROM disks can be cheaply produced by stamping them out like phonograph records. The drives are also inherently simple and inexpensive to make.

Types of Drives

An ordinary audio CD player cannot be used with CD ROMs. Although the basic technology is the same, quite different electronics are required. As with any hard disk, a controller card accompanies CD drives, along with device driver software. The price of these units is falling rapidly, and soon they should be no more expensive than a cheap hard disk drive. To make them more palatable, some manufacturers are designing CD ROM drives that double as an audio CD playback drive that can be plugged into ordinary hi-fi equipment.

Performance

One problem with optical disk technology is that most have slow average seek times compared to hard disk drives. CD ROM drives are especially slow in this respect: In 1990, the fastest commercial drives offered 340-millisecond seek times—some 30 times slower than the fastest hard disk drives! This is because a hard disk's read/write head is a tiny electromagnet, while CD drives must move a sizable optical assembly across the disk surface. Another problem with CDs is that, because the drives use only one single-sided platter, the cylinder density (number of sectors found at one head position) is low. But intense research will undoubtly push seek times downward, perhaps to hard disk performance levels. Some experts predict that future CD ROM drives will use a read/write head that is hardly more than a single fiber-optic strand wafting above the disk surface. Magneto-optical drives are faster than CD ROMs, but are still slower than hard drives for two reasons. First, they don't spin as fast, which means they wait longer for data to pass under the head. And, second, they take three revolutions of the disk to write data: one to erase the old data, one to write the new data, and one to verify that everything was written correctly. However, they do have seek times comparable to those of moderately priced hard drives. WORM drives vary in speed; most come out somewhere between CD ROMs and magneto-optical drives.

Market Trends

The spread of CD ROM technology is well underway. Industry-wide standards have been devised, opening the way for anyone to publish a disk that can be read by any drive. There have been many complaints that the standards are inadequate, however. It is not enough to just pack a lot of information on a disk. The information must be *indexed* so that the operating system can readily find it, and the information must be stored in a way that it can be understood and processed by application programs. For the moment, incompatibilities abound.

The first major CD ROM release was the *Grolier Electronic Encyclopedia*: an entire 20-volume, nine-million-word book transferred to disk and cross-referenced with a mainframe computer for spitfire lookups. Most major references have been released, such as the *U.S. Zip Code Directory* and *Books in Print*. Many business databases are available (with periodic updates), effectively replacing certain on-line services. PC special-interest groups have released huge public-domain software libraries. A variety of disks containing graphic images and laser fonts are also available. Finally, some publishing companies have collected small libraries of related books and images onto a single CD for educational use. One includes over 100 books about American History, with thousands of related images.

CD-I

The two companies that pioneered audio CDs, Phillips and Sony, have developed their own CD data standard called CD-I, for "Compact Disc-Interactive." The standard accommodates computer software, numeric and text data, sound, graphic stills, and primitive motion video. It was developed for the consumer electronics market. CD-I incorporates a Motorola 68000 microprocessor, providing the basis for elaborate interactive entertainments and educational programs. A group of engineers at RCA's Sarnoff Laboratory (taken over by General Electric and now part of chip maker (Intel) has developed DV-I, a way of storing 72 minutes of full moving video on a compact disk. Intel, birthplace of the microprocessors at the heart of all PCs, has licensed this technology and developed it further. Which technologies will ultimately sweep the marketplace is anyone's guess.

Future Trends

Opinions about the future role of compact discs in computing are as numerous as the grains of sand of the Sahara. Some describe CD ROMs as "a solution in search of a problem," believing that their use will be limited until low-priced read/write technology appears. Others claim that read-only CDs can revolutionize information processing. The truth could lie at either extreme, or anywhere between. It all depends on your view of computing.

Proponents of CD ROM see the technology as handmaiden to more advanced software—software that could not effectively exist without CD's help. They believe that the near-term application of CD ROM to reference sources and databases will be superceded by elaborate, graphics-based *knowledge bases* upon which software will rely for artificial intelligence processing. Only compact disks can fulfill this role, because only they can act as an inexpensive distribution medium for such vast amounts of data.

Solid State Storage

One way of getting around disk drive performance limitations is to eliminate the drives altogether, replacing them with banks of memory chips. One megabyte of chips becomes a 1M disk drive. The memory is organized as a **RAM disk** (also called a **virtual disk**). In RAM disks, 512-byte blocks of memory are treated as if they were disk sectors. Data is written into these 512 positions instead of a physical stretch of magnetic medium on a disk. Because there's no such thing as a read/write head in a RAM disk, every sector is instantly accessible. No time is wasted shuttling read/write heads from track to track, or in waiting for the right sector to rotate into view. For these reasons, RAM disks are very fast.

Memory Densities

RAM disks have benefitted from the continuing progress toward higher-capacity memory chips. One-megabit chips began shipping in quantity in early 1987, 4-megabit chips two years later, and 16-megabit chips are on the horizon. Note that these chips hold *megabits*, not *bytes*; it takes a set of eight chips to form *megabytes* (actually nine, since an extra chip is required for error-checking). New designs tend to be very expensive when they're first introduced. But if history is any guide, even the very high-capacity chips will ultimately become cheap. Two sets of 16M chips could form a 32M RAM disk at a price lower than a mechanical drive.

Drawbacks

The problem with RAM disks is that they lose their data when power is removed for only an instant. It's possible to make a RAM disk retain data when the computer is turned off by providing them with their own power supply; this is called a **non-volatile RAM disk**. And, to make sure that data isn't lost in the event of a power outage, most non-volatile RAM disks make provisions for batteries that can keep the chips "alive" until the power comes back on again.

Flash EEPROM

One form of solid-state memory that retains data without the need for a continuous power supply is called **Flash EEPROM**. Pioneered by Intel, these chips retain data for years without power and cost about as much as an equivalent amount of static RAM. And, like RAM, they're much faster than hard disks.

While at this writing Flash EEPROM is far more expensive per megabyte than hard disk storage, it's already being used in memory cards for palmtop computers. If prices continue to fall, it may replace hard drives in some notebook and desktop machines as well.

Where Is Hard Disk Technology Going?

Looking at the various optical and electronic storage options, it's tempting to conclude that the days of hard disks are numbered. But hard disk technology can be pushed far beyond the performance we are accustomed to. For example, the drives used in supercomputers may employ 14-inch platters and transfer data at 100M per second or more. The capacity of these drives is measured in *giga*bytes (billions of bytes) and cost tens of thousands of dollars (however, the price per megabyte of storage is comparable to an ordinary PC hard drive).

Not too many years ago, mainframe computers ran on 20M drives, and those drives were fantastically expensive. How much further can hard disk technology go? As we've seen, better electronics permits advanced RLL encoding technology that can double recording densities. And ever-better head designs can greatly increase the number of magnetic domains that can be packed along a track, and the number of tracks that can fit on a disk. Multiplied together, at least a tenfold capacity increase is in view. A 200- or 300-megabyte hard disk could be standard by the mid-1990s.

The question is, at what cost? We've watched the prices of all kinds of hardware drop terrifically in recent years. Price decreases result partly from the economies of scale associated with mass marketing. They also come from improved production techniques. But it's worth remembering that ever higher technology tends to be ever more *precise* technology. Production techniques tend to become more complicated with every advance, and that fact limits how far prices can drop. So a tenfold increase in disk capacities will probably not translate into a tenfold drop in cost per megabyte of disk storage.

Competition with Optical Drives

It's likely that, in the mid-90s, erasable optical drives will be available in the same price range as hard disks. But whether these drives will be as fast as hard disks is doubtful. Most likely, optical disks will *complement* rather than *replace* hard disks for a long time to come. Acting as *tertiary storage*, optical disks and high-capacity tape drives will take the pressure off hard-disk capacity requirements. They will become the primary distribution medium for reference materials, databases, and graphic images; and they will be the ideal archive medium for hard disk backups and business records. Meanwhile, the venerable diskette will continue to be used for software distribution, since no other medium promises to be nearly so cheap.

The Speed Bottleneck

By the mid-1990s, many microcomputers will function at what traditionally has been regarded as mainframe speed. They will run outlandishly complicated operating systems. Disk drive speed may become the critical bottleneck in a computer's performance, since advanced multitasking operating systems constantly access the disk. Consequently, there's going to be constant pressure on hard disk manufacturers to produce ever faster drives. And while solid-state storage is becoming denser and cheaper, it will still have a hard time catching up to hard drives, which currently offer 10 to 100 times as much capacity per dollar spent.

In summary, we can expect hard disks to continue to be the mainstay of secondary storage through the 1990s. They'll run faster and hold more data. And they'll come to possess more "smarts" that will make for greater reliability and higher performance. Unfortunately, they'll also go right on threatening our data. Since hard disks won't go away soon, you'll do well to understand them thoroughly.

What, Where, and How to Buy

In this chapter we'll discuss the bewildering array of options facing the hard disk buyer. Once upon a time, you merely had to decide whether to ask the computer store for a 5-megabyte or a 10-megabyte internal drive. Today, the decision has become much more complicated. You must anticipate how your own hard disk needs will change as new kinds of software enter the market. A move to desktop publishing, for example, completely changes your disk-capacity requirements. Equally important, you may need to consider how the disk fits into overall procedures. For example, *data security* may become the overriding factor in your hardware selection.

As you'll see, there is a seemingly endless parade of hardware options to choose from, both in features (types of media, encoding, head actuators) and in types of drives (hard disk cards, removable hard disks, Bernoulli technology). To make matters worse, manufacturers are defining themselves in a crowded market by advertising special features (such as "track buffers" and "on-board caching") that may or may not be useful to you. You, the potential buyer, are confronted with a wide range of prices, often for seemingly identical equipment. How do you judge quality? Should you pay extra for installation and support? What kind of warranty should you expect, and how useful will it really be? How do you protect yourself against unscrupulous dealers? Where do you take complaints? We'll try to answer these questions, and many more, in this chapter.

Unfortunately, some kinds of machines are designed in a way that severely restricts the buyer's options. Most laptops, for example, require a drive of an unusual design. The drive typically follows the usual hard disk standards, but its dimensions are unique to the computer. In addition, the drive may have the controller electronics built in. Or, instead of using the usual cables, the drive may have special connectors for joining to circuitry inside the machine. In these cases, you'll have a much narrower range of options, both in disk performance and capacity, and prices will be higher than in machines using conventional drives attached to a controller card in one of the machines' slots.

How Much Disk Capacity Do You Need?

The first question that enters a buyer's mind is, "how big?" If you are buying your first hard disk, any disk will seem large beyond all comprehension—even 10 megabytes. If you are buying your second hard disk, any disk will seem like only a stopgap against the rising tide of data that engulfs your life—any number of megabytes does not seem like it will be enough for long.

But infinity (or what seems like infinity) is beyond the pocketbooks of most consumers, so you must decide just how much hard disk to buy. This calculation is an *easy* one in the sense that it is largely independent of other purchase considerations, such as quality and performance. You need at least as much as you plan to use, and to buy any less is to invite troubles and distractions that could undermine much of the value of having acquired a hard disk in the first place. But the decision is complicated, for there are more factors to consider than you might guess.

Forecasting Future Needs

To accurately forecast how much hard-disk capacity you'll need over the coming years, we'd recommend that first you purchase a crystal ball. It's hard enough to anticipate how many megabytes of data will be churned out per year by the software you now use. If you plan to explore new genres of software, you can be sure that you will never have a very good idea of how much disk space you need to buy.

Perhaps your plans include nothing more than adding one more time-tested application to your work, such as an accounting package along with your word processing application. In this case, you can consult with someone who has experience in accounting packages and you'll get a pretty good idea of how much disk space your accounting files will consume. But, if you are thinking of moving into emerging, rapidly changing genres of software, such as desktop publishing or computer-aided design, your estimates of needed disk space could easily be off-target by a hundred percent or more. We'll explore the reasons for this quandry in a moment.

How Far Ahead Should You Plan?

First, it is important to ask just how far ahead you need to plan. Inexorably, disks fill. Although a hard disk may faithfully serve you for many years, like all computer equipment, it is racing toward obsolescence from the moment you buy it. The story is familiar: Programmers create applications that run acceptably only on the fastest, most capable hardware. Then, equipment prices fall, mass markets develop, and the price of leading-edge software also plummets. Old equipment and software is abandoned in response to the high utility and cost-effectiveness of the new products. Your one-time pride-and-joy is donated to the kid next door—sometimes before it is completely paid for.

The extent to which you can plan ahead depends on what you do with the machine, and on how much of a hacker you are. If you are a programmer and experimenter, avidly examining every bit of software you can get your hands on, you are unlikely to be able to predict the amount of data you'll be generating beyond about 18 months in the future. On the other hand, if you operate a stable small business in which the computer is strictly used for some bland accounting, you can look ahead with some clarity by as many as four or five years. Typically, however, three years is about the limit.

Equipment Generations

Three years is the limit because it is typically the time period of an entire microcomputer generation. During that time, the industry gestates a whole new level of software engineering, new microprocessors, operating system extensions, new video standards, higher-density RAM chips, new printer technologies, and—as we saw in Chapter 2—whole new disk technologies. Even if you feel completely content with the hardware and software you presently use, you're likely to adopt some of these introductions because they'll make your work easier.

So you should probably plan your disk capacity requirements on three years data accumulation, at most. Prices drop so quickly that it would be wasteful to spend money on capacity that wouldn't be used for several years. After a few years have passed, you may be able to keep the disk drive in service somewhat longer by adding a second hard drive, or by moving older data files to diskettes. Or, if you work in an office with a growing computer population, you can look forward someday to consigning your hard disk (and probably the whole computer) to a person further down the pecking order.

Problems of Inadequate Capacity

What matters is that you buy adequate disk space for the two- or three-year planning period in question. If you buy too much, you will have wasted money—perhaps a good deal of money if you are shopping for a high-capacity drive. But if you buy too little, you run the risk of undermining your whole computer productivity system (a topic we'll discuss in detail in Chapters 5 and 6). You will be inviting constant disk-management hassles, mistaken file erasures, slower disk performance, a return to the diskette shuffle, user confusion, and general, all-purpose calamity.

Consequently, it's best to err on the side of *too much* disk capacity. But there is such a thing as *way* too much disk capacity, and huge disks come with huge price tags. Indeed, you may have to settle for less capacity than you would like, simply out of affordability. If you go this route, plan on putting more effort into managing the disk.

Formatted versus Unformatted Capacity

Some vendors advertise the "formatted capacity" of a disk; others advertise "unformatted capacity." Formatted capacity is always smaller, usually by about 15 percent. Formatting lessens capacity because small sections of each track are lost to the spaces between sectors and to the identification codes that begin each sector. In either case, the specification is not exact. A "20M drive" might be 21,377,024 bytes in one case, and 21,272,576 in another.

Capacity Ratings

You may wonder why a "20-meg" drive is not *exactly* 20 megabytes. Actually, many factors can influence your disk's formatted capacity. Each operating system reserves a different amount of space for "bookkeeping" purposes. Also, different ways of low-level formatting a drive can yield different numbers of sectors, and different sector sizes, on each track. Finally, some disk controllers, accessory cards, and software drivers have the ability to compress the data that's written to your hard disk, making it appear to hold more data. Thus, the capacity of your disk will depend on your operating system, your disk controller, and the software you're running.

Nominal versus Actual Capacities

In calculating capacity needs, a natural impulse is to figure out how many kilobytes of software you'll place on the disk, add the number of kilobytes of data you'll generate with the software over some arbitrary period of time, add 20 percent for good measure, and then buy a hard disk at least that large. The general strategy is correct, but the specifics are more complicated than they seem.

In Chapter 2 we learned about *cluster size*—the minimum allocation of disk space DOS makes for any file. Recall that on hard disks, a cluster typically holds four sectors (2,048 or 4,096 bytes). This minimum unit of allocation applies to all files on the disk, including subdirectory files. For example, a disk filled with many short business letters can waste a good deal of space.

An Extreme Case

Say that a small business uses its computer mostly for correspondence. Twenty-four letters go out 250 days a year, with plans to keep five years' worth on the disk. That's 30,000 letters. Say that they are short ones, averaging 15 lines of 70 characters—about 1,000 bytes each. Now, 1,000 times 30,000 equals 30 million, or 30 megabytes. So it's only natural to run out and buy a 40M hard disk, confident that there's plenty of space to spare for the word processing software and a video game or two.

In reality, 40M would be far too little. When a word processor creates a new file, DOS allocates a 2,048-byte cluster of disk space. If the file turns out to be only 1,000 bytes long, the remaining 1,048 bytes of the 2,048 are wasted—they remain allocated to the file, even though no information is written upon them. If the file extends to exactly 2,048 bytes, every byte of the cluster is used and disk space is used optimally. But, if the file is lengthened by one more byte to 2,049 bytes, DOS allocates a second cluster of 2,048 bytes to the file, and 2,047 of them are wasted.

In our example of 30,000 short business letters, each 1,000-byte file would actually require 2,048 bytes of disk space, multiplying to 60 megabytes!

Indeed, 60M would be required even if each letter was but one word long. So the naive estimate of a 30M disk capacity requirement was wrong by half.

A More Typical Case

Generally, minimum disk-space allocation does not throw off capacity estimates by nearly so much. Most files are much larger than 1,000 bytes. When the average file is 7,000 bytes, four clusters of 2,048 bytes are allocated, giving 8,192 bytes. The first three of the four clusters are entirely filled, leaving 1,192 bytes unused in the last cluster. Thus, a 7,000-byte average file size wastes only about 15 percent of disk space, whereas a 1,000-byte average size wastes nearly half. The larger the average file size, the more efficiently disk space is used. A typical hard disk has about 20 percent wasted space.

Many applications produce very large files, making irrelevant this whole issue of minimum disk-space allocation. Database files can be immense, running into megabytes. Although they may contain numerous individual records, the records are not allocated disk space separately. Rather, they are laid out end-to-end within the single file; a record may reside half in one cluster and half in the next, leaving not one byte wasted.

Hidden Disk Capacity Requirements

Operating System Requirements

There are some additional requirements for disk space that are often neglected. First of all, the operating system will take up some space. The dual copies of the file allocation table on a 20M disk take up 30K. The root directory takes over 16K. And 50 subdirectories, each consuming an average of a cluster and a half, take up 154K of disk space. Add COMMAND.COM and other system files, essential DOS utilities, and perhaps the DOS Shell program, and we find that the operating system takes up two-thirds of a megabyte. Plan on devoting two megabytes, at the very least, to an advanced operating system like OS/2 (much more for UNIX) or an operating environment like Microsoft Windows.

Backup Files

Backup files can also take up a tremendous amount of space. Many text editors make file duplicates automatically, appending a **.BAK** extension to the file name. Proper backups should be kept on media other than the hard disk itself. But you'll still have to deal with megabytes of **.BAK** files. You'll need to allot disk space for them if you can't trust yourself (or others) to delete them when separate backups are made.

In some projects you may want to make a permanent copy of a file at various stages in its development—say, every day or two—so that you can return to an earlier version if things go awry. This can easily fill megabytes.

File Junkyards

While we're on the subject of backups, you might also consider keeping a kind of "junkyard" on your disk, a special directory where old files are put out to pasture—the sort of file that probably should be erased, but maybe ought to be kept for just a bit longer. As we'll see in Chapter 6, utility software is available to invisibly maintain junkyards. A file can be reclaimed at any time; the least-recently erased files are actually deleted only when disk space runs low. Such utilities make further demands on disk capacity.

Temporary Files

Finally, you should know that some software creates temporary files on the disk that you are completely unaware of. The program uses the files as a work area while it runs; when the program terminates, it erases them. For this purpose, DOS can supply a unique file name to a program so that the temporary file will not inadvertently overwrite an existing file.

Many word processors create temporary files when they format a text file for printing. As the document is copied into the temporary file, the formatting codes are converted into the code sequences actually used by the printer; then the data is sent from the temporary file to the printer. Such temporary files are usually larger than the data files they serve. Special hardware also may require temporary files. For example, tape backup units can need 100K of disk space to do their work.

By definition, temporary files make no demands on your disk *storage* capacity, but they can cause problems (an error message or—if the program is poorly designed—a software crash) when a disk is operated at the edge of capacity. They constitute one more reason to have more than adequate disk capacity at your disposal.

Emerging Requirements for more Disk Capacity

Open minded people will always think of new things to do with their computers. New genres of software arise. And existing genres that you always felt were meant for others find their way onto your hard disk. Let's look at some of the newer disk-hungry applications.

Bit-mapped Displays

Generally speaking, there is a movement toward *bit-mapped* displays on IBM-compatible machines. Bit-mapped displays write on the screen dot by dot, rather than character by character; the screen is always kept in a graphics mode, even when only ordinary text appears. All manner of fonts and special symbols may be used. When Apple released the Macintosh, it convinced many users that a graphical, bit-mapped interface makes computers much easier (and more fun) to use. IBM was slow to imitate this approach, but now endorses it with its support for Presentation Manager (OS/2's graphical user interface) and its alliances with companies like Apple and Metaphor. Graphical user interfaces are inevitably accompanied by many large files to hold fonts and other images.

Desktop Publishing

In this regard, desktop publishing is a good example of how a new and "unexpected" application can wreak havoc on the best disk-capacity calculations. For years, many users contentedly pecked away in text-based word processors, perfectly happy with daisy-wheel printers. Today, with the widespread introduction of laser printers, nothing short of designer graphics is acceptable. In place of a small ASCII text file, our disks now must hold several large page-description files. Worse, the disk may have to hold backup copies for these files.

Digitized Graphics

Higher-resolution bit-mapped screens have also given an impetus to the application of digitized graphics. Digitizers are becoming cheap and commonplace. Run a photo through, and the machine sends the image to your computer's memory—and then on to the hard disk for storage. When these images are stored in simple black and white (with no levels of gray), a full-screen digitization takes up 40K. But a gray-scale or full-color image may require much more disk space—perhaps a megabyte—unless it's compressed.

It is no wonder that graphics-oriented machines, such as those outfitted for computer-aided design, typically have hard disks in the 200- to 300-megabyte range. In time, the influx of desktop publishing applications will place similar demands on common PCs. Simply put, graphics is the wave of the future, and you had better be ready for it.

Using More Programs

Another concern is the proliferation of software. It's easy to count *data* files while neglecting program files. With time, you are bound to use more and more software, even if you do not branch into new kinds of work. Do you just use your computer for a little word processing? Consider the huge spelling checkers and thesauruses that have appeared. What of syntax checkers? Form letter libraries? Text databases? If it seems that there is no end in sight—well, that's right, there will be no end.

Utility Programs

You may also find that you'll be using more and more utility programs, especially *memory-resident* utilities. Programs that manage memory-resident utilities can automatically swap resident utilities in and out of random-access memory, allowing any number to be on-line, thus making it practical to have any number on disk. A couple of megabytes of dialers, notepads, calculators, and who-knows-what has become the norm.

Program File Size

There is another consideration. Program files are growing. As applications have become more complex, **.EXE** files of several hundred kilobytes have become commonplace. In part, this growth has occurred because compact programs have become more and more difficult to write. Finely crafted programs share bits of code between the many features the program offers. The part of the program that formats the screen may also format printer output. These interdependencies make programs more complex, more prone to errors, and harder to debug. It often is simpler to write two or three similar routines instead of one versatile routine. The result is larger programs, albeit programs that cost less to develop, contain fewer bugs, and get to market sooner.

The Impact of Windows and OS/2

Environments like Microsoft's Windows, as well as OS/2—IBM's intended successor to DOS—will impose new demands for disk capacity. For starters, its own files are big. But, more importantly, OS/2 creates large temporary files, especially when multitasking with large amounts of data. Both use a complicated memory-management technique called **virtual memory**. As memory fills, portions of data not currently in use are moved onto disk. When a program accesses the data again, the operating system shifts it back into memory. For all practical purposes, the machine has as much additional RAM as it has free disk space.

Of course, this technique can severely degrade software performance, and lots of RAM is still desirable. But virtual memory gets the job done, and it beats getting an "out of memory" error message. In any case, this technique imposes yet another burden on hard disk capacity (it also makes hard disk *speed* all the more important).

Fitting More Data onto a Disk

Often, files can be compressed so that they take up less disk space. We'll talk about data compression in Chapter 5. Some compression software can be loaded as a memory-resident program that silently goes about its business as applications software runs. It inserts itself between the application and DOS, invisibly compressing and decompressing data as files are written and read. Alternatively, the compression software can be hard-wired into the disk controller, so that data is automatically compressed and uncompressed during all read and write operations.

In some applications, you may want to take file compression into account in estimating capacity requirements. But it's hard to know how much your files will be reduced; some complicated data files may hardly shrink at all. Text files are usually reduced by about half. Certain kinds of data files, such as some spreadsheet files, may be cut by 90 percent.

File compression takes time and may slow disk access unless you buy hardware that accelerates the process. And compression utilities take up precious RAM. So it's not a good idea to acquire *less* disk capacity than you need by planning to store all files in compressed form. An exception to this rule is when you need to *archive* many files on the disk (store them for only occasional future access). In general, our advice is to save data compression for the day you discover that your capacity estimates were too low.

Assessing Capacity Requirements

If you're feeling a little overwhelmed by all this, you have a right to be. There really is no way to accurately anticipate your hard disk needs, particularly if you plan to keep abreast of new software developments. Still, a line has to be drawn, since a disk with hundreds of megabytes is clearly too large for most users, and prohibitively expensive.

Here are some guidelines for making the decision:

- Do not attempt to plan more than three years ahead. If you are a "power user," two years, or even 18 months, is more realistic.
- Calculate your data needs for existing and anticipated work loads, taking into account minimal cluster allocation if it is important.
- If you will be moving into desktop publishing, multiply by five your calculations of text data file sizes.
- If you will be using digitized graphic images, carefully research the storage requirements of the resolutions and colors you will be using, consider the need for multiple copies of an image, and figure out how many images will need to be kept on the disk at any one time.
- Add five megabytes for additional software you presently have no intention of buying. If you are a heavy-duty power user, add twice this much.
- When all of your needs are calculated, increase the estimate by 50 percent.
- This total should be regarded as 82 percent of your disk capacity requirements to leave extra space for temporary files, and to avoid performance degradation from overcrowding. So increase the total by another 18 percent.

Following these rules, you have a *conservative* estimate of your disk-space needs. You probably won't be able to buy a disk at exactly the right capacity, so buy the next increment above your needs. If you figure you need 26 megabytes, an additional 50 percent, plus 18 percent again, comes to roughly 52 megabytes. It would be unwise to buy a 50M disk in this case; spend a little more and get 60 megabytes. This outcome—a 60M drive to handle 26M of anticipated data—is not at all out of the ballpark. In the end, most people easily fill up twice the disk space they anticipated. This is why Microsoft, in its literature for Windows, recommends that you have at least 40M of disk space, even though Windows by itself consumes only about 18M of space. The rest will be quickly consumed by data files.

This leads us to one final rule: Never *ever* pass up inexpensive increments in disk space, even if you cannot begin to imagine ever needing the additional capacity. Sometimes an additional 50 percent of storage costs only 15 percent more. Think of the extra expenditure as an insurance policy against unexpected requirements—you may never need it, but if you do, you will save a lot of money and trouble by spending a little more to begin with.

Deciding How Many Diskette Drives You Need

Every computer requires at least one diskette drive. Diskette drives let you move software and data to and from the machine; diskettes may serve as a backup medium for your hard disk; and a diskette drive is sometimes required to hold a *key disk* in some copy-protection schemes (the software looks for the key disk in the diskette drive and refuses to run if it can't find it).

Once upon a time, all diskette drives were "full-height"—that is, they were twice as tall as the drives sold today and completely filled the disk drive bays at the front of the computer. Two diskette drives were necessary until cheap hard disks came along. Owners of early IBM PCs found that they had to abandon one of their diskette drives to make room for a hard disk. Since the mid-1980s, virtually all diskette drives have been "half-height" drives.

IBM introduced 3½-inch diskettes with the PS/2 line of products, and these drives quickly became incorporated into AT-style clones. Today, many top-of-the-line machines have two diskette drives in addition to a hard disk— one 1.2M drive to handle 5¼-inch diskettes, and one 1.44M drive to handle 3½-inch diskettes. Having both kinds of drives is by far the easiest way of transferring files between the two kinds of media. And, if you need to write 360K diskettes, you'll have less trouble reading them on other machines if you install a 360K drive—even if you already have a 1.2M drive installed.

Uses for Two or More Diskette Drives

Having more than one diskette drive is useful in several ways. If two drives are of the same type, they make it easier to use the DOS DISKCOPY command. Multiple drives are also useful when something constantly ties up one of the drives. If you often work with software that requires a key disk, it's handy to keep the disk in an extra diskette drive permanently. Similarly, additional drives are useful if you use software that automatically backs up the hard disk to diskettes while you work.

Diskettes and Backups

Probably the most important application of dual diskette drives is in high-speed backups of your hard disk. Since it takes as many as 33 1.44M diskettes to hold the entire contents of an 80M hard disk, you'll be kept plenty busy swapping diskettes. The time required for a backup can be cut in half by using two diskette drives, swapping diskettes in one as the other records data. Be aware that many backup programs require that both drives have the same capacity.

AT Incompatibility Problems

Unfortunately, the two kinds of drives found in IBM ATs also lead to compatibility problems. Early versions of the 1.2M drives introduced with the IBM AT brought headaches to many owners who did not understand their limitations. These drives use 1.2M diskettes for high-density recording, but they can also take 360K floppies for low-density ("double-density") recording. Low-density diskettes formatted and written on these drives are not always readable by 360K diskette drives, however. And 360K diskettes formatted on a 360K drive and written by an early 1.2M drive may not be readable by any drive at all. As if this were not confusing enough, a few models of diskette drives have special heads that can write both kinds of disks correctly—but there's no way to tell by looking at the front of the drive whether it has this feature or not. (There's one exception: If the machine is an original AT, it almost certainly can't write 360K disks in its high-density drive.) So beware: If you're writing 360K diskettes, the safest way to do it is with a 360K drive.

High-capacity Drives for XTs

If you shop around, you may be able to find a 1.2- or 1.44-megabyte drive for use in XT-class machines. These drives come with their own controller cards that replace the IBM diskette drive adapter (they can't function with an ordinary PC diskette adaptor card). If you have a 360K drive that will remain in the machine, it is connected to the new adaptor. Some of these cards require special control software (a *device driver*) to be loaded when the machine is booted, but good ones carry the required software on built-in ROM chips. This is a good solution if you need to access high-density disks, but, if you're doing backups, a streaming tape unit (discussed in Chapter 8) is usually a wiser choice.

Choosing among Hard Disk Options

So far, we've talked about "hard disks" as if the typical 40M or 80M controller-drive combination is the only option. But there are many choices. *Hard disk cards* make installation especially easy. *Removable cartridge drives* indefinately extend disk capacity. And *high-capacity drives* allow giant files. We'll look at each option in turn.

External Drives

One common distinction among all kinds of disk drives (except hard disk cards) is between *internal* and *external* units. Internal drives fit into the disk drive bays within the computer, and they draw their power from the computer's power supply. External drives have their own cabinet, a fan, and a separate power supply that is plugged into a wall socket. External drives are also useful when you want to add another drive and the machine's drive bays are filled.

Advantages

External units have a few advantages. They do not sap the computer's power supply or add to the machine's heat load. And, in computers already packed full of diskette drives, an external hard drive saves you from throwing out perfectly good hardware. But external units run at least $75 more than an equivalent internal unit, so these advantages do not come free.

Hard Disk Cards

Hard disk cards, sometimes called "card drives," place the hard disk drive right on the controller board. All components are miniaturized, and the drive electronics and controller electronics are integrated. The result is a hard-disk unit for which installation is (theoretically) merely a matter of dropping the card in a slot. Because the disk drive is mounted on the controller board, there's no cabling between controller and drive. Hard disk cards also have a reputation for being quieter than traditional 5 1/4-inch drives, although some are not.

Hard disk cards were introduced in 1985 by Plus Development Corporation under the trademark "Hardcard"; dozens of imitations quickly followed. They were made possible by the introduction of 3 1/2-inch disk-drive technology. Most hard-disk card makers buy the drives from a major manufacturer and create the controller electronics themselves.

This technology found immediate popularity when it was first introduced, particularly among owners of early PCs. These machines had not been designed to run hard disks, and they required modification of the built-in operating system (the BIOS) before a hard disk could be installed. This meant changing a chip inside the computer—an intimidating task for most users. By saving people this trouble, and making hard disk installation easier in general, hard disk card designers made a fortune. Interest has flagged, however, as drive installation has become easier.

Capacity

The first hard disk cards held 10 megabytes, and 20-, 30-, and 40-megabyte models quickly followed. Cards with 80 megabytes or more are available today. Most have two platters. The best drives use RLL encoding and run at a 1:1 interleave. The fastest may achieve average seek times approaching 9 milliseconds. Hard disk cards can be as reliable as ordinary hard disk drives.

Indicator Lights

Because hard disk cards are sequestered away in the inner depths of the machine, there is no indicator light that shows when the disk is active. This feature is not essential, but it may be useful for spotting disk malfunctions; an experienced eye can sometimes tell how well a disk is optimized by following the timing and pattern of red flickers. Some hard disk card manufacturers have gone out of their way to provide an indicator for disk activity. One strategy is to include an indicator light that is cabled to the hard disk card and adhesive-mounted to the front of the machine. In another approach, the hard disk card taps into the computer's video buffer and writes a tiny symbol in the upper-right-hand corner of the screen when the disk is active. Alternatively, the hard disk card can cause the system speaker to emit a quiet click with every head seek. Such features are user-selectable and may be disabled to avoid compatibility problems with other software.

Installation

Some hard disk card manufacturers have gone to great lengths to make hard disk cards easy to install. Often the cards come completely preformatted with the entire disk partitioned for DOS. Recall that high-level formatting places two hidden DOS files on the disk (IBMBIO.COM and IBMDOS.COM).

These files are under copyright, so they cannot be on the disk when you buy it. But space is set aside for them, and the DOS **SYS** command copies them over from the DOS diskette. When the hard disk card is first installed, you can't boot from it because these files are not present. But the drive can hold files, and it is fully functional. Manufacturers may place a batch file on the drive, and it will invoke the **SYS** command, and run other installation utilities as well. Installation may require nothing more from you than naming the drive specifier (such as **C:**) to be used by the drive.

At least one manufacturer has gone a step further and made the installation program set up an initial directory tree. As we'll see in Chapter 5, this is a highly personal business. You'll probably want to delete the entire structure and start anew with your own plan. Note that utilities for the drive may be included in one of the ready-made subdirectories, so these must be preserved.

Compatibility

Different hard disk card models are required for XT-, AT-, and PS/2-style machines. Some machines won't accept a hard disk card, especially if there's a disk controller card already present (either in a slot or built into the motherboard). Therefore, it's a good idea to ask about compatibility before buying and to make sure you can return the card if it won't work in your system.

PS/2 Machines

Hard disk cards have not fared well in the PS/2 world. The Micro Channel expansion slots used in most models are just too narrow to easily hold a hard disk card. Since these models all come with a hard disk installed, no market has developed. But hard disk cards are ideal for the low-end PS/2s, which use standard XT and AT buses. These have conventional slots and often lack a factory-installed hard disk. There are hard disk cards that can run in these PS/2s as well as in XT- or AT-style machines. But some manufacturers offer different versions for the two types of machines. When buying a hard disk card for a PS/2 machine, be sure that the card is specifically recommended for your model.

Power Requirements

Most hard disk cards are advertised as requiring no more power than a diskette drive. By disk-drive standards, they indeed *are* parsimonious with electricity, drawing as little as eight watts; but they nonetheless place an added load on a computer's power supply. The power-insufficiency problem is mostly confined to true IBM PCs, with their 63.5-watt rating. Most manufacturers claim that there is no danger of power insufficiency when their cards *replace* a diskette drive, but actual power requirements often slightly exceed those of a diskette drive.

Hard disk cards come in a bewildering array of shapes. Some form a sleek, inch-thick metal package, of fairly uniform thickness from one end to the other. Most hard disk cards, however, are very thick at whichever end of the card the disk drive resides, and very thin at the other, with the electronics exposed. Some poorly designed cards are little more than a traditional hard disk drive turned on its side and mounted on a controller card. Thin designs tend to be more expensive.

Placement

The assortment of shapes would merely be a passing curiosity were it not for their importance in installation. Very few drives are truly one slot wide (about one inch). To avoid taking up two, three, or even four slots, manufacturers have designed the drives for placement in particular positions. Facing the machine, some cards may fit in the leftmost slot, jutting out toward the computer case, as shown in Figure 3-1a. In certain cases, this configuration requires that you detach the system speaker in an IBM PC and move it elsewhere.

Other hard disk cards are designed for installation in the rightmost slot of a machine, with the drive reaching around the back of the diskette drive compartment (Figure 3-1c). This configuration may leave the drive overhanging the processor chip. This area around the processor may need to be clear if you ever decide to add an accelerator card to the machine.

Other cards squeeze the drive toward the end of the card closest to the front of the machine. Although the drive juts out over some of a second slot that would be used by another full-length card, the socket for the second card remains uncovered, allowing it to receive a half-length card designed for a short slot on an IBM XT. This configuration is shown in Figure 3-1b. You'll also find super-miniaturized, half-length hard disk cards made to fit in an XT's short slot.

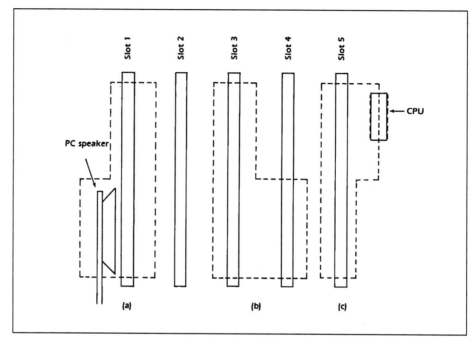

Figure 3-1. Hard disk card configurations

Installation problems

Some of these configurations undermine the much vaunted "ease-of-installation" that has drawn so many buyers to hard disk cards. An important rule is that adaptor cards should *never* touch, even if the point of contact seems non-conducting. There is no predicting what may happen when circuitry between two cards is accidentally joined; theoretically, every card in the machine *plus* the system board could be damaged. Various piggy-back cards (such as the memory expansion module for an IBM EGA board) have always been a problem in this regard, as have transformers and speakers protruding from modems.

To avoid this danger, you may find yourself shuffling your adaptor cards between the slots, seeking the ideal arrangement. If you must move the system speaker, you will find it a pretty clumsy task. And, if you fill the rightmost slot of the machine, you will have to move the diskette drive controller cables *over* the newly inserted card, which is safe in itself, but a nuisance when you remove or replace the computer cover, since the cables may catch.

Drawbacks

To most buyers, hard disk cards spell "convenience." But some buyers have not had it so easy. Installation can take more time than an ordinary drive-and-controller kit. Extra slots may be lost to card overhang, the power supply may require replacement after all, and, as a second hard disk for a machine, there may be serious configuration problems. The best hard disk cards, in fact, do drop right into an IBM PC, automatically set themselves up, and run beautifully. But, if the card is going to act as a second hard disk, you should call the manufacturer directly to ask whether the card will suit your needs.

Finally, do not assume that a hard disk card that works in a standard PC will work in any equivalent machine. Often the computer maker has its own hard disk products, and it will certify only these, making no comment on others. Not surprisingly, prices tend to run higher in this case. If you want to opt for a cheaper hard disk card, call the hard disk card maker and see if they keep a list of certified machines. And, if there is any question about the hard disk card's workability in your system, do all you can to secure a written money-back agreement.

Removable Hard Disks

Removable hard disks are enclosed in cartridges that are inserted into specially-designed drives. Like diskettes, any number may be used in a single drive. They combine the best characteristics of fixed hard disks and diskettes, offering both speed and high capacity, plus the ability to archive endless amounts of data. They also allow you to lock your data up in a safe place at the end of the day—an invaluable feature for government agencies and companies with important trade secrets.

The first removable disk drives were housed in external units; the cartridges are just too big to allow a drive small enough to fit into a computer's disk drive bay. These units robbed you of desk space (though some were able to fit under the computer), but the advantage was they did not drain the computer's power supply. Today, many units are internal, and they pose many of the same problems in installation as an ordinary hard disk drive.

Incidentally, the first hard disks were designed along these lines. Even today, a typical hard disk drive for mainframe computers uses giant "data packs" that are dropped into cabinet-size drives rather like a top-loading washing machine. They may hold *gigabytes* (thousands of megabytes) of data.

Platter-only Cartridges

There are two approaches to cartridge design. One technique places a single platter in the cartridge, with trap doors that open automatically when inserted into the drive, and close only after the drive stops turning. The read/write heads are lowered to the drive surface, and they fly over the disk on an air cushion, exactly like ordinary hard drives. Finely filtered air is constantly pumped into the drive to force out invading dust particles.

Cartridges Containing Complete Hard Drives

A second approach to removability places not just the drive platters, but complete hard drive inside the cartridge. These cartridges are much more expensive, of course; they may cost even more than a bare hard disk drive of like capacity. (Among the best deals is a kit that lets you build a cartridge around a standard hard drive you've bought separately.) Manufacturers that build cartridges with drives already built in often tout their shock resistance. But, since they're subject to the same kinds of damage as regular hard drives, they should still be treated with care.

Bernoulli Technology

We described the technical principle behind Bernoulli technology in Chapter 2. Iomega Corp. unveiled the Bernoulli Box in 1982 after the invention was rejected by several large companies, including IBM. Many tens of thousands of units have since been sold. The drives are popular because they offer an excellent compromise between speed, capacity, reliability, and data security.

The original Bernoulli Boxes used eight-inch disks held in flat cartridges measuring roughly 8½-by-11 inches. The cartridges have a write-protect switch (rather than a notch) to protect data from accidental overwrites. They can be partitioned for multiple operating systems, just like an ordinary hard disk. Gradually, smaller drives have been released that can be installed internally. Iomega now makes 5¼-inch models with capacities running to 90M.

Bernoulli Boxes use a separate controller card, so they require a slot in the computer. The drives use voice-coil actuators for 32-millisecond access, RLL encoding, and an SCSI interface that works through an Iomega-supplied controller card or through a standard SCSI adapter. Capacities of up to 90 megabytes are achieved by increasing both the density of data along the tracks and the number of tracks. Although the disks turn more slowly than standard hard disks—at about 2,000 rpm—higher data density makes for transfer rates of up to 1M per second.

Dual Disks

Many users prefer dual-drive units. By having matching drives, you can easily make identical copies of any cartridge. These may be the ideal backup medium because, if the original fails, the backup can be used "as is" without any complicated data restoration procedure. A tremendous advantage of Bernoulli Boxes is that a cartridge made in one machine can be used in any other Bernoulli Box of equivalent or greater capacity. Many removable disks drives are not nearly so compatible. This feature makes the medium ideal for transporting data.

Iomega has also introduced dual Bernoulli drives combined with a high-capacity hard disk. The hard disk is intended as a network file server, while the cartridge drives serve as an *archive* medium for large quantities of data. This strategy keeps the hard disk clear, prolonging its useful life by keeping disk space open.

Performance

The fast head access times and rapid data transfer rate would seem to point to exceptionally high performance. But remember that a Bernoulli cartridge can offer at most only two platter sides. This means that only two tracks reside at a given head position. While the makers have concentrated on fitting more data onto a track, the cylinder density is still considerably lower than on an equivalent dual-platter hard disk drive; thus, more head seeks are required to read a large file.

Installation

Installation is simple. Some units cannot be internally mounted, and so a controller card is inserted into a slot in the computer and cabled to the external unit. The cables are made long to let you place the unit well away from the computer, but they're also the right size to allow the unit to fit on top or under a desktop PC. Since the unit has its own power supply, it makes no demands on the system's. Internal drives install like an internal hard disk. A device driver (control software) must be installed on the system to manage the SCSI controller. Dual drives are typically named **C:** and **D:** in machines with no hard drive, or else **D:** and **E:**. A special utility is included to format the cartridges.

Interleave

An interesting problem arises when Bernoulli cartridges are shared between multiple machines. Because a fast machine can handle a higher data-transfer rate, the cartridges perform optimally with a lower interleave factor than is appropriate for a slower machine. Recall that too high an interleave keeps the controller waiting a bit longer than necessary until it can read the next sector; too low an interleave factor, on the other hand, costs a full rotation of the disk before the next sector may be accessed. In general, the cartridge should be set up to work the best on the machine it's used in most. (Interleave optimization is discussed in Chapter 7.)

High-capacity Drives

As we've seen, some computer systems require very high-capacity drives—drives of several hundred megabytes—particularly systems serving networks where the drive is shared between many users, or in stand-alone graphics-oriented systems used in computer-aided design or desktop publishing. Many manufacturers have rushed to provide these drives. Their select clientele is prepared to pay premium prices for the right mix of capacity and performance. Today, drives of more than 1,000 megabytes are available.

Cost per Megabyte

The cost per megabyte in high-capacity drives is similar to that of smaller drives. You might expect that you'd get a better deal on a large drive—as you do when you buy a large, economy-sized box of detergent—but this is not the case. Since there are fewer customers for very large drives, low demand keeps their cost per megabyte about the same, or slightly higher, than that of small drives.

High-capacity drives are almost never designed to operate with an IBM PC or XT. The eight-bit data bus used in these machines cannot handle the rapid data throughput these drives strive for. Some operate from the standard AT controller card, but most come with a specially designed card, often with a fast ESDI interface. Most high-capacity drives fit the standard 5¼-inch full-height form factor, allowing internal installation. Only the very biggest—usually intended for minicomputers, not microcomputers—come as external units, complete with their own power supply and fan. However, most vendors can supply an external case for a hard drive if there's no room left inside your PC.

High-capacity drives tend to be very fast. With many platters, and many sectors per track, they have a very high cylinder density. Far fewer head seeks are required to read a file, and the average seek time may be as low as 9 milliseconds. These drives tend to be at the cutting edge of microcomputer disk drive technology. When a tiny box can fetch a price as high as $8,000, engineers are free to do their very best. These are the sports cars of the hard disk industry. In fact, leading-edge technology *must* be applied if hundreds of megabytes are to fit in the standard full-height, internally mountable form factor.

Data Densities

Higher data densities on a track also pose limits. Recall that data densities may be raised by using higher-quality magnetic media with special read/write heads, or by using the more-advanced RLL data encoding methods. RLL technology was first applied to large mainframe disk drives; naturally enough, RLL first appeared in the PC world on high-capacity drives, where the expensive electronics were affordable. Hence, manufacturers of large drives "used up" some of the capacity gains from RLL years ago. While even more advanced RLL encoding is now appearing, using it to cram data at ever-higher densities along a track presents severe obstacles. In the most advanced drives, extremely small read/write heads fly even closer to the disk surface, and the magnetic medium has a very high *coercivity*, so that smaller tidbits of disk surface can act as magnetic domains. This technology is progressing rapidly by engineering standards, but not nearly rapidly enough by marketing criteria, where a doubling of price-performance every three years has become the norm.

Track Densities

Higher track densities are also promising. Thin film technology (plated media) have allowed designs using over 1,200 tracks per inch. The higher price of high-capacity drives allows the use of a dedicated servo surface. Recall that closed-loop voice-coil technology requires **servo bursts** between the tracks to keep the read/write heads on target. Most high-capacity drives have a **dedicated servo surface**, in which a whole side of one disk is devoted to servo information, and the **embedded servo data** is dispensed with. Without the servo data between the tracks, more can be squeezed on a platter.

The 1,024-Track Limit

High track densities make possible high-capacity disks with many cylinders. However, a fundamental flaw in the design of the IBM PC's BIOS—which has been carried over into most compatibles to this day—prevents it from handling drives sporting more than 1,024 tracks. Thus, if you buy a large RLL or ESDI drive, you may need to buy a "translating" controller. This type of controller makes the drive appear to the system as if it has fewer tracks (but more platters, more sectors per track, or larger sectors), circumventing the problem. (There are also software drivers that eliminate the problem by replacing the BIOS with code that can handle larger drives.) In either case, DOS never knows the difference. If you buy a late-model IDE drive, a translating controller is usually built right in.

Manufacturers' Specifications

You should be especially cautious about manufacturers' performance claims for their drives. Computer makers have advertised seek times of 1 millisecond or less, when in fact the extra speed was really provided by a hardware cache in the drive or its controller. Some hard disk controllers have disk management utilities built in, so that file layout is constantly optimized, data is compressed and uncompressed as it is written and read, and whole tracks are pre-read automatically. Any hard disk drive can benefit from these measures by applying readily available, inexpensive software utilities. But manufacturers who have built them into their systems may make unfair comparisons between their systems and others which could easily (and cheaply) be equipped with the same features.

Planning for Adequate Power and Ventilation

Disk drives and controller cards consume power. In most machines, the drive is fed by a cable reaching directly from the computer's **power supply**. A power supply is the large black or chrome box at the back-right of the machine in XT- or AT-style computers, or a chrome box along one side of a PS/2 computer. The box contains transformers and other circuitry that convert wall-socket power to the DC voltages that the computer uses. Some of the power is directed through the machine's slots, and this is how disk controller cards are powered.

Power requirements vary considerably from disk drive to disk drive. As capacity rises, less power is required per megabyte. Most computer dealers do not know how much power is consumed by the drives they sell; the numbers are printed only in a technical reference manual that must be obtained from the manufacturer. Also, it's important to find the correct number in the technical documentation. The most important figure is the drive's *startup* current, which can be as much as five times as great as the current drawn once the drive has revved up to full speed. (Typical startup currents are 5 to 7 amps; multiply the current by 5 volts to get the startup power, typically 25 or 35 watts.) Fortunately, most late-model PCs have power supplies large enough to handle one or two hard drives.

Power Supply Ratings

Power supplies are rated for maximum output. Ratings run from 63.5 watts in the earliest PCs to over 200 watts in most PS/2 machines and most AT-style compatibles. These values are only approximate; the actual power output varies from supply to supply. Most will output *at least* this much power, and perhaps five or ten percent more. The power supplies found in IBM clones cover a whole range of ratings from 63.5 watts to 250 watts or so.

The XT was given a larger power supply than the PC, mostly to support the hard-disk drive. Users had been filling their PCs with power-hungry add-on cards, and not enough power was left in many machines to handle the extra disk drive. Many who installed a hard disk in their PCs found that the machine crashed as soon as it was turned on. Happily, this problem has just about disappeared. These days, even the least expensive clones are given fairly large power supplies. Only by adding a second hard disk and filling the machine's slots are you likely to run into trouble.

Replacement Power Supplies

Many small companies make *replacement* power supplies that offer higher capacity. Except for the power rating, these power supplies exactly match IBM power supplies, so they are easily substituted. They cost as little as $50. We'll go into the details of choosing and installing a power supply in Chapter 4, which concerns hard disk installation. It is important to buy a power supply that affords adequate protection against electrical surges. Be sure to consult the discussion in Chapter 4 before buying.

Heat Load

Whether you'll need a larger power supply or not, you should keep in mind that all power consumed by the machine is ultimately converted to heat. You'll find that some disk drives consume considerably more power than others. Even if your power supply can easily furnish another 20 or 30 watts, you should consider that the machine will be burdened with that much more heat. Heat is the enemy of all computer components. Everything, including the disk drive, wears out more quickly because of it. And, when temperatures inside the machine rise too high, the disk drive is liable to go on the blink and refuse to function until the temperature lowers.

Merely adding a high-capacity power supply to your machine does not in itself increase the heat load. The wattage rating tells the maximum power that can be furnished; the increments of extra power are not actually supplied until computer components are added to the machine. So a power supply rating is not like a light-bulb rating or an electric heater rating, where a 500-watt rating means that 500 watts of electricity are always consumed.

Cooling

The fan at the back of the computer does its best to circulate cool air. But surrounding air is not always cool. If you run a heavily loaded machine, perhaps with two diskette drives, two hard drives, and all slots full, you may need to add a larger cooling fan, particularly if the computer sometimes operates in a hot room. (Don't try to replace your PCs original fan with a larger one, by the way. It's usually hidden inside the metal power supply case, which contains dangerous voltages and should not be opened.) Add-on fans don't cost much. We'll tell you about them in Chapter 4. For now, keep in mind that these "extras" may cost you more money when you go shopping for a drive.

Assessing Performance, Quality, and Convenience

We've described a wealth of drive designs and features. Which options are best for you? The decision is a difficult one because it's not obvious which features will complement the software you use. For example, compared to database files, text files benefit relatively little from fast seek times, but more from full track buffers. We'll look at such issues in this section.

How Important Is Disk Speed for You?

Not everyone really needs a high-performance disk. If you work long hours with word processors or spreadsheets that mostly access the disk only when you are loading and saving files, having a speedy disk is about as useful as keeping a Porsche for driving down to the corner grocery store. Your daily time savings may amount to milliseconds. Of course, a computer set up for high productivity may employ numerous utilities that are well served by a fast hard disk. But many people keep things simple, and, for them, extra dollars spent on a high-performance drive might be better devoted to more powerful software. If money is tight, a low-performance drive may be adequate. (If you need more speed later, you may be able to make up most or all of the difference with some RAM and a disk caching program.

The Worst Case

At the opposite extreme, if a drive is to serve a network, or if it is to function in a stand-alone multitasking system, it can never be fast enough. In networks and multiuser systems, the disk drive jumps back and forth, serving the needs of each user. In a single-user, single-tasking system, the read/write heads often hover over one cylinder, reading and writing in sequence. But in a multiuser system, control of the drive is constantly switched from one task to another. Not only is the drive kept especially busy by so many diverse demands, but it has to do additional work to *return* to the position from which it serves each task.

Further demands are made by **virtual memory**, which we mentioned earlier in this chapter. Virtual memory is a technique by which a multitasking operating system runs more applications than memory can hold by constantly swapping parts of programs and data between memory and disk. And sophisticated environments such as OS/2 and Windows often use **dynamic linking**, in which a program can enlist the help of utilities contained in files called **dynamic link libraries (DLLs)**. A program asks the operating system to "connect," or *link*, it to the library on request—that is, *dynamically*. Data is also swapped in and out of RAM. The hard disk runs helter-skelter to support all of this.

Virtual memory is an integral part of OS/2 (in fact, the Intel 286, 386, and 486 microprocessor chips are specially designed to support virtual memory). If you'll be using OS/2, UNIX, or some other advanced operating system, and you expect to be running several applications that are themselves large, and that need to load much data into memory, you really have no choice but to purchase a fast hard disk. By "fast," we mean a disk with a rapid average seek time. In these applications, the read/write heads tend to constantly scurry from one place to another, reading or writing only a little at each location. Most activity is *random access*, rather than *sequential*. Hence, the benefits of a high cylinder density are lessened, since whole cylinders are seldom read or written. A fast data transfer rate is also valuable, since a 1:1 interleave is highly desirable under these conditions.

Typical Performance Needs

If your computing needs fall somewhere between the extremes of simple word processing and high-powered multitasking, you'd do well to buy a drive with an average seek time in the 14- to 20-millisecond range. Increasingly, software is becoming too complicated to be satisfactorily served by slower drives. This is especially true if you plan on using Microsoft *Windows*, which uses a hard disk intensively. You may find even a 28-millisecond drive naggingly slow in some situations.

Assessing a Drive's Quality

It's been said that the everyday user's computer is the last beta test site for a hard disk. (In *beta tests*, ordinary users test a product before it is released.) These words may be a little unkind to hard disk manufacturers, who institute whole departments to test new hard disk designs under a variety of adverse conditions. But manufacturers cannot really know how well their drives will perform over the long run. Drive designs change from year to year, driven by a hotly competitive market and constant technical progress. Last year's experience becomes obsolete along with last year's technology.

Kinds of Drive Failure

Drive failures fall into two broad categories: *mechanical* and *electronic.* There are not many moving parts in a disk drive. But the parts must be aligned precisely; sometimes the slightest deviation causes the drive to stop working. Other failures are more blatant: The drive motor may simply burn out. The same can happen to a stepper-motor head actuator, or its drive band may go out of alignment. Tiny imprecisions can throw out a voice-coil actuator. There is no way a consumer can judge the quality of a drive on these points; the manufacturer's reputation and a good warranty are your only protection.

Another kind of drive "failure" may reside in the disk's coating or plating. The extreme thinness of the magnetic medium is hard to maintain. There may be overly thin patches that cannot support data reliably. An irregular disk surface may also invite a head crash. If a disk has too many flaws in its surface, it should not be sold. Particularly unacceptable are flaws on the outer track of a disk, which holds critical operating system information that can't be placed anywhere else on the disk.

Bad Tracks

When you buy a disk drive, you will find a **bad track table** written (usually by hand) on a label on the drive case, or on an attached sheet of paper. This listing tells which tracks failed the manufacturer's in-house tests. During low-level formatting you will need to enter these numbers into the format program so that it can mark off these tracks. We'll talk about this issue in detail in the next chapter. Today, many new disks have no bad tracks at all, but sometimes there may be a half-dozen. This is nothing to be upset about. You are losing only a tiny fraction of the disk's total capacity, and the rest of the drive ought to be as reliable as one with no flaws at all.

The MTBF

A disk drive's MTBF—Mean Time Between Failure—purportedly tells how many hours of operation a typical drive sustains before it fails in one way or another. The statistic applies only to the drive and the drive electronics. Controller card failures, though rarer, serve to decrease the actual MTBF. Many people regard the MTBF as a sort of "mean-time-to-crash." This conception is not really correct. On any number of occasions, data may be lost as magnetic traces fade or an electrical transient moves through the system. These "failures" may be recovered from without physically repairing the drive (in the worst instance, by reformatting the drive). From the manufacturer's perspective, the "failure" in MTBF means a situation where the disk must be sent to the shop. So don't interpret a 10,000-hour MTBF as a promise of 10,000 care-free hours.

MTBF Ratings

These days, MTBF ratings of 15,000 or 20,000 hours are typical, and some drive makers are advertising 50,000-hour MTBFs (nearly six years continuous operation). But 20,000 hours of what? Some disk drive makers say the number represents "typical usage," during which the drive is not turned on and off too many times. It might seem that you could increase the life of your drive by turning off the computer when it will not be in use for a few hours; but manufacturers are unanimous in asserting that drives will last longer if they are *never* turned off. The temperature changes ("thermal cycling") that occur during startup and shutdown inflict a lot of wear and tear.

You also can prolong the life of a drive by keeping its files *defragmented* (a topic discussed in Chapter 7). More important, see to it that the drive is kept relatively cool; heat degrades both mechanical and electronic components. Of course, as MTBFs rise toward several years, drives can be expected to die from obsolescence rather than mechanical failure. Still, the *M* in *MTBF* stands for "mean," and any drive can give up the ghost on its first day running.

You'll find that MTBFs are always given as a number rounded to five or ten thousands of hours. Even these suspiciously rounded figures may be grossly inaccurate. For MTBF ratings are not true statistics derived from experience. Technology changes too quickly for that. By the time a manufacturer could leave thousands of drives running for the tens of thousands of hours needed to establish an MTBF, years would pass, the technology would be obsolete, and the company would be bankrupt. Instead, a small number of drives are subjected to extremes of shock, vibration, and temperature change, and the resulting performance is statistically analyzed as the sum of the probabilities of failure of the drive's individual components. Because they are only estimates, MTBFs for new technologies may be even less reliable indicators of a drive's performance.

Shock Ratings

Sometimes you'll see a **shock rating** advertised. This number purports to tell how many "Gs" (multiples of gravitational force) the drive can sustain without permanent damage (1 G is the rate at which an object near the Earth's surface accelerates as it falls). The shock rating for a typical drive runs about 40 G. Obviously, hard disks in portable computers need more protection, and they tend to have higher ratings, typically from 60 to 100 G. Unfortunately, these ratings usually reflect the jolt a drive can take when it's not running. Most hard drives can withstand very little jostling while they're in use.

Noise

A final consideration is **noise**. Many first-time hard disk buyers are unpleasantly surprised to find that the gentle whoosh of their computer's fan is now accompanied by a high-pitched whine. The noise is less noticeable in a busy office. But, in a quiet room at home, the constant whirr can be distracting—even oppressive—if you sit before the computer for long hours.

You'll never find a noise rating for a hard disk. There is really no way of expressing one meaningfully, because it is often the quality of the sound, rather than its magnitude, that is annoying. During movements of the read/write heads, a drive may become noticeably louder, making a muffled rasping noise if you have a stepper-motor drive, a thumping sound with older voice-coil drives, or a chirp with some of the newer voice-coil designs. Not many people seem to mind these noises very much. It's the constant background whirr that drives some people to distraction.

If noise matters to you, your only protection is to find a drive to listen to before you buy. Keep in mind that a drive will seem at least twice as loud at home as in a busy computer store, particularly if you've acclimatized your ear to street noise on the way to the inspection. Once you've bought the drive, you're stuck with it. What you cannot do with a noisy drive is bury it away in a drawer or other compartment, using long cables. The drive *must* have ventilation.

Drive Manufacturers

The disk drive industry is fiercely competitive, and manufacturers often walk a fine line between producing substandard products and going bankrupt. In Asia, where upstart companies from Seoul to Singapore are making drives. These drives are "nameless," and their obscure origin is easily hidden behind the computer vendor's own label.

In the final analysis, the various manufacturers' quality ratings are not very helpful. In one case, drives with excellent MTBF ratings flooded into repair shops. Cutthroat competition hasn't helped the ratings game one bit, and it has become more and more difficult to sort out progress in technology from progress in advertising. Yet a loose correlation between ratings and quality does exist. Generally, when the ratings are especially high, the drive is superior. But drives with similar ratings may vary in quality considerably.

Like automobiles, one drive model may, on average, be more reliable than another model from the same maker. If you must have the greatest possible reliability, you might want to shop at a company that competes on quality rather than price. You can expect to pay a good deal more for the added margin of safety, especially since such drives aren't generally sold at a discount.

To a degree, you take your chances when you shop for a very large disk drive. These drives are designed at the cutting edge of technology. As capacities rise, so does the pressure to use ever-higher technology to cram more data on a track, more tracks on a side, and more platters into the standard drive casing. MTBF ratings may be next to meaningless. On the other hand, manufacturers seem to devote more loving care to the production of these drives; they are not quickly stamped out for mass markets. In a few years we'll know how good they really are.

Where and How to Buy

Once you've decided the type, size, and quality of drive you need, you must deal with a complicated marketplace. Should you buy from the cheapest mail order house or from the ritzy local dealer? How do you negotiate a deal? What should you expect in a warranty? How should you make payment to best protect yourself? And how do you go about returning damaged or unsuitable goods? We'll do our best to answer these questions in this section.

First, however, we'll overview absolutely everything that you might need to acquire to get your new hard disk up and running. Nothing is more frustrating than waiting days for a disk to arrive through the mail, only to find that you forgot to order a critical component. It happens all the time.

What You Need to Buy

When you buy, be sure to acquire all the little extras. Some hard disk vendors provide you with a "kit" containing a drive and various cables and hardware; others (especially low-priced mail order merchants) will sell you only the bare drive unless you ask for (and pay for) the accessories you need. You may or may not need a new controller card, depending on the kind of machine you own and what equipment is currently installed, and you may or may not get ribbon cables to connect the drive to the machine. MFM, RLL, and ESDI drives need two ribbon cables: The wider *control cable* can run to two drives, but a separate *data cable* is required for each drive. Whether a controller card is included depends on the kind of machine you own and what equipment is currently installed. The vendor customarily includes the two ribbon cables that connect the drive and card. The wider *control cable* accommodates two drives, but a separate *data cable* is required for each drive. Be sure to order another data cable when you add a second drive. IDE and SCSI drives use a single ribbon cable. You may also be a **bezel** (face plate) for covering over the unoccupied half of a full-height disk drive bay in XT-style machines. You'll need hardware to extend the dimensions of a drive if you're planning on slipping a 3½-inch drive into a 5¼-inch drive bay.

Mounting Rails

Owners of AT-style machines will require **mounting rails** for internally installed drives. These attach to the sides of the drives and ride along grooves in the side of the drive bays. They are widely available, and cost a few dollars a pair. Other machines do not require these rails. The rails are ordinarily shipped with screws to fasten them in place.

New Power Supplies

If you own an IBM PC or early PC clone, and you suspect that your machine is loaded lightly enough that it can handle a hard disk, give it a try. But test the system carefully before entrusting your most valued data to the new drive—just in case operation becomes erratic. If worse comes to worst, you may need to remove the drive until a replacement power supply arrives.

Power supplies in early IBM PCs send out two leads that supply power to disk drives. Later machines, and most clones, have four leads. If you'll be running two diskette drives along with the hard disk, you may need a Y-connector to split one power lead into two. Y-connectors are not usually included in hard disk kits. They cost only a few dollars. If power is insufficient, the replacement power supply you install will probably have four power leads, and the Y-connector won't be needed.

Formatting Utilities

Some drives have already been formatted at low-level when shipped. If this is not the case, you may need to do the low-level format yourself. The program that does this may be built into your hard disk controller (check the controller documentation to see if there is one—and, if so, how to invoke it) or may come on a diskette. (The IBM PC/AT's *Advanced Diagnostics* disk contains a low-level formatting program, for example.) If you buy a hard disk "kit," make sure that low-level formatting will be provided in one of these ways. If you want to avoid the (trivial) task of performing the low-level formatting yourself, ascertain that the drive comes preformatted. But it's probably better to do the job yourself, since the experience will come in handy if a major failure of some kind requires you to reformat the drive in the future.

Even if the drive comes preformatted, it's wise to request that a low-level formatting program be included, since it may be free for the asking. Formatting utilities are found in some disk toolkits. They're also available as stand-alone programs, some of which can take care of all parts of hard-disk setup, including partitioning, high-level formatting, and system configuration. But these utilities can be expensive, and you won't want to buy one just for the formatting program. So be sure to ask about low-level formatting when you buy a drive.

If you own a relatively fast machine, try to find out what interleave was used when you buy a preformatted drive. It may not be right for your machine. For example, for fast ATs, the 3:1 interleave used in most preformatted drives is suboptimal. By knowing the interleave, you'll know whether you need to go to the trouble of reformatting the drive when you receive it. Incidentally, in Chapter 7, we discuss utilities that calculate the optimal interleave for a drive.

The best time to apply these programs is when the drive is first installed, so you might want to order such software when you purchase a drive.

BIOS Replacement

If you own an early IBM PC, you may need to replace the ROM BIOS chip on the system board, since the BIOS in early PCs does not support a hard disk. Replacements are no longer available by mail order. To find out if your early PC needs a replacement chip, follow these instructions carefully. Start up the DOS DEBUG program. It will display a dash with the cursor beside it, and you should enter:

```
d f000:fff0
```

Then strike the Enter key. Several lines of symbols will appear, some of them random, some intelligible. At the bottom right you'll see a date. If the date is earlier than 10/28/82, you'll need the replacement BIOS. Then type the letter 'q' and press Enter to quit the DEBUG program.

High-capacity Drives

Similarly, if you buy a drive that holds more than 320 megabytes of data, or has more than 1,024 cylinders, you'll need to consider both BIOS and DOS support. Very-high-capacity drives are usually installed by dealers who know exactly how to make the operating system recognize the drive's geometry. Some drives may come straight to you from the manufacturer with specific installation instructions for your particular machine; this approach is fine as long as your computer is not souped-up in some nonstandard way. Be sure to avoid situations where your hand is not held the whole way. It takes considerable technical knowledge to install some high-capacity drives.

Large Partitions

On the other hand, drives larger than 30 megabytes are now the norm, so many users must deal with DOS's 32-megabyte partition limit without outside help. As we explained earlier, starting with Version 3.3, DOS lets you set up multiple DOS partitions on a drive, and DOS Versions 4.0 (and later) will let you create single partitions larger than 32 megabytes. If you're using a DOS version earlier than 3.3, or want to create very large partitions, you'll need to acquire either a more recent DOS version or else utility software that can accomplish these ends. Don't put off this purchase; it's required when you format the drive. You won't be able to change to a larger partition later without removing all your files from the drive.

Documentation

Too many hard disks are shipped without technical documentation. When you buy yours, see if the dealer has this information—and, if he doesn't, ask him to obtain it for you. You need this even if you feel you can't understand it, because someone else may need it someday. As we explain in the next chapter, when you install a second hard disk drive, a resistor pack called a **terminator** generally needs to be pulled off of one of the drives. You may not be able to find it without proper documentation.

Here is a list of all these requirements. Keep it handy when you order. You may drive the order clerk to distraction if you ask about every relevant item, but it's better to be safe than sorry. Sometimes it helps to explain the kind of machine in which the drive will be installed, and whether another hard drive is already in place. Then let the salesperson list exactly what will be sent, and compare it to the list.

A Shopping Checklist

Hardware

Drive
Controller (If you don't have one already or are changing drive interfaces)
Cables
Mounting screws (sometimes not included in drive/controller kits)

Original IBM PC Only

Replacement ROM (early PCs only)
Extension bezel (extends front of drive to top of the drive bay)
Replacement power supply
Y-cable (if three drives must work with an old, two-lead power supply)

IBM AT or Compatible Only

Mounting rails (if not included with your machine)

High-capacity Drives

> OPTION: BIOS extension hardware or software
>
> OPTION: High-capacity disk installation software

Software

> Low-level formatting program (may or may not be built into your control-ler)
>
> OPTION: General purpose hard disk installation program
>
> OPTION: Most recent DOS version
>
> OPTION: Special partitioning software for making large partitions or link-ing multiple drives into one logical unit

Documentation

> Installation instructions
>
> Drive and controller documentation
>
> Support phone number
>
> Warranty

Choosing a Vendor

You can buy a drive through a local retail store or by mail order. For some people, mail order has a poor reputation. Yet some of the best vendors sell mostly by mail. Local computer stores often give no discounts, but promise free installation and support. That can mean quite a lot to some people, but the difference in price can run to several hundred dollars, which is a lot to pay for a half-hour of a technician's time. On the other hand, if the drive will be installed in a network, or if the drive has an unusual geometry, you may save $1,000 in your own time by turning the job over to the experts.

Mail Order

Most mail-order firms make a profit by selling many units at very low margins. They're not likely to have much time to help you, or even talk to you about the order. This state of affairs is perfectly acceptable when you're buying an ordinary drive for an ordinary machine. If they offer you a "kit," it should provide everything you need to install the drive in an hour or two. But things may not go as smoothly in a more complicated upgrade, such as attaching a second drive to some existing controllers.

When your situation is an unusual one, you have to stick by your guns and *demand* the company guarantee that the drive will work, and that the company will take the drive back if it doesn't. Typically, the person taking orders over the phone will have little technical expertise. If all you hear are rosy reassurances without any explanations of *why* there is nothing to worry about, ask to talk to the in-house technician.

Systems Integrators

Some mail order advertisements are for a very different kind of service. These are **systems integrators**, who specialize in optimizing disk drives. They constantly test and compare new drives as they appear, matching them with the ideal controllers, or building controllers of their own. Sometimes they'll also match tape backup units to drives. Such vendors tend to offer only one drive-controller combination of given capacity for a particular machine. A good system integrator offers excellent support, including detailed installation instructions. Unfortunately, these days lots of firms are calling themselves "systems integrators" without any right to the title. You can spot a true systems integrator by the breadth and quality of the specifications sent when you request information and by the quality and quantity of technical help they are willing to offer.

Proximity of the Vendor

There's always an advantage in buying from a mail-order house that is within driving distance. On rare occasion, problems can't be straightened out over the phone. When it's not clear whether it's the drive or the computer that's malfunctioning, it's important for you to be able to take them in together. The vendor won't be terribly happy about this, but will usually agree to it rather than have you return the drive. Watch out that you're not charged unnecessarily for the visit. If your machine is at fault, you owe them a service charge—but not if the problem is due to their poor documentation. If they sell "hard disk kits," the documentation should be adequate by definition. Another advantage of being close to the vendor is that, should your complaints be ignored, you can make a nuisance of yourself until things are set right.

Technical Support

The documentation accompanying hard disk kits is often poor. Less-expensive products may be imported from abroad, and the vendor may add a single page of documentation as an afterthought. Generally, the lower the price, the more you need to think about how you'll handle problems if they arise. Inexpensive equipment is not necessarily more prone to problems; it's just that you can't count on adequate technical support.

When you phone a vendor to inquire about buying a hard disk, ask if they have a technical support line. What hours is it open? Does the vendor offer an 800 number? You might want to go so far as to ask questions more complicated than the usual salesperson can answer ("Do I have to change controller card dip switches to use this as a second drive?"); once you have a "techie" on the line, you'll quickly sense whether the vendor is able to give good support or not.

Try to have the drive delivered early in the work week, so that support will be available when you install it. If you do have problems, don't waste time trying one thing after another. Follow the instructions to a 'T.' If the drive doesn't work, get on the phone. It should be the *vendor's* problem that the instructions are inadequate, not yours.

Payment

Generally, you'll find the best prices on drives approaching obsolescence. When IBM standardized 20M drives with the release of the AT, warehouses full of 10M drives suddenly lost their perceived value and prices plummeted. Twenty-megabyte drives have followed suit. Conversely, you'll find that high-capacity drives will always be the most expensive.

When you order the drive, ask whether there is a surcharge for credit card purchases. (Some vendors advertise their prices as "cash prices," and add a surcharge to cover credit card company fees.) Also, if your drive is back-ordered, make sure your credit card will not be billed until the drive is shipped. In general, payment by credit card is preferable to using cash or a check, since it gives you many useful legal rights under the Fair Credit Billing Act (including, in some cases, the ability to withhold payment until a dispute is resolved).

Warranties

Be very careful about warranties. It's one thing to promise to repair or replace a drive, it's another to promise to do it promptly. Most drives come with a 12-month warranty for parts and labor. The figure is gradually going up as drives become more reliable. The warranty on the controller may extend to five years. It's important to note that the vendor's warranty may be longer than the manufacturer's warranty. This means that, if the vendor goes out of business, some of the warranty may be worthless.

Usually, the vendor cannot repair the drive in-house; he must send it back to the maker, or to a repair service. Since the drive must be shipped twice each way, with all the usual delays, a month can easily pass. Some warranties guarantee replacement of the drive if it is not repaired within a certain period of time. Be sure the wording in the warranty reflects the actual passage of time from the moment the drive leaves your door, and that it clearly states who pays for shipping. It should all be in writing.

Accepting and Rejecting Shipment

There's little danger of damage to a drive during shipment—if the heads are parked and the drive is packed well. (Incidentally, you should save the packing materials for the duration of the warranty so you can safely return the equipment, if necessary. Also, if the packaging shows signs of rough handling, you'll want it as evidence if you need to file a damage claim with the carrier.) Take a good look at the drive when you take it out of the box. Brand new drives carry a manufacturer's seal and logo on the metal shell—be suspicious if there's none. Unscrupulous vendors have been known to resell repaired drives that were returned under a replacement warranty. If you're in the mood to play cops and robbers, you can call the manufacturer and check to see if the serial number is recent.

If you need to send equipment back to the vendor for replacement or repair, phone them first and obtain an **RMA number** (returned merchandise authorization). Don't assume that the person receiving the package will have knowledge of your earlier conversations with the company. Write a detailed letter explaining the problems you've had, and write the RMA number on the letter. Be sure to also write the RMA number on the outside of the shipping container.

Mail order houses often impose a **restocking fee** against returned goods, often amounting to 10 percent of the cost of the goods. They're also unlikely to refund the money they charged for shipping the drive to you. So the refund check may be substantially less than you paid. When the error is entirely their own, they owe you a full refund, and you should demand it when you phone for an RMA number. Not many vendors will reimburse you for the money you spent returning the drive, even if the problem is entirely their fault.

We don't mean to put you off by pointing out so many hazards. Most buyers receive their drives quickly, install them without a hitch, and run them for years. But it's good to be prepared for the worst. Once you become reliant on a hard disk drive, you'll find it just about impossible to use your computer if the drive goes on the blink. The faster you can deal with emergencies, the faster you can get back to work.

CHAPTER 4

Installation and Setup

Depending on who you talk to, hard disk installation is either (a) "a snap," or (b) agony unto death. Having an easy time of it does not require any particular technical knowledge or experience; a little reading and a little common sense suffice. Those who have had an awful experience often turn out to have jumped in too quickly. Even dealing with a faulty disk drive need not be a terrible experience if you have learned how to recognize that the problem is in the drive and not in your attempts to install it.

An experienced technician can install and format a typical hard disk in under an hour, most of the time just waiting for the formatting programs to do their work. In most cases, a novice ought to be able to get through the process in under two hours, following the instructions we give here.

Self-reliance

If you buy a hard disk in a computer store, the vendor may install the disk for you if you'll bring in your machine. There's no denying the convenience, but, having foregone the experience of installing the drive yourself, you'll find yourself that much more reliant on the vendor in the future. Thereafter, if you have trouble with the drive, you may need to leave your entire system in a repair shop until someone gets around to looking at it. The same goes for diskette drives and expansion boards you acquire. By not learning the basics of connecting and configuring components, you leave yourself vulnerable to the schedules of others.

System Optimization

Hands-on familiarity with equipment is also useful to those who want to tweak their systems for highest performance. "Power users" need to feel at home with swapping boards, cabling equipment, altering DIP switch settings, and configuring DOS. If the very idea leaves you aghast, perhaps you should leave installation to the experts. But most people should take the plunge, particularly those who have better things to do with their money than pay $80 per hour to have someone twist a few screws and type some DOS commands. Fortunately, the vast majority of performance optimizations can be done with software, rather than by tinkering with the hardware.

Warranty Violations

Keep in mind that any installation of unapproved equipment may—technically at least—nullify a computer's warranty. This is particularly true of name-brand machines. Having a dealer install the equipment will not make it an iota more official.

Installing an Internal Hard Disk

Generally speaking, physically installing an internal hard disk entails (1) inserting a drive into a drive bay, (2) possibly inserting a controller card into one of the computer's slots, and (3) cabling the controller to the drive and the drive to the power supply. However, there are myriad variations on this theme. Some machines may have the drive controller built into the main system board. Others may provide a place on the system board into which a drive is plugged directly, with no cabling of any kind.

In the latter case, the machine requires a drive of a special design, and you may not be able to go to the marketplace for a discounted model. This is especially true of laptop computers. Drives made for machines of this kind are shipped with (what should be) detailed instructions for installation. You'll want to follow those instructions to a 'T,' rather than the ones we give here for an ordinary drive installation that applies to more than 90 percent of PCs.

Inserting a Drive

First you must get the cover off the machine. To begin with, unplug the computer. It's all right to run a machine with its cover off, but don't work in it while power is turned on! Next, move the monitor to the side of the machine if it normally resides on top. There's no need to disconnect it. Then pull the machine away from the wall or from any other obstacle that prevents easy access to both the front and back. If your machine has a security lock and key, be sure it is set to the "open" position; the cover will be locked into place otherwise.

Removing the Cover

The next step is to unfasten the cover. Most models have screws in the back of the machine that hold the cover in place, usually one at each corner and one or two at the center. It's easy to identify the corner screws, but sometimes a little harder to figure out which screws in the center fasten to the case and not to a component inside the computer. Look for screws that are identical to the ones on the corners. Some PS/2 models have screws on the sides of the machine, or use thumbscrews in back. Not all cases use screws, however. You may find that your machine uses some kind of latch that is opened just by pushing two buttons at the back or side of the machine, one button on each side. For most floor-standing models, you'll need to remove screws on one side of the machine, tilt the cover toward you, and then lift it.

If your cover *is* held in place by screws, a regular screwdriver will usually remove them. There's no need to unplug the various cables in the back of the machine. However, some machines have a "vanity plate" mounted at back. This decorative plastic plate is designed to spruce up a computer that sits on a desk with its back exposed to view. If a vanity plate is installed, you won't be able to get at the screws without removing it, and that requires pulling out all the cables. The plate is generally held in place by several strips of velcro. A few gentle tugs are all it takes to remove it.

Cables in Back

If you must disconnect cables, keep a sharp eye on which cable connects to which socket. It's easy enough to reinsert the power and keyboard cables, since these have unique plugs that can't be confused with others. However, the cables that plug into ports and expansion cards vary from machine to machine, so you'll want to keep track of what goes where. Most machines have unused sockets at back, and you could find yourself with several places that a cable could connect. You can attach a piece of masking tape to each cable to avoid confusion, writing on it the position of the card it plugs into. Even if you don't have a vanity plate to remove, you'll need to keep track of cables that aren't screwed in tight, since they may become detached while you're busy installing the drive. (This is especially likely to happen when you first pull the computer forward from its normal position.)

Now you can remove the cover. Again, designs vary, and you may have to experiment a little to find out how it opens. Most covers are completely removable, but there are designs that hinge upward without leaving the machine. Most covers surround the computer on three sides and are removed by pulling them forward and upward. There may be a little initial resistance if the cover fits tightly against the back of the machine. Tug at it firmly but carefully. If it won't give at all, take another look for additional screws holding it in place. Your best guide is your computer's manual, which should contain diagrams that show how to get the cover off.

The Catch

Once it's loose, pull the cover straight forward until it will go no further, then lift it upward from the front. The upward motion is required because there may be a catch at the top of the cover that stops the cover from sliding all the way forward. It's easy to get the cover off, but the catch can make it a little tricky getting it back on. When you later replace the cover, you must reverse the motion, approaching the machine with the cover tilted upward, then tilting it down flat and pushing it forward. Incidentally, sometimes cables from adapter cards run over the tops of other cards, and the catch may grab onto these as it is drawn forward. So pull forward very slowly, and reach back and loosen the adapter cables if there is a problem.

Inserting the Controller Card

When your machine is not already equipped with a controller card, you'll need to insert one into a slot. You'll find that it's easy to install an expansion card in a slot, even if you've never done this before. Choose a socket as close to the disk drive as possible. Because many expansion cards project sockets out the back of the machine, there is an opening behind each slot. This opening is covered by an oblong plate to keep dust out. Remove the plate, then place the controller card over the slot and gently rock it back and forth (towards the front and back of the machine) until it slips into the socket. Fasten the card with the screw that held the plate, if one is used, and store the plate someplace where it can be found if someday you need to replace it. The card may come with a plastic guide that attaches to the front end of the card slot. The guide, which you'll only need to insert if there isn't one already, stops the card from swaying when the computer is bumped. Be sure to snap the guide into place before inserting the adapter (the guide has a definite top and bottom, so see that it is oriented like others in the machine).

Be careful not to drop screws into the computer. If you do, be sure to remove them from the machine before switching on the power again. When a screw falls into a hard-to-reach nook, wrap a little masking tape around the tip of a screwdriver with the sticky side facing out. Then press it against the screw and carefully lift it out. Computer toolkits—available at dealers—contain a special "grabber" tool that makes it especially easy to recover a screw that's fallen into a tight spot. These toolkits also contain screwdrivers, nutdrivers, tweezers, and chip pullers; they cost about $18, and we strongly recommend that you buy one if you intend to work on your machine yourself.

The Disk Drive Bays

Empty spaces set aside for disk drives inside computers are called **bays**. Early drives—both diskette drives and hard disk drives—were twice the height of a typical drive today. Thus, an ordinary drive today is called a "half-height" drive. XT-style machines have two side-by-side bays, each capable of holding one full-height or two half-height drives. Both bays are open at the front. AT-style machines that imitate the early IBM AT models have a similar arrangement, but with the left-hand bay entirely enclosed (it held a full-height hard disk in the first ATs). The bay on the right was designed to hold up to three half-height drives.

Today, many clones, including machines using the 80386 and 80486 microprocessor, follow an AT-style design. But in most cases the internal full-height drive bay has been eliminated. Usually, a single bay is found at the right of the machine, and it can squeeze in *four* half-height drives. Four drives would seem more than adequate for any machine, but in some cases you can run out of space. The first two slots may go to diskette drives, perhaps one for each diskette format (5¼-inch and 3½-inch). A hard disk takes up the third slot; when it fills, a second hard disk goes into the fourth. No space may be left for an internal tape-backup unit (we discuss these in Chapter 8).

Sometimes the space provided *looks* like it can hold four drives, but actually fits only three. There is a standard dimension for the front panel of each drive, and manufacturers do a good job of following it. But the positioning of the panel in relation to the rest of the drive can make a panel reach a little too high or too low in some cases, so that it hits a drive above or below. When this happens, a drive can't be pushed all the way into the machine, and no amount of tugging can make it at peace with its neighbors. When this happens, it's usually possible to cram everything into the machine by changing the order of the drives, but this means you may not be able to position them exactly as you would like. If a drive just won't fit, you may have to opt for a hard disk card or an external drive instead.

PS/2 designs are more varied. Some have bays that hold only 3½-inch drives, while others hold 5¼-inch drives. These machines are smaller than earlier PCs, and offer less space for installation of peripherals of any kind. Some models provide space for just one 3½-inch drive, sometimes using a special drive design. The controller circuitry may not handle a second drive, and external installation may be necessary. Ironically, it is the top-of-the-line PS/2 machines that are closest to the earlier AT-architecture, following the traditional drive-cabled-to-controller-card system, and offering space for multiple units.

Inserting a Drive in an XT-style Machine

In a PC or XT, the drives slide into place and the mounting screws are attached through the metal siding. This would be simple enough were it not that it can be a terrible bother to get at all the screw holes. Only the outside hole for the rightmost drive bay is easily accessed. The screw holes between the two drive bays are accessible by removing a drive in the opposite bay and reaching through with a short screwdriver. The holes closest to the slots can only be gotten at by removing most of the cards. To stop the drive from wobbling, true XTs have an additional screw hole through the bottom of the machine.

In most XT-style machines, one bay is filled with two half-height drives, and the other is empty but for a face plate that blocks the opening in the front of the machine. Face plates install in different ways, usually with a screw or a clip that slides on and off with the help of a screwdriver or other pointed tool. Since the designs vary, you'll have to check the instructions, or just play around with it until you figure out how it is held in place. Most clones provide screw holes for two half-height drives in a bay, but early machines do not. For these, you may need to acquire an adapter kit that links the two drives together. The usual mounting screws then attach directly to this assemblage.

Inserting a Drive in an AT-style Machine

While disk drives are held in place by screws on PCs, IBM responded to the proliferation of half-height drives by introducing **guide rails** in ATs. These are strips of plastic that are screwed into the sides of disk drives so that rails run along both sides of the drives, from front to back. The sides of the drive bays are notched to receive these rails, so the drives slide in like drawers. Recall that in Chapter 3 we warned you to be sure that guide rails are included when you purchase a drive. To stop the drives from sliding out the front of the machine, small metal retainers are screwed in at the front of the notches, blocking the rails. These in turn are hidden by the computer cover. Note that the rails have a front and back, and that the tapered ends of the rails point toward the back of the drive.

Inserting a Drive into a PS/2 Machine

PS/2 machines present a wide variety of drive installations. Some require unique drive designs. The model 30, for example, uses a drive with a built- in controller. It installs directly onto the system board to which it connects by a special cable. On the other hand, a model 50 PS/2 installs the drive in a way that the back of the drive plugs directly into a controller board in one of the machine's slots.

PS/2 machines that use standard $3\frac{1}{2}$-inch drives mount them on plastic "sleds" instead of using AT-style rails. It's the same system used for diskette drives in these machines. The drive sits atop this sled and slides into place. A tab at the front of the sled latches it in place. To remove a drive, you pull the tab upward as you slide the drive forward.

PS/2 models that favor $5\frac{1}{4}$-inch drives use slide-on rails rather than plastic sleds. The drive bays are constructed as a sort of cage in which a second drive may be positioned toward the rear of the cabinet, *behind* the first. One drive blocks access to the other. The drives are locked firmly in place by tightening plastic knobs that hold them in place. No tools are required.

Cabling MFM, RLL, and ESDI Drives

In machines with MFM, RLL, and ESDI drives, two kinds of **ribbon cable** (flat, multiwire cable) stretch from a controller card to the drive, a **data cable** and a **control cable**. The control cable can connect to two drives, the data cable to only one. Hence, a computer with a second hard disk needs one control cable and two data cables. Systems with internal IDE and SCSI drives have a single ribbon cable that connects to all the drives in the machine. You must be sure that the drive or drives in your computer are connected to the right point on the controller cable. And you must take care that the orientation of the cables is correct so that they are not plugged in upside-down. Your equipment is not usually damaged when you connect cables the wrong way, but you can become terribly confused when this happens, since it's not obvious that a drive is wrongly cabled, and you may be lead to believe that the drive is not working because of some other aspect of installation.

Cables normally have different kinds of connectors at the two ends. The end that plugs into the drive uses an **edge connector**. It plugs into the back edge of the drive's circuit board at a point where a number of parallel traces (wires) come to an end. Usually there is a slot cut in the edge connector to match a plastic insert ("key") in the cable's socket. The cable's insert fits into the slot so that, if you try to plug the connector in upside-down, it won't fit. Unfortunately, some cables come without the key installed and *can* be plugged in the wrong way if you're not careful.

The opposite end of the cable plugs into a bank of protruding pins on the side of the controller card. It's easy to see how this works, and easy to connect the socket and pins, but occasionally the two parts will fit too tightly and it becomes difficult to unplug the cable from the controller card. When this happens, carefully use a knife or some other tool to pry the cable from the card in tiny steps. Don't just pull at the cable. If you do, pins may be bent or broken when the connection finally gives.

The wires in a cable are labeled from 1 upwards. Usually the side of the cable that corresponds to line 1 has a different color from the rest of the cable (typically red). Sometimes you can use this color code to orient the cable to the bank of pins it is connected to. On some controller cards, the pin blocks have tiny numbers printed on or beside them to mark the first and last pins. Alternatively, a pin may be missing and one of the holes in the connector filled so that the cable can't be connected upside-down.

The Data Cable

On MFM, RLL, and ESDI, the data cable carries data between the drive and controller. It is the smaller of the two kinds of cables, having only 20 conductors, as opposed to 34 in a control cable. It's easy to see where the data cable should meet the drive, since the edge connector won't fit where the drive joins with the control cable. However, finding the right connecting point on the controller card is another matter. There normally are two banks of 20 pins (each with 2 rows of 10 pins), one for each of two disk drives. The control card documentation will tell which bank to use. Often a label is printed on the board next to each bank of pins, with the labels J3 and J4 marking the pins for the first and second drives, respectively.

The Control Cable

The control cable carries signals by which the controller card operates the drive. Because the control cable may be shared by two hard disks, it has a second edge connector midway along the cable. Sometimes, hard disk kits are shipped with a control cable that accommodates only one drive. When you add a second drive, you'll need to replace the control cable with one that has two sockets. (On the other hand, you always need to obtain a second *data* cable when you add a second drive.)

In theory, a controller card can be designed to manage more than two drives. But nearly all controllers for IBM PCs (except for SCSI controllers) take only two disk drives (for a third and fourth drive, you'd need to add a second controller card to the machine). Since there's only one control cable for both drives, and it's a different size than a data cable, there's no problem finding the pin block at which the cable connects to the controller card.

The edge connector at the other end of the cable connects to the first disk drive in the machine (nominally, drive C). A second drive connects to the socket in the middle of the cable. When there is no second drive, this socket goes unused.

The Drive Select Setting

Most control cables have a twist in the section between the two sockets that connect the drives. Lines 25 through 29 are separated from the cable and join with the outermost connector in reverse order from the way they join with the middle connector. This ploy lets the computer distinguish between drives when two drives are connected.

All drives have a DIP switch or jumper on the drive circuitry that specifies whether the drive should act as drive #1 or drive #2. The switch or jumper makes the **drive select** setting. Drives destined for IBM PCs usually come from the factory set as drive #2. However, because of the twist in the cable, a drive joined at the end of the control cable is regarded as drive #1, despite the fact that its drive select setting is #2. Because the twist occurs after the middle socket, the drive joined at the middle is taken as drive #2. Ordinarily, there is no reason to alter the drive select setting on a drive, no matter whether it is to be drive #1 or drive #2.

The drive select setting may need to be changed, however, if you encounter a control cable that lacks the twist. These are sometimes called "straight-through" cables. In this case, the drive at the end of the cable needs to be set as drive #1, whether or not there is a second drive in the machine (the second drive would remain set as #2). The location of the drive select DIP switch or jumper is found in the drive documentation. Sometimes the two settings are numbered as #0 and #1 instead of #1 and #2.

Power Supply Connections

You'll also need to connect cables from the power supply. These are easily spotted protruding from the silver or black box at the right-rear of the computer in most AT-style machines, or along the side of most PS/2s. These connectors also are made in a way that they can't be inserted upside down. Incidentally, you'll find all sorts of harrowing warnings about imminent electrocution plastered all over the power supply. These refer to the inside of the metal box that you see. You can touch the box to your heart's delight without danger. But never, *ever* try to open the box, even when the machine is unplugged, and never insert tools through openings in a power supply.

Some early PCs have only two connectors coming from the power supply, and these may be taken up by diskette drives or additional hard disks. In this case, you'll need to acquire a Y-adapter—a cable that splits one connector into two. They cost only a few dollars at most electronic parts stores.

Computers that employ unusual hard-disk designs may not require that you connect a power cable. Instead, power reaches the drive along with the data and control signals.

Cabling an Activity Indicator

It's important to be able to see when a drive is active so that you won't switch off the machine before its work has finished. Most drives have an indicator light at the front for this purpose. But drives hidden inside a machine cannot display an indicator. To overcome this problem, some computers have an indicator light on the front panel that is shared by all hard disk drives. This light is usually called the drive **activity indicator**. A wire reaches from the front panel to connect to the controller card.

Sometimes, drive activity is indicated by software. For example, hard disk cards are hidden away inside a machine, and they are often installed in early PCs that have no activity indicator on the front panel. Some of these drives can display a special character at one corner of the screen whenever the drive is active. Similarly, you can use utility software that displays the letter of an active drive in the top-right corner of the screen. The letter disappears from view the moment drive activity stops.

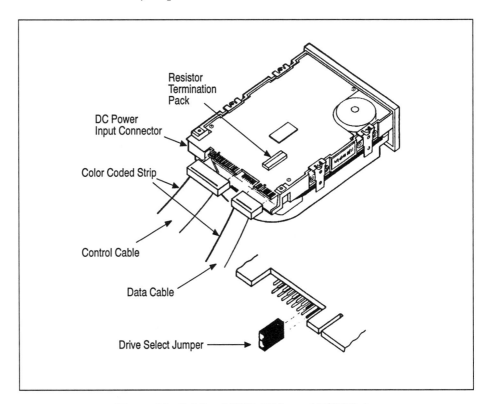

Figure 4-1. Cabling MFM, RLL, and ESDI Drives

Grounding Cables

Finally, some machines provide a **grounding cable** that electrically grounds the drive to the computer chassis. Many drives have a special connection for this ground wire—usually a tab that a connector at the end of the cable slides onto. Not all machines have grounding cables, and a drive will work without grounding. But if a grounding cable is available, take the trouble to connect it.

Connecting the Cables

You'll find that cabling is much easier with the drive protruding from the front of the machine. Push the drive all the way in and screw it in place only after the cabling is finished. Also take care to channel the cables behind the drives while you still have room to do so. When many drives are installed, there's barely enough room for all the wires, and it can be hard to reach drives installed deep in the machine. To get at one drive, you may need to disconnect others. If so, be very careful to keep track of which cable goes where.

Connecting RLL Drives

In Chapter 2 we discussed RLL encoding, which may write three or four times as much data along every track of a disk. Since it is the controller card that decodes the data, data moves at a much higher rate along the drive's data cable. For this reason, the cables are more sensitive to interference from other electrical sources. So take extra care when cabling an RLL drive. Ideally, the cables should be of the highest quality, even using gold-plated contacts in the cable sockets. More important, the cable should not be too long, since this increases the area over which the cable can pick up electrical interference. Keep the cable away from modems and network adapters. If your RLL drive is giving you trouble, try rearranging the cables.

Cabling IDE and SCSI Drives

IDE and SCSI drives are easier to install than MFM, RLL, and ESDI drives because there's only one cable to worry about. However, the second IDE drive on a cable may need to be jumpered as a "slave" drive (the first one must be a "master"), and each SCSI drive needs to be jumpered to have a different address (a number between 0 and 7). In addition, an SCSI drive in the middle of a cable must have its **terminator resistor pack** removed. (The documentation for the drive will explain how to set jumpers and remove terminators.) Power and grounding for IDE and SCSI drives are the same as for other kinds of drives. Many, but not all, IDE and SCSI host adapters provide the standard four-position connector for the LED in the front of the machine's case.

Installing External Drives

Installing an external drive is much easier than installing an internal one. You won't have to deal with mounting the drive, and there's no possibility of needing to install a new power supply, since the drive will have its own. But you *do* have to think about where you will place the drive.

Positioning the Drive

While the drive can be placed some distance from the machine using long cables, it must not be hidden away in a drawer or other sealed environment. It requires room-temperature air for cooling, and the air in any closed space will become quite hot. Even if the drive performs properly in confinement, high temperatures could lower its reliability.

Since external drives are smaller and less massive than your PC, they are more likely to be jostled about. If the drive sits beside the computer, see to it that it is not shoved around. *Don't* place the drive on top of the video monitor; by doing so, you'll block the monitor's cooling vents and increase the drive's own heat load. However, some units, such as the Bernoulli Box, have sturdy cases that let you place them under or on top of a desktop computer.

Adding a Second Drive

Adding a second hard disk drive is easy on most machines. The new drive is plugged into the connector at the center of the control cable; an MFM, RLL, and ESDI drive also gets its own data cable (see above), which runs directly to the disk controller. (IDE and SCSI drives don't need a second cable.) Two changes may be required on the drive's circuit board. You may need to add or remove a *terminator resistor pack* (which we'll discuss in a moment). The second change you may need to make will be to the *drive select* (MFM, RLL, ESDI), *master/slave* (IDE), or *address* (SCSI) setting, which we talked about in our earlier discussion on cabling. In every other respect, the drive is connected and formatted just like the first, except that the drive is referred to as drive #2 in low-level formatting and partitioning software (more on this later).

Terminator Resistors

Every drive (except for IDE drives) is equipped with a **terminator resistor pack** that is mounted on the drive's circuit board. When two drives are installed, the resistor must be removed from the drive that is connected to the middle of the control cable. The resistor usually looks like an ordinary integrated circuit chip. It actually contains eight parallel resistors, one for each of eight lines. Its location varies from drive to drive. The drive's documentation will tell you where to find it. If you have two drives of the same model, you can usually identify the resistor by looking for a socket that is filled on one and empty on the other.

It's best to pull the terminator resistor with a special tong-shaped chip pulling tool. These are available for a couple of dollars in any store that sells electronic parts and supplies, or as part of one of the computer tool kits we mentioned earlier. Place the tool around the ends of the chip and gently toggle it back and forth, lightly pulling upwards. You can pry a chip up with a small knife, but it must be done very carefully. If the chip suddenly comes loose at one end, pins will be bent or broken. Avoid touching any other part of the drive electronics, and be sure your clothing is free of static electricity before beginning.

Hang on to the terminator resistor after you remove it. If one drive goes bad and must go to the shop, you may need to reinstall the terminator resistor in the other so that it can operate alone in the machine. Also, keep the terminator resistor in mind when reconfiguring your machine. Because of it, you cannot simply change the cabling between the two drives to give them different DOS specifiers. This is true of diskette drives as well, which also have terminator resistors.

Problems with XTs

XT-style machines can pose special problems, since they descend from early IBM PCs, which were not designed with a hard disk in mind. These use a less-sophisticated controller card design than later machines. Many controller cards have a jumper that must be changed when a second drive is connected, and some will demand that the second drive be identical to the first. If you lack documentation for the controller card, you may have quite a headache on your hands. Worse, DOS may refuse to partition and format the drive when drive **C** already exists. The solution is to make the former drive **C** into drive **D** and format the new drive as drive **C**. This means that the older drive must be recabled, and jumpers and terminating resistors must be set accordingly (remember, the terminating resistor goes on the drive connected to the *end* of the control cable). DOS will readily format the new drive and accept the old one as **D**. Mistakes can occur easily in this process, so be sure to make a careful backup of the original hard drive before installing the second.

PS/2s

Most PS/2 machines will gladly accept a second drive, but not those such as the PS/2 Model 30, that are designed to hold only one drive that plugs directly into the machine's system board. You're left with no place inside the machine to add a second drive, no power source for the drive, and no controller connection. PS/1 machines are also designed this way, as are most laptops. A move to a larger-capacity drive may be the only solution.

Adding a Third Hard Drive

If you really get carried away and want to add a third or fourth hard disk drive, you'll ordinarily need to install a second controller card (however, SCSI controllers—which we discussed in Chapter 2—can handle more than two drives). Each controller card carries its own read-only memory (ROM) chips, and the ranges of memory addresses covered by these chips must not overlap. Controllers are factory-configured, so that the ROM begins at the memory address C8000x (memory addresses are written as *hexadecimal numbers*—it's not important if you don't understand them). But most controllers can be reconfigured by changing a DIP switch or jumper so that the ROM starts at D8000x. This is an easy matter, so long as some other adapter does not already occupy some or all of this memory range. If one does, you'll need to reconfigure that adapter's memory position in turn.

Replacing the Power Supply

Generally speaking, only IBM PC owners may need to replace the power supply when they add a hard disk. The 130-watt supply on an IBM XT (and many PC clones) should be more than adequate to support even two hard disks. You'll find a sticker on any power supply giving its rating.

Ironically, it's the machines that need power most that have the smallest supplies. The earliest PCs used 16K or 64K memory chips. By today's standards, memory was fantastically expensive in those days. A machine loaded to the 640K limit required as many as 360 chips! Power consumption was tremendous, and nearly every other component in the computer required more power than similar components do today. Still, some PC-class machines can run a hard disk drive without changing the power supply, particularly if the slots are not filled (memory and internal modems draw the most current).

Anticipating Insufficient Power

If power is insufficient, you may know it right away. If the machine freezes when you turn it on, it's time to shop for another power supply. Sometimes the power supply will seem to be adequate, but the machine crashes periodically. If the machine has worked flawlessly prior to installing the hard disk, and the disk has worked well since, repeated crashes indicate either that you are operating at the edge of the power supply's capacity, or that overheating is interfering with the drive. After a crash, quickly go into the computer and see if the air blown by the cooling fan is especially hot. (If it's overheated, it will be decidedly hot, not just warm.) If cooling seems adequate, your best bet is to install a new supply and see what happens. When crashes continue, it's time to seek outside help.

Sporadic Power Failures

You may be wondering why a power supply is adequate some of the time, but not always. One reason is that diskette drives add to the power burden, and they pull extra power when they start up. DOS uses only one diskette drive at a time, but it leaves a diskette spinning for a short time after it is finished using the diskette to avoid repeated starts and stops in close succession. Sometimes, one diskette drive starts up while a second still turns, pulling an exceptional amount of power. Two diskettes are seldom used simultaneously on a machine equipped with a hard disk. But one day this situation will occur and crash the computer. A second reason for occasional overload is that higher temperatures raise the resistance of electronic components, making them require more power. On a hot day, your whole computer may need a little extra power. If your machine is operating near its limit, it can lock up for no apparent reason.

You might want to save yourself some inconvenience and delay just by replacing the power supply on your early PC whether it's actually needed or not. Discount houses offer upgrades for as little as $50. But keep in mind that your new power supply may be as noisy as a vacuum cleaner, particularly if it's a cheap one. One reviewer found that the typical replacement power supply is five to ten times louder than the original, and actually two to four times louder once installed. There is good reason to try to keep the original supply if you can (the early PC power supplies were especially quiet).

Quiet Power Supplies

Some companies make super-quiet power supplies. These may reduce noise by as much as 90 percent. Paradoxically, this blissful quietude is achieved by using two fans instead of one. Because there are two, the fans can run more slowly, and this feature combined with a special blade design makes for much quieter operation. Unfortunately, a quiet power supply costs at least 50 percent more than an ordinary one.

Power Supply Quality

When a short circuit occurs in the machine, the power supply ought to shut itself off. All IBM power supplies are of this "total-shutdown" variety. But many models on the market are of the "current-limiting" type, which refuse to supply power beyond a certain level; others offer no protection at all. Short circuits can occur when someone pulls or inserts a card in a slot without first shutting off the power. This is a pretty dumb move, but an amazing number of computer aficionados admit to having done it absent-mindedly at one time or another. You should know that many, perhaps most, of the inexpensive power supplies on the market do not offer adequate protection from short circuits. If the worst happens, you could "fry" the electronics of your system board and every board in the slots.

Choosing a Replacement Power Supply

A good power supply does not have to be expensive. The problem is in knowing which ones perform "total-shutdown." Even those having this feature aren't ordinarily marked as such. Many vendors will assure you that the supply is "exactly like" an IBM supply, but most won't know for sure. A good supply may come in a plain brown box, a bad one in fancy packaging. Since most cheap replacement supplies are made in East Asia, you may require an Act of Congress to gain reimbursement for damage done by an inferior unit. Still, there haven't been many reports of damage from poor power supplies, so if you're on a very tight budget, an inexpensive unit should be all right.

Power Supply Installation

Installing a power supply is easy—if you bought the right one. In PC-style machines, the power supply has two connectors that plug into the system board, and many clones use plugs different from those in IBM machines. The IBM system board uses rectangular pins .095-inch by .036-inch. Some compatibles use .045-inch square pins. Since one variety of pin is square and one not, it's easy to tell them apart. Be sure to check the shape of the pins before you go shopping. (Many replacement power supplies have both kinds.)

First, you must remove the older supply. Do this only after you have unplugged the machine. The power supply will have a label on it adamantly warning you to keep out, you can get yourself killed. This message refers to the consequences of going *inside* the supply. The supply is contained in a metal box, and you can handle the box all you like without danger. Inside the box, high-voltage capacitors continue to hold power even after power is shut off or the machine is unplugged. So don't think that unplugging the machine makes it all right to break the rules. If you have insatiable curiosity to find out what's inside a power supply—*don't.*

Cabling the Supply

Four screws on the back of the computer hold the power supply in place. Before removing the screws, disconnect the cables joining the supply from disk drives and from the computer's system board. Two cables plug into the system board just beside the supply. The connectors snap into place; to remove them, push the end of a screwdriver between the snap and the plug to pull back the snap. The connector closest to the back panel is "P8," and the other is "P9." The replacement supply should have its two connectors labeled with these letters. If you can, check that they are labeled when you buy the unit. Be *very* careful not to mix them up when you insert the new supply. Should labels be missing, observe the color-coding of the wires on the original drive before you disconnect it.

Adding Extra Cooling

If overheating is crashing your system, you can increase ventilation by adding an auxiliary fan. These hang on the back of the machine, quietly forcing in extra air. In one test, this kind of fan reduced the temperature increase inside a computer from 30 to 15 degrees (Farenheit). Even without a specific equipment failure, you may want to add extra cooling if you find that components become noticeably hot to the touch. Overheating can shorten the lifespan of all parts of a drive, and heat contributes to the degeneration of electronic components, which is the leading cause of drive failure.

Sealing Empty Slots

Be sure to keep the back of your computer sealed. When the machine is new, a metal plate is installed beside each slot on the back panel. These plates are removed, one-by-one, as adapter cards are added to the machine. Often, when a card is later removed, the plate is nowhere to be found. Gradually, more and more holes are left open in the back of the machine. At first glance, these holes would seem to promote ventilation. Actually, the holes interfere with the internal ventilation scheme. Normally, air is drawn through the front panel of the machine, across the hard disk and other components. But, if there's a hole in the back of the computer, air may be drawn through it instead, reducing the amount of air that circulates over some components that need cooling. You should keep the plates in place when no card is installed.

Improving Ventilation

You can improve the ventilation in some early IBM PCs (not necessarily on clones). In these machines, you'll see a strip of slots along the *bottom* of the front panel when you remove the cover. Take one-inch wide plastic tape and block this strip across the entire width of the machine. Paradoxical though it may seem, this measure *increases* ventilation across the slots. Later IBM PCs were shipped with this modification already made.

Replacing the ROM BIOS

The BIOS in early PCs lacked an important routine that causes the operating system to search for hard disks and link them into operations. When hard disks were first sold for these machines, special code had to be loaded from diskette every time the computer was booted. But this approach did not allow booting from the hard disk.

Following the introduction of the XT, IBM made available a replacement BIOS chip that contained the special routine. Chapter 3 explains how to determine whether you need this chip. Alas, IBM discontinued shipments in mid-1987, so you'll need to turn to some other source for one. Instructions accompanying the chip will tell you how to install it.

Reconfiguring the System

When the computer starts up, the disk controller needs to know the geometry of the drives it will run. Recall that an AT-compatible's BIOS chips hold a table of standard geometries—a listing of the numbers of heads, tracks, and cylinders on certain drives. The controller needs to know which geometry to use. In XT-style machines, this information is contained on the controller card itself. This makes installation easy. There are no changes to the machine's DIP switches when a hard disk is installed. However, some XT-type controllers can handle fewer kinds of drives than AT-type controllers.

A new system was introduced with the IBM AT. In these machines and all that followed, including PS/2 machines, the code number for a drive's geometry is stored in **CMOS** memory. This memory resides on a special memory and clock/calendar chip powered by a lithium battery; it retains information and keeps track of the time of day even when the machine is turned off. After installing a drive, you run configuration software to initialize the proper value.

To make this initialization, you must know the proper number for your drive. Unfortunately, it's not always in the drive's documentation (though it's sometimes written on a sticker on the drive itself). If you can't find the number, you'll need to contact the disk vendor or manufacturer. Make sure you get the numbers of heads, cylinders, and sectors per track, as well as the *write precompensation cylinder* (the cylinder, if any, where write precompensation is turned on). This information may come in handy if you use third-party software (or a setup program that's part of your computer's BIOS) to configure your system for the drive. Just knowing the capacity of the drive will not help you since there may be several standard geometries for a drive of a given size, using different numbers of platter sides, tracks, and sectors per track.

The geometry you specify need not match the drive exactly. It just must not exceed the specifications of the drive you've installed. If you have a two-platter drive offering 720 tracks with 17 sectors per track, you could use a geometry for a 2-platter drive with the same number of sectors per track but only 680 tracks. The drive would work just fine, but the controller would not be able to access the last 40 tracks. Obviously, this reduces the effective capacity of the drive.

Add-on ROMS

When a drive's geometry is not described by the BIOS—as is often the case for drives of very high capacity—you can replace your BIOS with one that can handle your drive's geometry. (Some BIOSes have a built-in setup program that lets you configure them for any drive if you know the number of heads, number of cylinders, number of sectors per track, and the write pre-compensation cylinder.) Another solution is to install a ROM board that extends your BIOS to work with more kinds of disk drives.

Running Configuration Programs

Once you know the proper drive table number, and/or your drive's geometry, you need to run the computer's configuration program. On many AT-style machines, including numerous 386 or 486 clones, the program is called **SETUP** and is found on a diskette shipped with the machine. On true IBM machines, it is on the *Diagnostics Diskette* found in the *Guide to Operations*. Some clones store the installation routines on ROM chips inside the machine so that it is always on hand. When the machine starts up, you're offered an opportunity to launch the configuration program by typing a particular keystroke or keystroke combination.

The **SETUP** program is self-explanatory. It asks for the time and date and information about several kinds of connected hardware. Unfortunately, you need to go through all steps to get to the point of configuring a hard disk. Enter the code number when the program asks for the "drive type." Once all parameters have been set, the program reboots the machine. The job is easier in self-configuring machines, including PS/2 Micro Channel machines and EISA computers. When you run their configuration programs (found on the *Reference Diskette* in PS/2 models) they can figure out most installation information on their own.

Mopping Up

After your new pride and joy is merrily whirling along, do a good job of mopping up. Place the drive documentation in your **system library**. What? You don't keep a system library? All this means is that there is a single place for all of your computer documentation, including hardware documentation, DOS manuals, and software manuals. Small pamphlets or loose pages should go into clearly marked file folders or manila envelopes.

When you have trouble with a hard disk drive nothing will compound your exasperation more than not being able to find the documentation you need. It's a good idea to write on the documentation the address of the vendor, the duration of the warranty and its starting date, and the technical support phone number.

If a utility diskette accompanies the drive, you may want to make a copy—just in case. File the diskette away, and, if your diskette library is as messy as most people's, record the diskette's location in the documentation. Finally, set aside the original packaging in case you need to send the drive through the mail for repairs. If someone else might throw out the box, label it with a message. You may want to record the location of the packaging in the documentation. While few of us often rise to these sublime heights of organization, the effort is bound to be rewarded sooner or later.

Formatting

Once the disk is successfully installed, the machine will boot normally from a diskette in drive A. Although drive C now exists as a physical entity, DOS cannot recognize it, so you should resist the temptation to make the hard disk the default drive by entering **C:**. Before DOS can use the drive, it must be low-level formatted, partitioned, then formatted; and during these three steps the default drive will remain drive **A** (or some other already existing drive).

Recall from Chapter 2 that low-level formatting defines the sectors on the drive, that partitioning creates the master boot record and sets aside some or all of the cylinders for use by DOS (as opposed to other operating systems), and that high-level formatting writes the DOS boot record, root directory, file allocation tables, and system files—COMMAND.COM, plus the two boot files IBMBIO.COM and IBMDOS.COM (or IO.SYS and MSDOS.SYS in MSDOS).

Some drives are delivered with low-level formatting in place. There are even manufacturers (or vendors) who partition the drive and perform high-level formatting at the factory. In the latter case, the entire disk is invariably partitioned for DOS. While you may not have to bother with any formatting at all, it's worth understanding the process. This is because sometimes it's necessary to redo part or all of the formatting process, either in response to some kind of disk error, or in order to change partition sizes.

Low-level Formatting

As we explained in previous chapters, low-level formatting is performed by a special utility program that defines and labels the sectors into which a track is divided, and that then tests the media in each sector to see that it can successfully hold data. (Some drives, including many IDE drives, never need low-level formatting; make sure you find out if you're getting one of these drives when you make your purchase.) Low-level formatting programs are really very simple to run. But they can be intimidating because they seldom present an easy-to-use interface, and often employ technical terms. Reading just the next few paragraphs should be enough to let you understand these programs.

First, you need to find the program. It may be part of your disk controller's ROM (check the manual), or on a utility diskette supplied with your drive or system. If you need to reformat a disk and haven't got a low-level formatting program, you might try phoning the vendor to see if they're still willing to send you one. Otherwise, you'll need to buy one, usually as part of a larger disk utility package. IBM provides one in its *Advanced Diagnostics* package, which costs roughly twice as much as others. PS/2 machines have a low-level formatting program built in. It resides on ROM chips inside the machine. To start it up, just boot the machine from the *Reference Diskette* and press Ctrl-A at the main menu. You'll be lead to the *Advanced Diagnostics*, which offers low-level formatting as a menu choice.

As a general rule, if a disk drive is shipped with a low-level formatting program, you should use it instead of some other utility. This is because some disks have special information encoded on them that an ordinary format program will wipe out. Some, for example, have bad-track information written on the disk, and this information is used by the accompanying format program. Another example is found in some hard disk cards, which keep an extra sector on each track that can substitute for a defective sector so that a whole track does not need to be marked as unusable. A general-purpose formatting program will not be able to deal with these anomalies.

ROM Code

A few drives use an unusual, and potentially intimidating, approach to low-level formatting. They place the formatting program on a read-only memory chip (a ROM) on the controller card. There's nothing wrong with a program sitting in hardware instead of a diskette. But how do you get it going? It's launched by issuing a special instruction through the DOS DEBUG program. This program resides on a DOS diskette as DEBUG.COM. Once it's running, you type in a short sequence of keystrokes listed in the documentation that accompanies the drive. These keystrokes will seem like gobbledygook, so don't even *try* to understand them. Just type in *exactly* what the instructions say. This approach scares the gee-willikers out of computer novices, and fewer and fewer makers are resorting to it. But it's a perfectly good way to format a hard disk drive, and it has the added advantage that you can't lose the program since it's built in (however, you *can* lose the instructions for starting the program, so be sure they're filed away).

The Drive Specifier

Once loaded, low-level format programs prompt you for various information. The first task is to specify the drive that will be formatted. The program can tell the difference between a diskette drive and a hard disk drive. If there's only one hard disk in the machine, it will recognize the fact and just inform you that it has found only one disk and that is the one it will format. When it finds two hard disk drives, it will give you a choice.

There's a danger lurking here if you're installing a second hard disk. If the second drive is improperly installed and the formatting program cannot find it, it may assume that your first drive is the only one in the machine and that you want to format it. If a second drive has been installed, be sure that the formatting program has given you the option of formatting one of *two* drives. You might think that the program would recognize that the first drive has already been partitioned and (high level) formatted, and thus should not be touched. But there are times when a fully formatted drive needs to be low-level formatted, so the utility will gladly perform this task.

There can be some confusion in naming hard disk drives. Recall that a single *physical* hard disk can be partitioned into a number of *logical* drives. Perhaps half the drive will be recognized as drive **C**, and the other half as drive **D**. So it doesn't necessarily make sense for a low-level formatting program to refer to your first hard disk drive as drive **C** and a second hard disk drive as drive **D**.

Instead, the drives are numbered, with the first hard disk as drive 1 and the second as drive 2 (diskette drives aren't counted). This system is clear enough, but most users are accustomed to thinking of drives by their drive specifiers (like **C:**). And so a few low-level formatting programs attempt to be "user friendly" by referring to the drives by the letters **C** and **D**.

Bad Tracks

Most drives are shipped with a **bad track table.** This table lists all tracks that failed in the manufacturer's tests of the drive. The table is affixed to the drive casing, or is found on a separate sheet of paper that accompanies the drive (in the latter case, be sure to store it with the drive's documentation so that it will be available if you ever need to reformat the drive). By entering the track numbers, the formatting program is able to mark these tracks off bounds. You'll be asked for a **side (or head) number** and **track number**. The side number, of course, refers to the platter side on which the bad track resides.

You may be wondering why it's necessary to enter bad track information. After all, the DOS high-level formatting program (FORMAT.COM) looks for bad sectors and marks them as invalid in the disk's file allocation table. But DOS cannot test a drive nearly as well as a manufacturer's instruments can. The low-level formatting program leaves a special code (used to check for errors in the low-level formatting on each track as it works). When you have specified that a particular track is bad, the program intentionally writes an invalid number in this place. Later, the high-level formatting program encounters the number, understands it to mean that the track can't be used, and marks every sector on the track off bounds. Actually only a small part of the track may be bad. But, because no sectors are defined prior to low-level formatting, there is no way to specify where on the track the faulty media resides, and so the entire track is lost.

If you have a drive that works with an ESDI controller, the job is easier. A bad track list is stored electronically inside these drives, and the controller is able to find out the information without your help. In most cases, all you'll need to do is confirm that the information it read is accurate (you can also add the locations of any tracks you've discovered to be unreliable since the last low-level format). In the future, all drives will hopefully work this way.

Specifying the Disk Geometry

Once the formatting program knows which drive to format, it needs to learn with what kind of drive it is dealing. Ordinarily, the program doesn't care who manufactured the drive, nor is it interested in information like the drive's average seek time, whether the drive is internal or external, and so on. Rather, the formatting program needs to find out the *drive geometry*. As we explained earlier in this chapter, a list of geometries is held on ROM chips in the machine. You should be able to determine the drive's geometry from its documentation. Once this is done, you can enter the code number for that geometry—or, if your BIOS allows it, type the geometry directly into a setup routine.

Setting the Interleave

Most low-level format programs ask for an **interleave factor**. Those that do not may be able to figure out the optimum interleave for themselves, or may be tailored for a particular disk in a particular machine. In our discussion of interleave in Chapter 2, we expressed interleave values in the form **6:1** or **3:1**. But formatting programs usually take a single numeral, such as **6** or **3**. Generally speaking, a PC-style machine running at eight MHz or below will have a 5:1 interleave and a faster XT can have 4:1. A 286 machine running at six MHz takes a 3:1 interleave and faster 286 machines take a 2:1 value. 386 and 486 machines normally use a 1:1 interleave. Remember that a too-low interleave (such as using 1:1 when 2:1 is best) will slow down your machine much more than a too-high interleave.

Interleave Optimization

In our discussion of interleave in Chapter 2, we pointed out that the optimal interleave factor for a disk depends on the speed of the machine on which it works. In the days when there were only a few kinds of PCs available, the manufacturer could tell you the best interleave and that was that. Today, computers run at hundreds of different performance levels, yet the same disk drives can go into any computer. A computer's documentation sometimes gives advice about an ideal interleave. But, more and more, the only way to find out the optimum is to run interleave optimization software.

Interleave optimization may be a feature of a low-level formatting program. But most optimizers are designed to work *after* formatting—including high-level formatting—has been completed. This approach gives the program more flexibility, allowing it run on long-installed drives that are full of data, and to change the interleave if the machine is somehow made faster, perhaps by installing an accelerator. The data is preserved as the disk is tested for its best interleave and as the interleave markings (sector numberings) are subsequently altered. We discuss these utilities in Chapter 7, along with other hard disk optimization measures.

It's awkward to try to optimize the interleave factor without a utility designed for the task. You can repeatedly reformat the disk at different interleaves and try to time disk operations with a stop watch, but you'd spend a lot of time and get inaccurate results. Besides, interleave optimization utilities are becoming a standard part of disk "toolkits," making them quite inexpensive.

Testing

Low-level format programs test the disk after writing upon it, checking the integrity of the sectors created. As we'll see in Chapter 9, testing can be very elaborate, and most format programs fall far short of the state-of-the-art. Still, a good low-level format program will test and retest. This testing adds to the time that the format takes. Generally, a low-level format requires about one-half to one-and-a-half minutes per megabyte. So a 40-megabyte drive formats in about half an hour. However, a formatting program that performs extensive testing could take an hour or longer. Most programs give some feedback on the screen, telling which cylinder is currently being processed. Others make no changes on the display until the format is complete. These may leave you wondering whether the machine has crashed. Be patient—low-level formatting takes time. But if the format on a 40M disk isn't complete after two hours, and there are no changes on the display, it's time to seek help (unless the instructions tell you otherwise).

Partitioning

The DOS partitioning program is called **FDISK**. It is found on one of the DOS diskettes, as FDISK.EXE. Prior to DOS Version 3.3, partitioning was uncomplicated. FDISK simply marked the partition table in the master boot record, telling where the partitions begin, and it set up the boot record in the DOS partition (these concepts are explained in Chapter 2).

Primary and Extended Partitions

Starting with Version 3.3, two partitions may belong to DOS, a **primary partition** and an **extended partition**. The primary partition is exactly like DOS partitions in earlier DOS versions, and it is used for booting. Extended partitions hold data but can't be used for booting. Second hard disk drives may have only an extended partition. An extended DOS partition can be as large as the drive itself, but it may be subdivided, with each subdivision, or **volume**, acting as a **logical drive**. This means that each volume is given a drive specifier from **D** to **Z**, and, from the user's point of view, it acts as an independent drive with its own directory tree. In DOS 3.3, a volume may be as small as a single cylinder, and as large as 32 megabytes, but no larger. Hence, the 32-megabyte limit on partition size (and thus on file size) remains in force. Only starting with version 4.0 can you exceed the 32-megabyte limit in DOS.

Figure 4-2 diagrams this system. In the diagram, logical drives **C:** through **E:** are contained on a single hard disk. Note the introduction of **logical drive tables**. These are analogous to the partition table in the master boot record. They reside in the **extended boot record** that begins each volume of the extended DOS partition (note that calling these "boot records" is a misnomer, since they're not for booting). The logical drive table for the first volume tells the location of the next, and so on.

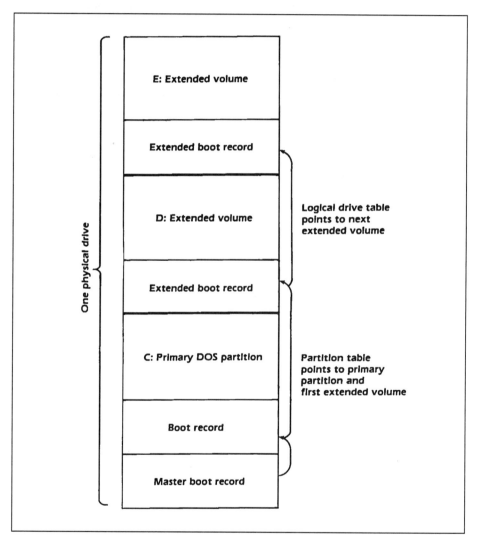

Figure 4-2. Partitioning under DOS 3.3 and later

The FDISK Menu

In our examples here, we'll look at FDISK in DOS versions 3.3 and 4.0. The same system continues in DOS 5.0. The exact wording of the menus varies between versions, but the functions are the same. DOS versions prior to 3.3 will lack the menu choices for extended partitions. Here is the basic startup menu.

```
FDISK Options
Current Fixed Disk Drive: 1
Choose one of the following:
    1.  Create DOS partition
    2.  Change Active Partition
    3.  Delete DOS partition
    4.  Display Partition Information
    5.  Select Next Fixed Disk Drive
Enter choice: [1]
```

The "current fixed disk drive" tells which drive FDISK is about to partition. The number #1 refers to the first drive in the machine (drive **C:**). If you need to partition a second drive that you've just installed, select menu choice #5 to direct FDISK to that drive (this menu choice doesn't appear when only one hard disk drive is installed).

The usual menu choice, #1, is preselected, so you only need to press Enter to get started. Then you're shown a second menu:

```
Create DOS Partition
Current Fixed Disk Drive: 1
    1.  Create Primary DOS partition
    2.  Create Extended DOS partition
Enter choice: [1]
```

Creating a First Partition

For a first partition on a first hard disk, you'll choose #1, otherwise #2. The message appears:

```
Do you wish to use the maximum size
for a DOS partition and make the DOS
partition active (y/n)........? [Y]
```

If your disk holds 32 megabytes or less, just press Enter to select "yes." But if you have more capacity, you've two options. If you're working in DOS 4.0 or later, you can type "y" and DOS will make an oversized partition automatically. You'll see a message like:

```
System will now restart
Insert DOS diskette in drive A:
Press any key when ready. . .
```

When you strike any key, DOS reboots from drive A:, presenting the usual date and time queries. The process takes only a few seconds, because only a few sectors on the disk are affected. When DOS 4.0 creates an oversized partition, it displays the message:

```
WARNING! SHARE should be loaded for large media
```

This reminds you that oversized partitions require that you load the DOS SHARE command when the computer starts up. Do this through your CONFIG.SYS file by adding the line:

```
INSTALL=SHARE
```

(If SHARE.EXE isn't in the root directory, be sure to specify a path for it.) The file takes up about 7K of memory. DOS 5.0 does not require this command for oversized partitions, but does if you're running some networks.

Creating Multiple Extended Partitions

Oversized partitions can confuse utility software, and even some application software but this is rarely a problem anymore. However, if your software can't deal with oversized partitions, you may want to confine yourself to creating multiple extended partitions of 32 megabytes or less. You do this by specifying "n" (no) when asked if you want to use the entire disk for the primary partition. FDISK then tells you how large the disk is:

```
Total disk space is 819 cylinders.
Maximum space available for partition
is 642 cylinders.
Enter partition size........: [642]
No partitions defined
```

It's up to you to decide how many cylinders to use. This example is for a 40M drive that will be split into two 20M partitions. FDISK displays the maximum number of cylinders that will fit in 32 megabytes—642. In this case, you'd type 410 (half the 819 cylinders) instead, then press Enter. The partition is created and the following message displayed:

```
Create Primary DOS Partition
Current Fixed Disk Drive: 1
Partition Status    Type  Start  End Size
 C: 1               PRI DOS    0  409  410
Primary DOS partition created
Press ESC to return to FDISK Options
```

This status information shows that logical drive C has been created, that it is the primary DOS partition (the one used for booting) and that the partition extends from cylinders 0 to 409. You press Esc to return to the main menu and then go on to make an extended partition from the remaining cylinders. Again, you select the first menu choice to "Create DOS partition" and then select "Create Extended DOS partition." The message appears:

```
Create Extended DOS Partition
Partition Status    Type  Start  End Size
C: 1                PRI DOS    0  409  410
Total disk space is 819 cylinders.
Maximum space available for partition
is  409 cylinders.
Enter partition size.........:[ 409]
```

As before, you're shown status information, and this time told how many cylinders are left. You can divide the remaining space into as many segments as you like, each with its own drive specifier, starting from D. FDISK specifies 409 cylinders as the obvious choice, and you select it by pressing Enter. Now the partitioning information reflects the new partition:

```
Partition Status    Type  Start  End Size
C: 1                PRI DOS    0  409  410
   2                EXT DOS  410  818  409
Extended DOS partition created
```

Setting the Drive Specifier

Notice that the second partition is not yet marked by the symbol **D:** to indicate its drive specifier. This is accomplished in the next step. FDISK displays the message:

```
Create Logical DOS Drive(s)
No logical drives defined
Total partition size is 409 cylinders.
Maximum space available for logical
drive is 409 cylinders.
Enter logical drive size........:[ 409]
```

At this point, just press Enter and you'll see:

```
Create Logical DOS Drive(s)
Drv Start End  Size
 D:  410   818  409
All available space in the Extended DOS
partition is assigned to logical drives.
Logical DOS drive created, drive letters changed or added
Press ESC to return to FDISK Options
```

You'll see the following warning:

```
WARNING!  No partitions marked active
```

The message means that you must tell DOS which partition to boot from. This task is performed automatically if you don't create an extended partition. But in our case, we must return to the main FDISK menu (by pressing Esc) and select the second menu choice ("Change active partition"). The usual status information appears:

```
Partition Status   Type  Start  End Size
 C: 1              PRI DOS    0  409  410
    2              EXT DOS  410  818  409
```

You're asked for the number of the partition to make active. You type 1 and press Enter, and that's that. If you choose this selection again, you get the message:

```
The only bootable partition on Drive 1 is already marked active.
```

Deleting a Partition

You're finished. The drive has been partitioned and now requires a high-level format. But before moving on to that topic, let's look at the other two options in the FDISK main menu. First, you may want to delete a partition from a disk. In this example, we'll delete an extended partition. Choose option #3 ("Delete DOS Partition") from the main menu and you'll be shown a screen like this one:

```
Delete DOS Partition
Current Fixed Disk Drive: 1
Choose one of the following:
    1.  Delete Primary DOS partition
    2.  Delete Extended DOS partition
    3.  Delete logical DOS drive(s) in
        the Extended DOS Partition
Enter choice:[ ]
```

To delete an extended partition (menu choice #2), you must first delete the logical drive assignment by selecting #3. Status information is displayed:

```
Delete Logical DOS Drive
    Drv Start End   Size
    D:  410   818   409
Total partition size is  409 cylinders.
Warning! Data in the logical DOS drive
will be lost.  What drive do you wish
to delete......................? [ ]
```

You type in the drive specifier (in this case, "D") and press Enter. DOS responds with the message:

```
Are you sure.....................? [n]
```

Type "Y" and Enter, and FDISK displays:

```
All logical drives are deleted in the Extended DOS partition
```

Then press Esc to return to the main menu. Select option #3 again ("Delete DOS Partition"). The same menu appears, but this time with only two choices:

```
1.  Delete Primary DOS partition
2.  Delete Extended DOS partition
```

After selecting #2, FDISK displays:

```
Delete Extended DOS Partition
Current Fixed Disk Drive: 1
Partition Status   Type Start End Size
 C: 1          PRI DOS   0   409   410
    2          EXT DOS  410  818   409
Warning! Data in the Extended DOS
partition will be lost. DO you wish
to continue...............? [N]
```

Just type "y" and Enter, and the partition is deleted.

Getting Partition Information

You can find out the current partitioning of a drive at any time by selecting option #4 from the FDISK main menu ("Display Partition Information"). You're shown the same information displayed by the other FDISK options. For example:

```
Display Partition Information
Current Fixed Disk Drive: 1
 Partition Status    Type  Start  End Size
   C: 1              PRI DOS    0  409  410
   D: 2              EXT DOS  410  818  409
Total disk space is 819 cylinders.
The Extended DOS partition contains
logical DOS drives. Do you want to display
logical drive information?  [Y]
```

Press Enter to see:

```
Display Logical DOS Drive Information
Drv Start End  Size
  D:  410  818  409
```

Partitioning Utilities

Prior to the appearance of DOS 3.3, large drives had to be partitioned with utility software that could create multiple DOS partitions on a disk, or partitions larger than 32 megabytes. These required you to load a device driver from your CONFIG.SYS file when the machine booted. Some of these utilities could pull off an even more amazing trick: They can cause a partition to *span* two hard drives. That is, two *physical* drives become one *logical* drive, accessed through one drive specifier, and one directory tree. This setup does not hinder disk performance, and in some cases actually helps it, since the single logical drive has two sets of read/write heads.

To work this magic, these programs must take the disk through every step of formatting, both low-level and high-level. Because they are often applied to super-high-capacity drives, they are specially designed to deal with the problems of unusual drive geometries. They can, however, be used with drives of any size. Your involvement in disk formatting is limited to entering bad track numbers and installing the DOS files through the SYS command. The rest is a breeze.

These utilities are gradually falling from favor as DOS acquires more capability. If you use one, you should be aware that some can interfere with the operation of certain kinds of software, particularly when they use a nonstandard sector size. Occasionally utility software, like file defragmenters and disk repair programs, won't work with drives formatted and partitioned this way. In some cases, the makers of partition extension programs have issued their own equivalents to some of these utilities.

High-level Formatting

High-level formatting takes longer than would seem necessary. All the program has to do is to write a boot record, the root directory, two copies of the file allocation table, and the DOS files IBMBIO.COM, IBMDOS.COM, and COMMAND.COM. But FORMAT.COM takes about a minute for every megabyte of disk space (or half that on fast machines). During this time, it takes a last look for bad sectors, and when it finds them, it marks them off bounds in the file allocation table.

Start the program by placing the DOS diskette (or, better, a copy) in drive A: and enter:

```
FORMAT C: /S /V
```

The /**S** switch makes the program move the three DOS system files to the disk, and the /**V** switch causes the program to prompt you for a *volume label* which we'll discuss in a moment. Then, when formatting drive C in DOS Versions 3.0 and later, the message appears:

```
WARNING, ALL DATA ON NON-REMOVABLE DISK
DRIVE C: WILL BE LOST!
Proceed with Format [Y/N]?
```

This message protects the disk from accidental reformatting (we'll talk about this problem at length in Chapter 9). Earlier DOS versions gave no such warning. If you use a pre-3.x DOS version and you find yourself about to accidentally reformat the hard disk, *get away from the keyboard.* While Ctrl-Break or Ctrl-Alt-Del ought to get you out of trouble, the precise timing of the keystrokes is important. If you hit Del before Ctrl and Alt, formatting may begin and continue for a fraction of a second—long enough to damage crucial DOS structures on the disk. The safest thing to do is to reach around the side of the machine and turn it off.

Once formatting gets underway, the screen displays only the message,

```
FORMATTING...
```

It won't give you any idea how far along the process has gone. Finally, you'll
see the message

```
Format complete
System transferred
```

When finished, the FORMAT program will tell you how many bytes are available on the disk, and how many are taken by the system files, the root directory, and the two copies of the file allocation table.

Formatting in DOS 5.0

DOS 5.0 completely revamps the FORMAT command. Whereas in prior DOS
versions FORMAT always destroys all data on diskettes, in DOS 5.0, FORMAT
normally treats a diskette the same way it treats a hard disk, reformatting the
root directory and file allocation tables, but nothing else. By doing so, DOS 5.0
opens the option of "unformatting" the diskette to recover data it previously
held. DOS 5.0 introduces the UNFORMAT command for this purpose; we'll
explain how it works in Chapter 9. Although FORMAT does not erase disk
sectors when it is used this way, it does check each sector to see that it holds
data properly.

If you want a format operation that isn't as easy to undo, add a /U switch (for
"unconditional format") to the command. The /U switch is useful when you
want to obliterate all data on a disk for security reasons. Otherwise, anyone
wielding data-recovery software can piece together your "erased" data. You
also should use this option if you've been receiving read and write errors. It
may help make the disk safe for further use, though it's far better to use a
program that performs an in-depth analysis of the disk surface for this
purpose.

DOS 5.0 also introduces the /Q switch (for "quick format"). A quick format is
like an ordinary one in that FORMAT merely erases the disk's root directory
and file allocation tables. But a quick format doesn't bother to test all disk
sectors to see if they can be read. Interestingly, you can combine the /Q and
/U switches for an even faster format. In this case, data is *not* obliterated. Use
the /U switch alone to expedite formatting of previously unformatted disks.

The Volume Label

Using the /V switch in the FORMAT command causes DOS to prompt you for a volume label after formatting is complete. A *volume label* is a tag up to 11 characters long that identifies the disk. These labels are useful with diskettes, as they let you identify a diskette without pulling it from the drive. On hard disks, volume labels can identify the purpose of each partition. They may also be useful for identifying backups, particularly in offices where there are many machines, since volume labels are normally recorded on backup media. A volume label takes up a slot in the root directory, and some people regard this as a waste. However, the root directory will never get anywhere close to full in a well thought-through file system.

If you do place a volume label on the disk, it will be displayed by the DIR, CHKDSK, and TREE commands. It also can be viewed at any time by entering **VOL.** DOS Versions 3.0 and later provide the **LABEL** command to change the volume label. The 11-character label is ordinarily restricted to one word, since DOS won't accept spaces in the label. You can trick some versions of DOS into accepting a space by using the /V switch and striking Enter when DOS asks for the label. DOS then issues another prompt asking for the label, and at that point you can enter a string with spaces in it.

The Cylinder 0 Problem

Occasionally, a disk has numerous bad sectors on the outermost tracks that hold the root directory, FATs, and DOS files. Some of these *must* be placed on continuous sectors. When the FORMAT program is barred from doing this, it issues an error message and quits. Try low-level formatting the disk. This will change the placement of the sectors, and bad spots on the disk surface may move outside sector boundaries, or to sectors that aren't critical. If you don't succeed after several low-level reformattings (and lots of exasperation), the disk is a dud, and it must be replaced.

Configuring the System

Once high-level formatting is complete, the disk is ready for use. But there are a couple of final chores. The machine will now boot from the hard disk (you must leave the door to drive A open, since the machine will always look for a DOS diskette there first.) Once you've booted successfully, take a few moments to configure the disk so that DOS can use it efficiently. There's no more to this than creating CONFIG.SYS and AUTOEXEC.BAT files and writing a few commands in them.

Creating CONFIG.SYS and AUTOEXEC.BAT

Both CONFIG.SYS and AUTOEXEC.BAT are simply ASCII text files. This means that they are made up of ordinary characters with no special formatting codes. The installation programs for DOS 4.0 and 5.0 automatically create these files for you. Otherwise, you can make the files or edit them using just about any word processor or text editor, including the DOS 5.0 *Edit* and Windows *Notepad* programs. Just be sure that the program you use doesn't insert any special formatting codes. If this is a possibility, use the software's "plain ASCII" *save* option.

If you need to create these files and they'll hold few lines, the easiest way to make them is by the DOS COPY command. To create CONFIG.SYS, you would simply enter:

```
COPY CON: \CONFIG.SYS
```

or, if drive C is not the default drive, then:

```
COPY CON: C:\CONFIG.SYS
```

Then write each line of the file in succession, typing Enter after each. For example:

```
BUFFERS=20
FILES=8
```

Finally, enter a Ctrl-Z character, which tells DOS that you've finished writing the file. Either press the F6 key, which causes DOS to output the character, or hold down the Ctrl key and press "Z." You'll see the symbols ^Z on the screen. Then press Enter once more and DOS writes the file to disk, displaying:

```
1 File(s) copied
```

Remember that merely creating an AUTOEXEC.BAT or CONFIG.SYS file does not put its commands into action. You must reboot the machine (via Ctrl-Alt-Del) and the commands in the files will be executed as DOS is reloaded.

Configuration Commands

Essential configuration commands go in CONFIG.SYS. These include the all-important BUFFERS and FILES commands that optimize file access. Starting with DOS 4.0, these commands are automatically written into CONFIG.SYS when you install DOS files on the disk using the DOS installation program. In fact, the installation program will create CONFIG.SYS in your hard disk's root directory if it does not find the file.

The BUFFERS Command

The **BUFFERS** command tells DOS how many buffers to set aside in memory to receive data from the hard disk. Each buffer holds one sector. Because programs tend to access the same sectors again and again, multiple accesses to the same sector can be avoided by *buffering* a number of recently used sectors in memory. In Chapter 7 we'll discuss in detail the logic behind this scheme. For now, you should know that the default value in all DOS versions prior to 3.3 is only two or three buffers—a value far too low for efficient hard disk performance. The command:

```
BUFFER=20
```

creates 20 buffers. Roughly 10K of memory is consumed by these buffers, but it's well worth it. DOS 3.3 sets a reasonable number of buffers based on the amount of RAM present. The DOS buffers are normally placed in conventional memory (that is, in the 640K normally available to DOS). Starting with DOS 4.0, you can add an /X switch to a BUFFERS command to place the buffers in expanded memory.

Deciding the Number of DOS Buffers

You may be tempted to create a large number of buffers to hasten disk operations. In many cases, the ideal way of handling disk files would be to read the entire file into numerous DOS buffers, operate on it there, and then write it back to disk in one operation. In fact, disk caching software (discussed in Chapter 7) does something like this. But two factors limit the number of DOS buffers that are practical:

- The buffers take up scarce memory. Enough buffers to hold a 100K file would, by definition, take up at least 100K of memory. Not all of us have so much memory to spare. (Most caching software can employ expanded memory or extended memory, consuming little of the 640K of conventional memory. However, as we noted earlier, DOS couldn't place buffers outside of conventional memory until version 4.0.)

- Whenever a disk read or write operation is performed, DOS must scan all buffers to see what they contain. Particularly in slower computers, the time required to scan many buffers can exceed the time needed to just go and read or write the sector on the disk drive. (Caching software, on the other hand, uses a much more elaborate means of detecting which sectors are in buffers, and in prioritizing which sectors should remain in buffers. In a word, caching software is just plain smarter than the DOS buffers.)

DOS documentation recommends the following number of buffers:

Disk Size	Recommended buffers
under 40M	20
40M to 80M	30
80M to 120 M	40
over 120 M	50

These numbers are approximate, and can be reduced if memory is scarce (50 buffers take up 25K of memory!). Note that you'll only need 1 buffer if you use disk caching, as we explain in Chapter 7.

Efficiency Concerns

When deciding on the number of DOS buffers, keep in mind that a large number of buffers is of little benefit when your application software works by reading a whole file into memory, operating on it, and then writing the whole file back to disk. Word processors and spreadsheet programs are good examples of this kind of software. By comparison, databases usually employ random access files that are read and written in bits and pieces, rather than as a whole. Such software gains much from operating with numerous DOS buffers. More and more, all kinds of software use a multitude of auxiliary files, and these files often benefit from having many buffers on hand.

The FILES Command

The **FILES** command causes DOS to set aside small blocks of memory, each of which is devoted to tracking a file when it has been opened. No more files can be opened at any one time than there are blocks that have been allocated. The default value is 8, and that would seem plenty. But five are used by DOS internally. A higher value is required if you start using your computer in complex ways. Many memory-resident programs (such as print spoolers) may keep files open while your application programs are at work. Programs may open *temporary files* that you never know about (they're erased when the program terminates). And some genres of software, particularly relational databases, are gluttons for file access. If you use your system intensively, you'll want to put into CONFIG.SYS the line:

```
FILES=40
```

(This is the practical minimum if you're using Microsoft Windows.) Older software may use a different method of file access that entails **file control blocks (FCBs)**. The number of file control blocks is selectable by the **FCBS** command. There's no need to concern yourself with it, but be aware that the command exists. If a program ever issues an error message concerning its inability to open a file control block, check the DOS manual under FCBS and place a line in CONFIG.SYS increasing the number available.

Device Drivers

CONFIG.SYS may also contain DEVICE statements. These load **device drivers** into memory. Device drivers are programs that intermediate between DOS and a device with which DOS is not equipped to deal, such as a mouse, a plotter, or an expanded memory board. When DOS asks for data from a device, the "driver" translates the command into instructions the device can understand. Conversely, when the device sends data to the computer, the driver converts it to a form that DOS can accept. A device driver held in the file MOUSE.SYS would be loaded by the statement:

```
DEVICE=MOUSE.SYS
```

The file can reside anywhere on the disk:

```
DEVICE=C:\DOS\DRIVERS\MOUSE.SYS
```

As you add more and more hardware to your system, you'll develop a small library of device drivers that must be loaded whenever their associated devices are used.

Limitations

Because some device drivers are quite large, you may have room in memory only for those absolutely required for the task at hand. If this is the case, you'll need to vary the devices installed by CONFIG.SYS (and possibly AUTOEXEC.BAT). DOS doesn't make CONFIG.SYS and AUTOEXEC.BAT interactive so that you can specify just how the system should be configured at startup. But there are third-party programs that can add this feature—and DOS allows interactive commands in CONFIG.SYS.

Another way to solve this problem is to make a series of CONFIG.SYS and AUTOEXEC.BAT files, but give them different names. Then create batch files that will copy the versions you want to the actual CONFIG.SYS and AUTOEXEC.BAT files. For example, say that you've created one CONFIG.SYS file that contains the line **DEVICE=C:\DOS\VIDEO.SYS** for an 80K device driver that runs a super-duper graphics card. Another CONFIG. SYS file, holds the line **DEVICE=C:\DOS\EMSDRVR.SYS** to load a driver that controls the expanded memory card that you only use when you run your spreadsheet program. Each file would be the CONFIG.SYS file for a particular application. Say that you named the first file **CAD.SYS** and the second file **SPREAD.SYS**. Then, you could make batch files named, say, **CAD.BAT** and **SPREAD.BAT**, that contain the lines **COPY CAD.SYS CONFIG.SYS** and **COPY SPREAD.SYS CONFIG.SYS**, respectively. By executing one of the batch files and rebooting, the machine is instantly reconfigured for the job before you.

And that's it! Your hard disk is ready to serve you. But don't just start off using it like a giant diskette. Devote a little extra time after installation to carefully organizing a directory tree that will keep your work orderly for months and years ahead. The next two chapters will show you how to do just that.

Navigating Around Directory Trees

Managing files in a directory tree ought not to be intellectually challenging. We all grew up around actual botanical trees, so it should come naturally to us to think about the consequences of loading programs and data files in remote directories. But a directory tree exists only in our less-than-perfect imaginations. When we use a hard disk, our minds are always burdened with keeping track of where files are and how to get to them. There's much you can do to lessen that burden, and that is the subject of this chapter.

In this chapter we'll be concerned with manipulating files within a directory tree. The aim is to find ways to:

- Move between subdirectories quickly.
- Keep track of the current directory on all drives.
- Temporarily alter directory trees to reduce the work required to navigate in them.
- Copy and move groups of files easily.
- Search for files, either by name or by contents.

- Let DOS find files automatically.
- Launch programs and their data files automatically.

For every one of these tasks, the number of keystrokes required can be substantially reduced. Not only will you save time and energy, but you'll make fewer mistakes. But before turning to specific techniques, let's take a look at *DOS Shells*, which provide shortcuts to many of these objectives.

DOS Shells

The inadequacies of DOS have spawned a genre of software called *DOS shells*. DOS shells add new capabilities to DOS and make existing capabilities easier to use. A good DOS shell makes DOS what you always wanted it to be. The shell is loaded like any other program. It takes you into a world of menus, tree diagrams, and fancy directory listings.

While a shell makes DOS appear to have grown in many ways, it does not actually modify DOS. In a sense, it *surrounds* DOS, and this is why it is called a "shell." Beneath, COMMAND.COM continues to manage memory and operate the disk drives. But the shell performs most DOS commands like COPY and ERASE, adding many powerful features to them. Furthermore, you can run programs from within a shell, exactly as if the program were loaded from the DOS prompt.

The Proliferation of Shells

These days, you cannot open a computer magazine without finding yet another DOS shell on the market. There are at least 100 in existence, some from well-established firms, some from seat-of-the-pants software houses, and some in the form of freeware or shareware. We'll be using *The Norton Commander* for some of our examples in this chapter. Starting with Version 4.0, DOS itself includes a shell. And, in its *File Manager*, Microsoft Windows provides standard shell features. We'll also be looking at these two programs in the pages ahead.

In view of all this activity, you might think that DOS shells are enormously popular. Although some have sold in large numbers, many PC users still go without. Yet this is one kind of software that nearly everyone can use profitably. The makers are wildly enthusiastic about the utility of their products while users yawn, shrug their shoulders, and demur, "It's nice, but I already know DOS."

Perhaps it's the manufacturers' own fault that DOS shells are seen as an aid for beginners. Their advertisements harp on the *ease-of-use* theme: "A rank beginner can master DOS in 30 minutes!" While these claims may sometimes be true, beginners tend to miss the opportunity of using a shell because they know too little about computers to realize what they are missing. Meanwhile, more experienced users, who pride themselves on their fluency in DOS, regard DOS shells as *sissy stuff.*

Capabilities

Too few people understand that a good DOS shell can automate complicated DOS chores that otherwise require lots of mental and manual energy no matter how well-versed the user. Many shells let you edit the directory tree; you can rename subdirectories and even move them around the tree. They'll make fancy searches across the whole tree for files of particular characteristics. And they'll let you *tag* selected files in subdirectories for copying and backups, saving endless typing. Even those of a puritanical bent who would rather just do it the hard way will find that a good shell helps avert errors, such as faulty file erasures, or copying bad files over good ones. For system managers, who must constantly mop up after others, a DOS shell is indispensable.

The frenetic competition among DOS shell makers has led to the most extreme *feature creep* of any software genre. You name it, and somebody has incorporated it into a DOS shell: data encryption, printer spooling, file recovery utilities, diskette cataloging. Some shells make the video display as complicated as a space shuttle control panel. In fact, for truly timid computer novices, a DOS shell may cause more confusion than it alleviates (a *menu generator*, which we'll discuss later in this chapter, is a better choice). But, in the hands of advanced users, a good DOS shell is always a powerhouse.

Trees and Directories

DOS shells are centered around the directory tree and directory listings. They may display the tree and directories differently, but all serve the same goal: to let you copy, move, erase, and rename files by marking their directory listings, rather than by remembering file names and laboriously typing them in.

Many shells are based on a diagram of the directory tree. These diagrams provide an instant overview of the shape and organization of your directory tree. A tree diagram may be scrolled up and down. Usually, a bar cursor moves through the tree, and you can change directories simply by moving the cursor to the desired tree position and striking a single key. Another keystroke opens a directory listing for the subdirectory. Some create combined tree-directory displays, with directory listings nested in a tree diagram.

All DOS shells let you easily create and remove subdirectories from the tree, often by moving the cursor to the desired position in the tree diagram. Some shells can rename subdirectories, and a few offer a tree grafting function that can move single subdirectories, or whole branches, from one part of the tree to another.

It takes several seconds for a shell to search an entire disk to assemble a tree diagram. Rather than perform this action every time the diagram is displayed, most DOS shells maintain a file that holds the tree structure. The file is modified whenever changes are made to the tree through the shell, but the file isn't always up to date if DOS commands alter the tree when the shell is not loaded. Most shells either notice the changes automatically or have a special command to update the tree file if it no longer corresponds to the actual tree. A well-crafted shell recovers gracefully from errors that occur when the tree diagram does not correspond to the actual subdirectory structure.

Directory Display

Like tree diagrams, directory displays may be scrolled up and down. This feature alone is worth the price of a DOS shell, since you're freed forever from the frustrations of executing the DIR command repeatedly to scan back and forth in a directory. Many shells offer special "wide" directory listings that fit numerous files on a screen. Some let you look at two separately scrollable directories side by side, or allow you to toggle between multiple directory listings.

Many shells provide more information about files than DOS does. They may show each file's attribute, or they may tell how many clusters a file takes, as well as the file's size. Besides the usual wildcard searches, many shells let you list files chosen by attribute, date, or time. Very powerful searches are made by combining these features. For example, you might be able to ask to see a listing of all read-only files with the extension **.TXT** that are dated between January and March. It's also useful to be able to see hidden files, since DOS directory listings won't show them, and they may be present in subdirectories that you want to erase.

Combined Directories

An especially valuable feature is the ability to combine many directory listings into one. Some DOS shells can create an amalgamated listing (a **global directory**) of a whole branch of a tree, or even the whole disk. These listings may also be made by wildcards and other search criteria, so that you could request, for example, a listing of every batch file on the disk. Of course, different subdirectories may hold files of the same name, so confusion can arise. Many shells overcome this problem by having you move a bar cursor to a file in question; its DOS path is then displayed.

Sorting Directories

The directory sorts that take great effort in DOS are performed easily in DOS shells. Most shells have a special sorting menu that lists the options. You need merely tick off the sort criteria you desire: file name or extension, date, time, file size, or attribute. Like DOS sorts, most shells do not actually change the physical order of the directory listings. The sort features may be applied to combined directories, letting you assemble, for example, an alphabetized listing of all *Lotus 1-2-3* files created in 1987.

Printouts

A good DOS shell lets you print out any listing it makes on the screen. Hence, it can be an invaluable tool for cataloging the disk. You can print out the tree diagram (usually with rather crude graphics). You can print out any of the various directory listings. And, if you like, in many shells you can sit back and have a complete catalog of every file on the disk printed out. Such a catalog may be very useful for recovering data when a serious disk failure occurs and your backups are not up to date.

Copying Files

Copying files is easy in DOS shells. In most shells you move the cursor to the file in a directory listing, strike a key, and then move the cursor to a position on the tree diagram and strike Enter. In some shells, all this moving about may actually be slower than typing an ordinary COPY command on the DOS command line. But in mass file transfers, DOS shells offer a decided advantage. They can select files not just by wildcards, but also by *tagging*.

Tagging

In tagging, you move the cursor up and down a directory listing and "tag" a file by striking the Spacebar or some other key. A symbol appears beside each tagged file. Some shells let you set the tags by wildcards. For example, you might have the shell tag all files with the extension **.DOC** by tagging for ***.DOC**. Then you could use the cursor to *untag* those few files that you don't want affected. You also may be able to *reverse* the tags, so that untagged files become tagged, and vice versa. This feature is useful when you want to copy all but a few files in a subdirectory. You need only tag the few, then reverse the taggings.

Backups

The COPY facilities in some DOS shells are so powerful that they may be used for a simple backup scheme. Some shells can span diskettes as they copy groups of files. When the first disk fills, the shell prompts the user for a disk change, then goes on copying files from the group. Some shells will copy files by any combination of wildcards, dates, and attributes, searching the whole directory for matches. So you could easily have the shell back up all files changed in the last week.

Moving Files

There is a command in virtually all DOS shells that really ought to have been included in DOS itself (and *is* provided by many software vendors as a command line utility). This is the MOVE command, which moves a file from one directory to another (or one disk to another). It does the same thing as a combination of COPY and ERASE, but it's faster (the file isn't actually copied unless it's being transferred to a different drive); it also saves keystrokes and confusion. The command sees to it that the file is erased only if it has been successfully copied. MOVE commands have all the flexibility of COPY commands, including tagging.

Properly designed, a MOVE command is extremely fast. Since there is no need to duplicate the file, all the shell must do is move the file's directory entry from one subdirectory to another. Using wildcards, dozens of files may be moved in the blink of an eye. Incidentally, you'll occasionally encounter "move" utilities in disk tool boxes, or on public domain bulletin boards. Use only versions from trustworthy sources, since files are easily lost if the software malfunctions, or if it handles errors badly.

Erasing Files

Tagging may also apply to a shell's ERASE command. Some shells offer special facilities for avoiding accidental file erasures. Often, they'll display all files about to be erased and ask your permission before going on. This feature is valuable when wildcard characters are used in erasures, since a mistake could cause dozens of files to be erased when only a few should have been. A good shell is able to extend an erasure to the entire disk, so that you can eliminate, say, all .BAK files in a single blow. In this situation, the shell may display the name of each .BAK file it finds, asking whether it should be deleted or not.

Viewing and Editing Files

Finally, nearly all DOS shells let you view files easily. Unlike the DOS TYPE command, which reads and displays a file line by line, shells load the whole file in memory and let you scroll back and forth in it. Consequently, most cannot handle files larger than available memory. Some have special facilities ("filters") for handling complex text files or encoded data files, which cannot be viewed at all by using the TYPE command. Usually, these filters display a file exactly as would the software that created it. Many shells also provide a full-screen editor that lets you make changes in files. Usually, these are only useful for altering simple text files, like batch files, or for jotting down notes. Even in this application, such editors won't take the place of a full-fledged word processor. In particular, printer output tends to be primitive in these editors.

DOS Access

While a shell is usually more convenient than the DOS command line, there are times when you need to enter an ordinary DOS command. Some shells let you type in, and edit, a DOS command in a window on the screen; it's then submitted to DOS for execution. Others load a copy of DOS's command processor, COMMAND.COM, letting you type your commands on a genuine DOS command line. It's a sort of Rube Goldberg way of doing things: DOS loads a DOS shell which loads DOS's command processor.

Memory Requirements

One common complaint about DOS shells is well-deserved. To put it indelicately, many DOS shells are *fat.* All those features take a toll on program size. Shells approaching 200K are not unheard of. It's no wonder Microsoft did not give COMMAND.COM as many capabilities. If the shell is kept in memory and programs run from within it, little memory may be left for data. On the other hand, if the shell is used only for managing the disk and you return to DOS before running a program from the command line, the shell doesn't cost you a byte of RAM.

Many DOS shells give you the best of both worlds—keeping the shell in memory yet not taking up any memory—by writing the program with a *reloader*. When a program is run from within the shell, most of the shell's bulk is abandoned, and only a small part stays in memory to execute the program. When the application terminates and control returns to the shell, the *reload module* reloads the rest of the shell from disk, returning it to its full splendor. The module that stays in memory may take up only a few thousand bytes of memory. While you must wait momentarily for the shell to reload, you're saved the trouble of constantly having to exit to DOS when you want to free memory to run a program, and then manually reloading the shell after you return from the program.

Miscellaneous Features

There are endless variations on the basic DOS shell design. You'll find "disk tool kits" that offer many DOS shell-like features in separate utilities. Some of the new memory-resident utility managers provide some DOS shell capabilities. For those who like the DOS command line the way it is, there are shells that replace COMMAND.COM with a version that offers many more services, all accessed in the usual command-line format. This approach is the opposite of simplification: It gives extra switches for the normal DOS commands, expanding their power. This solution may be preferred by technically adept users who dislike menus and icons. Some shells even include a special language for writing elaborate interactive batch files.

Every implementation has its own special features. You'll find data encryption, rudimentary menuing systems, password protection, printer control, screen blanking, keyboard macros, file unerasure—just about anything you can think of. Many provide varying degrees of on-line help, sometimes "context-sensitive help," which senses what your problems may be and advises you accordingly. Some help systems are practically tutorials.

Command Stacks

Another useful feature is a **command stack**—a list of all recently executed commands. You can review the stack to track the work you've done. And you may *re*-execute any command in the stack by moving the cursor to it and striking the appropriate key. Commands in the stack may be edited before being executed again, so you can avoid repeatedly typing long DOS paths by changing only parts of commands. Borland's SuperKey was one of the first products to offer this feature. More recently, it's become part of DOS, and is also supported by the DOSKEY program in DOS 5.0. We'll discuss it later in this chapter.

The DOSKEY program introduced with DOS 5.0 lets you view recent DOS commands, edit them, and reuse them. This memory-resident program is started just by typing DOSKEY. Once it is loaded, you can use the cursor-up and cursor-down keys to view earlier commands. Pressing cursor-up shows the prior command, and pressing it again shows the command before that one. Conversely, pressing cursor-down displays the command that followed the one currently displayed. You can see the oldest command used in your current work session by pressing Page Up, and the most recent by pressing Page Down.

DOSKEY lets you edit the command line, whether it holds a command you've just typed in, or an earlier command that you've recalled. The Cursor-left and Cursor-right keys move the cursor across the command line. Alternatively, you can use Ctrl-cursor-left and Ctrl-cursor-right to shift the cursor by whole words, or Home and End to jump the cursor to the beginning or end of the command. Once editing is complete, press Enter as always to put the command into effect.

Choosing a DOS Shell

For most users, the question is not "which DOS shell should I buy?" but rather "do I need a DOS shell at all?" Some shells are not very easy to use, and some have confusing documentation, so it's natural to avoid extra work when the benefits do not answer pressing needs. Even if you feel that you wouldn't gain much by having a DOS shell on line, keep in mind that a shell can be invaluable during periodic disk housecleanings. A shell is the best way to monitor the state of a hard disk, since it gives comprehensive statistics, shows the tree structure, gives full file listings, and lets you quickly look into individual files. The ability to apply wildcard operations across subdirectories can save you much time that would otherwise be used to move from directory to directory and repeat commands. Even when used only a few times a month, a shell may quickly repay its purchase price.

In the sections that follow in this chapter and the next, we'll sometimes discuss how DOS shells handle particular situations. And in some cases we'll show exactly how to accomplish tasks in the shells that accompany DOS 4.0 and 5.0, and in Microsoft Windows.

Helping DOS Find Files Automatically

Directory trees are a boon to file organization, but they create problems of their own. On disks containing only a root directory, all files are listed in the same place, so software can find any file by scanning that directory alone. In a directory tree, programs need a way of accessing files in subdirectories other than the one in which they reside. While DOS could have been designed to scan every directory in the tree automatically when a file is not found in the current directory, the process would be inefficient, and it would not cope with instances where several files of the same name are distributed in several subdirectories.

The Issues

There are two issues: First, software needs to be able to find files in directories other than the current directory; second, you need to be able to run a program when working within a directory other than the one holding the program file. Neither requirement is an obstacle if you are adept at writing DOS paths. If a program named TRASHER is in the subdirectory UTIL, and it is to work on the file BADIDEAS.TXT contained in the subdirectory NOTES, you can load the file from any directory by entering:

    \UTIL\TRASHER

Once in the program, you would specify the file as:

    \NOTES\BADIDEAS.TXT

The program might allow you to name the file on the command line, so that you could load the software and file by the command:

    \UTIL\TRASHER \NOTES\BADIDEAS.TXT

In this way, working from one directory, you can run a program in a second and have it load a data file in a third.

Obstacles

Unfortunately, you may not always remember the path to a file, and even when you do, it's tiresome to repeatedly type DOS paths. You can save yourself time and trouble by following various techniques for avoiding DOS paths, and we'll discuss them next. These techniques can be complex and they can lead to more confusion than they avoid. But one measure, the PATH command, should be part of every user's bag of tricks.

The DOS PATH Command

DOS provides the PATH command to help load program files from subdirectories other than the current one. You provide a list of subdirectories for DOS to search if it cannot find a program in the current directory. For example, say that you are working in the subdirectory WORD and want to load *Lotus 1-2-3* from the subdirectory \STATS\123. If you just enter:

```
123
```

DOS will look in the WORD directory and inform you that the file has not been found. But if earlier you had executed the PATH command:

```
PATH \STATS\123
```

DOS would proceed to search the subdirectory \STATS\123 for the *1-2-3* program file, where it would find it and load it.

Multiple Paths

Many file paths can be listed in a PATH statement, and they must be separated by a semicolon with no spaces between. The expression:

```
PATH \NOTES\OL;\STATS\123
```

would cause DOS to first search the **OL** subdirectory (containing the outline program), and then the **123** subdirectory. This statement lets you run both the outliner and *1-2-3* from anywhere on the disk.

There's generally no reason to name diskette drives in PATH commands. In fact, it's a bad policy, since you'll constantly turn up "not ready" errors when the drive is empty. However, when you have two hard disks, it's essential that you include a drive specifier with each path specification, as in the statement:

```
PATH C:\DOS;D:\NOTES
```

If there were no **C:** before **\DOS**, and drive **D** was the current drive, then the PATH command would look for the DOS directory on drive **D**, fail to find it, and refuse to carry out certain DOS commands.

You'll find that this command is not very flexible. You can't ask it to search all subdirectories in a branch of the tree, or the entire tree. Every time you enter a new PATH command, it replaces the prior one, so no more DOS paths may be included than will fit within a single DOS command. (Fortunately, there are path extension utilities available that get around this problem. They allow you to have a very long path, and add to or edit it at will.) You can find out the current path by entering only the word:

```
PATH
```

This action does not affect the current settings. To cancel the path settings, enter:

```
PATH;
```

Limitations

Unfortunately, the PATH command functions only for program files and batch files. Once a program is loaded, PATH will not help it find data files in other subdirectories. And even from the DOS prompt, PATH cannot help DOS commands find data files. For example, if you enter:

```
TYPE MYFILE.TXT
```

DOS will look for MYFILE.TXT only in the current directory, even if a PATH statement lists other subdirectories. DOS searches these directories only for files with an **.EXE**, **.COM**, or **.BAT** extension. Even when you name the data file along with the program file on the command line, as in:

```
WORD DOCUMENT.TXT
```

the PATH command won't help. A PATH command may let DOS find the program file in a directory other than the current one, but it won't find the data file, even when it is in the same directory as the program file.

Applications

The PATH command is useful nonetheless, particularly in its ability to locate and run batch files. Many users insert a PATH command in AUTOEXEC.BAT that (minimally) reads:

```
PATH C:\BATCH;C:\UTIL;C:\DOS
```

This simple command means that any batch file, any utility, and any external DOS file can be run from any directory on the disk.

Because DOS proceeds through the subdirectories named in a PATH command in the order they are listed, you can speed up file searches by naming the most frequently accessed subdirectories first. Avoid making PATH commands unnecessarily long.

The DOS APPEND Command

DOS offers the APPEND command to provide automatic tree searches for *any* kind of file, whether it is a program file opened from the command line, or a data file loaded from within a program. APPEND is an *external DOS command*, but when it is called, it permanently loads itself into memory, and is active in many DOS commands, such as DIR—but not without serious problems that we'll discuss in a moment.

Syntax

The syntax of APPEND is just like that of the PATH command. The expression:

```
APPEND C:\NOTES\TANK;C:\STATS\123
```

extends searches to two subdirectories. In this form, the APPEND command searches only for non-program files. To have it take on the role of the PATH command, so that it searches for files with .COM, .EXE, and .BAT extensions, you must add an /X switch:

```
APPEND C:\NOTES\TANK;C:\STATS\123 /X
```

The APPEND command was introduced with DOS 3.2, and in that version it is unreliable when the /X switch is used. The command has been improved in subsequent DOS versions. Also, note that APPEND commands are not cumulative. The contents of each command completely replaces those of the prior APPEND command. You can find out the current setting by simply entering:

```
APPEND
```

To clear the current settings for APPEND, enter:

```
APPEND;
```

Pitfalls

Be careful of how you use the APPEND command. Because it will automatically track down data files in remote directories, you can specify files by name only, without typing in directory paths. This is fine for looking at a file, but if you then save the file, your software will create a new copy of the file in the current directory rather than update the original file in whatever directory APPEND found it.

Matters become even more confused if you specify a directory path incorrectly (say, **C:\RODENTS\RATS.TXT**) and the file resides not in **\RODENTS** but in a directory specified by APPEND. In this case, the file is located by APPEND, not by the path you have specified. When you save the file, the altered version would be written into the RODENTS subdirectory and the original would be left unchanged. Starting with DOS Version 4.0, you can avoid this error by having APPEND suspend its search whenever you specify a directory path with your file name. This is done by adding **/PATH:OFF** to the end of the APPEND command, as in:

```
APPEND=C:\ONEDIR;C:\TWODIR   /PATH:OFF
```

Moving through the Directory Tree

It's important to know how to move about easily within directory trees. Lots of keystrokes can be wasted if you lose track of the current directory or where files you need are located. Once confusion starts, errors inevitably follow. Disasters are especially likely to occur when you think a directory is the default directory when it actually is not. In this situation, mass erasures can turn into mass catastrophes. Similarly, if you copy a group of files into the wrong directory, you can overwrite files of the same name, or just generally make a mess of things. Let's begin by looking at how you can always keep track of the current directory.

Tracking the Current Directory

When DOS displays only the austere **C:>** prompt, it's easy to become confused. The PROMPT command makes the DOS prompt display the name of the current directory:

```
PROMPT $p
```

If the current directory is **\ACCOUNTS**, the DOS prompt is transformed to:

```
C:\ACCOUNTS
```

As you can see, the symbol **C:** begins the command. The command changes the DOS prompt for all drives, so when you switch over to drive A, it becomes:

```
A:\
```

In this expression, the backslash indicates the root directory. (Diskettes can have directory trees—just like hard disks—and what is sometimes called a diskette's "directory" is actually its root directory.)

Displaying just the subdirectory name in the prompt leads to confusion, since the words you write on the command line become hard to read. For example, if you run CHKDSK; the command line might look like this:

```
C:ACCOUNTSCHKDSK
```

It's better to place a > symbol after the prompt. This is done with the expression **$g**. Thus:

```
PROMPT $p$g
```

results in:

```
C:\ACCOUNTS>
```

The DOS 4.0 and 5.0 installation programs insert this form of the command in AUTOEXEC.BAT. You can improve the command by adding a few dashes to make an arrow:

```
PROMPT $p---$g
```

giving:

```
C:\ACCOUNTS--->
```

You also can just type a few spaces at the end of a PROMPT command. DOS normally ignores trailing spaces, but in this case, it notices them and will insert the spaces after each DOS prompt.

Special Features

PROMPT can use other special symbols. The most useful are **$t** and **$d**, which print the time and date. **$_** inserts a carriage return. To make DOS show the time on one line and the current directory below, enter:

```
PROMPT $t$_$p---$g
```

The result:

```
12:06:28.78
C:\ACCOUNTS--->
```

If you feel that you can get along without knowing the time to the hundredth of a second, you can insert *backspaces* into the command using **$h**:

```
PROMPT $t$h$h$h$h$h$h$_ $p---$g
```

Other Methods

You can also find out the current directory at any time by entering the CHDIR command without naming a directory to move to. Just type:

```
CHDIR
```

or, using the abbreviated form of the command:

```
CD
```

and DOS will display the name of the current directory, such as **C:\MAMMALS\APES\GIBBONS**, on the line below. You can find out the current directory on a drive other than the current drive by including a drive specifier. If you are working at drive A and enter:

```
CHDIR   C:
```

DOS would display:

```
C:\MAMMALS\APES\GIBBONS
```

while drive A remains the default drive.

Alternatively, you can determine the current directory just by looking at a directory listing. Simply type:

```
DIR
```

and DOS will display the name of the current directory on the second line of the listing, such as:

```
C:\MAMMALS\APES\GIBBONS
```

for a subdirectory, or:

```
C:\
```

for the root directory (a single backslash with no directory names following it represents the root directory).

Changing Directories

When you perform complicated tasks that access files in several directories, you may find yourself changing directories repeatedly. The designers of DOS must have anticipated this, because they were kind enough to give a short form (CD) of CHDIR. But the real problem is in retyping long DOS paths. There are several ways of sidestepping this inconvenience.

Batch Files

One solution entails making batch files for your most active directories. Each file holds the single line:

```
CHDIR \LEVEL1\LEVEL2\LEVEL3
```

or whatever the DOS path is to the subdirectory. Place all of these batch files in the BATCH subdirectory, and set the PATH command so that DOS will always search for them. Then you can change to the directory just by typing its name.

The . and .. Symbols

Another way to change directories quickly is by the . (dot) and .. (double dot) symbols. Everyone has seen these at the top of subdirectory listings, but not many people know what they stand for. The first symbol, ".", refers to the directory itself. It's most useful for referring to a subdirectory without typing the entire directory path. For example, say that the current directory is the subdirectory COUNTY along the DOS path \REGION\STATE\COUNTY\ CITY. One way to change the current directory from COUNTY to CITY is to enter:

```
CD \REGION\STATE\COUNTY\CITY
```

But the "." symbol can save you some keystrokes by representing all sub-directories up to the current directory:

```
CD .\CITY
```

In this example, the "." is equivalent to **\REGION\STATE\COUNTY**.

The symbol ".." represents the *parent directory* of the current directory. Using the prior example, when the current directory is COUNTY, the command:

```
CD .. (or CHDIR ..)
```

makes STATE the current directory. The double-dot symbol can be used more than once to move to even higher subdirectories. For example:

```
CD ..\..
```

makes REGION the current directory.

The double-dot symbol is also useful for moving to parallel subdirectories. Say that the STATE subdirectory holds a subdirectory named DIVISION as well as COUNTY. When COUNTY is current, you could change the current directory to STATE by typing:

```
CD \REGION\STATE\DIVISION
```

But you could avoid some typing by using ".." to represent **\REGION\STATE**:

```
CD ..\DIVISION
```

Utility Software

There are also utility programs that can help you change between directories quickly. *The Norton Utilities* includes the *NCD* ("Norton Change Directory") program. It keeps a file that maps the tree, and which must be updated whenever you change the tree structure. The diagram it shows can be scrolled up and down, and you can position the cursor to add or remove sub-directories.

The *NCD* program lets you move to a subdirectory by typing just its name, without the DOS path leading to it. You can even use only the first part of the subdirectory's name, so long as it distinguishes it from all other subdirectories. For example, the command **NCD ELE** would take you straight to **\MAMMALS\ PACHYDRM\ELEPHANT**. In this case, no tree diagram is shown.

Moving About Using Simple Menus

We've seen how you can easily change subdirectories through batch files that are themselves stored within a BATCH subdirectory accessed by the PATH command. Of course, you could add more commands to these batch files to make them load software once the subdirectory change is made. The entire system may be streamlined by creating a master menu of batch file choices. A bit later we'll talk about complicated menuing software. But, for now, let's say that we want to create just a simple menu offering three selections:

```
1. Word Processing
2. Outlining
3. DOS
```

First, you need to create the menu screen. This is done by creating a standard ASCII text file using any text editor or word processor. None of the word processor's formatting commands can be used to make underlinings, center the text, or whatever. Rather, you must create a what-you-see-is-what-you-get image. Let's say that this file is named **MENU.TXT**.

Next, create batch files named **1.bat**, **2.bat**, and **3.bat**. The first of these files corresponds to the first menu selection. It moves to the word processing subdirectory on the proper drive, clears the screen, and loads the word processor (here named **WP**). When the program terminates, the next line in the batch file is executed, and this is a TYPE command that redisplays the menu screen:

```
C:
CHDIR \EDITOR
CLS
WP
TYPE MENU.TXT
```

Once the menu is displayed, the batch file is finished, and control returns to DOS. When a selection is made from the menu screen, and you press the Enter key, DOS interprets the numeral as a program name, searches for the program, finds a batch file by that name in the BATCH subdirectory, and starts executing the commands in the file. In this way, the menuing system helps you move from application to application.

After the menu is redisplayed, the DOS prompt appears. You can refine the menu by using a PROMPT command that asks for a menu selection. For example:

```
PROMPT Select a number and press ENTER--$g
```

The third selection in the menu exits the menu system and returns you to the DOS prompt. To achieve this, place nothing more than a CLS statement in the file 3.BAT. That's all there is to it.

Building Interactive Batch Files

If the simple menu scheme seems contrived, be assured, it *is*. DOS does not let batch files read a keystroke and execute particular commands on the basis of it. If it could, the command sequences of the separate files (1.BAT, 2.BAT, and so on) could be combined into one file. This can be done, however, using utility software. The *Ask* program in *The Norton Utilities* is called from within a batch file. It displays a menu like:

```
Run the (E)ditor, (D)atabase, or (Q)uit?
```

when it's written in the batch file as:

```
ASK "Run the (E)ditor, (D)atabase, or (Q)uit?", edq
```

The characters at the end of the line (edq) tell the ASK program the characters that represent the menu selections, and the order they appear in. ASK waits for a key to be pressed. And then it does a funny thing—it creates an *error condition*.

When programs are forced to terminate because they can't access part of the computer's hardware, they return an error code to DOS. Batch files may intercept these codes in the form of an *errorlevel*. Once a menu selection is made, the ASK program terminates and returns an errorlevel code that corresponds to the position of the menu selection within the menu listing. It does this even though no error has technically occurred. If **Q** has been struck, "errorlevel 3" is returned. **D** returns "errorlevel 1."

Batch files can make conditional branches for errorlevel codes. Look what happens in this batch file:

```
ASK "Run the (E)ditor, (D)atabase, or (Q)uit?", edq
if errorlevel 3 goto quit
if errorlevel 2 goto database
REM Not 3 or 2, so must be (E)ditor
REM Editor instructions begin here
:editor
  CLS
  CD\EDITOR
  WP
  GOTO QUIT
:database
  CLS
  CD\DATABASE
  DB
:quit
```

When **Q** is selected, errorlevel 3 occurs, and control jumps straight to the end of the batch file. When **D** is selected, errorlevel 2 occurs, and control jumps to the label **:database**. From there, a series of commands clears the screen, moves to the database subdirectory, and loads the database program. Finally, when **E** is chosen, errorlevel 1 occurs. There's no need to write a "goto" statement, since control will continue on to the editor's commands by default. After the editor has been run, another jump is made to quit the batch file (otherwise control would flow into the database instructions).

If you want more flexibility than this in your menuing system, you'll need to acquire a full-blown menuing program. We'll discuss such programs later in this chapter.

Moving About with Keyboard Macros

Until now, we haven't mentioned *keyboard macros*. You may have some experience with one of the many keyboard macro programs, such as *SmartKey*. These are memory-resident utilities that watch keystrokes as they arrive from the keyboard. You can associate a string of characters with any particular key, and when you press that key, the macro program replaces the keystroke with the associated sequence of characters. For example, you could link "antidisestablishmentarianism" with Alt-A. Then, as you're typing along in your word processor and feel an overwhelming need to impress, you can press <Alt-A>, and "antidisestablishmentarianism" is inserted into the document.

Keyboard macros can just as easily hold elaborate sequences of DOS commands and other instructions. In essence, certain keystrokes become menu selections—but no menu is displayed. The absence of a menu listing is, in fact, one of the disadvantages of keyboard macros. Over time, it's easy to forget what key does what. Another problem is that complicated commands can become difficult to modify. Still another problem is that a typographical error can suddenly send you off to the Twilight Zone. But keyboard macros offer one advantage over menuing: They don't insulate you from DOS. You're always working at the DOS prompt, in full control.

A feature to watch for when purchasing a keyboard macro program is the ability of one keyboard macro to load a set of different macros. Any keyboard macro program can save the keyboard assignments you make in a file. You can load one file for word-processing macros, another for spreadsheet macros. A first-rate program can have a macro load one of these files and pass control over to a different set of macros. This is an impressive trick. The software essentially pulls the rug out from under itself—and does it without crashing. When a macro program offers this feature, you can *toggle* between tasks with a single keystroke.

Macros in DOS 5.0 Dos 5.0 introduces the DOSKEY program to provide macros. Unlike the single-key macros described above, DOSKEY lets you define any word you like to represent an entire DOS command. You just type in the word and press Enter to have DOS execute the command. Say that you often use the command:

```
DIR *.TXT /W
```

to display directory listings tailored to a particular need. DOSKEY lets you tie this command to any expression you please, such as "QD" for "quick directory." Then all you need to enter is QD and the above command is executed (unfortunately, the DOSKEY macros won't work from within batch files). This particular macro would set up the command:

```
DOSKEY QD=DIR *.TXT /W
```

You can assign multiple commands to the macro by listing them all with the symbol **$t** inserted between. Also useful are the symbols **$1** through **$9**, which represent any additional information you want the macro to use. For example, you could rewrite the above DOSKEY command to read:

```
DOSKEY QD=DIR *.$1 /W
```

Now, when you use the QD macro you would need to specify what **$1** stands for. If you want a directory listing of .TXT files, you'd enter:

```
QD txt
```

and DOSKEY would convert the file specification to *.TXT. When you want .BAT files displayed, you'd enter instead:

```
QD bat
```

You may set up as many macros as you like, but DOSKEY normally limits them to as many as will fill its 512-byte buffer. To expand the buffer to, say, 2 kilo-bytes, add a **/BUFSIZE** switch the first time you use DOSKEY:

```
DOSKEY /BUFSIZE=2048
```

If you wish to use your macros again and again, write them into a batch file as a succession of DOSKEY commands. To see a listing of the macros, enter:

```
DOSKEY /DMACS
```

To make a batch file of the macros, add the **>** symbol and the desired batch file name to the command, as in:

```
DOSKEY /DMACS>MYMACROS.BAT
```

Then use a text editor to open the MYMACROS.BAT file. You'll see all of the commands, but without the word DOSKEY at the beginning of each macro. Type DOSKEY at the start of each macro so that each line will become a full-fledged DOSKEY command. Then save the file. Thereafter, you have only to enter:

```
MYMACROS
```

to have each DOSKEY command in the file executed so that every macro will be at your finger tips.

DOS Commands That Temporarily Modify the Directory Tree

One way to make it easier to move around a directory tree is to change its structure temporarily. There are commands that make DOS think that one drive is another, that a subdirectory is a drive unto itself, or that one drive is a subdirectory in another drive. This magic is accomplished by the ASSIGN, SUBST, and JOIN commands. Let's look at each in turn.

The ASSIGN Command

The ASSIGN command was developed to help old programs that *must* access drives A and B. Many of the first IBM PC programs were written before hard disks were available at all—a "fully equipped" machine had two diskette drives, and that was all. Often these programs required that the program diskette reside in drive A, and a data diskette in drive B. Such programs were easy to use, because you didn't have to specify so much as a drive, let alone a long path (this was before the days of tree-structured directories, in any case). Today, one of these programs may not work if it is used from a hard disk. It may look on drive A for auxiliary files, and try to write its data to a (possibly) nonexistent drive B.

ASSIGN comes to the rescue in these cases, since it lets you treat drives A and B as if they were drive C. The statement

    ASSIGN A=C

makes any operations on drive A be directed to the current directory in drive C. Hence, if you ask for a directory listing of drive A, you'll get the directory for C. To assign both drives A and B to drive C, enter:

    ASSIGN A=C B=C

That's all there is to it. To cancel the assignments and return all to normal, just enter:

    ASSIGN

Only DOS 5.0 provides a way to find out what assignments are currently in effect:

    ASSIGN /STATUS

Dangers

The ASSIGN command should only be used when absolutely necessary. It's a dangerous command, in that things can go mysteriously wrong. *Never* use ASSIGN with the BACKUP, RESTORE, LABEL, and PRINT commands, or with the other tree-modifying commands, SUBST and JOIN. FORMAT, DISKCOPY, and DISKCOMP ignore the new drive assignments made by ASSIGN.

The SUBST Command

The SUBST command was introduced with DOS version 3.1. It does all that the ASSIGN command does, and more. It can cause any subdirectory to be represented as a drive. For example, the subdirectory C:WATER\SNOW\ICE could be temporarily renamed **D:**. To make the files in the subdirectory C:DATAFILE\FILE5 available as **D:**, you'd enter:

```
SUBST D: C:\DATAFILE\FILE5
```

SUBST can be handy during disk housekeeping. When you copy files from all over the tree to a particular subdirectory, you can set up the subdirectory as a drive to save yourself the trouble of typing its path over and over again.

To undo a substitution, follow **SUBST** with the substitute drive specifier, and then **/D** (for "delete"). For example, if you've renamed a subdirectory on drive C as **D:**, then enter:

```
SUBST D: /D
```

To see the current list of substitutions, enter:

```
SUBST
```

For the case given above, it would return:

```
D: => C:\DATAFILE\FILE5
```

By default, DOS allows drive specifiers only up to **E**. You can extend the range to **Z** by placing a LASTDRIVE command in CONFIG.SYS. The statement:

```
LASTDRIVE = F
```

extends the range to F. Don't forget this requirement if you use the SUBST command several times over. Like ASSIGN, SUBST can cause trouble with commands such as BACKUP, RESTORE, FORMAT, DISKCOPY, and CHKDSK.

The JOIN Command

The JOIN command is the inverse of the SUBST command. Rather than regard a subdirectory as a separate (logical) drive, it treats an actual drive as a subdirectory in the directory tree of another drive. JOIN is usually used to link diskette drives into your hard disk directory tree. The statement:

```
JOIN A: C:\NEWDIR
```

makes the root directory of drive A appear as a subdirectory called NEWDATA that is listed in the root directory. Figure 5.1 illustrates this mechanism. JOIN creates the subdirectory if it does not find it. Any name will do, but you need to supply one since a root directory has no name of its own. If the diskette has a directory tree, all of it will be appended to the tree in drive C. JOIN can use an existing subdirectory only if the directory is completely empty. Otherwise an error message is displayed.

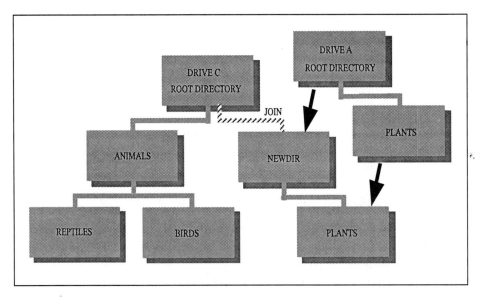

Figure 5-1. The JOIN command

To reverse a JOIN command, name the drive that has been linked into a tree and follow it with **/D** (for "delete"), as in

```
JOIN A: /D
```

The subdirectory **NEWDIR** would remain as an empty directory after the command is undone.

More than one JOIN command can be in effect at once. To see a listing of the current linkages, simply enter:

```
JOIN
```

JOIN must not be used in combination with ASSIGN or SUBST, nor should BACKUP, RESTORE, FORMAT, DISKCOPY, or DISKCOMP.

Dangers in ASSIGN, SUBST, and JOIN

Be very careful with ASSIGN, SUBST, and JOIN. There are many instances in which they can cause trouble and lock up the machine. Here are some special cases:

- DOS shells, menuing programs, and operating environments are likely to become completely confused.
- The commands may tangle up your system of batch files.
- You may overwrite files of the same name in different directories that have been linked together.
- The commands won't help you with the *key disk* problem, in which a program won't run unless its distribution disk is in drive A.
- You may temporarily lose access to data on a drive when the drive's specifier is assigned to some other purpose.

Copying and Moving Files

COPY is one of the most frequently used DOS commands. But many people fail to make use of some of its most powerful features. Let's go over the basics of this command and then we'll take a closer look.

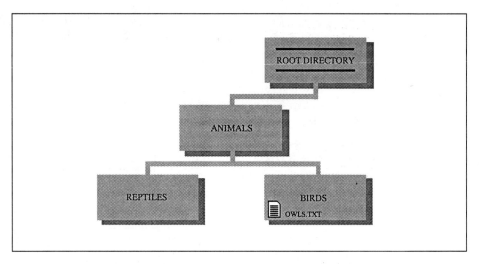

Figure 5-2. A two-level directory tree branch

When you copy a file from a subdirectory in a directory tree, you should first stop to ask which directory is the current directory—the directory to which DOS directs its actions by default. Consider the tree shown in Figure 5.2. Say that there is a file named **OWLS.TXT** located in the **BIRDS** subdirectory, and that you want to copy it to **ANIMALS**. If **BIRDS** is the current directory, DOS will automatically look for the file there, and you need only specify the directory to which the file will be copied:

```
COPY  OWLS.TXT   \ANIMALS
```

However, if any other directory is current, you must specify a directory path to **OWLS.TXT** also:

```
COPY  \ANIMALS\BIRDS\OWLS.TXT   \ANIMALS
```

Of course, you could make **BIRDS** the current directory, and then use the simpler command:

```
CHDIR  \ANIMALS\BIRDS
COPY  OWLS.TXT   \ANIMALS
```

When the directory in which the copy will be written (the *target directory*) is the current directory, there's no need to name it at all in the COPY command:

```
CD \ANIMALS
COPY  \ANIMALS\BIRDS\OWLS.TXT
```

Since no target directory is named in the command, DOS automatically directs the copy of the file to the current directory.

There is one case where this approach does not work. When the original file is in the current directory, as when **BIRDS** is current, then the command:

```
COPY  OWLS.TXT
```

results in the error message:

```
File cannot be copied onto itself
0 File(s) copied
```

because DOS would be copying a file with the same name as the original into the same directory as the original. Since two files in one directory can't have the same name, this action is not allowed.

Drive Specifiers

Of course, in any of these examples, you must add drive specifiers when the default drive is different from the one that you want to access. For example, if drive A is the default, and the tree shown in Figure 5.1 (page 176) is on drive C, then the examples given here would be written as:

```
COPY  C:OWLS.TXT  C:\ANIMALS
COPY  C:\ANIMALS\BIRDS\OWLS.TXT  C:\ANIMALS
COPY  C:\ANIMALS\BIRDS\OWLS.TXT  C:
```

Notice the lone **C:** at the end of the last example. It stands for, "to the current directory of drive C." Similarly, the expression **C:OWLS.TXT** in the first example refers to a file named OWLS.TXT in the current directory of drive C. When the current directory is other than the one in which you want the file copied, you'll need to either include a path to the proper directory, as in the first two examples, or you'll have to change the current directory of C using the CHDIR command. If you fail to take one of these measures, the copy will not be placed where you expected, and you may be left searching for it.

Shortcuts Using COPY

Earlier in this chapter, we described the dot (.) and double dot (..) symbols, which speed access to adjacent subdirectories in a directory tree. Using these symbols, you may copy files between adjacent subdirectories without typing long directory paths.

Copying to the Parent Directory

Say that you are working in the directory tree shown in 5.3, in which **SIAMESE** is the current directory, and you want to copy the file **CATLIST.DOC** from **SIAMESE** to the parent directory, which is **CATS**. Instead of typing:

```
COPY  CATLIST.DOC  \FELINES\CATS
```

you could accomplish the task by entering:

```
COPY  CATLIST.DOC  ..
```

The double period in this command represents **\FELINES\CATS**—that is, the whole DOS path up to, but not including, the current directory.

Copying to a Directory Above

Again using the directory tree shown in Figure 5.3, say that **FELINES** is now the current directory, and that you want to copy the file **PURR.TXT** from it to the **SIAMESE** subdirectory. Instead of:

```
COPY  PURR.TXT  \FELINES\CATS\SIAMESE
```

you could use:

```
COPY  PURR.TXT  .\CATS\SIAMESE
```

Here, the dot represents the entire directory path up to and including the current directory, which is \FELINES. If the copy were going to the CATS directory—a directory immediately beyond the current directory—you could enter:

```
COPY  MEOW.DOC  CATS
```

In this case, DOS assumes that **CATS** is a directory named in the current directory.

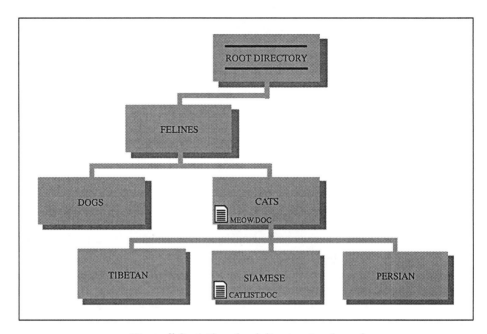

Figure 5-3. A three-level directory tree branch

Note that if you were to mistype **SIAMESE** with a word that does not name a subdirectory in the current directory, COPY would instead create a second copy of the file in the current directory and give it the name you actually typed. Before making a copy like this one, DOS checks the current directory for a subdirectory with the name you entered, and if it finds it, DOS copies the file to that subdirectory. Be careful, because if you make a typing error in the subdirectory name, the error may go unnoticed because DOS won't display an error message, and will copy the file to the wrong directory using the wrong file name instead. For example, if you wanted to enter the above command, but instead entered:

```
COPY  CATLIST  \FELINES\CATS\PERSION
```

The file copy will end up in the CATS directory and be named PERSIAN.

Copying to a Subdirectory at the Same Level

The double dot (..) symbol can help you copy files to *parallel* subdirectories, such as from **SIAMESE** to **PERSIAN** in Figure 5.3. With **SIAMESE** as the current directory, you could copy **CATLIST** from it to **PERSIAN** by typing:

```
COPY  CATLIST  ..\PERSIAN
```

Again, the .. represents the directory path up to but not including the current
directory—that is, it represents the parent subdirectory of the current directory. So, this last command is the same as:

```
COPY  CATLIST  \FELINES\CATS\PERSIAN
```

Utility Software

Any DOS shell helps you copy files between subdirectories with less effort. You
begin by selecting one or more files in a directory listing (perhaps several directory listings). In shells that support a mouse, this is done simply by moving
the mouse cursor over the file name and pressing a mouse button. Otherwise,
it's done by using a cursor key to move a highlight bar over the file name and
pressing some other key to mark the file.

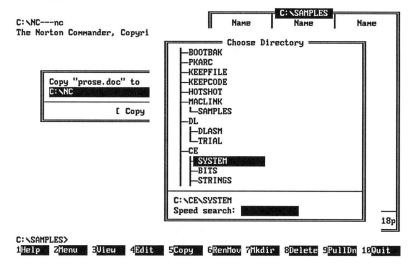

Figure 5-4. Copying files in The Norton Commander

Once the files are selected, most DOS shells display a dialog box and ask you to
enter the path to the directory to which the files should be copied. You type
the path, press Enter, and the files are copied. This approach is less than ideal,
since you still have to remember the directory path and go to the trouble of
entering it. A shell like *The Norton Commander* saves you this labor by letting you
first select files from directory listings and then select the target directory from
a directory tree diagram. The whole job can be done with a mouse. Figure 5.4

shows a file copied this way in *The Commander*. In the figure, the file SAMPLE.DOC has already been selected from a directory listing. Instead of copying the file to the current directory (C:\NC), the target directory C:\CE\SYSTEM is selected from the tree diagram.

The DOS 4.0/5.0 Shell

In the DOS Shell program that accompanies DOS version 4.0 and later, begin by choosing the *File System* from the startup menu and selecting the files you want to copy. Then pull down the *File* menu and choose *Copy*. (The Copy option is highlighted or appears as ***opy** when no files have been selected and the command can't work.)

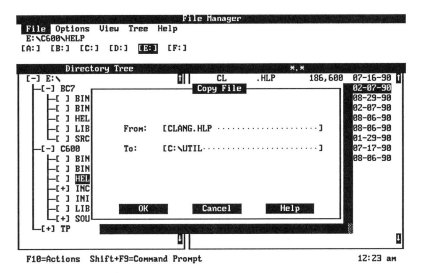

Figure 5-5. Copying files in the DOS Shell

You'll then see a dialog box (shown in Figure 5.5) that asks you to enter the path of the drive and directory to which the file or files should be copied. To save your copies in the current directory of drive B, you could simply enter **B:**. If you're not sure of the current directory then you should enter the entire directory path, exactly as if you were using the COPY command from the DOS command line. Remember that the root directory is denoted by a single backslash, as in **B:**.

The files are copied when you press (or mouse-click) Enter or OK. When a file of the same name already exists in the target directory, another dialog box will ask whether to copy over it (Figure 5.6). The cursor is set over the option that halts the copy operation, so you need to move the cursor to *Replace this file* and then press Enter or OK to make the copy. Keep in mind that, if you copy a new file over an old one with the same name, the contents of the old file will be lost wholly or partially in such a way that even the best "unerase" programs will be unable to recover your data. To disable this feature, pull down the *Options* menu and select *File Options*. A dialog box will appear displaying the line *Confirm on replace* with a symbol to the left if this feature is enabled. Toggle it off by clicking on the line with a mouse, or by using the cursor keys to move the highlight cursor to the line, and then pressing the Spacebar.

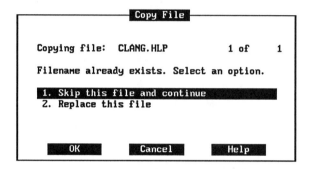

Figure 5-6. The Copy File dialog box

Windows 3.0

In Windows, enter the *File Manager* and select the file you want to copy. Then pull down the *File* menu and choose *Copy*. You'll be shown a dialog box like the one in Figure 5.7, asking you to type in the file's destination. You can use the Tab key to move the cursor to the place in the dialog box where this information is entered. Then type a directory path and press Enter. A full path is required; as far as copying files is concerned, there is no "current directory" such that you could type **C:** to have the file copied to a default directory on drive C. In fact, Windows will interpret **C:** as meaning **C:** and copy the file into the root directory.

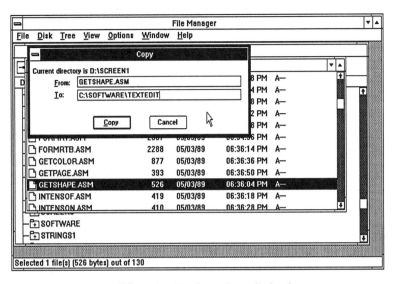

Figure 5-7. The Windows Copy dialog box.

When a file of the same name already exists in the destination directory, another dialog box (Figure 5.8) may prompt you to confirm that the file should be overwritten. This safety feature may be switched on and off by pulling down the *Options* menu and choosing *Confirmation.* You'll be shown a list of choices, including *Confirm on Replace.* The choice is enabled when an "X" appears in the check box to its left. To alter the setting, click your mouse on the check box, or use the Up Arrow and Down Arrow keys to move the cursor to the box, and then press the Spacebar.

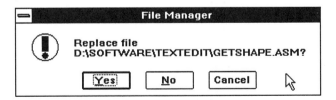

Figure 5-8. A confirmation box

Moving Files

DOS does not include a command for moving files from one location to another. You're forced to first copy a file, and then erase the original. Combining these functions in one command would make some errors less likely. In many instances the process would also be quicker, for in a file move between subdirectories on the same disk, there is no need to actually transfer the file from one disk location to another; simple changes in directory listings do the job. There are many MOVE utilities available on bulletin boards and in collections of free software.

A batch file can be used to move files, but it must be written and used carefully. At its heart are one command to copy the file and one command to erase the original. The danger is that something will go wrong when the file is copied. If the batch file fails to realize that the copy has not been made and goes ahead and erases the original, you'll lose data. Unfortunately, DOS is constructed in such a way that batch files can detect errors only for the XCOPY command, and not for COPY. XCOPY, which is discussed in Chapter 8, is more powerful than COPY in that, when you specify a nonexistent directory as the file's destination, it will create the directory and all directories leading to it. It would be better to receive an error message in this case, but nothing can be done to change the way the command behaves.

Here is a batch file for moving files:

```
@ECHO off
FOR    %%F IN (%2) DO GOTO Begin
ECHO   Error!  Format for MOVE is:
ECHO   MOVE   file   destination-directory
ECHO   For example:
ECHO   MOVE   c:\level1\myfile.txt  d:\
GOTO   Finished

:Begin
IF     NOT EXIST %1 GOTO BadFilename
XCOPY %1 %2
IF     ERRORLEVEL 1 GOTO ErrorOccurred
ERASE %1
ECHO   The file %1 has been moved to %2.
GOTO   Finished

:BadFilename
ECHO   The file could not be found.
ECHO   Be sure the filename is spelled correctly and include a
path to its directory if necessary.
GOTO   Finished

:ErrorOccurred
ECHO   Error!
ECHO   The file %1 could not be moved to %2.
GOTO   Finished

:Finished
```

We'll tell you in a moment how this batch file works, but you don't need to understand it to use it. Just type it into a file named **MOVE.BAT**. Then, when you want to use the batch file to move another file called **NOTAGAIN.DOC** from its current location to drive A, just type:

```
MOVE   NOTAGAIN.DOC   A:
```

Both the file name and it's destination may optionally take directory paths:

```
MOVE   C:\LEVEL1\NOTAGAIN.DOC   A:\FILEDUMP
```

To be useful, you'll want this batch file available no matter what the current directory. Place it in a subdirectory devoted to batch files and specify the name of that subdirectory in a PATH command.

How the Batch File Works

This is a complicated batch file; to understand it, you need to know batch file basics. The file begins with a FOR statement that tests whether at least two parameters (the name of the file to be moved and its destination) have been included on the command line. When a second parameter has not been given, the error message listed on the next four lines is displayed and a jump is made to the end of the file so that it terminates. Otherwise, a jump is made to the **:Begin** label to copy the file.

Before actually copying the file, a check is made to be sure that the specified file actually exists. This is done by the **IF NOT EXIST %1** statement, which looks for the file named by the first command line parameter (represented in batch files by the symbol **%1**). If the file is not found, a jump is made to the **:BadFileName** label, the error message on the following two lines is displayed, and a jump is then made to the **:Finished** label at the end of the file so that it terminates. Otherwise, the batch file goes on to make the copy with the statement, **XCOPY 1% 2%**.

After attempting to copy the file using XCOPY, an **IF ERRORLEVEL 1** statement examines the errorlevel code that is returned by XCOPY to verify that it successfully completed the copy. An errorlevel value of 0 is returned when all has gone well. The expression "ERRORLEVEL 1" refers to any other errorlevel code, such as might result from a disk drive error or a full-disk condition.

If an error has occurred, a jump is made to the **:ErrorOccurred** label, the error message on the following two lines is displayed, and the batch file terminates. However, if the copy has been made successfully, the **ERASE %1** statement is executed to delete the original file. Then, the next line of the file displays a message telling that the file has been moved. In this message, the file name is inserted in place of the symbol **%1** and the destination directory is inserted in place of **%2**.

Finally, a jump is made to the **:Finished** label at the end of the file and the batch file terminates.

A Pitfall

One limitation of this batch file appears when a full-disk error occurs before all files in a mass move are copied. For example, if you specify ***.*** as the file name when copying to a diskette, disk space may run short. In this case, some files are copied, but none of the originals are subsequently erased.

The DOS 4.0/5.0 Shell

Virtually all DOS shells can move files—including the shell shipped with DOS 4.0 and later—as can dozens of utility programs. Be certain that the software you use for this purpose comes from a reliable source. A *move* feature reaches into the heart of the file system, and a serious programming error could wipe out the entire directory system and all your data along with it.

In the DOS shell program, first choose the File System from the main menu (the Main Group). Then select one or more files to move. Once selected, you can pull down the *File* menu to choose *Move*. (If no files have been selected, *Move* is highlighted or appears as ***ove** to indicate that the command cannot function.) You'll proceed to the dialog box shown in Figure 5.9, which requests that you type in the path of the directory to which the file should be transferred. Some DOS shells let you perform this step by designating the target directory on a tree diagram. But in the DOS Shell you must return to the standard command line format. Remember that a single backslash denotes the root directory. Press Enter or OK (or click the Enter or OK symbol with a mouse) to begin the move.

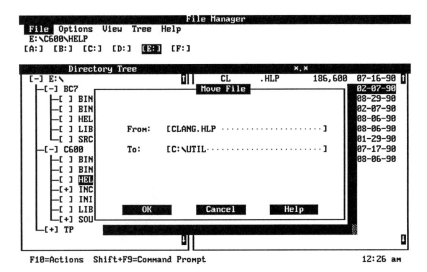

Figure 5-9. Moving files in the DOS Shell

Windows 3.0

In Windows, enter the *File Manager* and select the file you want to move. Then pull down the *File* menu and choose *Move*. You'll be shown a dialog box like the one in Figure 5.10, asking you to type in the file's destination. Use a mouse or the Tab key to move the cursor to the place in the dialog box where this information is entered. Then enter a directory path and press Enter. A full path is required because when copying files, there is no "current directory" in the sense that you could type C: and have the file copied to the last-accessed subdirectory. In fact, Windows will interpret **C:** as equalling **C:** and copy the file into the root directory.

When a file of the same name already exists in the destination directory, another dialog box may prompt you to confirm that the file should be over-written. This safety feature may be switched on and off by pulling down the *Options* menu and choosing *Confirmation*. You'll be shown a list of choices, including *Confirm on Replace*. The choice is enabled when an X appears in the check box to its left. To alter the setting, click your mouse on the check box, or use the Up Arrow and Down Arrow keys to move the cursor to the box, and then press the Spacebar.

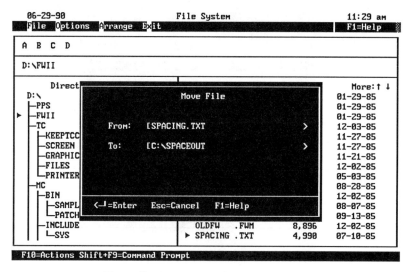

Figure 5-10. Moving files in Windows

Finding Files

When a hard disk has long been in use, keeping track of an ever-growing number of files becomes a serious problem. If you've organized the directory tree well, half the battle is won, because you can narrow the search down to a few subdirectories. But an extensive tree holding thousands of files makes a directory-by-directory search impractical. You must turn to utility software to search for a file, either by its name or by words found within the file.

Searching for Files by Name

Scanning directories is a perfectly good way of locating a file when you have a pretty good idea where that file resides. But it can be a very frustrating approach when the file could be hiding in any of dozens of subdirectories. Unfortunately, until version 5.0, DOS provided no way of making an automatic search of many subdirectories to look for the file. There *is* a way to perform a search in earlier DOS versions, however. Let's take a look at it.

DOS provides the ATTRIB command to alter file attributes. "Attributes" attach a certain status to a file, for example, that it is a read-only file, or a file hidden from directory listings. Besides changing attributes, the ATTRIB command can find out some of a file's current attribute settings. This is done simply by entering ATTRIB and then the file's name:

```
ATTRIB  FILENAME.EXT
```

or, using a directory path:

```
ATTRIB  C:\PROJECT7\FILENAME.EXT
```

The command responds by displaying the file's name and its directory path. The file's attributes are indicated to the left of the name. By ending the command with an /S switch, ATTRIB can be made to scan all directories beyond the specified (or current) directory in addition to searching the directory itself. The whole tree is searched when the root directory is specified. Thus, you can search the entire disk for the file **THATSIT.TXT** by entering:

```
ATTRIB  \THATSIT.TXT  /S
```

The initial backslash represents the root directory; it tells DOS to search subdirectories starting from the root directory. To search for **THATSIT.TXT** just in the subdirectory **\FELINES\CATS** and all subdirectories listed in CATS and beyond, enter:

```
ATTRIB  \FELINES\CATS\THATSIT.TXT  /S
```

When ATTRIB finds a file, it displays a message like:

```
R       C:\FELINES\CATS\THATSIT.TXT
```

telling you that the file **THATSIT.TXT** is in the subdirectory **C:\FELINES\ CATS** (and also, in this case, that the file is read-only, as shown by the R to the left). You can use this feature to search for groups of files by using global filename characters. For a listing of all files in a tree that end in .BAT, type:

```
ATTRIB  \*.BAT  /S
```

For all files named REPORT12 with any extension, enter:

```
ATTRIB  \REPORT12.*  /S
```

File Searches in DOS 5.0

DOS 5.0 adds the /S switch to the DIR command. This switch is familiar in earlier DOS versions in commands like XCOPY and ATTRIB. It causes a command to extend its actions, not just to the current directory (or the directory specified in the command), but to all directories held in that directory, all held in those directories, and so on. In this way, the **/S** switch can make a command cover a whole branch of the tree, or the entire tree when the command starts with the root directory.

To find the file **SAYWHAT.DOC** anywhere on the disk, you would enter:

```
DIR \SAYWHAT.DOC /S
```

The backslash before **SAYWHAT.DOC** indicates that the search should begin from the root directory. To search the subdirectory **\MAMMALS\AQUATIC** and all subdirectories beyond it, enter:

```
DIR \MAMMALS\AQUATIC\SAYWHAT.DOC /S
```

When used with the /S switch, DIR may find more than one instance of a particular file name as it scans multiple subdirectories. In this case, it lists all instances it finds, along with the directory paths of each.

Searching by the DOS 4.0/5.0 Shell

The DOS shells that accompany DOS 4.0 and 5.0 can search the entire disk for an individual file, or groups of files identified by global file name characters. In both shells, you choose *Display Options* from the *Options* menu. A dialog box appears, and in it you can type a specification for the files you want to appear in directory listings. Normally, this specification is ***.*** so that all files in a directory are listed. But if you list a particular file name instead, only that file will be listed. No listing appears at all if the file is not found in the current directory. Similarly, you can specify a group of files, such as ***.bat** for all batch files.

Once you've specified a file name, you need to extend the search for the file across the entire directory tree. This is done by pulling down the *Arrange* menu (in DOS 4.0) or View menu (in DOS 5.0) and choosing *System File List.* You'll see a composite listing for the entire directory tree, a listing that may include only one file if you've specified just that file under *Display Options.* Status information on the left side of the screen reports the directory in which the file is located. Be sure to return the *File Options* specification to ***.*** after you've finished searching.

Searching for Files in Windows 3.0

You can search for a file in Windows 3.0 by selecting the drive and directory from which you want the search to begin. Then pull down the *File* menu and choose *Search*. A dialog box appears asking for the file name. You may use global file name characters (* and ?) if you want to search for a group of files. You'll see a check box labeled *Search Entire Disk*. When it is checked, the search covers the entire disk, no matter what the current directory; otherwise it begins from the current directory. Press Enter (or click your mouse on the OK button) to begin the search.

Other Utility Software

Virtually all commercially available DOS shells provide advanced file-searching features. In *The Norton Commander*, for example, you may search for several files at once. A scrollable display of the file names can be consulted even as the search progresses to see which files have been found. When the search has finished, you can select a file from the list of those found. By doing so, the file's directory is displayed with the file highlighted so that it can be readily viewed, moved, or whatever.

There are also stand-alone utilities whose only job is to search for files. The FileFind program in *The Norton Utilities* looks for a file and all directories beyond it, or across the entire disk. It can also extend the search across multiple disks. FileFind lets you specify multiple search criteria, such as the file's date, size, or attribute. You can even specify a string of characters to look for inside the file (we'll talk more about this kind of file search in a moment). A utility like FileFind gives you much power when you're cleaning up a disk during periodic housekeepings. It lets you quickly look into files, and it lets you print out various statistics and lists of files from the searches you make.

Searching for Files by Content

Sometimes, you'll find that you've completely forgotten a file's name but know something about its contents. For example, correspondence directed to Mr. Rumplestiltskin is bound to contain the word "Rumplestiltskin." You can locate the file by using software that searches inside files, scanning every line for words you specify. The words are often referred to as the "target string," where "string" refers to a string of characters. This kind of utility software is not limited to text files. It can also look for text fields in spreadsheets, databases, and other kinds of applications.

The DOS FIND Command

DOS offers a primitive facility for such searches—the FIND command. Within text files, text is usually broken up into lines 80 characters or less. The FIND command could seek the word "Rumplestiltskin" in a file and show each line of the file in which the expression is found. Then you'd have to load the file into your word processor to confirm that it is the one you are looking for. To search the file **TALLTALE.TXT** for this string, you would type:

```
FIND  "Rumplestiltskin" TALLTALE.TXT
```

or , using a directory path:

```
FIND  "Rumplestiltskin"  C:\FABLES\TALLTALE.TXT
```

If "Rumplestiltskin" is found in the file, FIND might display:

```
----------  C:\FABLES\TALLTALE.TXT
Dear Mr Rumplestiltskin,
any other way.  Let me assure you, Mr Rumplestiltskin,
```

You can have FIND show the relative line number of each line displayed by adding /N (for "number") after the word FIND:

```
FIND  /N  "Rumplestiltskin" TALLTALE.TXT
```

Add **/C** (for count) at the same position in the command to make FIND report the total number of lines displayed (no lines are shown in this case), and **/V** for ("reverse") to display only lines that do not hold "Rumplestiltskin."

Restrictions

FIND has a number of limitations that greatly restrict its usefulness. First, until DOS 5.0, FIND was case-sensitive, meaning that it distinguished between uppercase and lowercase letters in its searches. If you specify "giraffes" as the word to find, and the word happens to start a sentence and thus is capitalized (Giraffes), FIND will miss it. DOS 5.0 introduces the **/I** (for "ignore case") switch to make searches case-insensitive.

Another problem is that FIND won't locate expressions divided between two lines of a text file. If you're looking for "blue moon" and "blue" is the last word of one line and "moon" is the first word of the next, FIND won't see it. FIND also sees every instance of an expression, whether or not it is a whole word. If you were to specify a search for the word "cat," FIND would report instances of words like "scat" and "catacomb."

FIND also has trouble viewing groups of files. You may specify multiple files to search by naming each on the command line:

```
FIND  "Rumplestiltskin"  FILE1.TXT  FILE2.TXT  FILE3.TXT
```

However, FIND cannot use global file name characters for searching large numbers of files. The command:

```
FIND  "Rumplestiltskin"  *.TXT
```

results in an error message rather than a search of all files in a directory with .TXT extensions. You can get around this limitation by applying the word FOR, which normally is used in batch files. To use ***.TXT** in your search, enter:

```
FOR  %F  IN (*.TXT) DO FIND "Rumplestiltskin" %F
```

This command works by executing the FIND command for every match made with the asterisk in ***.TXT**. Each time, the match is substituted for the characters **%F** so that the FIND command knows in which file to search for "Rumplestiltskin." The command is confusing, but you can use it without understanding it. Just enter the file name specification within the parentheses, and the search expression in place of "Rumplestiltskin."

Advanced Search Utilities

Complicated searches are possible with utilities devoted to just this purpose. These can use wild card characters in the search string, and may even perform a phonetic search for similar-sounding words. The utility may find strings that are split between two lines, even when hyphenated, and can search for more than one string simultaneously, using the logic of AND, OR, and NOT. Thus, you could ask for all sentences that contain "apples" or "oranges," but not "pears." You can even ask for occurrences of particular kinds of sentence structure or document formatting. In this way, you could have the utility make a file of all section headings in a document by describing the particular formatting codes your word processor uses to define them.

Perhaps most important of all, advanced search utilities let you specify how much text is displayed when a match is found. While simple programs merely return a "line" in the file (often corresponding to a line on the screen when the file is displayed), advanced utilities let you specify that the entire sentence or paragraph be reported, or all text up to specified border characters. The FileFind program in *The Norton Utilities* lets you view "found" files even as the search continues.

Search Tools for Programmers

Even more complicated search programs have been designed for programmers. These often mimic *grep*, the granddaddy of such utilities, which descends from the UNIX operating system. In their purest form, these are *pattern matching* programs. They use *metacharacters*—an extended set of wildcards— that can denote particular constructions. For example, a metacharacter could indicate an end-of-line position, and the utility would return a match only if the search string occurred at the end of a line. Programmers value these utilities because they give complete control over the interpretation of *control codes* embedded in a file. Such tools are not for everyone, but they can be invaluable in large programming projects.

Performance

A simple search program can move through 100K of files in about 30 seconds on a standard IBM XT. Only a few seconds are required by a fast 386 machine. In either case, an appreciable time would pass in searching all files on a typical hard disk. But most searches are limited to files specified by wildcard characters and the job is completed quickly. Of course, searches take longer when you use complicated search criteria.

Searching by Indexing

To make searches move more quickly, software can create a permanent index of the contents of all files on a disk. *Lotus Magellan* works this way. It scans the contents of all files of all kinds, looking for text, then makes an index of every word it encounters. As you might imagine, the index is quite large, amounting to roughly 10 percent of total disk space. Of course, files are constantly created, changed, introduced, or deleted, and so the index requires constant updating. This is done—with your permission—when the program is started up. In updating the index, only new or changed files are searched, so it doesn't take long.

The advantage of this approach is that a complex search can be made in a matter of seconds. Even when you specify a complicated combination of words, the program needs only to consult the index. The search can be "fuzzy," so that you can even track down words—particularly names—for which you may not be sure of the spelling. A list of all relevant files is displayed on one side of the screen, and you can quickly scan one after another until you find the right one. A collection of "filters" are provided so that you can view common file formats just as they appear in the application programs that create them.

Running Programs

A DOS shell can run any program. The shell employs a special feature in DOS (the "EXEC" function) that allows one program to run another. In most shells, you run the program by moving the bar cursor to the file's directory listing and typing a command code. Of course, many programs take information on the DOS command line when they are loaded; often, you type the name of the work file immediately after the program name, as in **WP CHAPTER7.TXT**. Most shells let you specify command line information in some way.

Utility Software

The *Norton Commander* uses a "point-and-shoot" approach to loading programs. It requires that you assign a particular filename extension to any data files used with a particular program. Then you can move the cursor (using a mouse, if you like) to any data file in a directory listing and "shoot"—the *Commander* uses the filename extension to figure out with which program the file runs, and it loads the program and the data file. To work this magic, you need to set up a simple file that tells which extensions match which programs. The data file may be anywhere on the disk; the *Commander* supplies the DOS path for the file when it loads the program.

This approach to linking data files to program files is inflexible in certain ways. If two programs use the same extension, the shell may start the wrong program when a data file is specified. Conversely, you may want more than one application to be able to access the same data file. In the later case, you can associate the extension to one of the programs that use it. When you want some other program to access the file, start up that program directly by name and then load the file from within the program. Remember that some programs automatically add a predefined extension to all files they create, and these should not be changed; you are free to devise your own system only when no extensions are added automatically.

The DOS 4.0/5.0 Shell

You can start up a program in the DOS Shell by moving the bar cursor to its directory listing and pressing Enter, or by moving the mouse cursor over the listing and double-clicking the mouse (striking the left mouse button twice quickly). If the shell is properly configured, you can also start a program by doing the same thing to the directory listing of a data file that you want loaded into the program. As in other DOS shells, this is done by associating the file's extension with the program that runs it.

Say that the word processor program file is named MYWORD.EXE. Find it in a directory listing and move the bar cursor to it, selecting it with a click of the mouse button or a strike on the Spacebar. Then pull down the *File* menu and select *Associate*. A dialog box will appear to ask you to enter the associated extension. In this case, you'd type in "DOC" and press Enter. Notice that the period that separates file names and extensions is not entered. Then you'd be asked whether to "prompt for options." Usually, it's best to specify "Don't prompt for options." Otherwise, when the DOS Shell starts up a program it will prompt you to type in codes for special options. Most programs don't require these options, which are explained in the DOS Shell manual.

Once the association has been made, striking Enter when a data file has been selected (or double-clicking on the file name) will start up its associated program and then load the file into it. It doesn't matter in what drive or directory the data file resides, for the DOS Shell will remember the location of the program file.

You may specify more than one extension that will invoke a particular program. The reverse, however, is not possible. Once you specify that files with **.DOC** endings belong to **MYWORD.DOC**, it's not possible to automatically load .DOC files into other programs. But you can always start up a program directly and then load any file you like into it. If your programs don't dictate particular file name extensions, make up your own.

Windows 3.0

In Windows, programs are started in two ways. You can either select the program from a directory listing and have Windows load it, or you can specify a data file belonging to the program. In the latter case, Windows automatically tracks down the program that created the file, starts the program, and then loads the file into it. Windows does this in the usual way by referring to the file name extension of the data file.

Figure 5-11. Associating data files with programs

To associate an extension with a program, enter Windows' *File Manager.* Call a directory listing to the screen and select a data file you want to associate with the application. Then pull down the *File* menu and choose *Associate.* You'll be shown a dialog box like the one in Figure 5.11, which would result from specifying an .OL extension. Then type in a complete directory path up to and including the program file, such as:

```
C:\PROGRAMS\OUTLINER\LINES.EXE
```

Be sure to include the filename extension of the program file itself (in this case, .EXE). Don't just type:

```
C:\PROGRAMS\OUTLINER\LINES
```

Then strike Enter, or click on the "OK" button in the dialog box. Thereafter, all files on any disk drive bearing the .OL extension are linked to the program named LINES.

You can also start programs in Windows by selecting one of the icons displayed in the *Program Manager* window. Each icon refers to what is called a group in Windows—a set of program and data files that can be accessed quickly, without going through the trouble of hunting them down in the directory tree. Standard groups in Windows include *Windows Applications, Non-Windows Applications, Accessories, Games,* and *Main* (the *File Manager* is found in the latter).

When the group icon opens into a window, every file in the group is shown as an icon with a title beneath, as Figure 5.12 shows. A bar cursor rests on the title of one of the icons. To start up a program from the keyboard, simply use the cursor keys to shift the bar cursor to the desired program and then press Enter. Working with a mouse, you need only move the mouse cursor to the program's icon and double click. Alternatively, you can start programs in Windows from the directory tree. You navigate the tree as usual, opening directories and selecting files. Once a program file has been selected, just press Enter to run it.

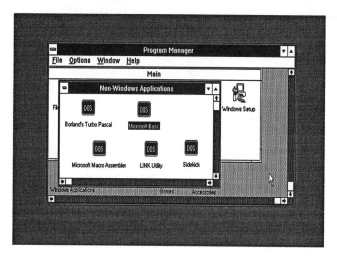

Figure 5-12. Programs listed as icons in Windows

Running Multiple Programs

Finally, keep in mind that Windows is multitasking, and that you can run several programs at once. Once they are running, you can move between them by clicking your mouse in the window of one program or another, or by repeatedly typing <Alt-Esc> to cycle from window to window. When you're working in one program and want to launch another, just move to any window from which programs can be launched, whether by a *Program Manager* group, by a directory listing, or by a menu selection in the *File Manager*. Then launch the program as always.

Menu Programs

Earlier in this chapter, we showed how batch files can form a primitive system of menus for running applications and DOS functions. Menus make computers very easy to use, and many businesses use them to insulate employees from the rigors of DOS. Menus take the user to the proper directory without any need to type a CHDIR command. No comprehension of the directory tree is required, and a menu system can help enforce a scheme for distributing files. It also may help avert disasters by channeling DOS commands, like ERASE and FORMAT. It doesn't make much sense to set up a menu program on a machine that only you use. If you're able to set up the menu system, you'll most certainly be able to handle a DOS shell, and that will give you much more power.

Menu systems have three disadvantages. First, the user cannot do any more than the menu system allows (short of leaving the menu system and returning to DOS). Second, the menuing system assures that computer users will remain computer-illiterate. And third, *setting up* the menu system usually requires a level of sophistication that far exceeds that required for the tasks the system will perform. Still, work must get done, and the world cannot stop while people learn to use computers.

Like many genres of software covered in this book, menu systems do not always fall into a neat and tidy category. Some DOS shells have menuing features, and virtually all **security systems** (which we'll discuss in a moment) are based on menus. Some systems completely take over the machine, and they cram the menus into only a few files. Other systems are mere extensions of DOS batch files, and they leave scores of files scattered across the disk.

Advanced Features

Menuing systems are as much a victim of *feature creep* as any other software genre. Some programs include editors, notepads, and calendars. Some can scan directories to find a file, or provide a more sophisticated equivalent of the DOS PATH command. Some have a built-in command language that is used in lieu of DOS batch files. Some provide an elaborate scheme for creating help screens as menu selections. Some mimic operating environments by offering overlapping windows and a cut-and-paste facility. Some are optimized for networks.

Such features are nice, but it's more important to find a program that gets the basics right. On the surface, most menuing systems look the same. But not all can achieve a high level of interactivity with the user. More important, there is a tremendous range in the ease with which menus may be created and maintained.

Most menuing systems are loaded by AUTOEXEC.BAT. Like DOS shells, some act as memory-resident programs. When a menu selection is made, the menuing program loads the program and runs it. Also like a DOS shell, only a small part of the program may remain in memory when an application runs, and the rest reloads when control returns to the menus. Some menu programs do not use this approach. Instead, they work through a series of DOS batch files, where the final command in each file returns control to the main menu.

A good menu program can be made to prompt the user for a file name, or other command line information, when a menu selection is made. For example, the main menu might read:

```
1. Word Processing
2. Spreadsheet
3. Outlining
4. DOS utilities
```

When the user types "1", a message would appear saying,

```
What is the name of the file you want to edit?
```

A first-rate menu system will be able to perform error checking on some kinds of user response—for example, that the input is a valid DOS filename. The ease by which a menu program can pass command-line information to a program is a measure of its quality.

Accessing DOS Commands

Nearly all menu programs make special provision for DOS commands. Some have a ready-made DOS command menu that you can alter very little. Others let you set up complicated DOS commands as a menu selection. But even when DOS access is flexible, no menu system will contain every possible DOS command. For this reason, some menu programs let the user exit to DOS; the subsequent return to the menu system may be automatic, or it may require reloading. In these programs, it is important that you be able to disable direct access to DOS if you want to be able to keep programs like FORMAT.COM out of the hands of inexperienced users.

Limitations

Menu programs vary greatly in their flexibility. Most limit the number of listings in one menu, as it's not practical to scroll menus up and down. Some limit the number of submenu levels. And some restrict a submenu to a single subdirectory. This means that the menuing system must exactly coincide with the directory tree structure. You can't set up a menu titled "Programming" that would branch to applications in several subdirectories. Some menu programs impose arbitrary constraints, such as the form of the main menu. Only a few give you complete control over the appearance and formatting of the menu screens.

Creating Menus

The hidden half of any menuing program is the part that creates the menus. These facilities are usually off-bounds to the person ultimately using the menus. They may be in a separate program, or they may be hidden behind a sequence of keystrokes. Because this part of the program is not used very often, it's doubly important that it be clear and easy to use. Otherwise, you'll have to study the documentation every time you want to change the menu system.

The best menuing software is itself menu-driven. It may present a series of prompts for information about filenames, paths, and command-line parameters. A few programs can display directory listings or a map of the tree while making menus. Another valuable feature is the ability to check that input information is correct—that DOS commands are valid, that program files are present in the directories you say they are, and so on. Some of the most capable programs are the easiest to use; some of the least capable are insanely difficult. Be sure that any menuing program you select has a good reporting facility that can both display and print the existing menu system lucidly.

Usage Tracking

Usage tracking is a particularly valuable feature of menuing systems. It creates a file that records how long particular users worked with particular applications. The program knows who is using the machine by asking for a name (or a password) before a menu selection may be made. At first sight, this may seem like spying, but such a record has many positive uses. It may be used as a record for billing clients, or for tracking computer use for tax write-offs. It shows how heavily the equipment is used, and who needs it most. And it tells which programs and data are accessed most, or not at all, so that disk space may be managed better.

A good menu program can sort the information about usage in various ways: by the user's name, the project number, the date and time, and the application name. Often these programs cannot report which data files were accessed, because the menu system is dormant while the files are loaded and an application is run.

It's hard to choose a menu program. From the outside, they tend to look much alike. But internally, some are a breeze to use, and others are a never-ending headache. Keep an eye out for reviews, which appear frequently. And if you *do* decide to set up a menu system, be sure that it does not become an impediment to those who want to learn more about computers.

Security Systems

Security systems are menu programs that limit a user's access to particular subdirectories or files. They remain in memory (and in control) the whole time the computer is turned on. Most work through a system of passwords that offer a tremendous range of capabilities and protection. Some do little more than stop people from accidentally erasing each other's files, but the most sophisticated programs protect data so well that, if the key password is lost, the data can never be recovered, not even by the software's manufacturer.

Passwords

Depending on the system design, passwords may be required in order to enter particular subdirectories, to use particular subdirectories, to use particular types of files, or to apply particular DOS commands. Conversely, a user can apply his or her password to a particular file to keep others out. When a file is protected in this way, no one can open it, erase it, or copy it to a diskette. In some systems, a special password is required to apply the COPY command to a program file; this makes software piracy more difficult. Passwords are also required for access to the facilities that create the menus. Finally, passwords may give access to particular peripherals, such as printers or diskette drives. This prevents someone from walking off with data that they have permission to work on. Passwords may also be used to limit a user's access to the computer at certain times of the day.

Intelligent Passwords

In some systems, users can create their own passwords; in others, the system manager assigns them. First-rate security systems use a system of *intelligent passwords*. In some, passwords age and must be replaced periodically. This measure stops password violations from extending indefinitely. A change in the access rights assigned to a particular password automatically extends to all menus. And a global lockout of passwords allows a system manager to disengage everyone from the system temporarily. The system watches illegal passwords carefully. If it finds someone trying passwords at random in an attempt to break in, it shuts him out.

Alternatives

You do not necessarily need to install a security system to reap the benefits of passwords. Some DOS shells have a built-in password system. Passwords are also sometimes incorporated into particular applications. Many database programs have some sort of access-denial scheme. These approaches are necessarily limited. Unless the entire system is protected, a technically sophisticated individual can always start up a debugger and peer into the files "through the back door."

Boot Security

The Achilles' heel of some security systems is that they can be penetrated simply by booting the machine from drive A. Since the system is brought into action by the AUTOEXEC.BAT file on the hard disk, all that's required is to stop AUTOEXEC from executing.

Many systems are free of this problem. Some use special hardware that occupies a slot in the machine. It holds passwords on read-only memory chips, and the machine is simply not allowed to boot from any drive without the proper password. Other systems work by making subtle changes to the hard disk. DOS cannot access the disk because of these changes. But when the security system is booted, it provides the help DOS needs.

Ctrl-Break

Often, a security system will disable the DOS Ctrl-Break key combination so that users cannot leave programs and get to DOS. Various other provisions stop people from starting up any software other than the approved programs. Without these restrictions, a clever hacker could find ways of sneaking illicit software into the system.

Audit Trails

Earlier, we discussed "usage tracking" in menuing software. The same feature exists in security systems, but the process is called an *audit trail.* Those who think of computers as Big Brother will have their worst fears realized. An audit trail keeps track of the names, programs accessed, the date and time of access, the time spent in each program, and so on. Reports may be generated that are organized by the various criteria. These reports help manage work, and also are designed to sniff out interlopers who are testing the system to see how it can be broken into. (Incidentally, most security systems have separate manuals for users and system managers, but anyone can buy a copy and experiment with the software to find a chink in its armor.)

Encryption

Sometimes restricted access to subdirectories, and even to individual files, is not enough. The next step is *data encryption.* Using a password as the basis, the file is scrambled. Most encryption is based on the DES (data encryption standard) developed for the United States government by IBM. It uses a seven-byte *key* that combines with eight-byte chunks of data to produce the encrypted file. The standard has gradually become dated as supercomputers evolve that are so powerful that they can simply try all possible combinations of the seven-byte key. In response, longer keys may now be used.

Encryption may be regarded as a second line of defense. It protects data when the machine is stolen. It also protects data that has been backed up from the hard disk. In less-sophisticated security systems, it stops people from accessing certain files in subdirectories to which they have access.

Most security systems offer encryption, and some automatically encrypt all files when written to disk. Encryption utilities also appear in just about any software genre you can think of. You'll find encryption in some keyboard macro programs, in DOS shells, and even within file defragmenters. *The*

Norton Utilities includes the *Diskreet* program for this purpose. It can work as a simple file-by-file encryption utility, or it can set up an encryption system that is always in operation. In the latter mode, *Diskreet* sets up something called an *NDisk*. An *NDisk* looks like another disk drive from the user's point of view. When you place a file on an *NDisk*, it is automatically encrypted. A password scheme controls access to the *NDisk* files. *Diskreet* can also keep an eye on all attempts to access *NDisks* and issue an audit report.

In a world harried by neophyte users and malevolent hackers, security systems offer nearly complete control over a system. But there are problems. It takes lots of work and time to build up a good security system. Some systems require that you reformat your disk. And the system can harrass users, who may constantly come in conflict with it. In particular, experienced computer users may feel themselves shackled by the system. Many of the DOS commands and software utilities they use to great advantage cannot be allowed within a security system. And exceptionally heavy demands may be made on the system manager, who must struggle to find a balance between security and productivity.

CHAPTER 6

Organizing Your Files

As file after file is added to a hard disk, a sort of data sprawl engulfs the directory tree. Long-forgotten subdirectories lie like ghost towns on the outskirts of the disk. Directory listings scroll on and on, filled with cryptic file names that made perfect sense when they were chosen, but not six months later. The root directory becomes a home to oddball files that fit nowhere else, gradually filling with hundreds of listings.

Amidst this chaos, trying to find a long-lost file can be a nightmare, particularly if you remember the file only by its contents and not its name. You may need to move from directory branch to branchlet to twig to twiglet, trying to keep track of which subdirectories you have covered. Within each directory you may have to look into scores of files. Multiple versions of files can deepen the confusion. And even after the file has been found, six months hence it will be just as lost again.

This sort of confusion is *the norm*. Few people take the time to set up a directory tree properly and to periodically "clean house" and catalog files. When a hard disk fills, half of it's bulk may be deadwood. But the more disorderly the disk, the harder the task of deleting superfluous files. When many people share a machine, this level of disorganization truly *begs* for disaster.

It takes time to manage files. Like backups, file maintenance is a process no one likes, because it bestows no immediately perceptible rewards. But you'll find that much less time is required to manage files than to recover from the consequences of not managing them. Equipped with the proper software utilities, it takes little effort to keep a disk in order. And you'll enjoy some hidden benefits: DOS is easier to use on a properly organized disk, and software may run more quickly.

Getting Organized

An orderly disk grows out of a well-conceived directory tree structure, good habits in file placement, and periodic housecleanings. When many people use a machine, the system can be maintained only through careful surveillance and thorough training.

There are a number of tried-and-true rules for disk organization, but there is no "best" way. The ideal scheme varies by many factors, including work habits, the number of people using the machine, the sophistication of the users (particularly their skill with DOS), the peculiarities of the software in use, the availability of disk space, and the system used to back up the disk. It's important to look ahead to the time when the disk fills and to have concrete plans for expansion to a second hard disk.

If you work with a much-used hard disk, you may find that hardly any of the rules have been followed. Indeed, your disk may be so chaotic that the best way to reorder it is by backing up all files, reformatting the disk, and starting all over. (If you do go to this extreme, be sure to make a thorough, *double* backup so that no data is endangered.) You won't regret the time invested in a major renovation.

These days, file management is greatly aided by software tools, including special-purpose utilities for specific tasks, such as cataloging files, and general-purpose file management programs, including DOS shells and operating environments like Microsoft Windows. In this chapter (and the next) we'll be giving a good deal of attention to using the features these programs provide.

Designing the Directory Tree

After only a year of use, the typical hard disk is frequently a sorry sight. Some users christen a newly-formatted disk by dumping the entire contents of the original DOS diskettes into the root directory—a mistake easily avoided by using the DOS installation program. Then subdirectories are created for the major programs that will be used—a *WordPerfect* subdirectory, a *Lotus 1-2-3* subdirectory, and so on. Sometimes, all files on all diskettes that accompany these programs are just poured into the respective subdirectories. Data files created by these programs quickly become intermixed with the program files themselves. Batch files, keyboard macro files, and various configuration files come to be scattered all over the disk, and utilities end up in odd places— often in the root directory—sometimes in whatever directory was current when the utility was first required and transferred to the hard disk.

What's wrong with this state of affairs? Just about everything. Megabytes of disk space can be wasted. DOS is slowed. Work is disorganized. Individual files are hard to find. Batch files won't work. Cataloging and maintaining the disk is made much more difficult.

We don't claim to know the ultimate system for hard disk organization, but there are some rules that are worth following until you know your own work habits so well that you can think of a better way of doing things. These are the principles that most consultants would impose on your hard disk—with good reason. Religiously followed, they ward off confusion that costs minutes every day, and hours every month. More important, they help avert the kinds of disasters that can cost you *weeks* of time. We'll step through them one by one.

Rule 1

Reserve the root directory for subdirectory listings. The root directory should serve as the master index to the directory tree. It is not a place from which to run programs, not a place to keep utilities, and most certainly not a place to store data files. The only files that belong there are COMMAND.COM, AUTOEXEC.BAT, and CONFIG.SYS—the files required to boot the machine. Ideally, the entire contents of the root directory can be displayed on a single screen.

Some users invoke COMMAND.COM from their \DOS directory instead of the root directory. If you want to do this, just make this the first line of your CONFIG.SYS file:

```
SHELL= C:\DOS\COMMAND.COM /P
```

However, since certain programs expect COMMAND.COM to be in the root directory, it's a good idea to leave a copy there. And, CONFIG.SYS and AUTOEXEC.BAT must remain in the root directory.

Many people place device drivers (utilities that run special hardware) in the root directory, since they are called for when the machine boots. The root directory is also a tempting place for utility programs that are listed in AUTOEXEC.BAT and started up during booting. These include any number of memory-resident utilities, such as an address book, keyboard macro program, or whatever. Any of these programs can be placed in other subdirectories. You'll find, however, that some utilities will create files in the root directory that can't be moved elsewhere.

Problems

When device drivers are located in the root directory, three problems arise. First, your root directory can no longer act as a single-screen "table of contents" for the disk. Second, all file searches are made longer, since DOS will scan the directory entries for these seldom-used files during every file request. And third, the utilities themselves may be separated from related files, making it harder to replace them with more recent versions.

Say that you're using a memory-resident program called *HyperZap*. You're far better off keeping the *HyperZap* program, **HYPERZAP.COM**, in a subdirectory with all other *HyperZap* files, say **\UTIL\HZ**. Then you can load the program by writing:

```
\UTIL\HZ\HYPERZAP
```

in AUTOEXEC.BAT. When you upgrade to a a new *HyperZap* version, you can easily erase all the old files and just as easily transfer all the new ones to the hard disk. This principle applies to all kinds of files, including device drivers loaded by CONFIG.SYS. To load the driver *ANSI.SYS*, which is a DOS utility that should rightfully reside along with other DOS files in the **\DOS** subdirectory, you'd include in CONFIG.SYS a line like:

```
DEVICE=C:\DOS\ANSI.SYS
```

Rule 2

Make the tree broad and shallow. It's tempting to create a grandiose logical design for the directory tree, subdividing files into categories, subcategories, sub-subcategories, and so on. (We'll refer to the first level of subdirectories below the root directory as *level-1 subdirectories*; they, in turn, are parent to *level-2 subdirectories*.) The result is a tree that reaches down five levels or more. There's a certain pleasure in the logical elegance, but it's outweighed by two drawbacks. First, you'll be forced to enter long path names repeatedly for many DOS commands, particularly the ones that are used most often. Not only is the extra typing tiresome, but you're much more likely to make mistakes.

The second drawback in many-leveled directory trees is that DOS takes longer to find files. To find a file five levels down, DOS must consult every subdirectory in between, which means that the hard disk's read/write heads must shuttle back and forth across the disk surface to the various subdirectory files. In addition, time is spent scanning the subdirectory entries until the listing for the subdirectory is found. For many kinds of applications, this may not be a major drawback. But programs that constantly open and close files may be slowed when the files are located deep in the directory tree. This inefficiency can be partially overcome, however, and we'll attack the problem in Chapter 7.

The Usual Recommendations

Our first suggestion was that the root directory should hold mostly subdirectory entries so that it acts as a "Table of Contents" for the disk. Some people recommend that level-one subdirectories should also contain mostly references to other subdirectories, and only a few files. In this system, level-one subdirectories should contain only program files (and certain auxiliary files). Data is kept in level-two subdirectories, as are utility programs for the software. Figure 6-1 shows this scheme.

Drawbacks

This approach has two drawbacks. First, it means that you'll repeatedly need to type paths containing at least two subdirectories. More important, your work becomes classified by the kind of software that works on it. Spreadsheets and database reports related to the same project end up in separate subdirectories belonging to the spreadsheet and database programs. This makes little sense.

Most software can get to any file in any subdirectory, so there's no technical necessity for this organization.

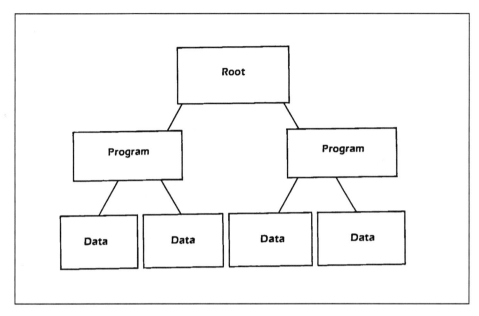

Figure 6-1. A conventional directory tree

As you gain experience with more and more software, your projects are likely to use files produced by various programs. For example, if you're busy writing a business report, you may have word processing files, outliner files, spread-sheet files, image files, and desktop publishing files, all of which will be combined in the final product. It makes no sense to have these files distributed to separate subdirectories residing under those holding the software that creates them, as shown in Figure 6-2.

Our Recommendation

Instead, subdirectories should be organized by project, and these should be placed immediately below the root directory. Files that are subsidiary to the project belong in subdirectories below those. Each software package ought to have its own subdirectory, also just below the root directory, as shown in Figure 6-3.

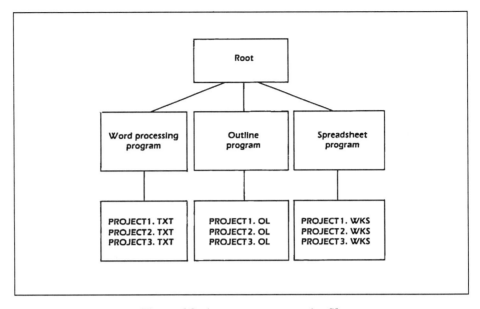

Figure 6-2. A poor way to organize files

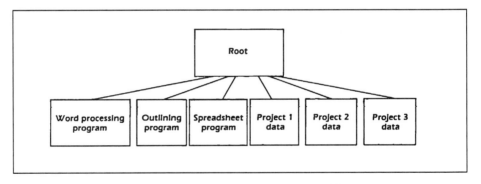

Figure 6-3. A better way to organize files

In fact, you may want to push software entirely out of the way. After all, your work centers around your data. The software that operates on it can be thought of as a plumbing system that ought to be kept as inconspicuous as possible. In this case, the tree diagram would look like that shown in Figure 6-4.

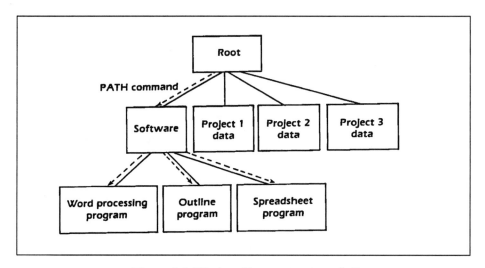

Figure 6-4. The best file organization of all

In this design, the root directory lists nothing but projects—except for the **SOFTWARE** subdirectory, which leads you into the basement where all the pipes and wires reside. You may complain that, in this scheme, the user is forced to type a long path everytime a program is loaded. But the DOS PATH command can be set up so that DOS can find a program file on its own, no matter the current directory (PATH was discussed in Chapter 5). By following this directory plan, you can keep all related files together, you can get at any program from any place, any program can get to any file in any place, and you seldom need to enter a DOS path that contains more than one subdirectory.

Rule 3

Build as much of the tree as you can before transferring files. DOS doesn't let you make changes in the directory tree easily. For reasons of efficiency and flexibility, it's a good idea to build as much of the tree as you can when the disk is freshly formatted. By doing so, you ensure that the subdirectories are compacted in a few cylinders near the outside of the disk; this makes for faster access. It also ensures that child directories will be the topmost entries in a directory listing. This approach lets DOS find files more quickly, since less time is spent scanning directories. (Chapter 7 tells how to make this optimization on an older disk in which subdirectory files are scattered.)

Rule 4

Create many small subdirectories. This suggestion amounts to saying, "Keep directory listings short." Subdirectories containing 100 files or more take a long time to search. On average, DOS would have to pass over 50 files before it finds the one it wants. It's also hard to scan a long subdirectory and grasp its contents. This is true even when you have a DOS shell at your disposal for scrolling the directory up and down.

Short directories are especially valuable when it comes time to clean house. You can quickly see what is new and what is old, and you're less likely to make deletions you'll later regret. You're also more likely to delete files at the time they become obsolete, since you can more easily spot them, and can more readily be sure that it's all right to delete them.

Rule 5

Use short directory names. Short subdirectory names are best. Drop as many syllables from the end of the word as you can while still being able to decipher the meaning. For example, a subdirectory called **UTILITY** is shortened to **UTIL** with little danger of confusion, since the word "utility" naturally comes to mind when you see "util." But substituting **CONT** for **CONTRACT** is riskier, since lots of words begin with "cont."

Avoid reducing long phrases to complex mnemonics. It's fun to decide that **NWOMRMC** should stand for "New Wave Outer-Mongolian Ragtime Music Criticism," but you won't remember it easily, and the fastest touch typist will slow to a snail's pace when entering it. It's better to create mnemonics that capture the essence of a subdirectory's contents: **MONGRAG**. Incidentally, you'll find it easier to remember names, and to type them, if you leave the vowels in.

Subdirectory Name Extensions

Many people are unaware that subdirectory names may be given three-character extensions, just like file names. For example, if you're working on the Great American Novel, you could create a subdirectory called **NOVELS**, and it could hold subdirectories called **AMERNOVL.CH1**, **AMERNOVL.CH2**, **AMERNOVL.CH3**, and so on—one subdirectory for each chapter. It's easy to think up grandiose schemes for classifying subdirectories in this way, but generally it's not a good idea. File paths are hard enough to type and read without inserting periods, as in:

```
NOVELS\AMERNOVL.CH2\NOTES.OLD\GARBAGE.OUT\BADIDEAS.TXT
```

There is one situation in which extensions for subdirectory names come in handy. Say that you name all subdirectories that contain Lotus *1-2-3* spreadsheets with the extension .**123**, such as **PROJECT1.123**, **PROJECT2.123**, and so on. You can quickly get a listing of all *1-2-3* subdirectories through a normal wildcard search: **DIR *.123**. However, this is an awfully small benefit for the extra typing you must do each time you enter a path to one of the subdirectories.

Rule 6

Don't give files the same names as subdirectories. Take care not to give matching names to files and to the subdirectories that hold them. DOS does a good job of keeping them straight, but you may become confused about whether a particular DOS command will operate on the subdirectory or the file. For example, if the current directory contains both a file named WP.TXT and a subdirectory named WP, the command **DIR WP** results in a listing of all files in the subdirectory WP; it doesn't search for files named WP in the current directory. DOS would have no trouble opening the file WP.TXT if a program requires it, so there is no true danger in crossing file and subdirectory names. But the practice is best avoided to keep things clear.

Rule 7

Keep utility software in one place. A common subdirectory is the *utility* subdirectory, often named **UTIL** or **UTILITY**. As your system grows, you'll acquire many software utilities. In addition, you'll find that many expansion boards are accompanied by a diskette that holds software used with the board, such as a RAM disk utility, a print spooler, or a head-parking utility. You may also have device drivers for a mouse or other input device, for an expanded memory board, and so on. Another class of utilities are disk maintenance tools, like disk cachers or defragmenters, which we'll discuss in Chapter 7. All of these should be kept in a common "tool shed" where you'll be able to quickly find them.

If you own an extensive tool kit, like *The Norton Utilities*, its files may be kept together in their own subdirectory placed below the general UTIL subdirectory. The installation program will let you place the subdirectory (or subdirectories) wherever you like. Don't mix utility packages in one subdirectory; software houses sometimes use the same file names, so confusion may result.

Unless you've gobs of open disk space, you shouldn't blindly copy over all files on utility diskettes to subdirectories on the hard disk. You'll find that much utility software is tailored for special needs you'll never confront. You example, you don't need drivers for a laser printer if you don't own one. Move what you need to the hard disk, and no more.

Rule 8

Create a subdirectory exclusively for DOS files. Create a subdirectory named **DOS** in the root directory and keep DOS files there. Then be sure to include the subdirectory in a PATH command (described in Chapter 5) so that DOS can find it no matter what the current directory. This approach lets you easily replace all DOS files when upgrading to a more recent DOS version—a task handled by the DOS installation program. Some users who don't know about the PATH command keep copies of certain DOS files in many subdirectories so that commands like XCOPY and CHKDSK will be on hand without typing a long DOS path. Not only does this approach waste disk space, it makes it more difficult to track down all old DOS files when replacing them with new ones.

Confronted with a new hard disk, some people dump the entire contents of the DOS diskettes into the root directory. As we explained above, the root directory should have almost no files at all. Unfortunately, some older DOS manuals actually instruct the reader to copy files to the root directory. It's not a good idea.

Many of the dozens of files held on the DOS diskettes have no business being on your hard disk at all. Of these, some may be of no value, such as an expanded memory driver in a machine that has no expanded memory. Other utilities would seem to be better placed in the UTIL subdirectory, (such as the RAM disk program, *VDISK or RAMDRIVE*), but they are better left with the

DOS files so that they can be easily updated. There's something to be said for having all DOS files on the hard disk so that they'll be on hand as you learn to use new commands. But, once you understand what the individual programs do, you can save a few hundred kilobytes of disk space by deleting the useless ones. Recent DOS versions include an installation program that prevents unnecessary files from being installed on your hard disk.

Rule 9

Keep batch files in one subdirectory. Just as the files for external DOS commands need to be on line from any directory on the disk, many batch files need universal access. For example, you may create a file called NOTES.BAT that changes the current directory to the NOTES directory and starts up a cardfile program. If NOTES.BAT is located in the BATCH subdirectory, and AUTOEXEC.BAT contains a PATH statement that includes this subdirectory, then you can type NOTES and be instantly conveyed to note taking no matter what the current directory. A system of batch files lets you readily change tasks without lots of typing.

Some batch files process files *within* a single subdirectory, and it might seem more natural to place them there. Sometimes this is a good idea, but there's much to be said for keeping all in one subdirectory. By doing so, you can survey the entire system easily. If changes are made in the tree structure, it's much easier to perform surgery on the files, since seldom-used batch files won't be overlooked.

Rule 10

Transfer to disk only the program files you need. When you acquire new software, you're often confronted with many disks full of unidentified files, sometimes amounting to two or three megabytes. That's 10 percent of a 20- or 30-megabyte disk. Usually about half of this amount can safely remain on the diskettes. Tutorials don't need to be on the hard disk; if moved to the disk, they should be removed once you're finished with them. Also, you'll need only one or two of the dozens of printer drivers that are commonly supplied with software. Don't fill your disk with them. No matter how small, each file will take up at least two kilobytes because of the minimum cluster allocation.

These days, virtually all large application programs are shipped with an installation program that will ask you questions about your system and then select the appropriate files for you. Always use this program when available. These programs are good at keeping unnecessary device drivers off your disk, but they may still introduce many files that you have no use for. Keep an eye out for files that contain data samples and templates. For example, some graphics programs may transfer large image files to your hard disk just to show off the program's capabilities. When you encounter files of this nature, take a look at them, learn what there is to learn, and then get them off your disk. You can always transfer them over to the disk later if you need them.

Rule 11

Make dangerous files hard to get to. On most machines, the most dangerous file is **FORMAT.COM**, which can accidentally be invoked to reformat a hard disk or diskette. (In Chapter 9 we'll discuss utilities that "unformat" an accidentally reformatted disk). If people will be using a computer who do not understand it well, it's a good idea to keep them away from this command, and thus from the file that carries it out. Other programs that can have disastrous consequences are low-level formatting programs, the DOS FDISK and RECOVER programs, and utilities that can graft or erase entire directory tree branches. It makes sense to keep these programs off the disk. But the DOS FORMAT program needs to be present so that you can format diskettes.

One way of keeping FORMAT.COM and other dangerous files out of the way is by making them hard to find. *Don't* keep them with other DOS files in the **DOS** subdirectory, where they can be easily called through the PATH command. Instead, place them in their own subdirectory listed in the DOS directory.

An even better way of hiding the FORMAT program is to rename it and call it from within a batch file. Say that you rename the program as **F.COM**. Then you can make a batch file named **FORMAT.BAT** that contains the single line **F A:**. When the batch file is called, it runs the FORMAT program, always directing it to drive A.

If you're *really* worried about accidental formatting, the safest procedure of all is to keep the program off the hard disk. Simply format all new diskettes when purchased (or buy them preformatted—it's only about ten cents more per diskette). In a business office, the original DOS diskettes, like all originals, can then be locked up by the system manager. Alternatively, delete FORMAT.COM from the disk and introduce a utility that formats disks safely. For instance, the *Safe Format* program in *The Norton Utilities* normally won't allow you to accidentally format a hard disk, and prior to formatting a diskette it saves crucial information on the diskette so that it can be unformatted if a mistake is made. We'll discuss these issues further in Chapter 9.

Viewing and Cataloging the Directory Tree

As a directory tree grows, it becomes ever more difficult to remember its structure. If you want to access a file three or four levels deep in the tree, and you can't remember the name or exact spelling of each subdirectory along the way, you've got to search along the path until to find the right words to type into your commands. What should be one command can become a dozen as you enter a succession of DIR and CHDIR commands.

Directory **tree diagrams** partially overcome this difficulty by showing the tree structure as an easily understood diagram. Figure 6.5 portrays a typical tree diagram. In DOS Versions 4.0 and later, a DOS command can display such a diagram, but the diagram cannot be scrolled up and down, greatly reducing its usefulness. Alternatively, utilities like the *NCD* (*Norton Change Directory*) program can provide a scrollable tree. Tree diagrams are at the heart of any DOS shell, including the *File Manager* in Microsoft *Windows*. They not only shown the tree structure, but allow you—to varying degrees—to perform DOS commands by referring to the tree instead of typing DOS paths.

Tree diagrams only partially help you around the difficulties of navigating directory trees because they operate outside of application software. Few applications include their own directory tree for searching for data files used by the program, and if you can't remember the path to a file, you must quit the program to search for it, or call up a memory-resident utility that displays a tree diagram. Only a true operating environment like *Windows* lets you more-or-less instantly move back and forth between tree and application.

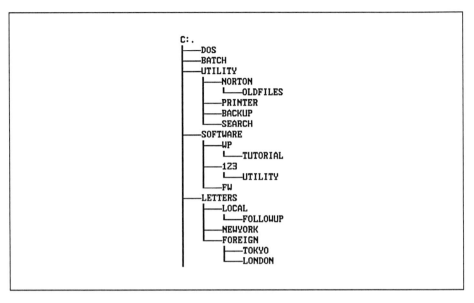

Figure 6-5. A typical tree diagram

The DOS TREE Command

Without the aid of a DOS shell, such as the one shipped with DOS 4.0 or 5.0, keeping track of the directory tree structure can be a nightmare. You can waste much time trying to find a particular subdirectory in a large tree, or worse, trying to find a particular file whose subdirectory you've forgotten. DOS shells can solve many problems by displaying a tree diagram and letting you obtain a file listing for each directory in turn with only a keystroke or two. But even without a shell program, there are some clumsy techniques for viewing directory trees. DOS includes the TREE command for obtaining a comprehensive listing of every subdirectory on a disk drive. In DOS 4.0 and 5.0, a graphical tree diagram, like the one shown in Figure 5.12, is displayed by the command. But in earlier DOS versions, TREE only displays the path to each subdirectory and a listing of all subdirectories it contains. For example:

```
Path:  \MAMMALS\FELINES
Subdirectories:   LIONS
   TIGERS
   CHEETAHS
```

Such listings are displayed in succession, starting from the root directory. All subdirectories of a branch of the tree are shown before going on to subdirectories in the next branch. Thus, after the root directory, you are shown the first subdirectory listed in the root directory, the first subdirectory listed in that subdirectory, and so on. If you want to view a tree diagram in DOS 3.3 or earlier, you need to use a DOS shell or some other utility software.

TREE is an external DOS command, meaning that it resides in its own file named **TREE.COM.** When that file is in the current directory, or is made available via a PATH command, all you need to do to have the tree for drive C displayed is to enter:

```
TREE   C:
```

This command works with DOS Versions 3.3 and earlier. The command always displays data for an entire tree and thus require nothing more than a drive specifier. In DOS 4.0 or 5.0, however, you should include a directory path. Since a lone backslash represents the root directory, you can display an entire tree in DOS 4.0 with the command:

```
TREE   C:\
```

Specifying a subdirectory, as in:

```
TREE   C:\AQUATIC\MAMMALS
```

results in a partial tree display consisting of only the directory MAMMALS and all subdirectories beyond it.

Listing Files

In any DOS version, TREE can also list the files contained in each subdirectory. Add the **/F** switch to the end of the command:

```
TREE   C:   /F
```

or, in DOS 4.0 or 5.0:

```
TREE   C:\   /F
```

The name of each file is displayed on its own line, with no information about size and date as in an ordinary directory listing. This feature makes the TREE listing much longer.

Printing Tree Listings

It's often convenient to print out the tree listing since the displayed data can't be scrolled up and down on the screen. To do this, just append **>LPT1** ("Line Printer #1") to the command:

```
TREE   C: >LPT1
```

or, in DOS 4.0:

```
TREE   C:\ >LPT1
```

In DOS 4.0, the diagram is drawn on the screen using graphic characters to form lines and corners. Most printers will substitute unrelated characters when the diagram is printed. You can have TREE replace the graphic characters with more presentable ones by adding **/A** to the command:

```
TREE   C:\   /A   >LPT1
```

Cataloging the Directory Tree

Even with a tree diagram in view, it's sometimes hard to track down files because subdirectory names may be too short to communicate a subdirectory's contents. What's needed is an *annotated* tree diagram bearing descriptive labels for each subdirectory. You can create one of these with little effort by making the TREE command write the tree data to a disk file instead of to the screen. Thereafter, you can load the file into your word processor and view it as you would any document, adding labels to the listing as you please.

The tree data is sent to a file by appending the symbol **>** to the command, followed by the name of the file that will hold the data. For example, to place the tree data for drive C in a file named **TREEDATA**, type:

```
TREE C:   >TREEDATA
```

or, in DOS 4.0 and later:

```
TREE C:\   >TREEDATA
```

As always, you can add a path to the directory where you want the file saved. Once the tree data is in a file, it can be loaded into any text editor or word processor and scrolled up and down. Add descriptive labels after each line of the diagram. Be aware that many word processors won't display the graphic characters used by the DOS 4.0 variation of TREE, so it may be a good idea to use the /**A** switch mentioned earlier.

If you use a version of DOS earlier than 4.0, you can use your word processor to pare down and modify the diagram it creates. Most let you delete an entire line with a single keystroke. Keeping one hand over that key, and the other over the down arrow key, you can quickly eliminate unwanted lines from the file. Then print it out as you would any document. The diagram will also be on hand for a quick look via the DOS TYPE command:

```
TYPE   \DOS\TREEDATA
```

Of course, later changes in your directory tree won't be reflected in this diagram. If you use the TREE command to create an updated file, earlier annotations in the file will be wiped out. Happily, most trees don't change very much once they are well-established. Just get in the habit of modifying the tree diagram file with your word processor whenever you use MKDIR or RMDIR to alter the tree.

Viewing, Sorting, and Printing Directory Listings

DOS's DIR command is the first command that many computer novices learn, but many don't realize how flexible it is. All too often, people look for a file in a directory just by typing **DIR** and then scanning the directory listing for the file. There's no need for all this eye strain, since DIR can look for just the one file. To search for the file, **WHATSIT.TXT**, enter:

```
DIR WHATSIT.TXT
```

Of course, you can use global file name characters ("wildcard characters") to look for groups of files. To find all files beginning with the letters "SE," type:

```
DIR SE*
```

Use the question mark when you want to match characters within file names. For instance, if you have a series of files named **CHAPTER1**, **CHAPTER2...CHAPTER9**, you can view them together by the command:

```
DIR CHAPTER?
```

DIR Switches

When you're not sure of the file name and need to scan the entire directory, use the /W switch, which causes DOS to display only file names—without file dates, times, and sizes—in a five-column format that fits many more file names on a screen:

```
DIR   /W
```

When there are more files in a directory than can be shown, use the /P switch with the command. This switch makes DOS stop after each screenful of file names is displayed, so that you have time to view it. Press any key to move on to the next screen, or Ctrl-break to cut the command short and return to the DOS prompt. For example:

```
DIR   /W   /P
```

DOS 5.0 DIR switches

DOS 5.0 adds four switches to the DIR command, two for customizing directory listings, and two that greatly increase the command's power. The /B and /L switches let you tailor the appearance of listings. Writing /B in the command causes DIR to omit the information it adds at the top and bottom of listings: the volume label, the number of files, and so on. This feature is useful when you want to keep all of a short directory listing on screen at once. The /L switch causes the listing to be displayed in lowercase letters.

The /A (for "attributes") switch gives you complete control over the kinds of files displayed, including the *hidden* and *system* files that the command will omit if this switch is not used. The switch is followed by a colon and then one or more symbols for the kinds of files you want listed, with no spaces placed between the symbols. For example, to view only hidden files, you would write:

```
DIR /A:H
```

The other symbols include **S** for system files, **D** for subdirectories, **A** for "archived" files (those with the archive bit set for backups), and **R** for read-only files. You could view both hidden and system files by the command:

```
DIR /A:HS
```

Any of these symbols may be preceeded by a minus sign to indicate that you want to see all files *except* those the symbol represents. To list all files, but not subdirectories, you'd enter:

```
DIR /A:-D
```

Finally, DOS 5.0 endows DIR with the ability to search multiple directories. This is done by the /**S** switch, which is familiar from certain other DOS commands, such as XCOPY and ATTRIB. When /**S** is used, DOS searches not only the specified directory, but all directories beyond it. In this way, DIR can search an entire branch of the directory tree, or the entire tree when the root directory is specified. To search all of drive C for the file COMEHERE.DOC, enter:

```
DIR C:\COMEHERE.DOC /S
```

Scanning Parallel Subdirectories

Another common waste of effort occurs when applying DIR to a succession of subdirectories. Many people will first make the directory the current one, and then enter a simple DIR command, as in:

```
CHDIR  \MAMMALS\AQUATIC\SEALS
DIR   SAYWHAT.DOC
CHDIR \MAMMALS\AQUATIC\WHALES
DIR   SAYWHAT.DOC
CHDIR \MAMMALS\AQUATIC\DOLPHINS
DIR   SAYWHAT.DOC
```

It's less work to write the directory path into each DIR command:

```
DIR \MAMMALS\AQUATIC\SEALS\SAYWHAT.DOC
DIR \MAMMALS\AQUATIC\WHALES\SAYWHAT.DOC
DIR \MAMMALS\AQUATIC\DOLPHINS\SAYWHAT.DOC
```

When you wanted to look for SAYWHAT.DOC in a parallel directory without changing the current directory and without typing a full directory path, you could use the "double dot" (..) symbol. It represents the entire path up the current directory. If the current directory is \MAMMALS\AQUATICS\SEALS, then you could search the parallel \MAMMALS\AQUATIC\WHALES directory by entering:

```
DIR ..\WHALES\SAYWHAT.DOC
```

Sorting Directory Listings

Sometimes it's useful to sort directory listings to help you find files. Perhaps you can't remember an exact file name but remember that it begins with an "A". DOS 5.0 makes it especially easy to sort directory listings: the /**O** switch in a DIR command does all the work for you. The command

```
DIR /O
```

lists all subdirectories, sorted alphabetically, followed by all files (also sorted alphabetically).

```
DIR /O:N
```

sorts by name (N). Instead of **N**, specify **E** for extension, **D** for date and time, or **S** for size. For reversed sorts, place a minus sign before the letter. Here are some more examples:

`DIR ./O:-N`	Sorts in reverse alphabetical order by name
`DIR /O:E`	Sorts alphabetically by extension
`DIR /O:-D`	Sorts in reverse order by date (newest first)
`DIR /O:S`	Sorts by size (smallest first)
`DIR /O:-G`	Groups files before directories
`DIR /O:E-D`	Sorts by extension (files with same extension appear newest first)

Note that several kinds of sorts can be combined, as in the last example.

Sorting In Older Versions of DOS

If you don't have DOS 5, don't despair; you can use the DOS SORT filter (SORT.EXE) to achieve similar results. Keep SORT.EXE in the DOS sub-directory and access it through a PATH command. This approach makes it available for any directory. SORT just sorts directory *listings*, not the directories themselves. The listing returns to its haphazard state when SORT is no longer applied. (In Chapter 7 we'll discuss utilities that actually sort directories on disk.)

To sort a listing's file names alphabetically, just enter:

```
DIR | SORT
```

Add an /R switch to reverse the sort so that it runs from "Z" to "A":

```
DIR  |  SORT  /R
```

Files may be sorted by extension with the command

```
DIR | SORT /+10
```

or by size with the command

```
DIR | SORT /+13
```

Unfortunately, the SORT filter won't sort dates or times correctly—at least not when they're expressed in the usual American format. SORT *will* work correctly on these fields if you use the COUNTRY= command (in CONFIG.SYS) to make DOS write dates and times using the conventions of certain countries (such as Sweden). But making this change can cause incompatibilities with other software, so it's not a good idea to do it.

Sorting In the DOS 4.0/5.0 Shell

The DOS Shell program that accompanies DOS versions 4.0 and later always sorts directory listings alphabetically by name. You can change the criterion for sorting by pulling down the *Options* menu once you have entered the file system. Choose *Display Options* from the menu. The resulting dialog box offers five sorting methods, as Figure 6.6 shows. The dialog box disappears as soon as you make a selection and the current directory listing is resorted. Notice that the last choice, *Disk order*, stands for the unsorted ordering found in normal DOS directory listings.

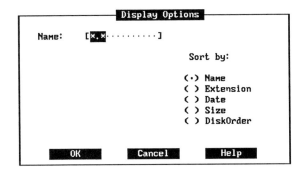

Figure 6-6. The DOS Shell dialog box for sorting files.

Sorting in Windows 3.0

In Windows, once a directory listing is in view, pull down the *View* menu and choose *Sort* by. The dialog box in Figure 6.7 will appear, showing the sort options. Choose an option by clicking your mouse on it, or by moving the cursor with the up arrow and down arrow keys and then pressing Enter. The directory listing is sorted once a selection is made.

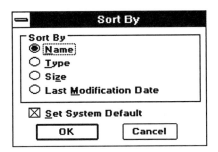

Figure 6-7. The Windows dialog box for sorting files.

Viewing and Printing Files

The cryptic file names used by DOS mean that you'll often need to look into old files to see what they contain. The best way to examine a file's contents is to load it into the software that created it. But this approach may be inefficient when you're searching through dozens of files. The software will probably load the entire file into memory and process it before showing it to you. It's much quicker to use a DOS command or utility to display the file. This is easily done with simple text files, which are readily displayed and understood. But data files for software like spreadsheets, databases, and outliners are filled with gobbledygook that only programmers can understand (and then only with great effort).

The TYPE Command

It's important to be able to view groups of files quickly. Sometimes you'll need to search through many to find the one you want. It's also useful to be able to browse through files while doing periodic housekeeping on a hard disk. The DOS TYPE command is a quick way of looking into files. You merely enter something like:

```
TYPE WHOSIT.TXT
```

or, using a DOS path:

```
TYPE \PRIMATES\HUMANS\WHOSIT.TXT
```

and the contents of **WHOSIT.TXT** is displayed, scrolling upward when the screen fills. The TYPE command reads straight through from the beginning to the end of the file. It reads only a bit of the file, displays it, and goes on reading more as scrolling continues; this means you can't scroll backwards.

The data is written as fast as DOS can manage, so when many short lines or empty lines occur in a row, the screen suddenly scrolls very quickly—too quickly to view. You can make TYPE pause after displaying each screen by appending |**MORE** to the command:

```
TYPE DATAFILE |MORE
```

Striking any key moves you on to the next screen. Instead, if you're quick, you can temporarily stop the scrolling by typing Pause (or Ctrl-NumLock on older keyboards); again, display continues when you strike any key. Ctrl-Break interrupts the TYPE command and returns you to the DOS prompt.

Limitations of the TYPE Command

Many kinds of data files resist inspection by the TYPE command. You need to understand a little about how files are constructed to understand why. All files consist of a string of bytes, where each byte holds a value from 0 to 255. When the sequence of bytes is displayed on the screen, each value from 0 to 255 is represented as its corresponding **ASCII character**, an arbitrarily assigned symbol from the ASCII standard. For example, the value **65** is represented as **A**, and the value **97** is **a**.

The uppercase and lowercase letters, plus numerals and punctuation marks, make up less than a third of the character set. Many of the remaining values are assigned to special European language characters, and to the box-graphic characters used to frame information on the screen. But some values have a special status. The lowest 32 characters, numbers 0 - 31, are treated by DOS as **control codes**. When DOS encounters certain control codes as it writes data on the screen, it interprets them as a command. For example, Character 9 causes DOS to tab the cursor, and character 13 brings about a "carriage return." Most control codes are not interpreted as commands, but instead are sometimes displayed as a two-character symbol like **^A** or **^B**. There are also single-character symbols associated with these codes, but DOS does not display them.

Impact of Control Codes

If you use the DOS TYPE command to examine an ordinary text file, the document scrolls before your eyes much as if it were viewed in the word processor that created it. These files contain control codes, but only those for tabs, carriage returns, and line feeds (in combination, the latter two end a paragraph and send the cursor to the beginning of the line below). But many programs insert other codes into files, whether command codes or special graphics characters. For example, a word processor might insert values before and after words that are to be italicized. When the word processor displays the information, it strips out the special characters so that only written text is seen. But when the DOS TYPE command displays the file, it is not privy to the special coding scheme for italics, so it just displays the special characters as if they were text.

Certain codes cause funny things to happen on the display. The cursor jumps around, writing the file here and there. The screen may suddenly clear. It becomes quite impossible to read the file. Another oddity is that DOS "beeps" the system speaker when it encounters character 7. This value represents the "normal" white-on-black color used to display characters, and some files contain many instances of this character; if you use TYPE to display such a file, the speaker beeps endlessly. Finally, when the TYPE command finds character 26 in a text file, it interprets it as an "end-of-file" marker, and it stops writing data on the screen. Often you'll find that if you use TYPE to display a very large file, it will display only a few lines and then abruptly halts. It has encountered character 26.

We've explained this phenomenon because it may interfere with your attempts to look into files to find the data you're searching for. Most word processor files are easily examined, but not all are. Some modify every character in the file, making it appear as nothing but gobbledygook. Most non-text files, such as spreadsheet files or outliner files, are filled with graphic characters and control codes that make it difficult to view the file. Program files are the extreme case; they present total nonsense when viewed by the TYPE command. But since there's no need to look into program files, this should be no problem. Still, you should know that when you look into an unidentified file that displays only gibberish, then the file probably contains code (program files always end with .COM or .EXE, but extra code may be stashed away in files that do not have these file name extensions). Incidentally, just because program files may be displayed as a series of random characters, you shouldn't think that program files are a kind of text file. They're made of a series of numbers, many of which are two or more bytes long, but DOS *displays* the numbers as sequences of ASCII characters.

Utility Software

The DOS TYPE command has become less useful as software has grown more complex. Today, few major programs keep data in simple ASCII text files. Often, to track down a missing file, you must start the program that created it and load one file after another until you find the one you're seeking. A DOS shell can do the job much more quickly by providing a library of filters for viewing particular kinds of data files. *The Norton Commander*, for example, has filters for all major word processors, databases, and spreadsheet programs. It can display their data files just as the data appears in the programs themselves—spreadsheet files look like spreadsheets, and so on. *The Commander* can also create or edit plain text files.

The DOS 4.0/5.0 Shell

To view a file in the Shell program that accompanies DOS 4.0, enter the *File System* and select a file (only one file can be viewed at a time). Then pull down the *File* menu and select *View*. A window opens to display the file, as Figure 6.8 shows. You can scroll the file up and down using the Page up and Page down keys (a mouse won't work). By pressing <F9>, the text may be displayed in an alternate form in which the characters are represented by code numbers. This feature is useful for computer programmers. In either case, the text can't be edited. Press Esc (or click on the Esc symbol) to return to the File System.

```
┌──────────────────────────────────────────────────────────────────────────┐
│                            File Manager                                     │
│  Help                                                                       │
│  ┌───────────────────────────────────────────────────────────────────┐    │
│  │                          File View                                  │    │
│  │                                                                     │    │
│  │   To view a file's content press PgUp or PgDn.                      │    │
│  │                                                                ▓    │    │
│  │   Viewing file:   C:\SAMPLES\PROSE.DOC                              │    │
│  │                                                                     │    │
│  │                                                                     │    │
│  └───────────────────────────────────────────────────────────────────┘    │
└──────────────────────────────────────────────────────────────────────────┘
```

When spring drew round, and with it the cold weather, during an icy Lent and the
  hailstorms of Holy Week, as Mme. Swann began to find it cold in the house, I us
ed often to see her entertaining her guests in her furs, her shivering hands and
 ·shoulders hidden beneath the gleaming white carpet of an immense rectangular mu
ff and a cape, both of ermine, which she had not taken off on coming in from her
 drive, and which suggested the last patches of the snows of winter, more persis
tent than the rest, which neither the heat of the fire nor the advancing season
had succeeded in melting. And the whole truth about these glacial but already f
lowering weeks was suggested to me in this drawing-room, which soon I should be
entering no more, by other more intoxicating forms of whiteness, that for exampl
e of the guelder-roses clustering, at the summits of their tall bare stalks, like
 the rectilinear tress in pre-raphaelite paintings, their balls of blossom, divi
ded yet composite, white as annunciating angels and breathing a fragrance as of
    ↵=Enter Esc=Cancel F9=Hex/ASCII   12:34 am

Figure 6-8. Viewing a file in the DOS Shell.

Windows 3.0

Windows does not provide a simple equivalent to the DOS TYPE command.
You won't find a *Type* selection in the *File* menu of the *File Manager*, although
most common DOS commands are found there. Instead, Windows includes
a complete text editor by which you can not only view plain text files,
but also edit them. The editor is found outside the *File Manager*. Access it by
opening the Accessories icon shown by the *Program Manager* (the window normally displayed when Windows starts up). Choose *Notepad* from among the
accessories, pull down the *File* menu, and select *Open*. You'll be shown a dialog
box in which you enter the file name and directory path. You can have Windows word-wrap the file by selecting *Wordwrap* from the *Edit* menu, as Figure
6.9 shows. If you already have a good word processor at your disposal, you
probably won't want to use the *Notepad* for much more than viewing files.
It's a complicated piece of software. You can learn its editing codes from
the Windows manual, or from the extensive online *Help* system that *Notepad*
provides (just pull down the *Help* menu and select the kind of assistance
you need).

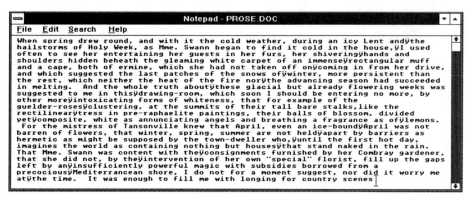

Figure 6-9. Viewing a file in Windows.

Printing Files

Normally, files are printed by the program that creates them. If you have created a file with your word processor, you print it by starting the word processor, loading the file, and using the program's *Print* command. However, there may be occasions when you want to print a file without using an application program. For example, you might find an unidentified text file on a diskette and want a printout. You could probably load the file into your word processor and print it, but it may be easier to have DOS do the job. To print a text-only file named **WHATSIT.TXT**, you'd type:

```
COPY  WHATSIT.TXT  LPT1
```

or:

```
PRINT  WHATSIT.TXT
```

The COPY command works by sending a copy of **WHATSIT.TXT** to a printer instead of to a new disk file. The expression LPT1 at the end of the command specifies that the data will be sent to the first parallel port—the one most printers are connected to. You could instead write PRN for exactly the same effect, or LPT2 if the target printer is hooked up to a second parallel port. Similarly, you may write COM1 in place of LPT1 if the printer is hooked up to serial port #1.

The PRINT command works differently, since it sets up a print spooler in memory to print one or more files "in the background" while you perform other work on the machine. This command does not usually require a specification of which printer port to use. Rather, the port is specified only the first time the command is used by adding a /**D** switch. One way to set the port is to execute an initial PRINT command that does not print a file:

```
PRINT   /D:LPT1
```

Alternatively, add the /**D** switch the first time you use the command to print a file:

```
PRINT   /D:LPT1   WHATSIT.TXT
```

You'll be prompted to name a port if you leave out the /**D** switch the first time PRINT is used. Note that PRINT (unlike COPY) is an external DOS command, meaning that it is kept in a separate file apart from the main DOS program COMMAND.COM. When the file PRINT.COM is not in the current directory, you must begin PRINT commands with a path to the subdirectory that holds this file, as in:

```
C:\DOS\PRINT /D:LPT1 WHATSIT.TXT
```

Alternatively, list the subdirectory holding the file (in this case, **C:\DOS**) in a PATH command so that DOS can find it automatically.

COPY and PRINT can be used this way only to print simple text files. Spreadsheet files, database files, and the like are out of bounds. The commands also cannot print text files that contain formatting codes. These are special characters that word processors introduce into files to control features such as typefaces, margins, and so on. You can tell whether a file contains formatting codes by having DOS display it with the TYPE command. When the displayed text contains extra characters, or appears in odd ways, formatting codes are present. Another sign of formatting codes is that the computer may beep as it displays the file (press Ctrl-Break to stop the display).

On the other hand, some programs include formatting using ordinary characters. For example, a program might italicize the word heaven's in "for heaven's sake" by having you write:

```
for @italics(heaven's) sake
```

Because all of the characters are ordinary text, DOS will have no trouble printing out files formatted in this way. But the printout would contain no italics; instead, the text would appear exactly as it does on the screen.

Among word processors that employ special formatting characters, each has its own system. When a program prints a file, it converts the codes into the instructions required by the particular printer in use. DOS, on the other hand, simply sends the codes to the printer as if they were part of the text. The printer becomes confused and prints out random characters; it may interpret certain codes in the wrong manner and begin formatting the text in bizarre ways; or the printer may run wild, beeping and spewing out paper.

No harm is done to your equipment or files when such mistakes occur. However, you may have difficulty regaining control of the machine and the printer. The proper way to deal with an out-of-control printer is first to strike Ctrl-Break to stop DOS from transmitting data. Once the DOS prompt returns to the screen, turn off the printer, wait a few seconds, and then turn it back on. Don't deselect the printer using one of the buttons on the printer case. Although it has stopped moving, the printer will continue to hold characters DOS has sent to it, and it will again run amuck when you strike the select button a second time. The printer must be reinitialized to regain control of it; turning it off and on is the easiest way of accomplishing this. (Many printers can be reinitialized by using the printer control buttons; consult your printer documentation to learn whether this is an option.)

Another disadvantage of using DOS to print files is that it does not insert page breaks into the text. If your printer uses continuous-feed paper, a lengthy text document is printed in a long scroll. Text may fall on top of the crease where the paper is torn apart. Sometimes you can get around this problem by setting dials on the printer to force automatic page breaks. But not all printers offer this capability. Note that PRINT advances the printer paper to its "top of form" position when it finishes printing a file. COPY just stops mid-page.

Generally, DOS is best used for printing single-page files for quick reference. The COPY and PRINT commands offer a convenient way of printing system files, including CONFIG.SYS, AUTOEXEC.BAT, and other batch files. Any other kind of file is best printed out by the software that created it so that it may be properly formatted. There also are utility programs that can print simple text files and format them to a limited extent, setting page margins and line spacing, and letting you add page headers, page numbers, and so on. But this kind of utility cannot interpret formatting codes that are kept within the text to mark italicized words, alternate fonts, and so on.

The Ctrl-PrtSc Trap

Incidentally, you can also copy files to the printer by striking Ctrl-PrtSc (or Ctrl-P) at the DOS prompt. This activates the "printer echo" feature, which sends everything DOS sends to the console to the printer as well. When you then enter "TYPE MYFILE", the file displayed by TYPE is also directed to the printer. Striking Ctrl-PrtSc or Ctrl-P a second time toggles the feature back off. This is a very clumsy way of printing out files, but it works. Unfortunately, computer novices have a way of inadvertently striking these key combinations. If the printer is turned off, the machine freezes up and issues a printer error message—one that Ctrl-Break can't get you out of. In despair, most people reboot the machine and lose the work that was in progress. Instead, you can turn on the printer so that the message is printed, and then press the key again (pressing Ctrl-PrtSc or Ctrl-P without turning on the printer won't do the job). It's good to know about this little gremlin, and a good idea to inform coworkers of its existence.

Cataloging Files

A file name is a tiny thing. Although over a quintillion file names are possible (count them and see), it's very hard to find 11 characters that describe the *content* of a file. Finding *another* name for a related file is even harder. Unfortunately, DOS does not yet allow descriptive tags for files.

Using DOS to Catalog Files

Within the confines of DOS, there are two strategies for cataloging files: through directory tree structure, and through file-naming conventions. In directory trees, keep subdirectories small, with only related files in each. For example, if your correspondence grows to hundreds of letters, don't just dump them all in one large directory. Divide the files into categorized subdirectories.

Allow the names of higher-level subdirectories to partially define the content of lower-level ones. For example, a subdirectory containing documents about factory safety regulations could be named something like FACSFTRG ("FACtory SaFeTy ReGulations")—a name that, with time, would be undecipherable even by the person who created it, not to mention other people. Instead, place the subdirectory along a directory path in which the entire path defines the meaning of individual directories: \FACTORY\SAFETY\REGULATN.

Coding File Names

File names may be coded with special characters for the purpose of cataloging them and locating them by global file name characters. In this technique, particular positions in file names are reserved for particular codes. For example, the file name extension may be regarded as three separate codes. The first character might represent the name of the person who created the file, with "S" for Sally, "M" for Mike, and so on. The second character could associate the file with a particular topic or project, such as "P" for plastic and "A" for aluminum. And the third character could tell the content of the file, such as "M" for memo, "L" for letter, and "R" for Report. Finally, the eight-character file name would be devoted to the best-possible description of the file's contents: **OVERRUN, WARNING, NEWPLAN**. The result would be filenames like **OVERRUN.SPL, WARNING.MAM**, and **NEWPLAN.SAR**. You could then use global file name characters to request, for example, a listing of all reports written by Sally:

```
DIR  *.S?R
```

One problem with this system is that many application programs require predefined extensions; they won't be able to recognize files if you replace the mandatory extension with a special coding system. In this situation, you're forced to use characters from the file name itself for codes, preferrably starting from the last character and working toward the first. Unfortunately, this solution makes file names harder to read. Perhaps a greater problem is that once you start such a system, you must maintain it. This takes discipline and care, plus forethought about how to deal with unusual situations. For example, in the scheme described above where the third character of a file's extension tells whether it is a memo, letter, or report, you'd need to keep that code in that particular position even when other codes (such as the author's name) aren't required for a particular file. Try using dashes or underscores to replace unused codes. Instead of labelling a file as a "report" by naming it **COSTING.R**, you'd have to type **COSTING.--R**.

Cataloging Files with Utility Software

As you can see, DOS won't help you much in cataloging files. True catalogs require utility software. One way of making a catalog is to create a text file holding file names and descriptive labels. Many memory-resident utility packages include a simple editor that can be used for this purpose. Keep a separate catalog file in every directory for this purpose. When you create a file, quickly call up the resident editor and enter the file name and a note about its content. Don't forget to edit the catalog file when you delete files.

Cataloging Utilities

There are utilities that set up their own files in each directory to hold information about other files. The *FI* (File Info) program in *The Norton Utilities* accepts comments of up to 65 characters for each file. It places the comments in a file, and you can call upon this file for an annotated directory listing (using wildcard characters, if you like). The comments are created at the DOS command line. For example, if you've just created a file named **GODZILLA.DOC**, you might enter:

```
FI GODZILLA.DOC Field report from July herpetology expedition
```

If you have exceptional cataloging needs, you may want to acquire a utility that lets you associate keywords with a file, or attach lengthy notes to it. You can then search for combinations of keywords, asking, for instance, for all files keyworded with "Final report" and "Refinancing" but not "1991." Searches may also encompass a choice of words found within descriptive labels or notes. Some software includes facilities of this kind, but they apply only to that software's own files. For example, the Windows versions of *Microsoft Word* lets you specify title, subject, author, keywords, and notes for a file.

When cataloging is done through a utility that operates outside application software, you may need to quit the program whenever you create a new file so that you can type in the cataloging information. This drawback can be circumvented by making the utility a memory-resident program. The utility can be "popped up" on the screen through a hot key whenever required. Or, it can link itself into DOS in a way that it automatically comes up whenever you create a new file from within application software.

Archiving Files

You have three options when a hard disk fills. You can add another disk to the machine and cope with the problems of working in two directory trees. You can buy a file compression utility (discussed below) to try to stave off the full-disk problem a while longer. Or you can take matters in hand and move less important files over to diskettes in a process called archiving. Archives are data files that are not required day to day—allowing them to be removed from your hard disk—but which are still important and must be available if needed. Don't confuse archives with backups. Backups keep spare copies of files that remain on your hard disk. Archived files, on the other hand, are completely removed from the disk. And while backups are just copies of files identified by their file names, proper archives are cataloged in some way so that you can easily locate files by their contents.

Building an archive index

When transferring archives from your hard disk to diskettes, you may be tempted to preserve the directory structure under which the files are organized. For example, if correspondence of a certain nature is found in the subdirectory MISSIVES, a subdirectory of that name can be created on a diskette, and the entire contents then copied to it. It's hard to set up and maintain an archive system this way. A better approach is to simply fill diskettes with files at random. Use empty diskettes and number them consecutively: 1, 2, 3... When a diskette is filled with archived files, say on drive A, execute a command like this:

```
DIR  A: >C:\ARCHIVES\ARCH001
```

This example assumes that you've set up a subdirectory named **ARCHIVES** in the root directory of your hard disk, and that the diskette in drive A is disk #1 (001) in the series. For the next diskette, the command would be:

```
DIR  A: >C:\ARCHIVES\ARCH002
```

These commands redirect the output of directory listings from drive A to a series of files named **ARCH001, ARCH002, ARCH003,** and so on. Open these files one after another in your word processor. Delete the directory headings and other information so that the files are reduced to nothing more than file listings. Then annotate the listing for its content, beginning keywords with a # sign. For example:

```
ARCHIVE DISKETTE #1
#Correspondence to #Italy
MYLETTER.DOC 3405    03-12-87        12:34p
YOURLTTR.DOC 2019    09-07-89        08:44a
HISLETTR.DOC  568    12-01-90        11:01a
#Correspondence to #France
HERLETTR.DOC 5401    01-28-88        02:03p
OURLETTR.DOC 3999    11-11-90        10:30a
```

Your hard disk now has an index to each diskette. But separate indices are not very useful, so combine them into one large file (say, **ARCHIVES.LST**), preferrably in the order they were created. Any word processor can do this, or use the DOS COPY command, appending a file like **ARCH023** to **ARCHIVES.LST** by the command:

```
COPY  ARCHIVES.LST+ARCH023
```

With this index on hand, you can search for a file by loading **ARCHIVES** into your word processor and using its search command to find the annotations you've placed in the files. Once you encounter a reference to a desired file, look for its associated diskette number and you'll know just where to find it. One advantage of this approach is that related files may be spread across many diskettes, and yet they are just as easy to find as when they have been meticulously grouped on one diskette.

Notice that there is no limitation on how much information you can enter about each file. If you're up to the job, a line-by-line explanation of each file will result in a crystal-clear catalog guaranteed to be useful years later when your memories of the files have dimmed. By making a habit of starting keywords with a symbol such as the # sign (#France instead of "France"), your search commands can avoid extraneous appearances of keywords.

Utility Software

A number of software companies have published diskette librarians, which are intended to organize diskettes. These programs vary widely in their capabilities. Virtually all can inspect floppies and print out directory listings on labels that may be affixed to the diskette. However, not all of these programs maintain a disk-based composite index of files that can be searched. Nor will most let you make annotations about file groupings and contents. By all means, find out what utilities the marketplace currently offers. But before buying one, be sure that it will do more than you can easily do with your word processor.

Managing Disk Space

The secret to hard disk management is spelled, D-I-S-C-I-P-L-I-N-E. It makes much more sense to put files where they belong when they are first created and to erase them the moment they become obsolete than to run a periodic housecleaning. You might want to argue the virtues of procrastination in the name of "economies of scale." But eight-character file names provide flimsy descriptions of a file's contents. If you put off dealing with files at the time they are created or modified, you'll later face the huge *dis*-economy of having to look into each file to find out what in heaven's blazes it is—if you can figure it out! And when you misjudge an old file's value and delete it, the dis-economies loom larger.

Installing New Software

When you acquire a new piece of software, you must almost always install it before you can begin to use it. Installation means to set up the files that hold the program (or that are used by the program) so that they can find each other. You may also need to configure the software so that it works with your particular printer, display, extended or expanded memory, and other equipment.

As software has become more complicated, it has come to be shipped with dozens, sometimes hundreds of files, filling many diskettes in some cases. Having all essential files on hand can be a problem in machines equipped only with diskette drives.

Most software includes an installation program. You simply run this program (the software's documentation will tell how) and it prompts you to insert the distribution diskettes one by one. Usually the program will ask you questions about your system or the kind of work you will be doing, and on that basis it selects certain files to copy out of the many contained on the diskettes. While an installation program would seem to protect you from every problem, many things can go wrong, in part because installation programs are often poorly designed. Keep these suggestions in mind:

- Place the software in appropriately named subdirectories. Frequently, the software's installation program will create these directories for you, or you may be instructed to create subdirectories of particular names at particular positions in the directory tree. Don't rename directories made by the installation program unless the documentation specifically allows it, because the program may be designed to look for files in a subdirectory of that name only.

- Once the software's subdirectories have been created (either by you or by the installation program), add a subdirectory for data files. Don't get into the habit of placing data files in the same subdirectory as the program files. Data files should go into their own subdirectories so that they can be conveniently viewed in their own directory listings. By keeping them apart from program files, you'll also avoid future confusion about the identity of various files. And when you later need to install an updated version of the software, you can do so without confusion and without endangering your data.

- Make copies of your AUTOEXEC.BAT and CONFIG.SYS files before running the installation program. Many installation programs open these files and insert lines into them. For example, they may place a DEVICE statement in CONFIG.SYS to cause a device driver to be loaded when the computer is booted. Unfortunately, not all installations are "well behaved" in this regard. They may write statements in the files that nullify those that you have written yourself. In the worst case, the file may simply be replaced with one generated by the installation software. By making copies of the two files before running the program, you'll be able to recover quickly if undesirable changes are made.

  Be particularly wary of changes made by installation programs to a PATH command in your AUTOEXEC.BAT file. Some programs require this command for proper operation. Installation programs may simply replace the existing command with one of their own. When this happens, other software in your system may mysteriously stop functioning.

- Avoid placing unnecessary files on the disk. It is astonishingly easy to fill up a 20- or 40-megabyte hard disk, so be sure that the files you place on it are actually used. Printer drivers are particularly wasteful of disk space. These are the small files that let software work with the printer you own. There may be more than 100 shipped with the software, but you will be using only one or two. Most installation programs ask for the name of your printer and install only the appropriate file. Still, you should verify that the disk has not been packed with useless printer drivers. A file holding a printer driver usually has a name resembling that of the printer it serves.

Other candidates for elimination are software tutorials and software demonstration files. Run the tutorial, and then delete it from the disk. The same applies to demonstation files, which are ready-made data files that can be loaded into the software to show it in action. These often are included for software salesman rather than software customers. Again, take a look and then get rid of them.

When you are unsure whether a file can be eliminated or not, rename it and then see if the program runs properly. A good way of doing this is to change just the first character of the file name to the next highest letter of the alphabet. For example, the file **WHATSIT** is renamed to **XHATSIT**. If you find that you need the file after all, you'll have no trouble remembering what the original name was. Be sure to make a thorough run-through of the software before eliminating files, including printing.

- Keep a sharp eye out for files that use the same names as those employed by other programs on your hard disk. Certain names tend to be used again and again. If two programs use a file named **STARTUP**, you certainly don't want them to read the wrong one, for they would probably become fatally confused and cause the machine to freeze up. Even when the two files are safely tucked away in their own subdirectories, a poorly thought-out PATH command or APPEND command could lead to confusion. Since such file names may be built into a program and may not be changeable, there often is nothing you can do about this situation except to be careful.

Copy Protection

When you buy copy-protected software, you should examine the documentation closely to find out if it limits the number of times it can be installed on your hard disk—and, if so, how many hard disk installations are allowed (installations are limited to hinder software piracy). In the chapters ahead we will discuss a number of techniques for optimizing the disk and backing it up. Several of these can interfere with the copy protection scheme. This happens when utility software inadvertently moves around copy protection data that has been installed at particular positions on the disk. When a copy-protected program can't find the information where it expects, the program assumes that it must be a pirated copy and refuses to function. When this happens, you must reinstall the program to get it going again, and that means using up one of the few installations you are allowed.

Key Disks

Key disks are another problem. These are used in a copy protection scheme where one of the distribution diskettes must be in a diskette drive (usually A) for the program installed on drive C to work. In this approach, utility software cannot interfere with the copy-protection scheme. But often you'll want that diskette drive available, especially for backups.

Mass File Deletions

Paradoxically, people often delete files accidentally because they don't use the DOS ERASE (or DEL or DELETE) command *enough*. Users need to get into the habit of getting rid of files when they're no longer needed, either by archiving them on diskettes, or by erasing them once and for all. When directories become clogged with obsolete files, confusion blooms and mistakes happen.

DOS Safeguards

DOS protects you from certain kinds of catastrophic mass erasures. The RMDIR command can't delete a subdirectory unless it is emptied of all files and references to child subdirectories. Without this safeguard, in a few keystrokes you might wipe out a major portion of the directory tree and all the files it contains. DOS also won't let you simultaneously erase every file in a subdirectory (DEL *.*) without first answering "Yes" to a query as to whether you really want to do that.

Remaining Hazards

But you may still inflict gross damage through the use of wildcards. DEL *.TXT could wipe out a whole novel in one blow. Many people do not properly understand the use of the asterisk as a wildcard. The statement:

```
DEL ZZZ*.WKS
```

erases all worksheets (.WKS) for which the first three letters of the filename are ZZZ. Files named **ZZZWKS** and **ZZZABC** are deleted, but not **ZZ.WKS**. Now, imagine a case where you have two files named **AZZZ.WKS** and **BZZZ.WKS**, and you want to delete both with one command. If you enter:

```
DEL *ZZZ.WKS
```

the DEL command will erase *all* files with a .WKS extension in the directory, not just the two you desire. It interprets every character following the asterisk as a wildcard. This mistake could cost you scores of files. To avoid it, *never use an asterisk at the beginning of a filename.* To delete just the two files, use the question mark instead:

```
DEL ?ZZZ.WKS
```

Note that a file called AAZZZ.WKS would not be affected by this command. A question mark, unlike an asterisk, substitutes for exactly one character.

Typing Errors

Another common error arises from careless typing. Many programs generate duplicate files with a .BAK extension. These should be deleted as soon as work on the file is complete. Otherwise they clog directories and may be unnecessarily copied during backups. They are eliminated from a directory by typing

```
DEL *.BAK
```

but you may inadvertently enter:

```
DEL *.BAT
```

...or...

```
DEL *.BAS
```

in which case you'll lose all batch files or all BASIC program files, in the directory. To avoid this error, make a one-line batch file containing DEL *.BAK, place it in the batch file subdirectory with the PATH command pointing to it, and name the file something like **KILLBAK.BAT**. Then you can routinely eliminate the BAK files from any subdirectory without raising your blood pressure.

To protect yourself against all sorts of wildcard erasures, make a batch file named DELETE.BAT that contains these lines:

```
CLS
DIR %1
PAUSE --- STRIKE ANY KEY TO ERASE %1, or CTRL-BRK
ERASE %1
```

If you were to enter DELETE *.WKS, this batch file would list all files about to be erased, then it would ask your consent, offering the option of using Ctrl-Break to abandon the erasure. When Ctrl-Break is used, the message "Terminate batch job (Y/N)?" appears, and you must press "Y".

Deleting Whole Directories

In addition to the ***.*** wildcard combination, you can erase all files in a subdirectory by naming the subdirectory alone. For example, to erase all files in the subdirectory **PAJAMAS** along the path **\CATS\PAJAMAS**, just enter:

```
ERASE \CATS\PAJAMAS
```

Before making the erasure, DOS will prompt you with the usual "Are you sure(Y/N)?" message. Now, say that you really want only to erase the file **MEOW.COM**, but you make a little mistake and leave out the backslash between it and PAJAMAS:

```
ERASE \CATS\PAJAMAS MEOW.COM
```

Because of the error, DOS doesn't know how to interpret the end of the line. In Versions 3.0 and 4.0, DOS just goes along as if the expression MEOW.COM was not there. And so it tries to erase all files in the subdirectory, asking "Are you sure(Y/N)". Of course, to the inexperienced user it appears as if DOS is checking whether MEOW.COM should be erased, and so he or she may answer "Yes." Be aware that DOS asks "Are you sure?" *only* when it's about to erase everything in sight.

Problems with RMDIR

Incidentally, sometimes you'll want to use RMDIR to remove a subdirectory and will dutifully delete all files in it beforehand by DEL *.*. But RMDIR won't work. This happens because there is a *hidden* file in the directory (a file in which the attribute for "hidden" status is turned on). The DOS ERASE and DEL commands don't operate on hidden files, and the DIR command won't list them. You'll need to change the file to "normal" status before DOS can get rid of it. We'll explain how to do this in a moment.

The DOS Shell

The Shell program in DOS 4.0 and 5.0 provides an added measure of both versatility and safety in making mass file erasures. Besides letting you select files using global file name characters, you can move through a directory listing and select multiple files that are not related by the way they are named. For example, the files ELEPHANT, GORILLA, and CHIPMUNK could not be specified as a group using global filename characters (unless a directory held only these three files). Three separate ERASE commands would be required from the DOS command line. But the DOS Shell lets you tag the three files from within a listing of many files and then erase them with a single command.

To tag multiple files in the DOS 4.0 shell, move the bar cursor to a file name and press the space bar (or click a mouse over the file name). In the DOS 5.0 shell, press <Shift-F8>, make the selections with the space bar, then press <Shift-F8> a second time when you have finished (or click a mouse over the file names while the <Ctrl> key is held down).

One advantage of tagging files is that files in different directories may be selected simultaneously. Once all of the files you want to erase have been chosen, pull down the *Files* menu and select *Delete*, exactly as if you were erasing a single file. A confirmation box then appears and the name of each file is displayed as the file is about to be erased; a keystroke or click of the mouse verifies that the erasure should proceed. Figure 6.10 shows an example. Confirmation boxes are quite helpful in avoiding mistakes during mass erasures; however, the feature can be disabled by pulling down the *Options* menu, selecting *File options*, and changing the *Confirm on delete* setting in the dialog box that is displayed.

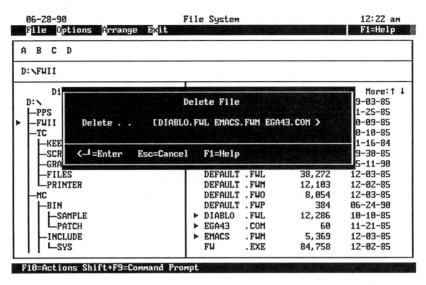

Figure 6-10. File deletions in the DOS Shell.

Windows 3.0

In Windows, begin by entering the *File Manager* and selecting the files you want to erase. Then pull down the *File* menu and select *Delete*. A dialog box like the one shown in Figure 6.11 will appear to show the names of the selected files. These are listed one after another with a space between. When many files are selected, their names won't all fit into the box. But you can use the cursor keys to scroll back and forth along this horizontal listing, editing it as required. Alternatively, you may write a specification into the box using global file name characters, as though you were working from the DOS command line.

Then click your mouse on the *Delete* button or strike Alt-D. For safety's sake, Windows will prompt you for further confirmation with yet another dialog box. You'll need to specify "Yes" or "No" for each file as it comes up for deletion. This feature is enabled or disabled by pulling down the *Options* menu and selecting *Confirmation*. The resulting dialog box offers a check box labelled *Confirm on delete*. To change the current setting, click the check box with your mouse or use the cursor keys to move the square cursor to the check box and strike the space bar.

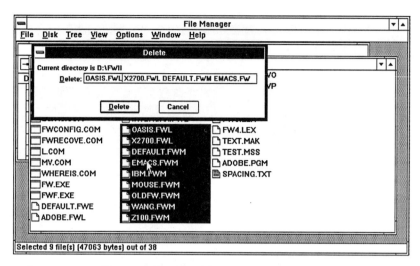

Figure 6-11. File deletions in Windows.

Advanced Erasure Utilities

There are special erasure utilities that are far more capable than DOS. Some can erase hidden and read-only files, traverse the directory tree during wild-card erasures, and be made to query the user before completing erasures. The tree-traversal feature is extremely dangerous in the hands of the inexperienced, but it can be very useful for general housecleaning tasks, like removing all .BAK files. Be wary of public domain file-erasure utilities. If you can't find a qualified recommendation, don't use them. These programs must be extremely well-crafted, lest they run amok and wipe out scores of files.

File Junk Yards

If you're tempted to erase a file, but want to keep it a bit longer, consider squirreling it away in a "junkyard" subdirectory. This batch file would do the job, providing there's no danger of a "full-disk" error:

```
REM Moving the following files to the Junk Yard:
DIR %1
COPY %1 \JUNKYARD
ERASE %1
```

If the batch file were named **DISPOSE.BAT**, you'd need only to enter **DISPOSE OLDFILE.TXT** to move **OLDFILE** to the junkyard subdirectory.

Some utilities perform this service automatically. The *FileSave* program in *The Norton Utilities* saves deleted files for a specified number of days or until a specified amount of disk space is filled. It works as a memory-resident program loaded from your AUTOEXEC.BAT file. In configuring the program, you can dictate which drives it will save files from. You may specify that all files be saved, or only files with particular extensions. At any time you can call up the program for a listing of deleted files it has stored. The files are out of view otherwise, since they're kept in a hidden directory that the DOS DIR command won't display. It takes only a few keystrokes to bring back the file.

Setting File Attributes

In Chapter 2 we learned about the *attribute byte* that resides in the directory entry of every file. Ordinarily, the attribute byte is set by software. But there are occasions when you may want to intervene. By changing the *archive bit*, you can determine whether backup utilities or the DOS XCOPY command will include the file when they transfer data. Second, you can change the file's *read-only* status to protect it from changes and from accidental erasure.

Utilities

DOS provides the ATTRIB command to change file attributes. It can change only the archive and read-only attributes. It uses the expression **+A** to *set* the archive bit (turn it "ON") so that a file will be readied for backup. The expression **-A** *resets* the archive bit (turns it "OFF") so that backup software passes over the file. Similarly, **+R** makes a file read-only, and **-R** returns it to normal status. To reset the archive bit in the file **2NDCOPY.BAK**, type:

```
ATTRIB -A 2NDCOPY.BAK
```

To make the file read-only:

```
ATTRIB +R 2NDCOPY.BAK
```

Starting with Version 3.3 of DOS, the ATTRIB command uses the /S switch to change all files in the current directory and all subdirectories below it. To set the archive bit of every file on the disk in preparation for a global backup:

```
ATTRIB +A \*.* /S
```

As you can see, ATTRIB can take wildcard characters. In this example, the expression *.* /S means "all files in the root directory, and all files in all subdirectories below."

The DOS Shell

In the DOS Shell program (DOS 4.0 and later), begin by selecting one or more files for which you want to change the read-only, archive, or hidden attributes (the DOS 5.0 shell can also change the system attribute). Then pull down the *File* menu and choose *Change attribute*. A dialog box will offer two choices:

```
1.  Change selected files one at a time
2.  Change all selected files at once
```

The first choice results in a succession of dialog boxes, requiring you to confirm each file in turn before its attributes are changed. In either case, you'll be shown the screen in Figure 6.12. The three attributes are selected in the same way as files are in directory listings. Either click the mouse over the attribute name, or move the bar cursor over the name and press the Spacebar. An arrowhead appears to the left of the name when it is selected. Repeating this action deselects the attribute. When the proper attribute combination is set, press (or click) Enter and the attributes will be changed (use the Tab key to move the bar cursor to the "Enter" button).

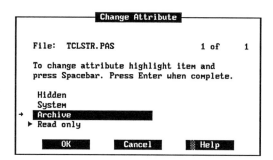

Figure 6-12. Changing file attributes in the DOS Shell.

You can find out the current attributes of a file simply by following this procedure to the last step, but then pressing Esc instead of Enter. Arrows will mark the current attributes. More conveniently, select *Show Information* from the

Options menu once a file has been selected. The second line of the displayed information reports the file's attribute, listing "r" for read-only, "a" for archive, and "h" for hidden.

Windows 3.0

In *Windows*, begin by entering the *File Manager* by clicking on its icon, then select one or more files in which to change the attributes. Pull down the *File* menu and select *Change Attribute*. You'll be shown a dialog box like the one in Figure 6.13. When one of the four boxes contains an X, that attribute is selected. Change the settings by clicking on the boxes with the mouse, or by shifting the cursor between the boxes using one of the cursor keys and then pressing the Spacebar. Once the desired combination of attributes has been specified, press Enter (or click the mouse on "OK"), and the attributes will be changed.

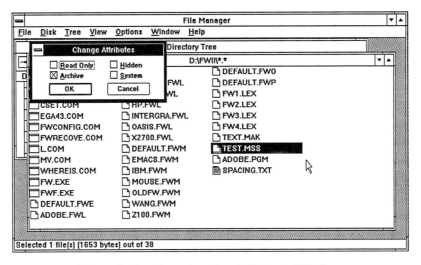

Figure 6-13. Changing file attributes in Windows.

You can find out the current attributes of a file by following the same sequence to see which attribute boxes have Xs. Then, instead of pressing Enter or clicking "OK", cancel the command. Note that, when more than one file has been selected, none of the four boxes will contain Xs, as if no attributes were set. In fact, any number of attributes may be shared between the files. However, rather than display a composite listing, in this case, Windows gives no information about current attribute settings.

Data Compression

Data compression is often the simplest solution to dwindling disk space. It is certainly the least-expensive solution, since compression utilities usually cost only $50 to $75. Often a file's size may be cut in half. In some cases, half of disk space can be reclaimed by compressing all applicable files. It's as if a 20-megabyte disk suddenly becomes a 40-megabyte disk! Data compression can also be very useful in data transmission across phone lines. A file reduced to half its former size takes only half as long to send. Of course, the parties at each end must own copies of the compression/decompression utility. But these are quickly paid for by the savings in long-distance charges.

Memory-Residency

The programs that achieve the best file compression, like PKZIP, run from the DOS prompt and take several seconds or even minutes to compress a file. However, some faster but less powerful compressors are speedy enough to be used in a **memory-resident mode**. The program is loaded by AUTOEXEC.BAT when the machine is booted, and it links itself into the operating system's disk-access routines, just like the path programs discussed earlier in this chapter. (If they're well designed, the two kinds of programs ought to be able to peacefully coexist.) When a file is loaded, the compression utility automatically decompresses it as it is fed to DOS; when the file is saved, it is recompressed.

Compression Techniques

Compression utilities use several techniques to squeeze the air out of files. It may surprise you that files are compressible at all. Upon inspection, a 10,000-byte text file contains fully 10,000 characters (spaces are characters, too). But nearly all files contain *patterns* and *redundancies*, and it is the compressor's job to find them and represent them more economically. Here are some important techniques:

ASCII compression. A byte of memory holds a pattern of eight bits ("ONs" and "OFFs"). Not all bits are always used, and some patterns occur much more often than others. The standard ASCII system for representing characters may be rearranged so that frequently used characters are encoded in only a few bits, while seldom occurring characters are encoded in longer bit strings.

Dictionary lookups. Some utilities are optimized for English-language text-file compression. They use a small dictionary of the most common words to substitute codes for these words.

String compression. Words not found in dictionary lookups may occur repeatedly in a file. Once the first occurrence has been identified, subsequent instances may be replaced by a *pointer* to the first; that is, a code tells the compression program to go find the first instance and insert it in place of the second. This technique is particularly effective in very long files.

Digraph encoding. Certain vowel-consonant pairs (called digraphs) occur frequently in English; these are encoded as single bytes.

Run-length. The utility seeks out sequences of the same character or pattern and encodes them as a repetition count. Many database and spreadsheet files contain long sequences of zeros or other "filler" characters that may be eliminated in this way.

Software-specific analysis. Some software may encode data in special ways. WordStar, for example, slightly changes the standard ASCII character set for its own purposes. For popular software, a compression utility may offer a special mode that deals with just those special files.

If you look into a compressed file, you'll see mostly gobbledygook. Text files may hold a few remaining English words that couldn't be compressed by any of the techniques at hand. This means that your files are even less browsable than before, and that file organization and cataloging is more important than ever. The files are nonetheless perfectly ordinary DOS files, so they may be copied, compared, and checked by any standard DOS utilities.

Specialized Utilities

Some compression utilities are dedicated to only one kind of file. *SQZ*, for instance, operates only on *Lotus 1-2-3* worksheet files. Like database files, spreadsheet files often contain much unused space. Data fields are sized for the largest data item that will occur, and most fields are only partially filled. Such files are packed full of zeros that may be quickly eliminated. Some *1-2-3* files may be compressed to as little as 5 percent of their original sizes, and most can be reduced by more than half. *SQZ* comes with a built-in communications option that reformats spreadsheets specifically for modem transmission. It also includes a password provision that keeps snoops out of your files.

General-Purpose Compressors

Most file compressors are general-purpose. These programs can deal with any kind of file, although they are much more effective with some than others. You choose which files will be compressed by first going through the disk with a utility that makes an initial compression. Some let you choose groups of files by wildcards, whole directories, or even the entire disk.

Effectiveness

Typically, general-purpose utilities can reduce text files by 60 percent (50 percent to 80 percent), database files by 75 percent (70 percent to 90 percent), and spreadsheet files by 30 percent (much less than the results achieved by a special-purpose utility like *SQZ*). Files containing graphic images vary widely in their compressibility; some, like GIF files and certain kinds of TIFF files, may already have built-in compression; they can't be squeezed any more. Most utilities report how much they've compressed a file. It may seem that there's no point in compressing a file smaller than one disk cluster, but there is if you pack several of them into one compressed archive. Besides saving space due to compression, this technique can help you reclaim some of the space DOS wastes by insisting that files take up a whole number of clusters.

Program files have less redundancy than other kinds, but do have patterns that lend themselves to compression. Some compressors, such as PKLite and LZEXE, are specially designed to compress programs. These utilities accept a program file and output a much smaller one that decompresses itself when it's run.

Performance

At first sight, file compression seems like an ideal solution to dwindling disk space. But all the processing required in compressing and decompressing files can exact a heavy toll on performance. The time required by compressors varies greatly by the kind of file, and by the compressor's own strengths and weaknesses. A 100K text file might require 15 seconds to compress. This time penalty is not very great when one loads a few business letters every hour. But if you are a programmer whose compiler must work with dozens of program files, the delay is completely unacceptable. Database sorts can take five times as long when the data files are compressed. On the whole, decompression takes less time than compression, since the search for patterns has already been performed.

Amazingly, in certain cases, file compression can actually *speed up* disk access. When a compression utility does little more than strip zeros from a spreadsheet, it takes very little time to reinsert the zeros when the file is read. Since the file is held on far fewer disk sectors, less time goes into the actual disk read operation. This gain may outweigh the time lost to decompression. This is especially true on systems with fast CPUs, as well as in systems where compression and decompression get a boost from special boards or chips.

Memory Requirements

Another disadvantage of memory-resident compressors is that they take up precious memory to use as a work area. A resident utility could take up as much as 40K of scarce conventional memory unless it's loaded high using the special features of DOS 5.0—or with a memory manager like 386MAX. If you're shopping for a memory-resident compressor, ask if it's capable of being loaded into high memory.

Hardware-based Compressors

Data compression is sometimes built into disk controller cards. Files are automatically compressed and decompressed as they pass through the card. These compressors are much faster than software utilities, but sometimes gain their speed by sacrificing some degree of compression. Still, they typically reduce files by about 25 percent to 50 percent.

Data compression is a valuable tool to help you through a period of insufficient disk capacity. If you're strapped for disk capacity and you own a particularly fast machine, it may be worth compressing most of your files. But, unless you own a very fast machine, you should avoid data compression if you can. You're far better off spending more for a larger disk than clocking in tens of hours of extra disk-access time.

Optimizing Speed and Productivity

People who use computers all day become *speed junkies*. Somehow, having a tool that performs tasks in milliseconds makes people *more* impatient. And impatience grows as ever more complicated software configurations bring the hard disk to its knees. Advanced users sometimes expect more from microcomputers than they were designed to deliver. An IBM PC wasn't intended to support real-time spelling checking within a multitasked, multi-file word processor running under Microsoft Windows. The higher a user pushes his or her productivity, the heavier the hard disk's burden.

Each generation of computers is faster than the previous one. Depending on the application, from one third to one half of the increase in performance may be attributed to a faster hard disk. No wonder speed junkies drool over rapid seek times, track buffers, and other technical goodies.

Developing Speed

There's no denying that money can buy speed. But you also can *develop* speed through thoughtful optimization of your system. The world's fastest hard disk will slowly degrade in performance if steps are not taken to keep it optimized.

As heavier and heavier demands are placed on disk performance, just buying the fastest hardware is not good enough. You need to work at optimizing the disk drive's throughput. Some of the optimization is done when the disk is first formatted. Some is done by periodic maintenance. And some is done on an *ad hoc* basis, adopting techniques that are appropriate for some tasks but not others.

Technical Skill

Once upon a time, disk optimization was a difficult and time-consuming task. It took considerable skill and patience to tweak a disk into high performance. Today, matters have changed. A broad offering of disk analysis and optimization utilities are available, mostly at low cost.

Relative Gains

Some disk optimization measures give large gains. The improvement is apparent immediately. Other optimizations are more subtle. They may lead to only a 10 percent gain. But the benefits are cumulative, and a half-dozen 10 percent gains multiply to a doubling of performance. Sometimes, what should be a small gain becomes a large one, because a bottleneck in the system has been opened and other performance factors are given free rein. Conversely, a single bottleneck can severely hamper a disk that should be quite fast.

You need to understand disk drives pretty well to use all the optimization strategies open to you. If you're not familiar with the contents of Chapter 2, you should read it before going on. We begin with an overview of the path data travels from its origin in magnetic domains on the disk surface to its final destination in system memory. Then we'll tackle the optimization solution for each step along that path. Finally, we'll try to sort through the conflicting claims about the relative value of the various optimizations.

Fifteen Factors in Hard Disk Performance

Let's begin by examining 15 determinants of hard disk performance, starting with the disk surface.

Cylinder density. The greater the number of sectors per cylinder, the fewer head moves required to read or write a file.

File defragmentation. Files compacted onto as few cylinders as possible are read more quickly than those scattered across the disk.

Average seek time. A fast average seek time maximizes the percentage of disk-access time that is spent reading or writing data.

Interleave. An optimum interleave minimizes the number of the disk turns required to read all sectors on a track.

Data transfer rate. Disk access on very fast computers may be speeded by faster data transfer by the disk controller.

Processor speed. A faster processor speeds up DOS, influences the data transfer rate, and allows software to process files more rapidly as they are read or written.

Track buffering. Whole tracks may be read in one rotation of the disk, even when the processor cannot handle a 1:1 interleave.

RAM disk support. A hard disk may be unburdened by placing certain repeatedly read files on a RAM disk.

DOS buffers setting. Selecting the right number of DOS buffers helps DOS avoid reading the same data again and again.

Caching. Disk accesses may be greatly reduced by a caching scheme that's more efficient—and can hold more data—than the one provided by the DOS buffers.

Directory tree design. The directory tree can be designed in a way that minimizes the disk activity required to search for a file.

Subdirectory layout. Subdirectories can be compacted into only a few cylinders to minimize the time DOS needs to trace through a directory path.

File layout. Placing certain files near the outer edge of the disk gives modest performance gains.

PATH and APPEND commands. The DOS PATH and APPEND command can be tailored to quicken directory searches.

FASTOPEN command. Starting with Version 3.3, DOS can be made to remember the location of recently accessed files so that it can reopen the file
without searching directories and the file allocation table.

Of the 15 factors, four are limited by hardware. Average seek time depends on
the drive itself; neither a new controller nor special software can change it.
The cylinder density and data transfer rate can sometimes be altered by switching to a different controller card, and the processor speed may be changed by
an accelerator card. Many of the remaining factors rely on software, but some,
such as track buffers and disk caching, may be hard-wired into the drive controller. A few performance gains are made entirely by managing the disk well;
these cost nothing.

Disk-level Optimization

Optimization at disk-level is directed toward minimizing time spent in *mechanical motion.* A high cylinder density means that a file can fit into fewer cylinders,
reducing the number of head seeks required to read it. File defragmentation
compacts files into as few cylinders as possible. Fast seek times lessen the time
the controller is kept waiting while the read/write heads shuttle between cylinders. And an optimal interleave reduces the time spent waiting for sectors to
rotate beneath the read/write heads.

Cylinder Density

Cylinder density is increased by adding more sectors per track, or more tracks
per cylinder. Of course, the number of tracks per cylinder depends on the
number of platters in the drive. There's nothing to do to increase this factor
except buy a larger drive.

Many people do not sufficiently appreciate the benefits of higher cylinder
density. Two drives, one with two platters and one with four, may have the
same average seek time. But the drive with four platters may be said to have an
average access time that is only half that of the other, since only half as many
seeks may be required to read a file (less benefit results with *random-access files,*
such as database files, since the heads move between cylinders after reading
only a snip of the file.) This advantage argues for buying a large drive up front,
rather than adding capacity later.

The number of sectors per track on some ST506-type drives can be changed
on some drives by substituting an RLL controller card (but only if the drive is

RLL-certified, as explained in Chapter 2). Depending on the encoding system used, the sector density per track may increase by 50 or 100 percent. A 100 percent gain means that head seeks may be cut in half—the effect is the same as doubling the number of platters.

Keep in mind that gains from a higher cylinder density are completely defeated by allowing your files to become very fragmented (we'll talk about defragmentation in a moment). A file that is spread across many cylinders requires numerous head seeks, no matter the cylinder density.

You may be able to achieve a pseudo-increase in cylinder density by compressing files. Since compressed files take up fewer sectors, less head movement is required to read them. File compression makes for important performance gains only in special cases where a simple utility can collapse a simple file structure. For example, some spreadsheet compressors simply strip out thousands of zeros from the file and insert codes telling how many have been removed from a particular location (we're oversimplifying). Files compressed in this way can be uncompressed quickly, and the job can be done automatically when the file is read or written (we discussed compression utilities in Chapter 6). Elaborate file compressions may take more time to perform than they save in disk access time, particularly on slower computers.

Reducing File Fragmentation

When you distribute files to a freshly formatted hard disk, each file is laid out in contiguous clusters, filling each track on each side at any given head position, and moving on to the next cylinder only when the current cylinder is full. Ideally, DOS would do its best to confine a file to as few cylinders as possible. For example, a 35K file can fit in one cylinder on many two-platter disks (four tracks of 17 512-byte sectors comes to 34,816 bytes). But DOS does not optimize the file's layout; it simply uses the next available sectors. Unless the file happens to begin in a completely empty cylinder, the 35K file would reside on two adjacent cylinders, thus requiring a head seek when it is read or written. Still, the file is said to be "contiguous" even if it is not optimally located.

Loss of Contiguity

But a file may not stay contiguous for long. Because no space is left between files as they are deposited on disk, when a file grows, the additional sectors required must be allocated at non-contiguous positions. On a newly formatted hard disk, DOS allocates disk space starting from the outer edge, and additional space for growing files is allocated from available inner tracks. But once all cylinders have been used, additional space must come from holes opened by file erasures. (DOS versions prior to 3.0 use a simpler scheme in which disk space is *always* allocated from whatever clusters are available closest to the disk's outer edge—even on a freshly formatted disk.)

The result is chaos, pure and simple. On a "mature" hard disk that has had many erasures and reorganizations, files can become very fragmented. Consider how this might happen with only a few files if each is constantly growing. Say you're writing a report with several chapters and that you add a few hundred words to each chapter every day. The disk has already been filled and additional clusters are found wherever files have been erased. In this way, each day another non-contiguous fragment is added to the file, and reading or writing the file requires an additional move of the drive's read/write heads.

Inefficiency

Because of these needless head movements, much of the performance gains of a fast processor, fast controller, and an optimized interleave are wasted, for the disk does not read data quickly enough to push these features to their limits. The degree of performance degradation depends on the kind of file in use. Large random-access files naturally require a lot of head movement, but program files, text files, or spreadsheet files are loaded in sequence, and severe fragmentation greatly reduces the speed at which they are read or written.

Fragmented *subdirectory* files are especially a problem. Recall that subdirectories are files like any other, except that they are marked as subdirectories in the attribute byte of their directory listing. When you search for a file in a third-level subdirectory, such as *MAMMALS\PRIMATES\OLDWORLD\ GIBBONS.APE*, DOS looks for the subdirectory called *MAMMALS* in the root directory, reads that file, searches for the entry **PRIMATES**, reads that file in turn, and so on. A four-sector cluster holds 64 directory entries. Subdirectories with more than 64 files require a second cluster, and it may be discontinuous with the first. Just *finding* a single file can take a lot of head movement when subdirectories are badly fragmented. This is especially true when many directories are searched automatically by the DOS PATH command.

Defragmentation

The obvious remedy for this chaos is to *defragment* the files, packing each into as few cylinders as possible and using adjacent cylinders to minimize the distance a head must move. True optimization is an impractical ideal, since it requires grouping files in a way that minimizes the "wrap-around" of files from one cylinder to the next. For example, a file that fills exactly two cylinders of disk space usually stretches across three cylinders, since it is unlikely to begin at exactly the first cluster of the first cylinder it occupies. To achieve perfect optimization, DOS would need to leave parts of cylinders empty, and that would waste a lot of disk space. But it's not hard to get near the optimum distribution of files.

Defragmenting a disk is one of those inherently futile undertakings in life, like raking up leaves or washing the car. Chaos begins creeping in again only moments after you've finished, since DOS takes no pains to avoid fragmentation.

Hidden Benefits

Defragmented files extend some hidden benefits. Utilities that unerase accidentally deleted files work flawlessly when used with a perfectly contiguous file. Even massive erasures can be reliably restored without requiring you to piece the files together. Defragmentation also makes file-by-file backups proceed more quickly, and it helps tape backup units achieve *streaming* for longer periods (a topic we discuss in Chapter 8). A third advantage is that defragmented disk drives live longer. Fewer head seeks means less overall wear and tear on the drive. A defragmentation utility may well pay for itself in this way.

There are two strategies for defragmenting a disk. You may acquire a defragmention utility (a "defragmenter," or, as some hackers call them, a "defragger"), or you may back up the whole disk, reformat it, and restore the files. You're probably thinking that it must be a lot easier to spend a few dollars on a defragmentation utility. You're right—the backup method is a very inconvenient way of doing the job.

Defragmenters

Let's take a look at defragmenters. They analyze file layout and copy clusters back and forth until every file is contiguous. They require some open disk space to do this, since they tend to produce large temporary files. Some operate more quickly than others; the time required depends on the capacity of the disk and the degree of fragmentation. On a 386 machine with a 40M disk, the process typically takes 20 or 30 minutes. Some defragmenters are included in general disk utility packages; others are sold as stand-alone programs.

Features

The defragmenter in *The Norton Utilities* is called *Speed Disk*. We'll use it here as an example of how a defragmenter works. *Speed Disk* defragments files and compacts them on outer cylinders. In doing so, it essentially defragments unused disk space, leaving an unbroken band of unused clusters starting from the inner edge of the disk. *Speed Disk* also optimizes directory access by placing all subdirectory files on the outer edge of the disk and sorting them (more on this in a moment). You can ask *Speed Disk* to perform any of these optimizations individually or all together. Sometimes there's no point in going through all of the optimizations. When you start up *Speed Disk*, it analyzes the disk and displays a screen like that shown in Figure 7.1 recommending which optimizations to perform. If you want a close-up look at individual files, you can request a "File Fragmentation Report," like the one in Figure 7.2.

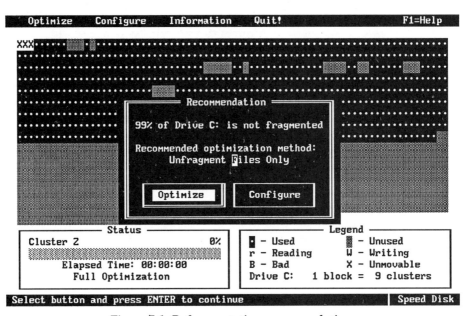

Figure 7-1. Defragmentation recommendations.

Speed Disk can be customized in a number of ways. You can specify which files should be placed at the outer edge of the disk, closest to the root directory and compacted subdirectories. It's a good idea to specify that all files with .EXE and .COM extensions—that is, all program files—should be positioned this way since they never change their sizes. You also can name files that should not be repositioned. By default, *hidden and system* files are considered unmovable since they sometimes take part in copy-protection schemes that depend on finding them in the same location each time they're accessed. Other options let you specify the degree of error checking made during the defragmentation. You can even ask *Speed Disk* to erase the data within unused sectors so that no one can view it with utility software.

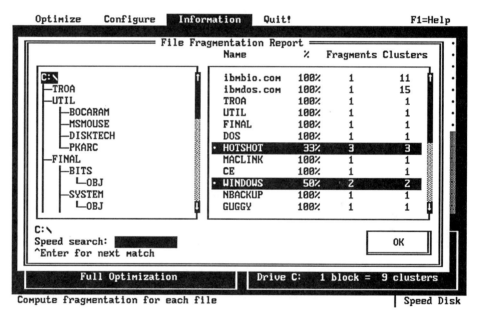

Figure 7-2. A file fragmentation report.

Dangers

You may be a trifle alarmed at the prospect of a program cutting up and reassembling your precious files. And well you should be—defragmenters perform major surgery. One point you needn't worry about is a power failure. Most defraggers write a second copy of a sector before erasing the original. But it can be a little messy recovering from a system crash during defragmentation, since you may need to weed out temporary files left by the defragmenter.

When to Defragment

How are you to know when it's time to run a defragmenter? As we've seen, the software itself will tell you whether defragmentation is required. The DOS CHKDSK can also give a clue, since it can report the degree of fragmentation of individual files. Just include a filename on the command line with CHKDSK, as in: (CHKDSK \NOVEL\CHAPTER1.DOC). When CHKDSK returns its usual information, it tells how many blocks the file is broken into. You won't want to test many files this way, however, since you have to wait for CHKDSK to analyze the whole disk each time.

When a disk becomes severely defragmented, you'll notice that files take longer and longer to load and save. The disk drive's indicator light will blink more and more for the same amount of work. You can avoid this degradation by applying the defragmenter periodically, whether or not the disk seems to have slowed. Generally speaking, a heavily used disk can benefit from defragmentation about once a month. This is also just about the right period for a global backup of the disk, so it is sensible to schedule them together. (*Incremental* backups—those affecting only files that have been changed—should be made more frequently, as we'll explain in Chapter 8.)

A few commercially available controller cards attempt to do defragmentation behind the scenes without DOS's knowledge. This, however, is a stopgap measure. Ultimately, the problem will be solved by operating systems like UNIX and OS/2, which organize the disk so that it's less subject to fragmentation in the first place.

Defragmenting without Utility Software

We mentioned above that defragmentation is not a problem with freshly formatted disks, because nothing but contiguous sectors are available for DOS to allocate to each successive file. The same benefit accrues if you back up all of your files on diskettes or tape, reformat the disk, and then restore the files. DOS lays them out one after another. (Incidentally, it's for this reason that you can speed up diskette access just by making a direct file-by-file copy to a second diskette: **COPY A:*.* B:**. Note that the DOS **DISKCOPY** program doesn't defragment a diskette, since it creates an exact sector-by-sector image of the original.)

But why *reformat* the disk? Isn't erasing all the files good enough? In Chapter 8 you'll learn that a good backup utility can preserve an entire directory structure, recreating every subdirectory when it restores each to a reformatted disk.

It is simply easier to exploit this capability than to go from subdirectory to subdirectory, erasing files. And since subdirectories are themselves files, they also require defragmentation, which means tearing down the subdirectory tree and then recreating it. It's really a *lot* easier just to reformat the disk and have a backup utility do the work for you. This entails only a high-level format, as explained in Chapter 4.

Problems

Of course, this technique does not work if you use a streaming tape drive to make an image backup of a disk (as explained in Chapter 8). If you use tape, make a file-by-file backup. These days the distinction between image and file-by-file backups on tape is blurring, and some tape units can restore file-by-file from an image backup. Even if your tape drive can do this, it would be very inefficient, and it is not advised.

To do the job right, you should make *two* global backups. It's a pain, to be sure. But if you make only one backup, you will have only one copy of your data when the disk is reformatted. Backups sometimes go awry, and you'll be sorry not to have a *backup to your backup* when you have trouble restoring data to the reformatted disk. Be sure you know your backup software well before defragmenting your disk this way.

Seek Times

We discussed average seek times in Chapter 2. There is not much more to say about this factor in connection with optimization. We'd like to warn you again about misleading manufacturer's claims for very fast seek times that actually represent a "virtual" seek time achieved by hardwiring into the controller some of the optimization techniques presented here—particularly defragmentation and sector caching. Having these facilities built into the disk electronics is handy, saves labor, and conserves precious RAM. But you won't have the flexibility offered by utility software that provides the same services, and you may pay much more.

Benefits

How much does a fast seek time matter? Or, putting it differently, how much will performance suffer if you opt for a slower stepper-motor drive? Naturally enough, the answer depends on how much head movement the drive must make to serve the particular software you use. You can judge this simply by watching the indicator light on a disk (for an accurate reading, you should first defragment the disk). Running the software from a diskette gives an even more dramatic indication of the importance of seek time.

Tasks that use many small files benefit greatly from fast seek times. Programmers are in the greatest need, since large programs are created from dozens of files. The files are likely to be spread all over the disk, and each requires a search from subdirectory to subdirectory to find it.

Another role in which fast seek times make a big difference is in disk-based data sorts. Lacking enough memory, software dumps the data into large temporary files. These files span many cylinders, particularly if recent erasures have left the disk badly fragmented. The result is a non-stop churning of the read/write heads. Database users know well the seemingly endless grinding of the drive and flicker of its indicator light.

Advanced Operating Systems

If you're using OS/2, or some other multitasking operating system, fast seek times are extremely important. When multiple large tasks are run at once, available memory quickly fills, and the operating system starts to swap data and program modules in and out of memory. All of this occurs *in addition to* normal file reads and writes. This activity may defeat other performance optimization measures. For example, even if a series of records are packed into one cylinder and are accessed in sequence, the read/write heads may have to constantly leave the cylinder to take care of various operating system demands. Also, the heads may need to scamper back and forth to serve the input-output needs of several programs at once.

Remember that drives with very high cylinder densities make average seek time less important, since they fit a file into fewer cylinders. Ironically, the highest cylinder densities are in high-capacity drives, and these tend to have the fastest head seeks of all. But these drives are often intended to serve networks, where *no* drive can ever be fast enough.

One way to determine a drive's performance is by running a disk performance test. *CORE International* publishes such a test. It takes only a few seconds to run, and it displays the information shown in Figure 7-3. Since it measures more than average seek times, it is a valuable tool for comparing drives. It is available from CORE for a nominal fee, or it can be found on many electronic bulletin boards free of charge. If you use this test, however, make sure to disable any software or hardware caches in your machine first. Otherwise, you may be measuring the speed of the cache—not the speed of the disk.

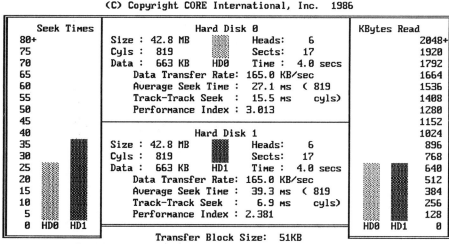

Figure 7-3. The CORE disk performance test

Optimizing the Interleave

In Chapter 2 we explained how the disk sectors on a track are numbered discontinuously, allowing time for the electronics to "digest" the data from one sector before accessing the data at the next. Since *logically* adjacent sectors are not usually *physically* adjacent, they are said to be *interleaved*. An interleave factor of 3:1 means that sectors numbered #100 and #101 are three sectors apart on the disk surface (that is, there are two sectors between them). Hence it takes three complete rotations of the disk to read all sectors in a track, using this interleave.

A Too-Low Interleave

Recall that the interleave is set during low-level formatting, which creates and labels tracks and sectors. The formatting program prompts you for an interleave factor. The number you enter is quite an important decision. If the interleave is too high, the electronics end up waiting an unnecessarily long time until the next (logical) sector spins under the read/write head. If the inter-leave is too low, the electronics will not be ready, and an entire turn of the disk will be inserted between each sector access. Clearly, a too-low interleave factor is a far more serious problem, since it creates delays much larger than a too-high interleave.

An improper interleave setting can greatly degrade overall disk performance. Consider a disk formatted at a 1:1 interleave that should be at 2:1. It rotates 17 times to read every sector on a track, when it could instead read all sectors in only two revolutions. That's 15 extra rotations. At 60 revolutions per sec-ond, this amounts to a quarter of a second, or a full second when all sectors are read from a two-platter cylinder. Fast head seeks (say, 1/30th of a second) are lost amidst this inefficiency. An over-large interleave is not as inefficient, but it still may add appreciable fractions of a second to every cylinder read or write operation.

The Proper Setting

Finding a proper interleave setting has become more of an issue as hardware has differentiated. The optimal setting depends in part on the speed of the computer's processor. Of course, many different processor speeds are found amongst the IBM machines and clones. In fact, some machines can run at literally *thousands* of different speeds, since continuously variable add-on clock crystals have been introduced to allow users to push the speed as high as other components in the machine will allow.

Even an already formatted disk shipped in a new computer may not necessar-ily be set at the optimum interleave. This may occur when the manufacturer is overly cautious in setting the rate. Or, in the case of some clones, the com-puter's components are not carefully matched and tested to find the optimum setting. The interleave will also be thrown off if you change the processor speed by introducing an accelerator card or inserting a faster clock crystal.

Finding the Optimum

Since you have no way of monitoring the disk's activities from microsecond to microsecond, how are you to know which interleave factor is optimal? Indeed, how do you find out the interleave factor your drive currently uses? It's a lot of work to reformat a disk and reinstall files, and it's hard to time disk operations.

Fortunately, there are utilities that will do the job for you. These work by saving the data in several cylinders and then reformatting the cylinders again and again using different interleaves. Once the utility determines the optimum interleave, it reformats the entire disk in that interleave without disturbing the data. Starting with Version 5.0, *The Norton Utilities* includes the *Calibrate* program for this purpose. We'll use it as an example here.

How the Utility Works

Normally, *Calibrate* begins by performing interleave-optimization tests. It figures out the current interleave and tries a number of others, all the while preserving data on the tracks it tests. When it has finished, it displays a bar chart like the one shown in Figure 7.4. Relative interleave performance is measured by the number of revolutions required to read all data on a track (shown by the vertical axis in the figure). If your drive is not able to handle a low interleave, you'll find that low interleave settings take longer than intermediate ones. You're also told how large a performance gain can be made over the current interleave.

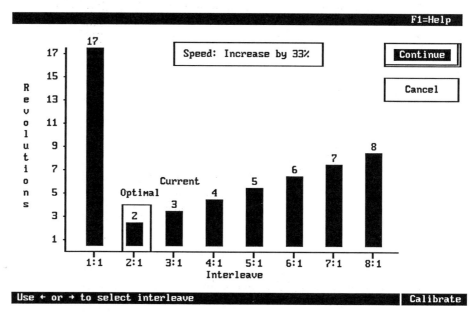

Figure 7-4. Interleave analysis.

While it's at it, *Calibrate* can run a number of tests on the drive and drive media. It performs **seek tests** to check the accuracy of read/write head motions (there's seldom a problem of this kind). It runs **data encoding tests** to find out the charactertistics of the drive and its controller, and to gain access to disk controller commands that let the utility test the hard disk even more thoroughly. Finally, *Calibrate* can run **pattern tests** to verify the quality of the media in each sector. It does this by writing bit patterns—sequences of 0s and 1s— and then reading them back. *Calibrate* uses the "worst case" patterns that are most difficult for the drive electronics to read and write without error. Data found on faulty or failing media is relocated to good sectors. You can choose to have up to 80 patterns tested if you want to be especially thorough.

Time Requirements

Calibrate can take quite a while to do its job if many tests are performed, ranging anywhere from several minutes up to many hours if you choose to run many of the pattern tests. Time requirements also vary by the size of the drive, the speed of the controller, and the clock rate of the computer's processor. When it's going to be a big job, it's a good idea to set the program in motion at the end of the day, just as you finish work. It can be stopped at any time, however, and it will pick up where it left off when you run it again.

A *disk test map* keeps you informed of how much has been done. No data is lost if a power outage crashes the machine. In fact, you can terminate the program at any time and run the disk with two different interleaves. The disk controller has no problem with this situation—it merely reads the sector numbers as they pass the drive's read/write heads and reads or writes the required sector when it appears.

Pitfalls and Limitations

There are a few pitfalls to avoid when running an interleave-optimization utility. First, you should remove, or switch off, other software that might simultaneously run in the background, including certain kinds of memory-resident programs (TSRs) and device drivers. For example, a communications program working in the background would have to be disabled, since incoming data could activate it at crucial moments when *Calibrate* requires complete control over the machine.

Background programs may be loaded automatically by your CONFIG.SYS and AUTOEXEC.BAT files when you start up the machine. The easiest way to disable them is to just boot the machine from a DOS diskette in drive A. Remember, though, that certain device drivers loaded by the CONFIG.SYS file may be essential to your machine, including those that manage hard disk drives or the video display. So you may need to create a temporary, minimal version of CONFIG.SYS on the boot diskette.

There are certain situations in which this kind of program cannot work. *Calibrate* works only with *physical* disk drives, not those that are *logically* created by software. It can't be applied to network drives, RAM disks, or drives that have been created by the DOS ASSIGN or SUBST commands (discussed in Chapter 5). It won't work with diskette drives, nor with those that use *translating controllers* that make the drive appear to have a different number of sectors per track than it actually has. There are also some kinds of drives, including those using SCSI controllers, that won't allow interleave modification. If there's any question at all about the suitability of your drive for this kind of utility, you should make a full global backup of all data on the disk before running the utility the first time.

Other Uses for Interleave Optimizers

It would seem that you'd only need to run an interleave optimizer once on a drive (or perhaps twice if you somehow change the machine's processor speed). But this software also can work as one kind of disk-repair utility. When a disk has intermittent problems reading or writing data to certain sectors, and the problem is not remedied by an ordinary disk-analysis utility that checks the media within disk sectors, then fading format markings may be the culprit. If this is the case, running a program like *Calibrate* will solve the problem. In fact, you can periodically run the program as a sort of preventative medicine. Particularly on older disks, once every three months is about right.

Controller-level Optimization

When data is read from the disk surface, it is buffered on the controller. Controller-level optimization speeds the transfer of the data to DOS. Recall from Chapter 2 that the ultimate determinant of transfer speed is the number of sectors on a track. A typical 17-sector hard disk turns 60 times a second. At 512 bytes per sector, that comes to 4.18 million bits per second. Add to this the formatting information stored between sectors, and you've got the nominal 5-million bits/second rating of the ST506 controller used in most machines.

So long as a controller is properly matched to a drive, it will be able to handle the drive's maximum data output. So you can't normally improve the data transfer rate by buying a faster controller. But you may be able to replace the controller with one that fits more sectors on a track (an RLL controller). There are also fancy controllers that automatically apply compression techniques to data as it is written so that more will fit within existing sectors. The controller uncompresses the data as it is read back. DOS never knows the difference. Track buffers see to it that all data on a track is buffered by the controller so that all subsequent accesses to the track are made at electronic speed. RAM disks take this process a step further by eliminating the mechanical disk and storing files as if they were entirely buffered on the controller. And caches save recently accessed data in fast RAM in case it's needed again.

Increasing the Data Transfer Rate

Some disks can be made faster by replacing the current MFM controller with an RLL controller. As we explained in Chapter 2, RLL encoding typically places 50 percent more sectors on a track. To handle the greater workload, the controller typically runs at 7.5 megabits per second. This optimization entails backing up all data on the disk and reformatting it using the new RLL controller card. The backups must be made before the new controller is installed.

As we explained in Chapter 2, not all disk drives can work reliably with an RLL controller. The drive electronics must be able to handle the high data rate. If you already own a drive and want to add an RLL controller to your machine, call the drive manufacturer and see if you can find out whether the drive is approved for RLL use. You'll find that retail dealers are apt to claim that a drive will work properly with RLL, but manufacturers are more cautious. Malfunctions tend to be sporadic, making it very hard to locate the offending hardware when the machine crashes because of an RLL problem. You're more likely to avoid problems if you buy a drive and controller combination that has been well-tested and already shipped in large numbers.

Increasing Processor Speed

The speed of the computer's system clock sets the rate at which the processor and other circuitry functions. A faster clock hastens disk transfers in two ways. First, it increases the rate of data transfer between the controller card and main memory. Second, it speeds disk access by making software, including

DOS, run more quickly. Once directories and file allocation tables are read into memory, DOS can scan them more rapidly. DOS can also transfer data from its buffers to programs more quickly. Productivity software also must process incoming data. For example, text editors break up text files into one-line units and place each unit at a separate memory location. A faster processor cuts the time required.

There are two strategies for increasing system speed. One is to increase the clock speed of your machine by replacing the crystal that generates the clock. This is risky, and we don't recommend it; it can cause your system to crash, lose data, and possibly corrupt your hard disk with no warning. A better approach is to upgrade the processor (and related circuitry) to a different, more efficient model.

Accelerator Boards

One way to do this is by installing an **accelerator board**, which fits into one of the computer's slots. Accelerator boards have a faster, more powerful processor that supercedes the computer's. If the original processor chip is used at all, it is as an auxiliary processor to handle input-output. Accelerators typically substitute the next-highest chip for the current one, replacing an 8088 chip with a 286, and 286 with a 386 model, and so on.

An accelerator board has its own clock crystal on board, and this chip does not affect the clock rate in other parts of the computer. If a 4.77 MHz PC receives an accelerator card that runs a 286 chip at 8 MHz, *only* the circuitry on the card runs at 8 MHz. Data transfer across the system bus (across the slots) continues at the 4.77 MHz clock rate, as does access to system memory. This means that the DMA chips that perform data transfer between the disk controller and memory will work no more quickly when an accelerator is installed. Similar limitations accrue to machines that use the processor to transfer disk data, since the data must pass across the system bus, and the bus runs no faster.

Hidden Benefits

While accelerator cards cannot help with disk transfer rates, they *do* make a difference in how quickly DOS can scan directories and file allocation tables once these are loaded into memory. And, of course, software can process incoming and outgoing data much more quickly. Some accelerator boards achieve faster memory access by keeping a memory *cache* on the card. Special, super-fast memory chips hold copies of the most-recently accessed memory locations. Since the same memory addresses tend to be read repeatedly, the boards save time by going to the onboard cache, rather than by constantly rereading data from slower RAM chips.

Replacement Motherboards

A better way to increase your system's throughput is to replace the motherboard altogether, moving from, say, a 286-based unit to a 386SX, 386, or 486. As you check prices, you may be surprised to find out that a replacement motherboard costs less, not more, than an accelerator board. Why? Because motherboards are produced by the millions, while accelerator boards do not sell in large numbers. Of course, you may have to buy RAM for the new motherboard, and you may be tempted to add other features while you're upgrading your system. Still, odds are that a replacement motherboard offers the most bang for the buck if you want to boost your system's CPU speed.

Track Buffering

Recall from Chapter 2 that track buffers are a feature built into some hard disk controller cards. When a request is made for a single sector, the controller reads the whole track on which the sector is located, starting with the sector closest to the read/write head. It reads the sectors in their physical sequence, as if the disk had a 1:1 interleave. Then it takes the requested sector from the buffer and sends it to DOS. The next request for a sector from the track can then be delivered instantly, at *electronic speed*, since there is no need to wait for the sector to swing under the read/write head.

Writing Data

Of course, track buffering may be employed for writing data as well as reading it. In this case, when DOS "writes" a sector, it is inserted into the track buffer. Under ideal conditions, every sector on the track is given new data, and the data is physically written on the disk only when the track buffer is full. However, to avoid data loss through power outages and other glitches, the track is actually written after a specified delay, or when a request is made to move the read/write heads to another cylinder. The delay is typically a few seconds. No performance degradation occurs, even when more sectors on the track are subsequently written, since the delay period is quite long compared to data transfer times, and it's unlikely that another sector will be sent to the buffer just as the track is written out. Track buffering may be made *more* efficient during write operations by sorting out which sectors have changed and by writing less than a full track.

There is another reason why track-buffering software does not wait long before writing data to disk. When the last sectors of a file are sent to the track buffer, the data could remain in the buffer for several seconds or longer. From the point of view of the application software, the file has been completely and successfully written to disk. The program might immediately terminate, perhaps through some sort of "save and quit" command. A moment later the track buffer begins to spill its contents onto the disk surface and—bang!—it runs into an unrecoverable disk error of some kind—perhaps a full diskette. But the program is gone, so its built-in error-recovery facilities cannot come into play. The file is lost.

Applications

Track buffering is of most use in machines that cannot handle a 1:1 interleave. Theoretically, it lets disks using a slower interleave work as fast as one with 1:1 interleave—data is supplied as fast as the processor can handle it. Even a machine with 1:1 interleave can benefit, because sometimes a fast interleave is undermined by the software accessing the disk. If software processes data as it is received, it introduces delays in the request for the next sector. The next sector may pass by the read/write heads before it can be read, and an extra turn of the disk is required to get to it. No waiting is required when this happens with a track-buffered controller.

Track buffering is most useful for sequential files. Random access files benefit less, since the next required sector is more likely to reside on another track. In either case, the benefits will be greatly reduced if the files are allowed to become highly fragmented.

Software-based Buffering

Track buffering can also be performed by certain disk caching utilities. Instead of buffering the track on the controller card, it is kept in the computer's memory. If it is well-designed, the software will make use of idle circuitry, so that the computer's overall performance is not slowed, even when it turns out that other sectors on a track are not required. Be aware that there are situations in which this feature can slow down a machine, such as when you work with widely-dispersed records in random access files. In this case, you can turn the buffering feature off by pressing a hot key to bring up the memory-resident caching software.

RAM Disks

One way of getting around slow head seeks is to eliminate them altogether by using a RAM disk. We discussed RAM disks in Chapter 2 as one of the alternate data storage options, and described *non-volatile* RAM disks that maintain their data even when the computer is turned off. Because non-volatile RAM boards are still quite expensive, and because they may lose data if the power is off for a long time, not many users opt to add megabytes of RAM storage to their systems. But smaller, transient RAM disks can play an important role in improved disk performance.

How They Work

A RAM disk sets aside part of memory and divides it into sections that correspond to disk sectors. A device driver (control program) sits in low memory, performing the same functions as a disk drive's electronics. From DOS's point of view, it is just another disk drive. But there is no waiting for read/write heads to move across the disk surface, and no waiting for platters to turn. Completely fragmented files are read and written as quickly as perfectly contiguous ones.

RAM Disk Speed

It is the processor that makes data transfers in most RAM disks. The data moves from the RAM disk part of memory to the microprocessor chip, and then to a DOS buffer. Special-purpose RAM disk boards may be equipped for DMA (direct memory access) transfers, which move the data directly from one memory location to another.

RAM disk boards are often equipped with their own power supply and line to a wall socket. When the computer is turned off, they retain data, making them *non-volatile.* Most come equipped with a backup power supply that will maintain data in the event of a power outage.

Software-based RAM disks are created by a device driver or memory-resident program. Usually this is done at startup, but some RAM disk software can be brought into play at any time. Then files are copied to the RAM disk from a hard disk or diskette. When work is finished, the altered files must be copied back to disk.

Dangers

RAM disks are notoriously risky, since the files they hold are destroyed by the slightest power disruption. While power outages are rare, instances where software malfunctions force you to reboot the computer are not. When important data is kept on the RAM disk, it must be constantly backed up. This is very easy to do by stopping work periodically and executing a simple batch file that copies the endangered files over to your hard disk.

Read-only Files

Rather than risk your data, it's better to reserve a RAM disk for *read-only* files that are under more or less constant access. *Program overlays* are an example. Overlays are parts of a program that remain on disk while the main program is loaded. As various program functions are called upon, the corresponding overlay is loaded from disk onto an area in memory reserved by the program for this purpose. By *overlaying* the same section of memory with different modules of code, a program occupies less room.

Reference Files

RAM disks are also good for holding the electronic dictionaries used by spelling checkers and thesauruses. When spelling checkers constantly watch for errors during text entry, the hard disk holding the dictionary never stops working. Performance may degrade to the point where the screen does not echo characters as quickly as they are typed. And the incessant flicker of the hard drive's indicator light tells of excessive wear and tear. Both problems are completely eliminated by placing the dictionary on a (quite large) RAM disk.

Temporary Files

Temporary files also benefit from RAM disks. Word processors often create temporary output files containing special formatting codes for the printer. Much disk access may be required to fill in cross-references between pages. Directing the temporary file to a RAM disk can greatly speed the process. Similarly, the compilers and linkers used by computer programmers may create elaborate temporary files that are under constant random access. The entire cycle time from source text to finished code can often be cut in half just by moving the process over to a RAM disk.

Program Files

Finally, RAM disks may make a big difference in system performance when you move back and forth between programs. It is easy enough to create batch files or keyboard macros that will shut down one program and begin another, but waiting for the programs to load can be onerous. By placing the program files on a RAM disk, the load time is made as fast as possible.

An important point to note about all of these applications is that none places critical files on the RAM disk. If power is interrupted, all that is lost are unchanging program files or data files that can be easily reloaded from the hard disk. There's no need to back up this RAM disk at all.

Drawbacks

The problem with RAM disks is that they greedily consume the one resource that hardly anyone has enough of: memory. It's usually practical to devote only a small part of conventional memory to a RAM disk. But even a 64K RAM disk can hold many program overlays, a large printer output file, or the temporary files made by a compiler.

Extended Memory

Fortunately, there are two ways to set up a large RAM disk using almost none of your precious 640K of conventional memory. The RAM disk may reside in **extended memory** or **expanded memory**. Extended memory can be installed only in 286, 386, and 486 machines. It is made up of RAM residing at memory addresses above one million. The 640K of conventional memory resides below this mark. The processor used in XTs cannot get at memory in this range, and even the more advanced chips require an advanced operating system to use it with programs. But a RAM disk can be installed in extended memory and run with DOS.

Expanded Memory

Expanded memory is easily confused with extended memory, but it is quite different. It works in all kinds of machines, using special memory boards in XTs and 286-type ATs. In 386 and 486 machines expanded memory may be created from extended memory using special emulation software.

XT-style machines are limited by DOS to 640K of memory, but the processor can, in fact, reach a full 1,000K of memory addresses under DOS. Some of the unused memory range is reserved for special needs, but most is left open. Expanded memory normally takes over a 64K stretch of addresses in the high end of memory and uses it as a "window" for passing data back and forth to programs. While many megabytes of expanded memory may be installed in the machine, at any moment only 64K is accessible to the processor through this 64K window. When a program requires a particular piece of data, the section of expanded memory holding the data is shifted into the 64K window so that the processor can get at it. (Actually, the window is divided into four

16K sections, so a program can get at four sections of expanded memory at once.) This process is called **bank switching**. The scheme is diagrammed in Figure 7-5. Programs must be specially written to keep data in expanded memory.

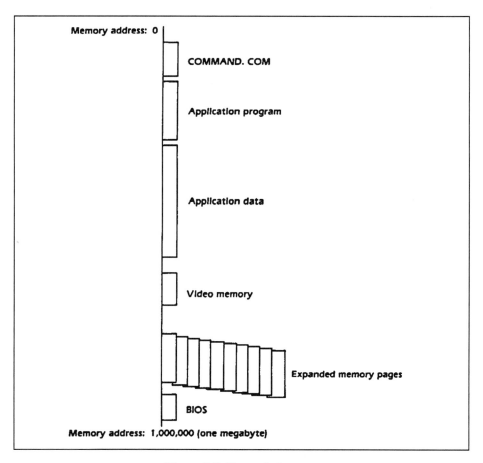

Figure 7-5. Expanded memory

Today, numerous memory expansion boards are available that can be set to work as conventional memory (640K), extended memory, or expanded memory. Most of these boards let you use part of the installed memory in one way and the remainder in another. A portion might be devoted to expanded memory to be used by programs that keep huge files, and the rest could be used as extended memory to support a large RAM disk. Many people have unused extended memory but never bother to allocate it to a RAM disk, wasting a valuable productivity resource.

RAM Disk Software

RAM disk programs are available from many sources. DOS Versions 3.0 and later include a RAM disk program. Many add-on memory cards provide a RAM disk on their utility diskettes. And myriad commercial and public domain offerings are available.

Each program is tailored differently. While nearly all allow you to size the RAM disk in 1,000-byte increments, some also give you control over sector size, the number of directory entries accommodated, and other specifications. A few let you avoid these complications by demanding the simple equivalent of a single-sided or double-sided diskette.

Some RAM disk programs come as device drivers that must be installed via CONFIG.SYS when the computer is booted. Others can be loaded at any time. Several RAM disks may be created if you prefer smaller disks under multiple drive specifiers. No matter how the RAM disk is created, or in what kind of memory it resides, a few kilobytes of conventional memory is devoted to the device driver. You must reboot to remove a RAM disk from memory.

Positioning the RAM Disk

Most RAM disk programs create the disk under the next highest available drive specifier. For example, if you have a diskette drive as **A:** and a hard disk as **C:**, the RAM disk will be created as **D:**. Some programs let you specify the name for the disk, in which case you could make it **B:** if your system lacks a second diskette drive. Some RAM disk programs let you *insert* the drive between others. In a machine with two diskette drives, inserting a RAM disk as **B:** makes the second drive **C:**. (Be warned that doing this invites confusion.) You may even be able to "replace" a disk drive with the RAM disk, so that a RAM disk named **B:** completely hides from view the diskette drive normally at **B:**. This feature can be useful when a drive goes out of whack and your batch files and software are configured to rely upon it; a RAM disk can sometimes stand in for a drive until it is repaired.

The DOS RAM Disk Program

DOS includes a RAM disk program named *VDISK* or RAMDISK in IBM DOS and *RAMDRIVE* in MS DOS. It is held in the file **VDISK.SYS** or **RAMDRIVE.SYS**. The program can only be used when the computer is booted. This is done by adding a line to your CONFIG.SYS file. To create a 128K RAM disk in conventional memory, write:

```
DEVICE=VDISK.SYS 128
```

or:

```
DEVICE=RAMDRIVE.SYS 128
```

If the program file is not in the root directory, you'll need to include a directory path for it, as in:

```
DEVICE=C:\DOS\VDISK.SYS 128
```

The drive specifier assigned to the RAM disk will be the next available above the highest drive specifier currently used. For example, if you have a diskette drive A and a hard disk drive C, and no drive B, the RAM disk will appear as drive D, even though B is free.

Creating a 128K RAM disk this way means that 128K of conventional memory will no longer be available for your programs. If you have extended memory installed in your machine then you can have the RAM disk placed there instead. Just add /E at the end of the statement:

```
DEVICE=VDISK.SYS 128   /E
```

Be aware that placing a RAM disk in extended memory may cause problems with communications hardware, such as modems and network adapters. You can be sure of compatibility only by experimentation.

Installation in Expanded Memory

A RAM disk can also be placed in expanded memory by appending an /X switch in IBM DOS (Version 4.0 or later) or an /A switch in MS DOS:

```
DEVICE=VDISK.SYS 256   /X
```

or:

```
DEVICE=RAMDRIVE.SYS 256   /A
```

The /X and /A switches may not be used in the same command as an /E switch, since a RAM disk can't operate in two kinds of memory at once.

You may make the RAM disk as large as you please within the confines of available memory. However, VDISK and RAMDRIVE won't let you shrink remaining conventional memory to less than 64K. Note that the actual size of the RAM disk will be slightly smaller than the amount you specify, because some space must be devoted to the directory and other DOS structures.

Unless specified otherwise, DOS limits the number of drive specifiers it can use to the letters A through E. In a complicated system you may need to extend this range to accommodate one or more RAM disks. You can do this with the LASTDRIVE command. To extend the range of drive specifiers to H:, you would place this line in your CONFIG.SYS file:

```
LASTDRIVE=H
```

RAM Disk Performance

RAM disks are useful, but they are not infinitely fast. Because they rely upon the processor to transfer data between memory locations, their performance very much depends on how fast a machine you own. Perhaps your work does not entail the sorts of constant disk access that can be easily moved over to a RAM disk. But if your work *can* benefit from a RAM disk, it is one of the easier and cheapest means of improving performance.

DOS-level Optimization

A disk is optimized at DOS-level by minimizing the work DOS must do to find its way to a file, or to extract data from a file. We saw in Chapter 2 that DOS reads disk sectors into an adjustable number of buffers. Setting the number of buffers correctly is the easiest and most important of all optimization measures. Buffering can be taken much further through disk caching utilities, which may keep hundreds of sectors in system memory.

DOS finds files much more quickly when the directory tree is designed to complement the process. Files, including subdirectory files, may be laid out on the disk in particular patterns that minimize head movement. Also, the DOS PATH and APPEND commands can be set up in a way that helps DOS find a file in the shortest time. Finally, starting with DOS Version 3.3, the FASTOPEN command can greatly reduce the time it takes DOS to find and open a file.

Optimizing the Number of DOS Buffers

DOS uses buffers to minimize physical disk accesses. When an application program requires only a few bytes of information from a sector, and then a few more, it would be senseless to read the same sector repeatedly from the disk surface. DOS keeps the most recently accessed sectors in memory, and before going to disk for data, it first checks to see if the data is already on hand in one of the buffers. Similarly, when a program sends data items to disk, DOS waits until a sector is filled with data fragments before actually writing the sector on the disk surface.

An Example

For example, say that in a random-access data file every record is 128 bytes long. Data is entered for a record and "saved." Only a quarter of a 512-byte sector is changed, and if DOS writes the sector to disk, three-quarters of the data will be an exact copy of what is already written. Since the disk drive must write an entire sector at once, there is no way to write just the data that has been changed.

Say you were to continue entering new data into the next three 128-byte records in the database. The same sector would be written to disk four times in a row, each time changing a different part of the sector's contents. Obviously, if all four records were entered before any disk access was made, three of the four disk accesses would be eliminated.

This is the rationale for sector buffering. When data is entered into one of the buffers, DOS waits to see if more is coming. It writes out the data only if the buffer is required for some other sector, or if a delay period has elapsed without disk access (lest data be lost if the machine crashes or is turned off).

Writing Data

Applications programs have a way of assuring that all buffers holding new data are recorded on disk before the program terminates. You may have had the experience of losing power while working in a database, only to find that when you restarted the program, data that you thought had been saved was nowhere to be found. The data was lost because the software did not have the opportunity to "flush" the buffers on to disk during a normal program termination. This is one reason why you should always quit a program through the proper exit command, and never by rebooting or switching off the power.

The BUFFERS Setting

DOS lets you choose how many buffers it sets up when the system is booted. This is done by including the line **BUFFERS=number** in either CONFIG.SYS or AUTOEXEC.BAT. DOS allows from 1 to 99 buffers; as we'll see in a moment, **BUFFERS=20** is about right for many systems. You'll need to reboot to bring the new command into action. When no BUFFERS setting is made, DOS defaults to two buffers on a PC or XT, or three on an AT. Starting with Version 3.3, DOS checks the amount of system memory installed and sets an appropriate number of buffers. In DOS 4.0 and later, the DOS installation program automatically creates a CONFIG.SYS file and writes a BUFFERS command into it. Like many DOS default settings, these numbers were chosen to conserve memory, and they are extremely conservative, even from the standpoint of a diskette-only machine.

It's easy to see the advantage in having many buffers. When there are only a few, DOS is forced to empty buffers before the sectors they hold have been completely processed, since other sectors are momentarily required. The discarded sectors must be written to, or read from, the hard disk a second time, and perhaps *many* times. Much time is wasted on unnecessary disk accesses.

However, as useful as buffers are, it's possible to have DOS create *too many*. It takes time to search for a particular sector among the buffers, and if it is not found, a disk access must be made anyway. When many buffers are searched, the time required may exceed that taken by simply going to disk without any buffering scheme at all.

The Optimal Value

There is no single "optimal" value for the DOS BUFFERS setting. It varies by the way particular applications process files, and it depends somewhat on a computer's speed, since a faster CPU can search the buffers more quickly. Those who have run tests on buffer settings recommend values between 15 and 20 for most machines. Each buffer takes up 528 bytes—512 for the sector and 16 for DOS's bookkeeping—so 20 buffers take up about 10K of RAM. If you have a hard disk and you've relied on the DOS default settings of two or three buffers, you'll notice an immediate improvement in performance with most applications when you increase the number of buffers to 20.

DOS Versions 3.0 and later search the buffers more quickly because the software is better-crafted than in earlier versions. If you use an earlier DOS version, 15 buffers may be optimal. Here is yet one more reason why you should upgrade to the latest DOS version, if you have not already.

Relative Performance

Having more DOS buffers does not help all software. In fact, some applications are slightly slowed by a larger buffer setting. When sequential files (such as text files) are read or written, no sector is repeatedly accessed, and hence the whole buffering system serves no purpose. But the processor overhead for the buffer searches remains. Conversely, *completely random* file accesses are not helped by having many buffers, as nearly all accesses require a sector not currently held in the buffer pool. Fortunately, most "random" accesses are not all that random—the software tends to work on only a few file locations at once—and having more buffers generally benefits data throughput.

Some application software opens many files at once. It may be tempting to increase the number of DOS buffers to accommodate them all, but if you think about it, you'll see that this makes no sense. The BUFFERS setting is a kind of gambling. You are setting *odds* that, on the average, a specific unit of data is more likely to be in memory than not. In essence, you are agreeing to risk wasting time looking for data that may not be in memory, rather than undergo the certitude of losing many milliseconds to a disk access. The balance is set by a contest between CPU speed and disk speed—the number of sectors or files involved has nothing to do with it. Similarly, it's erroneous to think that the larger the disk, the more DOS buffers it needs.

Applying Disk Cachers

Disk caching (pronounced "cashing") combines the best features of RAM disks and DOS buffers. A section of memory is set aside to hold frequently accessed disk sectors, and when DOS issues a command to look for a sector on disk, disk-caching software first searches through the cached sectors; if it finds its target, it supplies the sector to DOS from the cache, saving the time it takes to read data from the disk surface. The logic is the same as for DOS buffers. But disk caching programs can keep *megabytes* of sectors in memory when extended or expanded memory is used. And in this way it is more like a RAM disk—whole files may be kept in memory.

In our discussion of the DOS BUFFERS command, we cautioned you against creating too many buffers because DOS could spend more time searching them than it is worth. You may wonder how a disk caching program could possibly be efficient when it keeps many times as many sectors in memory as would be prudent for the DOS buffers. Disk cachers are much smarter than DOS in this regard; they maintain logic that ensures that only minimal processing time goes into the search. And because the cacher can keep so much of a file in memory, a more protracted search is less risky than with DOS buffers, because a program is much more likely to find the sector it needs.

The Role of DOS Buffers

The cache sits between the physical disk and the DOS buffers, as shown in Figure 7-6. It does not replace the DOS buffers. Its role is more like that of a RAM disk, in that it acts as a sort of pseudo-disk that can supply sectors to the DOS buffers more quickly than a physical disk access can. When a cache is operating, it is redundant for DOS to keep many buffers of its own and search through them. Accordingly, set the number of DOS buffers to 1 or 2 when you are using cache software.

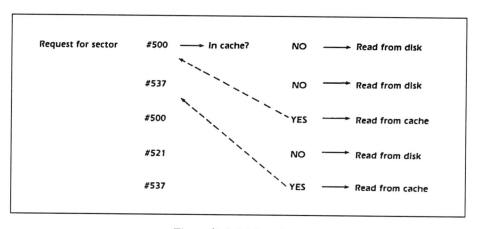

Figure 7-6. Disk caching

Sector Selection

When DOS reads a new sector, it is forced to give up a sector held in one of the buffers. It allots the buffer on a "least-recently used" (LRU) scheme. Discarding the least-recently used sector makes sense, but it is not the optimal logic. Disk cachers use a combination of least-recently used logic and least-frequently used logic; a cacher may hang on to a sector that has been "hit" many times, even if it is the least-recently used.

Why isn't DOS made as smart? It's certainly not for lack of ability on Microsoft's part. Disk cachers take up 20 to 30K of memory—extra code that would bloat DOS. DOS needs to run in systems with too little memory to devote to a disk cache, and too little to hold a larger rendition of DOS. Even in systems equipped with 640K, memory shortage is a persistent problem, and it is much better to purposely allot a portion of memory to disk caching for some applications, and not for others.

Performance

The benefits of disk caches are apparent very soon after they're loaded. Odds are the File Allocation Table (FAT) will quickly be stored in the cache, speeding all DOS file operations. A disk cache increases the speed of disk-intensive operations (such as database sorts) by as much as 100 to 200 percent. The greatest gains are made using random-access files in which the software constantly accesses physically distant points in the file.

In some rare circumstances, a disk cache can actually slow software down slightly. If a file's sectors are read only once, extra time is performed to move sectors through the cache. The slowdown is usually not noticeable, however, and is far outweighed by performance gains.

FATs and Directories

Because disk cachers may use large amounts of memory, they usually end up holding the whole file allocation table, the root directory, and recently used subdirectories. This lets DOS search for files more quickly, particularly when the directory tree is complicated and subdirectories are fragmented. This performance gain is particularly noticeable to programmers when they compile or link numerous small files.

Reading vs Writing Data

Theoretically, a disk caching program should be able to achieve performance gains when writing data as well as reading it. For example, when a database program changes one record held in a sector, the sector can remain in the cache for a few seconds before being physically written to the disk; this allows time for further changes to the sector, saving the trouble of multiple disk accesses. Most caching programs write data directly to the disk, however. It's considered too dangerous to leave data loitering in memory, especially since FAT sectors or other crucial information could be destroyed if the machine is turned off or rebooted. Instead, cachers write sectors directly to disk, but they keep a copy in the cache in case it's used again. These programs are called **write-through cachers**, because in a sense they write data *through* the cache.

The IBMCACHE Program

PS/2 machines are shipped with a disk caching program called IBMCACHE. To install it, place the Reference Diskette in drive A and enter **IBMCACHE**. A menu with four choices is displayed:

```
1. Install disk cache onto drive C:
2. View disk cache settings
3. Change disk cache settings
4. Remove disk cache from drive C:
```

By selecting the first menu choice, the file IBMCACHE.SYS is copied to the root directory of drive C. In addition, a line like the following one is added to your CONFIG.SYS file to start up disk caching when the machine is booted:

```
DEVICE=\DOS\IBMCACHE.SYS  64  /NE  /P4
```

This creates a 64K cache in conventional memory, using a page size of four pages (the page size is the number of disk sectors the cache program reads or writes at once). You may create a larger cache by changing the value 64. Delete the **/NE** switch (which stands for "not extended") to have the cache located in extended memory. Alternatively, you may alter the cache parameters by making the appropriate selections in the menu shown above.

The MS DOS Cache Program

MS DOS includes a disk caching program starting from Version 4.0, as does IBM DOS starting from Version 5.0 (it's also packaged with Windows). This program is held in the file SMARTDRV.SYS. To create a 128K cache in conventional memory when SMARTDRV.SYS is in the root directory, you would place a command like the following one in your CONFIG.SYS file:

```
DEVICE=\DOS\SMARTDRV.SYS 128
```

Adding **/A** to the end of the command causes the cache to be created in expanded memory, or, if you have extended memory, to have your extended memory board used as expanded memory by the cache. Using /A without preceeding it with a cache size causes all of expanded memory to be devoted to the cache.

Advanced Disk Cachers

Quite advanced features are available in some disk cachers. There may be a "high priority" mode in which you can allocate portions of the cache to particular files, whether or not they are currently in use. This allows you to switch back and forth between tasks without constantly reloading the cache with the files used by each. The "high priority" configuration can be saved in a file for use at another time, and the entire system can be reconfigured on the fly, without rebooting. Some caching programs can also be made to read whole tracks at a time in anticipation of requiring other sectors from a track; it creates a sort of *full track buffer*.

The disk caching program that accompanies *The Norton Utilities* comes in two versions. One is intended for machines that have lots of memory available. Its emphasis is on speed. The second version is intended for machines that have no extended or expanded memory on hand. The program itself is smaller, and it uses fewer buffers. It won't work as quickly or as intelligently as the other version. But it can greatly improve performance, even with only 5K of conventional memory given over to it.

Most caching programs issue reports that help you assess their effectiveness. They tell how many disk accesses were made by DOS, how many were handled by the cache, and how many required physical reads or writes. Using these data, you can determine whether the cache is worth the memory devoted. Caching software is not very expensive, particularly when you consider that in many instances it can impart voice-coil speeds to stepper-motor drives. However, using a cacher is inexpensive only if you already have spare memory on hand.

Optimizing Directory Tree Organization

File searches are a particularly time-consuming aspect of disk access. When a file is listed in a subdirectory that is several levels below the root directory, the read/write heads must jump from subdirectory to subdirectory as DOS traces its way to the file. Little time is lost when only a file or two are opened. But some applications repeatedly access scores of files.

Subdirectory Size

There are three ways to minimize file search times. First, keep the size of sub-directories to one cluster. Recall that a directory entry takes 32 bytes. A 512-byte sector holds 16 such entries, so a four-sector cluster holds 64. Since two slots are given to the *dot* and *double dot* entries, a single-cluster directory can hold 62 files. This amounts to nearly three screens in a directory listing. It's more files than most subdirectories should hold.

When subdirectories are restricted to one cluster, the entry for the next sub-directory along the path can always be found without moving the read/write heads to another track. Subdirectories tend to be fragmented, since clusters are usually allocated gradually as more and more files are listed in it. The one-cluster restriction also means that DOS never has to search further than 62 entries to find the subdirectory's listing. (DOS searches directories top down, and it quits the search once it finds its target).

Reordering Listings

In Chapter 5 we mentioned utilities that sort a directory by physically reorder-ing it on disk. Properly designed, one of these utilities can help speed disk searches by placing all entries for child subdirectories at the top of the direc-tory, as shown in Figure 7-7. While seldom-accessed subdirectories might not deserve a priority position, on the whole this is the optimum way to order directories.

The second benefit of utilities that permanently sort directories is that they will move all unused directory slots to the end of the directory sectors. DOS scans each sector before reading the next. If sectors early in the directory are mostly filled with empty slots made by file erasures, the search takes that much longer. One minor inadequacy of DOS is that it does not discard sectors once it allocates them to a subdirectory file. If three clusters are allocated to hold many files and all files are then erased, the subdirectory file continues to take up three clusters. While DOS always assigns a new file to the topmost available slot, a lot of empty space may separate actual file entries, putting your disk drive through unnecessary head seeks.

Tree Leveling

Finally, subdirectory access is quickened by creating a tree with as few levels as possible. If a programmer places 40 code modules in the subdirectory **PROJECTS\PASCAL\DATABASE\REPORTS\MODULES**, DOS will have to perform (in the worst case) seven head seeks to get to the start of each file, or 280 seeks to link all modules. Even at a 40-millisecond average access time, that's over 11 seconds wasted in head movements—not to mention the time spent scanning each subdirectory. (In a moment we'll see how the FASTOPEN command makes an end-run around this inefficiency.)

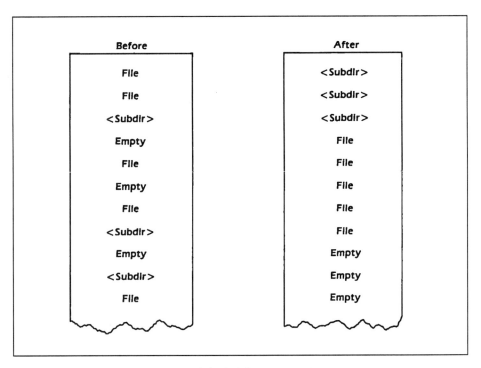

Figure 7-7. Subdirectory sorting

Optimizing Subdirectory Layout

By grouping all subdirectory files in only a few cylinders at the outer edge of the disk, you can greatly reduce head movements when DOS looks up a file nested several levels down the directory tree.

An ordinary 17-sector-per-track, two-platter disk drive has 68 sectors in a cylinder. RLL encoding increases that number to 100 or even 136 sectors. Sixty-eight sectors equals 17 clusters, or 17 subdirectories. Hence a well-developed directory tree made up of 68 subdirectories can fit on only four cylinders, or only three cylinders using RLL 2,7 encoding.

When subdirectories are compacted in this way, subdirectory-to-subdirectory searches proceed much more quickly. DOS is much more likely to find the next subdirectory in the chain in the same cylinder, averting the need for a head move. Even greater speed is attained by positioning the subdirectory cylinders as close to the outer edge of the disk as possible. This measure limits the *distance* of head movements to and from the root directory and file allocation table. Many defragmenters, including *Norton Speed Disk*, perform this optimization.

Optimizing File Layout

Modest performance gains can sometimes be made by positioning crucial files as close to the outer edge of the platters as possible. The point is to minimize the *distance* the read/write heads must travel to reach the file. Of course, DOS will access the file's directory immediately before moving to the first cluster of the file, so the presumption is that the directory will also be near the outer edge. This is necessarily true for files listed in the root directory; otherwise, you must follow the prescriptions in the preceeding discussion of subdirectory compaction.

This measure is useful for files that are frequently and repeatedly accessed, such as overlay files. You'll see more difference on stepper-motor drives, where the seek time is proportional to the distance the heads are moved. Many people do not have such high-priority files in their system, and for them this optimization measure is a waste of time.

Without the help of utility software, you have real control over file layout only when a disk is empty and first filled with files. In this case, you set up as much of the directory tree as possible, and then copy over high-priority files. But there's no way you can *maintain* an ideal file layout without help from utility software. Again, it's defragmenters that do the job.

Optimizing the PATH and APPEND Commands

In Chapter 5 we examined the DOS PATH command. Recall that this command automatically searches a list of DOS paths for a file you wish to load. Starting with Version 3.3, DOS added the APPEND command, which extends the search to data files. In both commands, you list a series of paths, and DOS searches them in that order.

You can optimize path searches by listing paths in the PATH and APPEND commands in their order of importance. If the first path listed is **\IDEAS\NOTIONS\INKLINGS\INSIGHTS,** and the second path is **\BATCH,** DOS must search through five subdirectories everytime a batch file is used. If batch files are used often, the path sequence should be the reverse. The same logic applies when you list paths in an APPEND command. As a general rule, you should place short searches before long ones in the PATH sequence.

The value of this optimization varies from day to day, depending on the work you do. If you have a fast computer and a short PATH command, you probably won't notice the difference.

Using the FASTOPEN Command

Starting with Version 3.3, DOS provides the FASTOPEN command to speed repeated accesses to files. Normally, every time DOS opens a file, it must work its way through the directories that comprise the file's path. When FASTOPEN is activated, it stores in memory the locations of recently accessed files, including subdirectory files. For example, when **\PLANTS \FLOWERS\ROSES.DAT** is loaded, FASTOPEN saves the cluster number of the data file **ROSES.DAT,** and of the subdirectory files **PLANTS** and **FLOW-ERS.** Next time you open the file, DOS is able to send the read/write heads directly to **ROSES.DAT** without shuttling through the subdirectories. Similarly, if you then ask to load **PLANTS/FLOWERS/BUTTRCUP.DAT,** DOS can find it's way straight to the **FLOWERS** subdirectory to look for the file.

To activate FASTOPEN for drive C, you must enter:

```
FASTOPEN C:
```

By default, up to 34 files and subdirectories may be recorded. This number may be changed from any value from 10 to 999. To set it to 100, enter:

```
FASTOPEN C:=100
```

Thirty-five bytes of memory are taken for every file. The number must be at least one greater than the most levels of subdirectory you'll be using. FASTOPEN must never be used with the JOIN, SUBST, and ASSIGN commands discussed in Chapter 5.

FASTOPEN is a welcome addition to DOS. It can make a significant difference in certain applications, especially when overlay files are repeatedly called, and the cost in memory is negligible.

Choosing Optimization Measures

We've looked at 14 factors in disk performance, and only a few can't be changed once you've bought your disk and controller. So which measures make the most difference? And how does a measure's cost compare to its gains? If you've been reading closely, you can probably guess that the answers to these questions vary not only from machine to machine, but also from application to application. For example, if you work with large databases that are accessed fairly randomly, file defragmentation will be of less benefit to you than to users who access many sequential files.

Tradeoffs

You'll find that some optimizations nullify the benefits of others. Conversely, some optimizations are undermined when other optimizations are not performed in tandem. Let's take a look at these tradeoffs:

Cylinder density. A doubled cylinder density cuts in half the number of head seeks required by most applications, making fast seek times less important. However, the benefits of a high cylinder density are defeated by file fragmentation.

Average seek time. Faster seek times make less difference on drives with a higher cylinder density, on drives kept defragmented, on drives in which the subdirectories have been compacted, and on drives used with a substantial amount of disk caching.

Interleave. Track buffering makes the interleave irrelevant. The addition of an accelerator card may undermine a previously optimized interleave. Slow software can undermine an effective interleave by inserting additional delays between sector reads and writes.

File defragmentation. File defragmentation is less important when disk caching is used; it is entirely irrelevant when files are kept on RAM disks.

Interface type. A fast interface is useless if the processor cannot handle the higher data rate. Its benefits are largely squandered when the disk has not been optimized to minimize head movements.

Processor speed. A faster clock speed hastens data transfer from the controller to memory, allowing a faster interleave. It also speeds up the processing of data in DOS buffers, caching software, and so on. The benefits of accelerator boards are more limited. Their greatest impact is made when inefficient software creates delays that interfere with the disk's interleave optimization. An accelerator board may also hasten searches of DOS buffers and disk caches.

Track buffering. Track buffers may significantly increase performance accessing sequential files, but have minimal effect with random access files. Disk caching partially duplicates the benefits of track buffering. Track buffering is undermined when files have not been defragmented.

RAM disk support. In applications that read many small files, transferring them to a RAM disk can cut access time greatly. However, an intelligent disk cacher can do the job just as well, using approximately the same amount of RAM.

DOS buffers setting. For those using DOS versions prior to 3.3, failure to change the default **BUFFERS** setting to a value from 15 to 20 undermines most optimizations, since the disk is forced to do unnecessary work. However, when disk caching software is used, the **BUFFERS** setting must be kept low to avoid redundant searches.

Disk caching. By keeping much data in memory, disk caching reduces the benefits of all measures that optimize mechanical access to files, including fast seek times, high cylinder densities, track buffering, and file defragmentation. Conversely, a disk cacher would slow a RAM disk, as the RAM disk already operates at electronic speed.

Directory tree design. An optimized tree design makes the most difference when your software opens and closes many files, or a few files repeatedly. Disk cachers, subdirectory compaction, and the FASTOPEN command reduce the value of this optimization.

Subdirectory layout. The benefits of compacting subdirectories into a few cylinders are lessened by a shallow directory tree design, the FASTOPEN command, and disk caching.

File layout. File layout makes a minor contribution to disk speed. There is even less gain when RAM disks or large disk caches are used.

PATH and APPEND optimization. This is a minor optimization that becomes totally inconsequential when FASTOPEN is used, or when a large disk cache keeps the relevant subdirectories in memory.

The FASTOPEN command. The FASTOPEN command matters only when files are repeatedly opened. It makes less difference when tree organization, subdirectory compaction, and disk caching increase the speed of directory searches.

Cost Effectiveness

Now, let's look at the relative costs of the various optimization measures. We'll use typical retail prices where actual dollar values are given. Most products are available at discounted prices.

Cylinder density. This measure is very expensive when it results from the purchase of a very high-capacity disk, since these disks tend to cost more per megabyte. It is inexpensive when acquired through RLL encoding, since RLL controllers cost only about $50 more than ordinary MFM controllers. However, a disk drive that can use RLL encoding may be more expensive.

Average seek time. Fast seek times are associated with higher-capacity drives. These days, the cost per megabyte for a 100-megabyte drive is not too different than for a 40-megabyte drive, so the extra speed comes for free. But not everyone needs so much disk capacity. Faster small drives are available, typically at a 15 percent premium.

Interleave. Interleave optimization utilities exist as stand-alone programs retailing for about $75, or as part of a general disk toolkit package costing $125 to $150.

File defragmentation. Many defraggers are available at a reasonable price. You can still buy stand-alone utilities (for about $50). Or you can go for economies of scale and buy a general disk toolkit that includes a defragger.

Interface type. The faster ESDI interface is found only on expensive, high-capacity drives. Currently, a switch to RLL encoding in a standard MFM drive is the cheapest way to have a higher data rate.

Processor speed. Higher processor speed may come very cheap or very dear. Accelerator cards can run from a few hundred dollars to over a thousand. Simpler accelerators that fit into the microprocessor socket may cost only about $150. On the other hand, a replacement clock crystal for older AT-style machines costs only a few dollars at an electronics supply store.

Track buffering. Track buffers tend to be a luxury feature used to promote more expensive controllers (and their accompanying drives). Disk caching utilities that can create a software track buffer are available for about $50 to $75.

RAM disk support. DOS provides **VDISK** or RAMDRIVE for free, and, you'll find that RAM disk software is included with many add-on memory boards. Commercial programs are available, but you shouldn't need to buy one.

DOS buffers setting. The DOS buffers setting costs nothing.

Disk caching. Disk cachers, like defragmenters, come as stand-alone packages, or as part of a general disk toolkit. They run $50 to $75 alone, or less when included in a utility package. Remember that they're also included as part of new DOS versions, so you get one "free" when you upgrade.

Directory tree design. The tree design costs nothing. But it takes a lot of careful thought. Utilities that reorder subdirectory listings are usually found within disk tool kits, such as *The Norton Utilities*.

Subdirectory layout. Again, the optimization is free, but it requires time for planning.

File layout. There's no cost, unless you use a defragmenter that can rearrange files by a specified plan.

PATH and APPEND optimization. **PATH** is standard to all DOS versions from 2.0 onward. The **APPEND** command appears starting with DOS 3.3. So both are free if you use DOS 3.3 or a later version.

The FASTOPEN command. Available starting with DOS Version 3.3., so it also costs nothing.

Recommendations

All in all, too much attention is given to hardware solutions for optimization, and too little to software solutions. In particular, fast seek times have taken on mythical proportions. There's no point in owning an 18-millisecond drive if it's run in an unoptimized system.

A file defragmenter is the most important optimization measure open to you. It costs little, and it's likely to give at least a 50 percent boost in performance even on a drive that has long been filled with data. *Everyone* should have one of these programs, and should use it regularly.

Disk caching is second in line, especially if you have expanded or extended memory that often sits idle. In some applications, disk speed may triple or quadruple from just these two optimization measures. If you don't already have this software, you can acquire it for under $100. A hundred dollars of added hardware investment will not buy nearly so much speed.

The importance of other optimization measures depends on your applications. If you often find yourself waiting for the disk to stop churning, stop and think about what's happening. How many files are accessed? If only a few, perhaps a RAM disk is the solution. In what way are the files accessed—sequentially or randomly? Perhaps a larger cache is what you need. Do the files remain open, or are they repeatedly opened and closed? Maybe FASTOPEN will do the job. Now that you understand the principles behind disk optimization, you should be able to experiment effectively and push your hardware to the limit.

Backups without Pain

Hard disk backups may be the most boring topic in all computerdom. It's not that backup techniques are inherently dull—quite the contrary, there are lots of interesting tricks and strategies. But it's hard to sustain interest in something so seemingly unproductive. Like military expenditures or health insurance, the most desirable outcome is when the effort is a total waste.

Unfortunately, backups have a way of being useful all too often. In a moment we'll survey the dozen-odd ways that people lose data day in and day out. So many data-munching monsters inhabit the world, it's hard to work with computers and not suffer occasional loses, either by your own hand or through various hardware or software calamities. And no real respite is in sight. Even as these words are written, a prominent software company begins a massive recall of a popular program that "in certain instances" erases hard disks at random. Your data is never *completely* safe from attack.

Risks to Your Data

It would be nice to begin this chapter without the usual lecture about the importance of backups. But forgive us if we indulge. A decade after the appearance of the first IBM PCs, most data still goes without being backed up. It is as if every newcomer must learn the hard way. Studies show that only a third of hard disks in offices are backed up. Yet the average office PC is used by 3.6 workers, making it all the more difficult to reconstruct lost data.

One way of looking at the expense and effort devoted to backups is to regard them as an insurance premium. A good backup utility program and a few boxes of diskettes cost about $150. A discounted tape backup unit with a couple of cartridges might run $500. For a 20-megabyte hard disk, a monthly global backup plus two incremental backups per week take up roughly 25 hours per year using diskettes, or 15 hours using tape (assuming unattended operation during the global backups). At $20 per hour for the time, and amortizing the software and equipment costs over three years, we arrive at $550 per year for diskette backups, and $475 per year for tape.

Putting a Price on Data

Now, what is the value of your data? If you write only letters and you keep paper copies of each, your data is hardly worth anything. On the other hand, if your accounts receivable are entrusted to your hard disk, a data loss could easily cost you tens of thousands of dollars directly, and thousands more scurrying about trying to reconstruct your business. It's harder to put a price on the damage to your reputation among customers and colleagues. Most priceless of all is the inspiration lost when you obliterate several chapters of the Great American Novel. An already-precarious project may never recover from such a disaster; it's just too dispiriting to go on.

For data worth $10,000, a year's backup costs about five percent of its value. This figure is higher than common full-replacement insurance premiums. But for $20,000 worth of data (or $20,000 worth of chaos-avoidance), backups start to seem cheap. In fact, in a typical business, backups are by far the cheapest insurance premium paid. The time required to make backups increases only slightly as disks (and their holdings) grow.

Most people tend to think of backups as a precaution against a *crash*. True, most haven't a clue about what exactly constitutes a crash, but we all know about auto crashes and plane crashes, and we certainly don't want something like that to befall our data. The fear is not unjustified: sooner or later, all hard disks fail. Yet for every out-and-out hard disk holocaust, hundreds of individual files are maimed or erased by well-meaning users. Backups are every bit as valuable as protection against user failure as against hardware failure.

File-Recovery Tools

Many users seem to acquire a false sense of security from owning file-recovery tools. We'll look at these tools in depth in Chapter 9. They certainly can be valuable. But all file-recovery tools have limitations. In many situations they can make only a partial data recovery, and what they recover may be so garbled that, well, all the king's horses and all the king's men won't be able to put it back together again. Having a backup is nearly always preferable to trying to reverse the damage.

Aversion to Backups

But for all their utility and all their cost-effectiveness, backups are avoided. They may be an endless source of apprehension, guilt, and angst, but somehow the resistance to sitting down and making the backups survives. Do we need an Eleventh Commandment?

The answer, we fervently believe, is "no." Making backups can be trivial, but organizing a system in which backups are trivial is *not* so trivial. People avoid backups because they are not organized. A small, but ample investment of time is required to set up the backup procedures. And that investment needs to be approached as a distinct project. Otherwise, you'll be too disorganized to make proper backups when they are needed. You won't want to stop for backups because they'll take much longer than the 5 or 10 minutes they ought to. And so there will be no backups at all.

Dangers to Your Data

You may already be making regular backups, and may feel that this chapter should be left for the sinners. Perhaps your backups are adequate for your needs. But before taking your leave, consider all that can happen to your data:

- A disk sector can go bad, wiping out part of a file. You can use a repair utility to mark the sector as off limits to DOS, but the data is gone for good.
- You may erase one or more files accidentally. If the files are badly fragmented, and the disk has many scattered unallocated sectors, an unerase utility may not work, particularly on non-text files.
- You may modify a file in a regrettable way and not be able to reverse the damage.

- You may accidentally reformat a disk. As we'll see in Chapter 9, utilities that undo the damage of a reformatting may be only partially successful.
- The hard disk may suffer an unrecoverable head crash, mechanical failure, or electronic blowout.
- A power outage occurring at the moment a file is being saved may cause loss of the file both in memory and on disk.
- You may copy a file to another subdirectory, overwriting a different file with the same name.
- You may purposely erase files you would want to keep, but have misidentified. This happens often during disk housecleaning, particularly when hurriedly trying to make space on a full disk.
- You may inadvertently destroy a file while working on it, say by deleting most of it accidentally and then saving it.
- Malfunctioning software may mangle its own files or unrelated files. Or it may write into DOS buffers in main memory; when the buffers contain file allocation table sectors, both copies of the FAT are rendered useless and everything on the disk is lost.
- As part of your education as a computer programmer, you may murder a disk directory or file allocation table.
- You may give the wrong command to a disk-management utility program and wipe out whole branches of the directory tree.
- A disgruntled employee may erase scores of files, or reformat or repartition the disk (perhaps at low level).
- A computer virus may enter your system and wipe the disk clean.
- Thieves, fire, or some other calamity may claim your whole machine (*and* your backups, if you're not careful).
- Your meticulously crafted system of batch files and software configuration files may be wiped out in a general crash, leaving you to recreate the whole system by going back to the manuals.

  Regular backups can save you from every one of these situations. But the backups must be made intelligently. Otherwise the backups themselves can turn on you.

- You may repeatedly back up a file, but not be able to find the most recent version.
- You may make backups that are useful for restoring all data to the disk, but not for restoring only a few files.

- You may make a global backup that cannot be restored following damage to the disk surface.
- You may back up files with the same name and not be able to tell which is which.
- You may back up data files, but not the tree structure, system files, and batch files.
- You may corrupt important files without realizing it, and then record them over your good backups.

What It Takes

There's a lot to learn to put together a good backup system. For starters, you need to read this chapter. Then you must sit down, think through the options, and decide just how detailed your backups need to be, and what hardware you'll use for them. Once decided, you'll have to begin research on the latest offerings in the marketplace. After the shopping is done, there's software study and practice, followed by some busy-work setting up record-keeping for the system. Finally, you've got to put your plans into action on a regular basis.

We'll lead you through all of this in the following pages. The whole process should take about 10 hours, perhaps more if you invest in a tape unit. That's a lot of time—as much as you can expect to invest in six months' worth of backups once the system is established. After that, backups will be a tiny afterthought in your work schedule. And they'll be out of mind, not because you can't face up to the precariousness of your data, but because you'll know that, no matter what happens, you're safe.

Some General Concerns

Before we launch a discussion of various hardware and software options, we want to lay out the basic issues and methods of backup. You'd think that copying some files wouldn't require a lengthy dissertation. We certainly don't want to make matters more complicated than necessary. But, alas, they *are* complicated. Seeing only part of the problem may lead you to backup procedures that won't do the job you actually require.

Hardware versus Software

The first point to understand is that backups are a software phenomenon. You may want to buy special hardware to help with backups, such as a tape unit or removable cartridge drive. But the flexibility and reliability of your backups is largely entrusted to software. No matter how slick and powerful the hardware may appear, it is mostly the accompanying software that determines whether or not the hardware can meet your needs.

Tape Backup Software

For this reason, you will find that most of what we have to say about diskette-based backups applies to tape-based backup. Each is run by similar utility software, and the only real difference is that with one medium you must diligently swap diskettes, whereas the other allows you to walk away while the backup proceeds. If tape cartridges had much smaller capacities, there would be little distinction between the two media. The same logic applies to high-capacity removable disks.

We'll look long and hard at software in this chapter. While "ease of use" is a nicety for most software, it becomes a life-and-death issue of "likelihood of use" with backup software. When backup software is user-unfriendly, backups tend not to be made at all. Software also varies in its flexibility and error-correction capabilities. Inflexible software may require lots more work to achieve the same backup plan. Flexible software can accomplish much with a few keystrokes, and it can remember your backup scheme and repeat it automatically. Software with good error-correction can help avoid the double-whammy of damaged backups from damaged originals.

Choosing Software

There are many well-designed backup utilities on the market, so you might end up with a good one by sheer chance. But perhaps you won't. You'll be using this software hundreds of times. The street (discount) price for a typical utility is roughly $75, so it will cost you less than 25 cents each time you use it. That's not much compared to the time (and grief) a good utility can save you. So *you* should choose the utility; don't let it choose you.

Unfortunately, many tape drives operate only with the software that accompanies them. The tape unit may look great, but the software can be awful (or vice-versa). This danger makes it much riskier to buy a $1,000 tape unit instead of a $100 diskette-backup utility. If the software is no good, you're stuck.

Speed versus Flexibility

One issue we haven't mentioned so far is *speed*. Most people so thoroughly detest backups that they're suckers for speed. The sooner it's over, the better. There's no denying that backup speed is important, particularly for backups made on diskettes, where the time between changing disks may be too short to divert one's attention, but too long to keep one occupied. But speed is only one feature of many, and flexibility, reliability, and ease-of-use should not be neglected just because one program runs a little faster than another. You'll find that most good backup software falls in roughly the same performance range, and that a 10- to 20-percent advantage is hardly noticeable.

DMA

In Chapter 2 we discussed DMA, or *direct memory access*. With DMA, data is moved between the computer's memory and a peripheral like a disk drive without passing the data through the processor. When a not-very-clever backup utility like the DOS BACKUP command copies data from hard disk to diskette, it first transfers a block of the data from hard disk to memory, and then it shifts the data from memory to diskette. But high-performance backup utilities can keep both processes going simultaneously through clever DMA programming. As the processor moves data into memory from a hard disk, a DMA channel constantly copies it to a diskette. On ATs and faster clones, transferring data via DMA is actually slower than transferring it via the CPU. However, because DMA can continue while the processor is doing other things, it still offers a speed advantage.

Going Around DOS

Software that works in this way usually uses DOS to read the hard disk, but bypasses it when writing the information to a diskette or tape. The backup program takes over the diskette (or tape) controller and pushes the hardware for the very last drop of performance. Rather than read files one at a time (which entails lots of time-consuming head movements), these programs use all available RAM as a buffer. It takes some pretty complicated programming to pull this off efficiently.

Incompatibilities

Like all computer electronics, the circuitry that handles DMA has gradually improved. The first IBM PCs used relatively slow DMA chips. Later versions were faster. Backup software is designed to run on all of these machines. But if it demands too much performance from a machine, DMA *overruns* occur, and data is lost. Accordingly, some software comes with a DMA test utility that checks the data transfer rate of the DMA circuitry. The software then adjusts its timing to suit. Early PCs may require a replacement DMA chip. Incompatibility with early PC clones has occasionally been a problem.

Because most backup utilities go around DOS, you should be especially wary of unknown software for which you have no positive recommendation or review. Software can malfunction without giving any signs. If it errs in making the backup, you'll be wasting time diligently making useless copies. If it errs during data restoration, all of your data is at risk.

Ease of Use

As we'll see in a moment, the majority of backup sessions are quite short, as only a small portion of the disk's data is copied. In these quick sessions, the time it takes to get the software moving is significant. A terrible user interface can send you scurrying back to the manuals again and again. Inflexible design may force you to specify individual files for backup manually. And software that can't remember your backup plan may require you to type in long code sequences each time you repeat the backup. What good is a five-minute backup when it takes a half-hour to get it going?

Manufacturer's Claims

Be wary of manufacturer's claims of backup speed. These benchmarks are sometimes made with hard disks organized in a way that optimizes the program's performance. Data verification (double-checking) is turned off. Head movements are reduced by using only one level of subdirectories. Large files are employed to avoid the added overhead of looking after many small ones. And the disk is completely defragmented before the backup begins. Sometimes, the advertised speed will be for a whole-disk *image* backup, rather that a more time-consuming *file-by-file* backup (we'll get to this topic in a moment).

Conversely, computer magazines may sometimes test a backup utility with an artificially complex tree structure, perhaps using 1,000 subdirectories. This is done to see if the utility can manage extreme cases where its memory management skill is pushed to the limits. Software that performs admirably under ordinary circumstances may fail when confronted with very large files, or numerous small files.

Performance

To some extent, backup speed is set by hardware rather than software. If you own a fast hard disk, backups will proceed more quickly. You can accelerate backups by optimizing your hard disk's performance, as described in Chapter 7. Having lots of RAM available helps too, since it provides more work area for the software. If you have a 1.2M or 1.44M diskette drive, backups to diskettes work more quickly than with lower-capacity diskette drives. This is because the drives work faster, and because fewer disks need to be swapped. Finally, as we'll see later in this chapter, some kinds of tape drives operate more quickly than others because of the way they format data.

Image versus File-by-file Backups

In Chapter 2 we explained how DOS allocates disk space in a way that causes files to be spread across many areas of the disk. When files become fragmented, DOS takes longer to read or write them, since more head movements are required. Similarly, when backup utilities copy files, the backup takes longer when the files are badly fragmented. For rapid backups, files need to be compacted into contiguous disk space.

Image Backups

The fastest possible backup moves the read/write heads to each cylinder only once, starting from the outer edge of the disk and moving inwards cylinder by cylinder. Backups made in this way are called *image backups*, since they make an exact copy of the surface of the disk without regard to the distribution of files. Image backups are necessarily total, or *global*, backups, since there is no simple way of assuring that any given file will be completely backed up unless every disk sector is copied.

File-by-File Backups

Image backups used to require an *image restore*, in which every sector is rewritten to exactly the same location from which it was originally recorded. This approach does not work well when only one file has been damaged. Other files on the disk will have changed since the last backup, and the image restore will return them to their prior state. For this reason, products that do image backups can frequently scan the image and restore only an individual file.

In file-by-file backups, whole files are recorded one after the other. This kind of backup takes longer than an image backup, but restoring individual files is much simpler and quicker.

Relative Performance

Because of the necessary increase in head movements, file-by-file backups may take much longer than image backups. But more advanced software can close the performance gap. Intelligent backup programs may analyze the directory listings and file allocation table, and then read whole cylinders of data at once, filling memory with bits and pieces of various files. The software will process groups of files this way, greatly reducing head activity.

Some software lets you make a file-by-file restoration from an image backup. The software examines the file allocation table, which always resides at the start of an image backup. It learns the location of the parts of a file, and then moves through the image in sequence, copying the parts of the file into memory, where it reassembles it and then rewrites it to the hard disk.

DOS versus Proprietary Formats

Backup programs save data on diskette or tape in a variety of formats. In the simplest (and usually slowest) case, individual copies of each file are made in standard DOS format. If you like, you can insert the backup diskette in a drive, scan its directory, and copy a file right back to the hard disk. However, many programs use **proprietary formats** in which the data is compressed into a sort of gibberish that only the restore program can understand. Sometimes, many files are linked into one giant file to make best use of disk space.

All backup formats require some way of storing the directory paths of the files they contain. Even DOS-like backups may have special files on the diskettes to hold this information. Alternatively, they may recreate part of the tree on the backup media. By knowing the directory paths, the restore program can return the file to its rightful place. If the file's subdirectory no longer exists on the hard disk, the restore program will recreate it.

Data Compression

You'll find that proprietary formats do not compress files to the same extent that a compression utility might. Rather, the great advantage of proprietary formats is that they may include advanced error-correction codes. When diskettes are damaged, the restore program is able to use these codes to recreate the corrupted data, providing not too much has been harmed.

It's a little scary having your data encoded in a proprietary format. If serious problems arise during data restoration, there's no way to fish your data off the diskettes using a word processor or a recovery utility. This is not an unreasonable fear. As we mentioned above, backup software sometimes does not perform as well in restoring data as in backing it up. Early versions of the DOS BACKUP command sometimes refused to restore data. Because BACKUP uses a special format, some unfortunate users lost all of their data. Today, backup utility software—BACKUP included—tends to be much more reliable.

Backup versus Restore

Backup programs are actually backup-and-restore programs. But we tend to neglect the restore part, since almost all of our experience with the program is making backups. This emphasis influences our thinking when we choose backup hardware and software. Priority is given to features that make backups quick and flexible. But it's important to give adequate attention to the problems of restoring data after some kind of calamity has passed.

You can work out the world's most reliable and easy-to-use backup system only to find that you can't easily recover your data in the way you need it. As we've learned, total data loss is the least likely event in which you'll call upon your backups. More often you'll want only a single file. Or you may use backups to archive data and may want to restore an entire subdirectory to the directory tree. Perhaps you'll need to restore only files of a certain extension that have dates which fall in a particular range. And, in mass-restore operations, you'll need some way of stopping older files on the backups from overwriting more recent versions on the hard disk. It also happens that you'll want to restore a file to a different directory than the one from which it was originally taken. Some restore software can manage these requests, some cannot. Feature-mania has not carried over to restore functions to the extent it has permeated backup functions.

Major Issues

Besides the flexibility that abundant restore features make possible, several broader issues must always be kept in mind:

- It's hard to made a file-by-file restoration from an image backup. Image backups are ideal for restoring the entire disk following a major calamity, since every sector in the backup is in the order it will be rewritten to disk. But when files are fragmented on the disk, they are scattered around the backup. One cluster may be at the beginning of track 3 of a tape, the next cluster may be at the end of track 5. More and more tape backup units come with software that can make file-by-file restorations from an image backup, but the process is time-consuming. Fancy feature-filled restorations of groups of files may be impossible.

- Some backup software, whether for diskette- or tape-based backup systems, does not cope well with errors in the backup media itself. Poorly designed software may refuse to continue when it encounters an error. This problem can normally be overcome when restoring from a file-by-file backup. But you can lose everything if the software balks during an image restore. Backup utilities that store data in a proprietary format are all the more dangerous, since ordinary recovery utilities may not be able to help you repair your backup diskettes, which may not use ordinary 512-byte DOS sectors.

- Most backup software has trouble making an image-restore to a disk that has more bad sectors than when the backup was made. This is just the situation that often follows a head crash and reformatting. Although a different layout for the data could be arranged, the software is confronted with more sectors on the backup than it can fit on the hard disk. Good software keeps track of which backed-up sectors are unallocated so that it can safely put them to use, if required.

Practice Backups

You should check out the restore features *before* you actually need them. This is a simple matter when it's done with only a few files. But it's scary if you try restoring the entire disk. Watching the backups slowly overwrite every disk sector is enough to make anyone's blood pressure rise. Yet, if you're not willing to go through a trial run, how can you possibly trust the backups over the long term?

Attended versus Unattended Backups

To many, the ideal backup system is invisible. Backups are made automatically with no human intervention, sometimes at night when no one is using the computer, sometimes "in the background" as the computer continues to be used for other purposes. Except for small incremental backups, diskettes can't be used for unattended backups since no one is on hand to swap them in and out of a drive.

Manufacturers have introduced an array of special hardware for making unattended backups, including tape drives, high-capacity cartridge disks, and special hard disk cards.

Background Backups

Background backups operate as memory-resident programs. They periodically kick in, scan the disk for changed files, and make backups. The backup utility may postpone its actions if the machine is especially busy. When backups begin, they are *multitasked* with whatever else is going on in the machine. Work can continue, but it may be slowed. The software used by background backups can tell only if a file has been changed. It cannot know whether the changes have been substantial. So it may back up the same file repeatedly. Some background backup software overcomes this problem by making backups only at preset times.

Off-hours Backups

Off-hours backups have certain advantages over background backups. The backup software does not need to be memory-resident at all times. Instead, a small module can reside in memory to watch the computer's real-time clock and initiate the backup when the right moment arrives—typically in the wee hours of the morning. Only then is the backup software loaded. Alternatively, the backup software can be loaded at the end of the day and set to go off at some later hour. Of course, the machine must be left on and the system clock must be set properly.

It's important to understand that most "automatic" backup schemes still require some aid from human hands to set up the system. Software may need loading. Blank disks or tape cartridges need inserting. And power must be switched on for external units. Only the completely internal systems using a second disk drive are truly automatic. And they suffer from the disadvantage that the backups themselves are not safe from dangers like theft or fire.

Error Checking

You'll often hear that backup software has "excellent error-checking." There are many kinds of error-checking, and not all programs perform them all. They are:

- Testing that data has been correctly read from the hard disk during backups.
- Testing backup media for faults while writing to it.
- Testing that data has been written correctly to backup media while the backup is going on.

- Testing (during a restore) that data has not been corrupted while it resided on the backup media.

- Testing the hard disk for bad sectors when data is restored.

- Testing that the data has been correctly written to the hard disk when data is restored.

Proprietary formats give the best error correction, because the embedded error codes can tell if the backups have been corrupted, and often they can help reconstruct it. Many backup programs offer a "verify mode" in which data is read or written twice for safety's sake. These modes nearly double the time a backup takes, so you may or may not want to use them very much.

Backup Pitfalls

A number of pitfalls can interfere with backups, no matter what the backup medium. One problem is backing up hard disks that have been partitioned in an unusual way. Backup programs are designed for a specific operating system. They expect sectors of a particular size, and files and directories to be organized in a particular way. A backup utility can't work if the disk deviates from this organization in any way. If you have created a partition larger than 32 megabytes, either through the FDISK program in DOS 4.0 or later, or through utility software, you need to be sure that your backup software can deal with it. Similarly, if you've delegated partitions to different operating systems, you'll need a different backup program for each. An image backup of the entire disk can overcome these difficulties, but it will be of little use if you desire only a partial restoration of data.

Flexibility

Another difficulty is that many backup utilities cannot support all hard-disk-like devices. While many can service the ubiquitous Bernoulli box, many have trouble with unusual removable disk drives, very-high-capacity diskettes, and the like. If you're considering buying unusual equipment, think about how you'll back it up. On occasion, the only practical way is to buy an identical second unit so that you can make a direct copy from one to the next.

LANs

Local area networks (LANs) are another instance of non-standard hardware. Many backup utilities can function on a LAN, but only when the entire network is off-duty. All LAN makers offer a solution to the backup problem, but whether it will be flexible, speedy, and reliable is another question. Make backups an integral part of your research when considering which LAN to purchase.

Copy Protection

Copy protection is another common backup problem. There are many schemes for "installing" copy-protected software on hard disk. Most place certain parts of a program at particular locations on the disk surface. When data is restored to the disk, the copy protection scheme is not reinstituted, and the program becomes unusable. It's easy to exhaust the limited number of hard disk installations allowed by some copy-protected software. Most programs allow a second installation for just this situation. But you may be out of luck if the problem occurs a second time.

Processor Speed

Finally, be careful of variable processor speeds around backup software and hardware. The intricate machinations of high-speed backups may be very dependent on precise timing. Many PC clones have a variable clock speed selectable from the keyboard. Sometimes backup utilities will run only at the slower speed, particularly when they format diskettes at the same time they make backups.

Varieties of Backups

Back in the days when a dual diskette-drive system was the norm, "backups" usually meant copying everything from the source diskette to the backup diskette, either by the DOS DISKCOPY command, or by using the COPY command with global file name characters (such as *.*). Today, 40-megabyte hard disks are the norm, and disks 10 times that size are not uncommon. Copying so much data is time-consuming and it's just not practical to back up that much information frequently. For this reason, backups seldom include everything on the disk. We don't mean to make matters complicated, but we count fully *five* kinds of backups, and each has its unique application. They are:

Global backups. A backup of all data on the hard disk, including the tree structure and system files.

Incremental backups. Copies of all files that have changed since the last backup.

Differential backups. Copies of all files that have changed since the last *global* backup.

Temporary backups. Creation of second copies of files which are kept on the hard disk along with the originals.

Serial backups. A series of backups of the same files, capturing each stage in the file's evolution, such as successive drafts of a report.

Let's look at each kind of backup in turn.

Global Backups

Global backups copy everything on the disk. This may sound straightforward, but the word "everything" is open to definition. Sometimes backups are considered "global" when confined to all *data* files on a disk. Program files (those with .COM or .EXE extensions) may be omitted from the backup because copies are found on the diskettes on which the software was distributed.

The point of copying absolutely *everything* on the disk is that it is easy to get back to work after a total data loss, in part because the directory tree can be restored along with data. Much work goes into setting up a directory tree, distributing the files among subdirectories, installing and configuring software, and working out batch files and other utilities. This work is performed over many months and years, and the hours invested in it tend to be undervalued. Yet all this work must be renewed if your hard disk fails and must be completely rebuilt. A global backup will do the job for you.

Incremental and Differential Backups

An **incremental backup** copies all files that have been changed since the last backup. Normally, a number of incremental backups follow a global backup to record changes that have occurred since the global backup. When the changes become far-reaching, another global backup is done and the incremental backups are then discarded. If all data must be restored to a disk, first the global backup is restored, and then the succession of incremental backups. This procedure can be inefficient, since successive versions of the same file may be written one atop the other until the most recent version is restored.

Differential backups overcome this drawback by including all files that have changed *since the last global backup*. This means that some files will be backed up repeatedly, even though they have not recently been changed. Thus, differential backups take longer than incremental backups, and they consume more backup media. But they are more convenient when it comes time to restore data.

Backup software may approach incremental or differential backups in two ways. It may *append* new backups of changed files to old backups, or it can *overwrite* the old backups. Overwriting old backups uses media more economically, since you keep only the most recent version of every file that has changed since the last global backup. Incremental backups made this way amount to the same thing as a differential backup.

The various backup programs handle incremental backups differently. Some keep a master catalog of all backups, updating the file after every appended incremental backup. This approach makes it easy to find the most recent version of a file during data restoration. Other programs create a new catalog file with each backup, leaving numerous old catalog files that must be culled periodically.

The Archive Bit

The *archive bit* is at the heart of incremental and differential backups. From Chapter 2, you may recall the *attribute byte* held in the directory entry of every file. The attribute byte sets various characteristics for the file, making it read-only, for example, or hiding it from directory listings. A byte consists of eight *bits*, and one of the bits is devoted to telling whether the file has been changed since it was last backed up. This is the **archive bit**.

When DOS writes to a file, it sets the archive bit to "ON." A backup program can scan directories for files with this attribute setting, copy the files over to backup media, and reset the archive bits to "OFF." The difference between an incremental backup and a differential backup is that the archive bit is not turned off after a differential backup is made. Since the bit goes unchanged, the file is backed up again and again until a global backup finally switches the bit off.

It's worth knowing that when you view a file in application software but do not save it, the archive bit is not changed to "ON." But if you happen to save a file *without* changing it, the bit will be turned on and the file will be backed up needlessly the next time you run a backup utility.

Special utilities can alter the archive bit setting of any file. DOS Version 3.2 and later offers the ATTRIB command for this purpose. But fooling with archive bits is not a sensible way of managing backups. A good backup utility will let you quickly tag files you want to include or exclude from backups. Only a primitive backup program like DOS's BACKUP could give you reason to alter a file's archive bit manually.

Temporary Backups

Temporary backups are fleeting copies of a file that are kept in the same subdirectory on the same disk, usually with the extension **.BAK**. Many programs, particularly text editors, create .BAK files as a matter of course. They protect you from damage you make to your own files. If you have a change of heart about your modifications to the file, or if you damage it irreversibly, as by an inadvertent deletion of part of the file, you need only copy the .BAK version over the original and you're back to square one. Of course, temporary backups do not help you in the event of a global data loss, since both copies of the file would be lost.

Software that makes automatic .BAK files does so by erasing any prior .BAK file, renaming the current file with a .BAK extension, and then writing the new version. Some programs overwrite a prior .BAK file everytime you use the program's "Save" option. Others change the .BAK file only when the program starts up or quits.

Serial Backups

The final type of backup is related to temporary backups, but it carries the process further. This form of backup has no customary name; we'll call it a **serial backup**. Serial backups are a sequence of backups of the same file made at intervals. They allow you to recover work that has been accidentally damaged through modification. Computer programmers often have this problem. They'll make a change and save the file, make the next change and save it again, and so on. Only later does it become apparent that one of the many changes caused a serious bug that cannot be traced easily. It would be easier to abandon a few hours work and start anew, but the original condition of the file is lost forever. Had a separate copy of the file been made every half hour or so, it would be easy to find the point at which the bug was introduced, and recommence with the file that preceeded.

In this approach, sometimes all files related to a particular project or theme are backed up together. You capture the state of a project at any one time. When data is lost, you can restore all files together, safe in the knowledge that the file versions complement each other. This approach is superior to saving only changed files by *incremental* backups, since you may have trouble sorting out the proper versions.

Diskette-based Backup

Diskettes are the "poor man's" backup medium. They are inexpensive, but diskette-based backups are much less convenient than using tape or removable disk cartridges. The problem is not just the ennui of endlessly swapping diskettes; you have got to *manage* the diskettes, keep them properly labeled, ordered, and boxed. Otherwise, multiple backups quickly fall into chaos, and there's a good chance that errors will occur when you restore data.

Diskette-based backups can be made using the DOS COPY command, or its more sophisticated cousin, XCOPY. However, unless you have exceptionally simple backup requirements, you'll need to use a full-fledged backup utility. Your DOS diskette holds the BACKUP program, which can do a passable job of backing up a large hard disk—if you have the time to wait for it. Since we're firm believers in frequent backups, we strongly recommend that you pass up BACKUP and acquire one of the many backup programs available on the market today. They are inexpensive, and the time they'll save you will quickly repay your investment.

Backups Using COPY

Some people rely on nothing more than the DOS COPY command for making backups. It may seem like a perfectly good way of protecting your data if you work on only a few files at a time. But we advise against reliance on COPY. With time, you'll have a gigantic stack of disorganized backups, with little indication of which file versions are most recent. In the event of a major head crash, restoring your data will be a nightmare. You'll have to recreate the directory tree from scratch, reinstall all software, and recreate keyboard macro files and other work that would likely be exempted from the backup scheme.

The COPY command is also the least flexible of all backup options. It's useful only for making partial backups of files in a single subdirectory. When the files are related by file name or extension, wildcard characters (* or ?) can move the files by a single COPY command. Otherwise you are reduced to entering a separate COPY command for each file, constantly changing subdirectories or typing in long path names.

Limitations

COPY can locate files only by the characters in their file names. It is oblivious to the file's time and date, and oblivious to the setting of its archive bit. Sophisticated backup programs keep track of the subdirectory from which files were copied; COPY keeps no such records, so you must manually set up an identical directory structure on the target diskette. Files of the same name kept in separate subdirectories are easily confused.

COPY is useless for backing up files larger than the backup medium can hold, and it can't handle a group of files larger than can fit onto one diskette. If you enter **COPY *.* A:** in a subdirectory containing 500K of files, and drive A holds a 360K diskette, after a while COPY will issue a "disk full" message and quit. There's no way of specifying the remaining files after a disk change. Since the copy command won't let you *exclude* files by a syntax that would mean, "copy all files except *.DOC," you can't move some files by wildcards and then move the remainder manually.

Error Checking

COPY also does little to protect your data from corrupt media. You can use the /V switch to verify that data has been written correctly. After data is recorded on the diskette, it is read back and the error-checking information tested. This option increases the time required substantially, and it won't protect you from damage done to the diskettes after the backup is made (unlike most backup utilities).

Applications

Although grossly inadequate for general backups, the COPY command works for hour-to-hour backups of a project for which all files reside in a single subdirectory. Tag the files with an identifying extension so that you can use global file name characters. Placing the COPY instruction in a batch file makes life all the easier. When files can't be grouped by extensions, list them individually in a batch file to avoid typing their names and paths again and again.

Backups Using XCOPY

Many users are unfamiliar with the XCOPY command. Like COPY, it can move one or more files between disks. But it can operate on more than one subdirectory at once, and this feature makes it very useful for backups. XCOPY is designed for mass copies; if you omit the file name, it assumes ***.*** (the global file name characters that specify "all files"). As with COPY, you can specify a name for the new version of the file, renaming it as it is copied. For example:

```
XCOPY  C:*.DOC  A:*.BAK
```

copies files named *.DOC from the current directory to drive A, changing the file name extensions to BAK. By adding the /**S** switch to the command, as in:

```
XCOPY  *.DOC  A:  /S
```

XCOPY is made to search for files in not just the current directory, but also in all subdirectories beyond—meaning subdirectories listed in the current directory, subdirectories listed in those directories, and so on. This way, a single branch of the tree can be copied. When the XCOPY command is used while the root directory is the current directory, or when the root directory is entered as the directory from which to copy, the /**S** switch makes XCOPY copy matching files from the entire directory tree.

XCOPY expects to find a parallel tree structure on the disk to which it is making the copies. If it does not find it, it automatially creates subdirectories of the same name as on the source disk. XCOPY works only in this manner; you can't have it take files from several directories on the source disk and make copies in one directory on the target disk.

How the Directory Tree Is Copied

XCOPY is not always an easy DOS command to use. Because it can work on just a branch of the source tree, it is essential that you exactly specify the subdirectory that is the starting point of that branch. Just as important, you must tell XCOPY the name of the subdirectory on the target disk at which it should begin transferring copies of files and making new subdirectories to hold them (if necessary). Consider the command:

```
XCOPY  C:\CATS\*.*  A:\  /S  <enter>
```

In this case, all files (*.*) are copied from the directory tree branch on drive C beginning from and including the subdirectory **\CATS**. The target drive is specified as **A:**. This means that the files contained in the **CATS** subdirectory are copied into the root directory of the target diskette. XCOPY does not create a subdirectory named **CATS** on drive A. The subdirectories branching out of **CATS** on the source disk (drive C) instead branch out of the root directory on the target disk (drive A). When subdirectories of these names (**SIAMESE, PERSIAN, TIBETAN**) already exist on the target disk in the same positions, they'll be used for the copies instead of creating new subdirectories. Figure 8.1 illustrates this process.

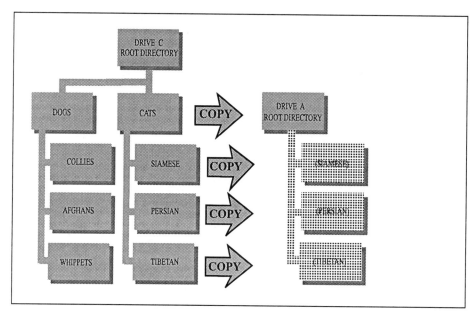

Figure 8-1. Backups using the XCOPY command.

You can also specify a directory other than the root directory for files to be saved into on the target disk. For example, the command:

```
XCOPY  C:\LEVEL1\LEVEL2\*.*  A:\FIRSTDIR  /S
```

would place the files from the subdirectory called **LEVEL2** into the **FIRSTDIR** subdirectory on drive A, creating **FIRSTDIR** if it is not already present. Subdirectories extending from **LEVEL2** on drive C would be created—if they didn't already exist—beginning from **FIRSTDIR** on drive A. Again, XCOPY will place the file copies in existing directories of the same name, but only if they are in the correct position relative to the starting subdirectory; otherwise, XCOPY will create new subdirectories to accommodate the transferred files.

This example could be simplified by making the source drive the current drive and by making the starting directory on the source drive that drive's current directory:

```
C:
CHDIR  \LEVEL1\LEVEL2
XCOPY *.*  A:\FIRSTDIR  /S
```

It is essential that you specify the beginning target directory fully. You can rely on defaults—the current directory of the target drive—but if you make a mistake, XCOPY will go right ahead and transfer the files, creating numerous subdirectories in the wrong positions. Undoing the mistake can be a lot of work.

If you want to copy a branch of a tree to a disk that does not contain identical subdirectories and you'd like the copied branch to originate from the root directory but don't want any new files actually placed in the root directory, you could use a command like this one:

```
XCOPY  *.*  A:\EXTRADIR  /S
```

The contents of the current directory on the source diskette are placed in a new subdirectory on the target, EXTRADIR, which XCOPY will create in the target's root directory.

XCOPY and the Archive Bit

By adding an /M switch to an XCOPY command, only files whose archive attribute is set (switched "ON") are copied. The command:

```
XCOPY  *.*  /M  A:
```

copies to drive A all files that happen to have their archive attributes set, and:

```
XCOPY  \FISH\SALMON\*.DOC  /M  A:
```

copies files from **\FISH\SALMON** that have .DOC extensions and archive attributes that are turned on.

Like a backup program, XCOPY turns the archive attribute off after making the copy. This feature can be used to let XCOPY back up a group of files to multiple diskettes. Imagine that all the files you want copied have their archive attributes set. You enter:

```
XCOPY  *.*  /M  A:
```

and the copying begins. When XCOPY runs out of diskette space for copying the files, it displays an "Insufficient disk space" error message and quits, just as the COPY command would. But it will have turned off the archive attributes of all files that have been successfully copied. When you change diskettes and reenter exactly the same command, the files already copied will be skipped over. You need only repeat the command as many times as are required to copy over all files (typing <F3> <Enter> causes DOS to reuse the previous command line). You may still use an /S switch to extend the backup across multiple subdirectories.

The DOS BACKUP and RESTORE Commands

The DOS BACKUP command is the most commonly used backup utility, but not deservedly so. It is slow and inflexible. In the past it has also been unreliable, but the bugs seem finally to be removed (versions prior to DOS 3.1 should be avoided). BACKUP can copy one, some, or all files from any or all directories to diskettes. It stores the data in a proprietary format, without embedded control codes. The only measure of error checking it allows is the use of the standard DOS VERIFY command, which roughly doubles the already-excessive time it takes to make a backup.

If we sound overly critical of the BACKUP program, it is not out of disrespect. When you buy DOS, you are buying an operating system. It's nice that a backup utility is thrown in, but it cannot be expected to compete with specialized programs that may fill a whole diskette and require a lengthy manual.

Syntax

The BACKUP command resembles other DOS commands, like COPY and XCOPY. You may list a source and a destination. For example:

```
BACKUP BIGFILE.DOC A:
```

backs up the file **BIGFILE.DOC** in the current directory on to the diskette in drive A. Wildcards may be used. To back up all files with a **.DOC** extension in the current directory, enter:

```
BACKUP *.DOC A:
```

Or, to backup all files in the directory:

```
BACKUP *.* A:
```

Of course, you may use full DOS paths:

```
BACKUP \LEVEL1\LEVEL2\LEVEL3\*.* A:
```

The BACKUP command's power arises from the **/S** switch, which applies the command to the source subdirectory and all subdirectories below. To make a backup of all files on the disk, you merely enter:

```
BACKUP \*.* A: /S
```

The Format

In DOS versions prior to 3.3, every file is backed up as a separate file on the backup medium. However, a special **header field** is placed at the start of the file to hold its DOS path and directory information. Each diskette also holds a file named **BACKUPID.@@@** that contains reference information.

Starting with DOS Versions 3.3, BACKUP writes the backups into one giant file on the backup media. The file is named **BACKUP.XXX**, where 'XXX' is a number from 001 upwards corresponding to the backup order. Each diskette also holds a file named **CONTROL.XXX**, using the same format. It saves paths, file names, and other directory information for each file.

Tracking Diskettes

BACKUP creates a volume label reading BACKUP XXX on each diskette. When each diskette fills, BACKUP prompts you for a disk change, and then continues writing. Hence, even small files may stretch across two diskettes. Files larger than a diskette are readily copied. In fact, the BACKUP command is the only way in DOS that you can copy a file that exceeds diskette capacity in order to transport the file to another machine.

Incremental Backups

Incremental backups are made via the /M and /A switches. The 'M' in /M stands for "modified," meaning that the file has been modified since the last backup, and its archive bit has been set. BACKUP automatically resets the archive bit to zero (turns it off) after the backup is made. Use the /A switch to make a sequential backup, in which the newly copied files are *appended* to whatever data is already recorded on the backup diskette in the drive. Thus, to make an incremental backup of the entire disk, enter:

```
BACKUP \*.* /S /M
```

and to append the backups to earlier ones, enter:

```
BACKUP \*.* /S /M /A
```

Date and Time

Starting from DOS 3.3, you can specify files by their time of creation. Earlier versions can specify the date. The switches for these specifications are, appropriately enough, /D and /T. The expression

```
BACKUP \*.* /S /D:1-10-88
```

backs up all files created *on* or *after* January 10, 1988. The /T switch works similarly. There's no flexibility in these commands. You can't back up files from earlier dates and times, or from specific dates and times.

Logging the Backup

Also starting from DOS 3.3, the BACKUP program can be made to create a log file in the root directory of the hard disk (of the source drive). It contains the date and time of the backup, names and paths of all backed up files, and their corresponding diskette numbers. When another backup is made, the log information is appended to that of the previous backup. Over time, the log file can become quite large.

Diskette Formatting

A final improvement added to BACKUP in DOS 3.3 is the ability to format diskettes while the backup progresses. Earlier versions could not do this. If you ran out of diskettes, you had to terminate the backup session, go to DOS, and run the FORMAT program.

Performance

The BACKUP program is unacceptably slow for general backup needs. On slower machines, a global backup of a 20-megabyte disk takes from one to two hours, depending on the number of files and complexity of the tree structure. The tedium has to be experienced to be believed. You can save so much time by instead using a sophisticated backup utility that the cost of the software may be repaid in your first backup session.

The RESTORE Command

Because BACKUP uses a proprietary file format, you can only use the RE-STORE command to reclaim your files. It prompts you for the appropriate diskettes and lets you know when you insert the wrong one. RESTORE uses basically the same syntax as BACKUP. For example, to restore all files in the subdirectory \LEVEL2, you must enter:

```
RESTORE A: C:\LEVEL1\LEVEL2\*.*
```

To additionally restore files belonging to the subdirectories below \LEVEL2:

```
RESTORE A: C:\LEVEL1\LEVEL2\*.* /S
```

And to restore every file to a disk, recreating the tree structure if required:

```
RESTORE A: C:\*.* /S
```

Features

Some of the switches differ between BACKUP and RESTORE. In RESTORE, /B specifies the date, and (in DOS 3.3) /A specifies the time. /M causes only files that have been modified or deleted since they were last backed up to be restored. /N restores files that no longer exist on the hard disk (this switch must not be used with /A or /B).

Dangers

In DOS versions prior to 3.1, BACKUP and RESTORE have had more than their share of bugs. There are reports of conflicts with memory-resident programs in Versions 2.1 and 3.0. Files have occasionally been scrambled. And, most notoriously, RESTORE has refused to do its job in some cases, leaving you high and dry, with your backups in an otherwise unreadable form. The programs appear to have improved in recent versions. But they are still not nearly a match for even a second-rate full-scale backup utility.

Backup Utility Software

The computer software market is awash with backup programs. Competition is keen, and features abound. Backup utilities tend to be a little pricier than the DOS shells discussed in Chapter 5. As with all software, there is no hard and fast relation between price and performance. The best-known may not be the best.

At any price, a good backup program pays for itself quickly: it pares down the time required for backups, helps avert mistakes, provides better error-correction, and creates records of the backup. While DOS shells have an (unwarranted) reputation as being for beginners, backup utilities are a tool for novices and power users alike. They can be customized to cut backup time to a few minutes.

Backup programs have been crossing boundaries with other utility software genres. Some have DOS shell features; others provide file-recovery features. The furious competition causes individual products to continually evolve. The product that leads in spring may be left in the dust by fall. To decide which is best at any given moment, you need to keep an eye out for reviews and recommendations. You'll learn here which features are important for your own backup needs. Keep a list of your requirements and take it with you when you go shopping.

Performance

For some years, backup programs tended to compete on speed rather than features. Since most people loathe making backups, the opportunity to get them over with more quickly seems irresistible. Performance is important, but you should not regard the fastest program as necessarily the best. Ease-of-use may save you more time up front than rapid data transfer does during the backup. And *flexibility* is all important. Good software lets you easily specify particular kinds of files for backup so that your backups won't be filled with files that aren't required and can't be sorted out. Fewer files makes for faster backups; in this sense, a well-designed but relatively slow backup program can outperform the supposed "winner."

Performance Strategies

Some backup programs are *speed-demons*. To work quickly, they rely on DMA channels to move data between diskettes and hard disk *simultaneously*. Some read whole hard disk cylinders at once to avoid excessive head movements; afterwards, they sort the data into files as it is written to diskettes. Another ploy is to keep diskette drives spinning during disk changes. A disk change takes only about five seconds, and the fastest utilities, running in the fastest machines, can keep you continuously swapping diskettes in and out of dual drives. Turning the drives on and off would slow down the backup because diskette drives take time to come up to speed. There's no harm in changing disks while the drives turn; the diskettes disengage when the drive door is opened. Diskette drives normally are shut off to save wear and tear on the diskettes, which are abraded by the diskette envelope.

The fastest backup programs can make astounding claims. Even on a slow computer, 10 megabytes can be recorded on 1.2-megabyte diskettes in 4 minutes. However, statistics like these are for optimized conditions, rather like the gas consumption ratings for automobiles. Sometimes the measurements are made using especially fast disk drives that hold a small number of large, completely defragmented files. Advanced error checking may be shut off. So advertising claims may be exaggerated.

Proprietary Formats

As we discussed earlier in this chapter, some backup utilities produce DOS-readable files while others employ proprietary formats. Disks that use a proprietary format may elicit a "bad disk" error message from DOS. Even disks readable by DOS may not allow DOS access to the files backed up on them. Sometimes the hard disk's files are crammed into a single giant file, with information about their subdirectory locations intermixed. Another strategy is writing a catalog at the end of the backup.

On the other hand, some utilities replicate the DOS format exactly. They copy from the source disk as much of the directory tree as is used by the files written on a given diskette. In a global backup, each diskette holds different parts of the tree. The same subdirectories tend to be created on several diskettes. For example, say that a hard disk's root directory has a child directory that holds numerous files—enough to fill two diskettes. Two backup diskettes might each hold a corresponding subdirectory file, using the same name and location in relation to the root directory. But each will list only part of the files contained in the hard disk subdirectory. When the utility restores data, it *combines* the subdirectory listings to create a subdirectory matching the original.

That diskettes use the standard DOS directory format does not necessarily mean that backup programs employ DOS to make the copies. DOS is notoriously slow, and many programs directly control the hard disk and diskette hardware for faster data transfer. But DOS is also reliable, and the backup software may be less so if it goes it alone.

Operation

Like all software, backup utilities may be *command-driven* or *menu-driven*. The DOS BACKUP program is an example of command-driven software. All specifications for the backup are given from the command line when the program is called. The advantage in this approach is that the program can easily be used from a batch file. You might set up one batch file named **FULBAKUP.BAT** and another named **INCBAKUP.BAT**, placing the appropriate command lines for full and incremental backups in each. Then you'd only have to type FULBAKUP or INCBAKUP, and the job would proceed.

Most backup utilities are menu-driven. Let's look at the *Norton Backup* program as an example. At the beginning of a backup, it presents a screen like the one in Figure 8.2, allowing you to select the drive to be backed up, the kind of backup (global, incremental, and so on), the kind of diskettes used, and so on. It analyzes the disk quickly and tells you how many diskettes are required and roughly how long the backup will take. If you like, you can call up a dialog box to set certain options, including whether the backup should be verified, whether data should be compressed, whether error-correction codes should be inserted, and so on.

By choosing "Select Files" from this screen, you move on to a screen like the one shown in Figure 8.3. It looks like a DOS shell, with a directory tree diagram on the left and a directory listing on the right. You can tag files using global file name characters or by moving the cursor over individual file names. This feature is as useful for excluding files from a backup as for including them. For example, you could begin by selecting all files in a directory by specifying the global file name characters *.*, and then manually delete a few from the backup.

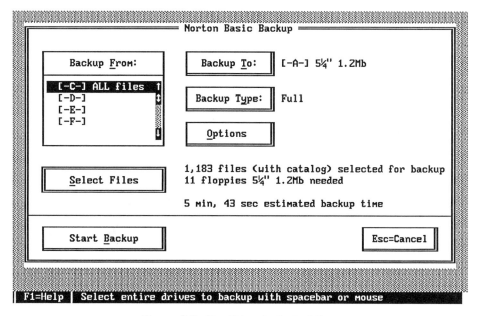

Figure 8-2. Specifying backup options.

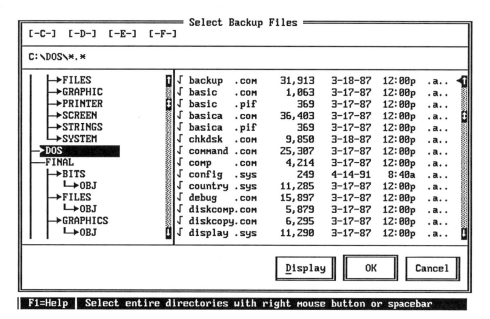

Figure 8-3. Selecting individual files for backup.

Once you start the backup, the status report shown in Figure 8.4 appears. The directory listing at the top right tells which file is being backed up, and the tree diagram on the left tells where it resides in the directory tree. The bottom left prompts you to make disk changes. It also times the backup and tells you how far it has progressed. Finally, the bottom right of the status screen presents overall statistics about the numbers of files backed up and diskettes used.

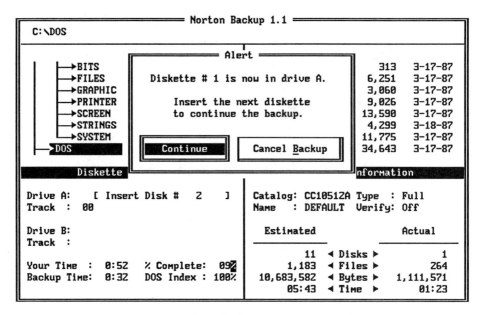

Figure 8-4. Diskette backup with Norton Backup

Menu-driven backups like *Norton Backup* are much easier for beginners than command-line backups because there's no complicated syntax to remember. And menu-driven backups usually can be automated just as easily as command-line backups. As we showed above, the DOS backup command can readily be invoked from a batch file. The same applies to any good backup utility. In the case of the *Norton Backup*, you can save the current backup settings, including file selections, and assign a name to the settings. One group of settings would be for a global backup, another for a weekly incremental backup, and a third for a special-purpose project backup. Thereafter, you can run the entire backup just by naming the program on a line in the batch file and following it with the name of the backup settings you want to use.

Some programs, including *Norton Backup*, let you automate backups even further by incorporating *macros* into the program. Just like keyboard macros, you start "recording" a sequence of commands, type them in carefully, and then stop the recording. Thereafter, you can play back the entire command sequence.

Data Restoration

Most programs use the same interface for restoring data as for backing it up. Files move from diskettes to hard drive instead of vice-versa. With the *Norton Backup* you encounter screens quite similar to those used for backing up data, complete with tree diagrams and directory listings. It's possible to assemble these listings because the program makes a backup catalog that it can consult when data is restored. One copy of the catalog goes on the hard disk and another is written at the end of the backup in case the hard disk should fail completely. Working from the catalog, you can select to restore individual directories or files grouped by global file name characters. If you like, you can hunt down a particular file, select it, and then restore it in only a few seconds.

Diskette Requirements

The number of disks required for a global backup varies between backup utilities, but not greatly. A 20-megabyte backup might take between 12 and 14 1.44M diskettes. Diskettes of other sizes require proportional quantities. Many utilities begin the backup by scanning the hard disk and telling how many disks are required. Not all can format disks on the fly, so you'll want to have more than enough ready. Programs that use proprietary formats tend to fit more data on to a disk, perhaps as much as 20 percent more. They may accomplish this by using larger disk sectors, so that less space is wasted between sectors.

Programs electronically mark each diskette so they can know its position in the backup sequence when data is restored. Since you can't see electronic markings, you still need to carefully label a series of diskettes before its first use. Some utilities come packaged with numbered labels.

Error Checking

A variety of errors can occur during either backup or restore operations. Errors that occur during data restoration are obviously serious—your data is at stake. But even errors during backup can be very troublesome. Since incremental backups clear a file's archive bit once it has been copied, an interruption of the backup can leave you with no way of restarting; you're forced to make a global backup the second time through. A good backup program can deal with many error conditions.

Backup programs deal with bad sectors on diskettes in varying ways. Some don't notice bad sectors at all and write data on top of them. A few stop the backup abruptly when they encounter a bad sector. DOS-oriented programs may use the DOS VERIFY feature when data is recorded. But most programs check every sector before writing to it, and when they find a bad one, they mark it off bounds in the file allocation table and continue with the backup.

Backup utilities may also test a diskette for errors when data is restored. Some programs are completely at a loss when they encounter a bad sector. In the best case, they'll give up trying to restore the file that is partially stored in the bad sector. In the worst case, a utility can refuse to go on restoring files at all, and you may suffer massive data loss.

Error Recovery

Fortunately, this failing is rare. Most utilities can recover from data loss and continue restoring files. Many programs that use proprietary formats write extensive error-correction code on the diskettes. Damaged data can often be restored using these codes. In fact, even data on a *physically* damaged diskette may be resurrected this way.

Bad sectors are not the only gremlin that can interrupt a backup session. A program should be able to recognize when the diskette drive door is open and issue a message. And it should be able to identify a diskette in the backup series that has already been filled with data and has been inserted inadvertently into the drive a second time. Similarly, during data restoration, a program should be able to recognize instantly when the wrong diskette has been placed in the drive.

Flexibility

Be sure that a backup utility is coordinated with your computer hardware. Programs that work through DOS should be able to handle any kind of drive (however, remember that a DOS-like disk format does not necessarily indicate that DOS is used). A critical advertising phrase to watch for is, "backs up any logical device." This expression implies that the backup program operates through DOS, and that it can copy files to any kind of diskette drive, to any removable cartridge drive (including Bernoulli boxes), to another hard disk, or to tape backup units that work with DOS-like commands. Programs that go around DOS may not be able to handle any device, but they will work faster.

Utilities that can alternate backups between two diskette drives are preferable, since work is done while you change diskettes. Many can run two drives, but don't expect them to be able to handle two drives of different capacity. This may be all for the better, since mixing media can lead to no end of confusion.

Tape Backup

To many, tape backup seems like a panacea for backup woes. What could be more convenient than pushing a button, walking away, and returning minutes later to a fully backed-up disk. In many situations, tape backup can be just this simple. But, like everything else in computerdom, there are many intricacies to tape backup; headaches (and even data-loss) can arise from choosing the wrong tape unit, or from using it the wrong way.

Tape's weakness is its *linearity*. Any two bytes of data on a hard disk are separated by only a few inches; on tape they may be separated by hundreds of feet. Random access is a possible, but slow. It's for this reason that tape is used for archiving data on mainframe computers, and seldom used for direct access. Unlike a diskette drive or a removable cartridge disk drive, a tape unit is less likely to be used for purposes other than backups and distribution of large amounts of data.

Fundamentals of Tape Technology

With only a few exceptions, all tape units use tape cartridges, which make handling tape as easy as handling a diskette. The tape is usually coated with a reddish-brown oxide much like that on audio tape. The surface may be divided into a number of tracks, which run the length of the tapes, or may be scanned in diagonal stripes like a videotape. Tapes with longitudinal tracks are usually read in serpentine fashion. The tape isn't rewound after each track is read or written; at the end of a track the drive motors reverse direction and access continues on the next adjacent track.

Tape Formats

Every drive uses a particular **tape format**. This refers to the tape dimensions, the number of tracks used, the way data is organized, and the method employed for cataloging files. Tracks are divided into logical units called **blocks**. For example, a block might record a dozen disk sectors end-to-end and follow them with error-correction code. Some formats require that the tape be preformatted, just as all disks are under DOS.

Technology

Tape units have a read/write head that, in principle, resembles the read/write head in a disk drive. The head creates a magnetic field across a gap, and that field affects, or is affected by, magnetic particles on the tape surface. Typically, several thousand bits of data are written per inch of track. When the tape comes to an end, the head shifts to an adjacent track.

What makes tape units special is the rapid speed at which they move tape across the read/write head: usually 90 inches per second. This is a lot faster than audio cassette tape, but it's necessary to make backups at a reasonable speed. By computer standards, it's not very fast at all; the read/write heads of a hard disk cover the circular tracks at roughly 10 times this rate. A DC-600A tape cartridge is 600 feet long. Using nine tracks, the effective length of the tape is 5,400 feet, or 64,800 inches. At 1,000 bytes per inch, the tape has an (unformatted) capacity of about 60 megabytes. At 90 inches per second, the tape could theoretically be filled in just 12 minutes. In reality, backups proceed more slowly for reasons we'll explain in a moment.

A tape drive connects to the machine in much the same way as a hard disk. If an interface board accompanies the drive, and it communicates with the computer through DMA (direct memory access) or via the CPU.

Streaming

You'll often encounter the expression "streaming tape" in advertisements. Streaming is not a particular technology or tape format. It is an ideal for tape performance that all kinds of tape drives strive for, but seldom attain. **Streaming** refers to *continuous* data transfer to the tape. This condition is achieved more easily with image backups. Head movements in the disk drive are minimal in this case, so there are few interruptions in the supply of data. But in file-by-file backups, data can not always be transferred at the rate tape can absorb it and **underruns** occur.

Underruns

Drives that use unformatted tape can continue turning during underruns. Because the tape is unformatted, recording can recommence at any moment. But this approach wastes tape, possibly reducing a cartridge's effective capacity to below requirements. Formatted tapes, on the other hand, must stop when underruns occur. Repeated starts and stops are very time-consuming and they make for slower performance in these drives.

One study of tape drives found that the majority could not stream consistently. As with most aspects of tape-drive performance, the ability to stream is largely dependent on the tape drive-software. It must be very fast. Well-crafted software approaches a file-by-file backup by reading groups of files into memory, reading all in a single pass across the disk surface. Once the files are buffered in memory, the drive can embark upon a long period of streaming. Often, when backup software has much memory available, it can achieve streaming for longer periods. Some software tells how many underruns have occurred when it issues status reports.

While consistent streaming offers a certain theoretical satisfaction, it is of no real importance in itself. It is simply another factor in determining how long a backup will take. Since optimal streaming occurs with image backups, it's tempting to think an image backup must be "best." But an image backup is simply faster.

Misconceptions About Tape Backup

Many are willing to pay the price of a tape backup unit in the fond hope that all the cares and woes of backup will magically disappear. The idea of solving all backup problems with the push of a button is irresistible. Unfortunately, life is not so simple. While you *can* buy a tape unit, plug it in, and start making daily image backups of the whole disk, you may be in for a rude awakening when you eventually lose some data. While tape backup is superior to diskette backup in nearly all respects, it still requires careful forethought to be used adequately and safely.

Tape Standards

Tape backup involves two kinds of standards. On one hand, there are *physical standards* that describe the size of tape cartridges, the number of tracks they use, and the rate that tape moves through the drive. On the other hand, *format standards* determine exactly how data is laid out on the tape, how error correction is handled, and so on. Physical standards are based on the various kinds of tape cartridges that have been devised. Let's begin with them.

Cartridge Types

Like any other kind of computer equipment, tape cartridges have gone through generations of improvement. The earliest mass-market cartridge was called the DC300A. It held 300 feet of tape that could be divided into two or four tracks, writing 1600 bits per inch of track. These cartridges are large, measuring six by four inches. Today, this standard has been superceded by the DC600 cartridge. As its name implies, it holds 600 feet of tape. While streaming, these cartridges move tape at 90 inches per second. Originally they were divided into 9 tracks, but advanced drives can write 32 tracks to cram 120 megabytes of data onto a tape—just the ticket for backing up a medium-sized hard disk.

The problem with these cartridges is the size. Tape drives that hold them can't readily be miniaturized so that they can be mounted internally in one of a PC's drive bays (least of all a PS/2's 3½-inch bays). In response, the basic DC600 design was reduced to 3½ by 2½-inches, holding 205 feet of quarter-inch tape. This is the now-ubiquitous DC2000 standard. Typically, these cartridges hold from 40 to more than 150 megabytes. But advanced technology can push them to double that. There are also DC1000 cartridges, which vaguely resemble audio casettes. By using thinner tape, they restrict the tape capacity to about 20 megabytes.

The QIC-40 Standard

The great virtue of DC2000 cartridges is that they appeared on the scene after years of compatibility problems among DC600 cartridges. In consequence, several far-reaching format standards have been devised. The first of these is called **QIC-40** ("QIC" stands for "quarter-inch cartridge"). QIC-40 was developed in response to the need for an inexpensive tape backup system for ordinary PCs with ordinary-size hard disks. The tape is divided into 20 tracks, each of which can hold roughly 2M. This gives a 40M capacity, which is adequate for a complete backup of a small hard drive.

To keep the price of these drives low, they plug directly into a computer's diskette controller. In essence, they take the place of a second diskette drive. While this measure assures that the drives are compatible with DOS, it also condemns the drive to relatively poor performance, because diskette data transfer rates are not very high. Generally speaking, QIC-40 backups proceed at half the rate of those directed toward a DC600 system. It's also worth knowing that these drives require formatted tapes, and formatting can take as long as an hour.

Another problem is that the QIC-40 standard does not dictate exactly how individual files should be recorded on the tape. Thus, you can exchange cartridges between various QIC-40 drives and the drives will be able to read them. But they may not be able to make sense of the data and deliver files as you require them. Fortunately, third parties often make backup software for many vendors' tape drives. If the software that runs both drives is made by the same vendor, the tapes are likely to be interchangeable.

When the QIC-40 standard was devised, few users had hard drives much bigger than 40M. Nowadays, however, more and more users need to back up drives with capacities of 100M or more—and QIC-40 can be too slow and too small for the job. As a result, another standard—called QIC-80—has arrived. QIC-80 tapes can store a minimum of 80M—more on extended-length tape cartridges or when data compression is used. Also, because it uses a dedicated controller card rather than a floppy controller, QIC-80 is much faster than QIC-40. Therefore, while QIC-40 enjoys a price advantage because it doesn't require a controller card, QIC-80 is likely to become popular among users of moderate-sized hard drives. Higher-capacity QIC standards—including QIC-150 and QIC-320—will also become popular as hard disks grow.

Helical Scan Drives

For disks larger than a few hundred megabytes, the best backup solution is either 4 or 8mm helical scan tape. Like videotapes, the cartridges in these drives are written and read by heads attached to a quickly rotating drum. As the drum spins, the heads scan the tape in diagonal stripes that cover nearly the entire width of the tape.

Both the 4 and 8mm technologies are based on existing non-computer media. Four-millimeter drives use cartridges similar to digital audio tapes (DATs), while eight-millimeter drives use cartridges all but identical to eight-millimeter camcorder tapes. At this writing, all 8mm drives are made by a single company—Exabyte—which holds an exclusive license to use Sony's tape transports in its products. (Other companies that sell 8mm tape backup systems buy the drives from Exabyte and remarket them under their own names.) Four-millimeter drives, by contrast, are made by several manufacturers and conform to one of two format standards. The first, DDS (Digital Data Storage), is licensed by a consortium of vendors including HP and Sony. The second, Data/DAT, is free to all comers and offers something DDS doesn't: special provisions to work as a slow—but relatively inexpensive—random-access medium.

Eight-millimeter drives have the largest capacities and are used to back up mainframes, minicomputers, and servers on local area networks. Four-millimeter drives hold about half as much data, but the drives are more economical and are available from multiple sources. The software for 4 and 8mm drives is similar to—and often made by the same vendors as—the software that runs QIC drives.

Tape Backup Performance

Tape drives are marked by a wide range of performance. Some are *very* slow, particularly in file-by-file backups. Most drives are capable of a data transfer rate between 25 and 90 kilobytes per second, with higher speeds typically accompanying larger-capacity drives. But poor software can severely hamper streaming. The drive may constantly stop and restart, or tape may be squandered on *inter-record gaps* (IRGs). It takes a drive roughly a third of a second to come up to speed, so numerous stops quickly add up to minutes and even hours. In the mid-1980s, a review of a drive produced by a premier electronics company found that 2.4 megabytes of small files required *two hours* to back up; the company promised it would soon release software that made the drive run 20 times faster! Software is that important in tape drives.

You must be cautious about manufacturers' claims for the performance of their drives. A typical advertising claim may state that a drive "backs-up a 20-megabyte hard disk in four minutes flat!" Usually, statistics like this are for an image backup, done without optional read/write verfication. Such backups bring a drive as close as it gets to streaming, so the statistics are for the best case. Depending on both hardware and software, file-by-file backups may be much slower. Claims for file-by-file backup performance are also suspect, since tests are sometimes done on atypical disks. The disk is defragmented, it is filled with large files to avoid numerous directory accesses, and the directory tree may have only one level of subdirectories to shorten searches.

Comparative reviews show quite a range in performance. A 10-megabyte image backup may take from $1\frac{1}{2}$ minutes to 13 minutes. Image restores take about the same time as a backup. File-by-file backups for 10-megabytes range from 5 minutes to 35 minutes, with complete restorations taking two to four times longer (12 minutes to 75 minutes).

File-by-File Backup

In a file-by-file backup, the backup software traces through the disk directories, shuttling the read/write head back and forth. The added head movement makes for slower overall data transfer, particularly on badly fragmented drives. Since the tape is capable of recording data as fast as the drive can supply it, the time spent on head seeks leaves brief periods during which the tape drive has nothing to record. During these moments, the drive can temporarily stop the tape, or it can go on moving tape but record nothing over it. In the first instance, much time is wasted starting and stopping the drive. In the second case, tape is wasted, and the effective capacity of the tape drive is reduced.

Increasingly, makers of tape drives are writing smarter software that undergoes an initial scan of the whole disk. The software copies groups of files into memory, sometimes going around the usual DOS facilities for extra speed. When available memory is filled, the tape starts turning, the files are disgorged onto it, and then the tape is stopped until the next group of files are loaded in memory. Faster computers may be able to move files into memory quickly enough to achieve sustained streaming. Running a file defragmentation utility before the backup begins helps greatly.

The Ideal

The ideal tape backup combines the speed of an image backup with the flexibility of a file-by-file backup. Indeed, some tape drive software can restore individual files from an image backup, although with difficulty. Because the image backup begins with cylinder 0 (the outermost cylinder on the disk), the disk's root directory and file allocation table is found at the start of the tape. The software reads the FAT and stores it in memory. Then it searches for the subdirectories leading to the desired file, and finally searches for the file itself. All of this requires moving back and forth along the tape, making the restoration quite slow. The software speeds up the process by retrieving any clusters belonging to the file as they are first encountered, assembling the complete file once all clusters have been found.

Restoring a file from an image backup can be painfully slow, particularly when the file was highly fragmented on the disk from which it was recorded. But if the need is only occasional, the delay ought to be acceptable.

As tape drive software improves, some manufacturers are supplying software with their drives that *only* performs file-by-file backup, leaving image backups in the dust. Comparative tests show that the best software can achieve file-by-file backup times only marginally greater than those required for an image backup. Such high performance is possible partly because the software ignores empty clusters during file-by-file backup, whereas it backs up *all* clusters during an image recording.

Buying a Tape Drive

Buying a tape drive is harder on the nerves than buying a hard disk. At bottom, hard disks are much alike. But tape drives vary in many ways, and you'll be buying software that is barely mentioned in tape drive advertisements. Generally speaking, the same rules apply that were described in Chapter 3 for buying hard disk drives. But, unlike a hard disk, you are buying both hardware *and* an elaborate software package. It's impossible to test the full range of features at a dealer's showroom, and you are all the more vulnerable when you buy through mail order.

Do not buy a tape drive until you have either found a positive recommendation for the drive, or have negotiated a return agreement so you can experiment with the drive and return it if it proves unsuitable. Manufacturers may try to tempt you by offering free DOS shells, cache utilities, and other goodies. Don't become distracted from your real requirement: to be able to make fast, frequent, reliable backups with little effort or resistance. A cheap drive is not cheap if you won't use it. Most have a one-year warranty; avoid those that offer only 90 days.

Capacity Requirements

When you finally buy, go for large capacity if you can afford it. A 60-megabyte unit costs only about a third more than a 20-megabyte unit. This is a good idea even if you have only a 20-megabyte drive to back up. You'll be able to append many incremental backups to a single tape. More important, you'll be ready to handle a larger disk drive when you inevitably acquire one. Although tape backup units will undoubtedly become faster, they are used infrequently enough that you'll want to go on using a drive for many years.

If you can't afford a high-capacity unit, you may find that a smaller one can do the job anyway. Some drives are accompanied by software that can span a global back up across two or more cartridges. Alternatively, you may be able to back up part of a directory tree to one cartridge, and part to another. Of course, incremental backups should have no trouble fitting onto low-capacity cartridges.

Tape units share many of the concerns that accompany buying a hard disk drive. You must decide whether to opt for an internal or external unit, and sometimes must choose between full- and half-height drives. External units have their own fans, which may be noisy. Some drives can also be noisy when they wind tape at high speeds.

Utilities

Most tape drives come with various utility programs. Diagnostic software may check out the drive, and perhaps test the computer's DMA channels. **Certification utilities** test the integrity of blank tape cartridges by writing data and reading it back. Some drives have tape erasure utilities. And most have a **retensioning utility** that steadily runs tape from reel to reel to equalize the tension; this measure helps avoid instantaneous speed variations that lead to errors; the utility should be run after every few backups.

We've mentioned an awful lot of concerns about both tape hardware and software. Yet most advertisements for tape units mention the barest details. To avoid unpleasant surprises, we recommend that you follow these four suggestions when shopping for a tape drive:

Shop for software. Figure out the backup system you want, and then buy a drive to fit it. Be sure that the software that accompanies the drive is powerful, flexible, and easy-to-use. Alternatively, find a drive that can be run by some of the backup programs offered by other companies.

Don't buy without a recommendation. Don't buy only by brand name. One of the worst-performing drives ever released came from an internationally prominent electronics company. And don't buy the cheapest drive available on the assumption that it may be a only a trifle less convenient. Remember that bad software can render a tape drive useless for some kinds of backup. Watch computer magazines for reviews, talk to people who use tape, or seek out informed advice at user-group meetings. The time spent on homework will be repaid handsomely over the years you use the drive.

Secure a return agreement. Unless you have a dependable good review of a drive, don't buy it without a return agreement. Ten days is adequate, but 30 is ideal if you can find someone willing to agree to it. Some manufacturers have advertised 30-day money-back offers. Naturally, dealers don't like these arrangements, and they may try to hit you with a *restocking fee* of up to 15 percent of the drive's price, plus shipping charges. The shipping fees ought to be your responsibility, but not the restocking fee; demand a *full* refund. Explain that you must examine the full range of software capabilities before agreeing to keep the unit. Sooner or later you'll find a dealer who will agree, providing you maintain the packing materials in pristine condition.

Buy the unit when you have time to experiment with it. Once you've secured a return agreement, make use of it. Spend half a day putting the software throught its paces in *all* kinds of backup and restore operations. If performance is too slow, send it back. Don't keep the drive out of inertia, thinking that it's poor performance is unimportant since it's use is only occasional. Any features that discourage your using the drive make your purchase that much less valuable.

Installing a Tape Drive

Installing a tape drive is much like installing a hard disk. Internal drives must be inserted into the machine, with all the attendant fiddling with guide rails, bezels, screws, and power cables. The drive's controller card is inserted in a slot close enough to the drive to make cabling easy. And then the data and control cables are attached. All of the principles discussed in Chapter 4 apply.

Device Drivers

Since DOS does not control tape drives, many tape units come with a device driver (others are directly controlled by their accompanying backup software). When a device driver is used, it is supplied as a small program that must be loaded into memory when the machine is booted. The loading is done automatically by listing the driver in the CONFIG.SYS file with the DEVICE command. If the driver file is called **TAPEDRV.COM**, the expression **DEVICE = TAPEDRV.COM** must be placed in CONFIG.SYS. The documentation accompanying the drive will tell you exactly what to write if there is any confusion. Some tape units include an installation program on the diskette that automatically inserts the DEVICE command in CONFIG.SYS. Similarly, most drives require that you allocate a certain number of DOS buffers for the drive to perform optimally. This is done by the BUFFERS command, which we described in Chapter 7.

Once listed in CONFIG.SYS, the tape device driver is loaded whenever you start up your computer. It takes up memory (usually less than 20K) whether or not your tape drive is in use. While most of us can spare 20K, many other memory-resident programs may make demands for scarce memory. You may want to institute a system of flexible configuration files to load the tape device driver only during backups, or arrange to load it into high memory.

DMA and Port Addresses

Earlier, we talked about how tape drives use the various DMA channels. Some tape units let you set which channel is used. Similarly, there is a range of **port addresses** the tape drive may employ. "Ports" are the gateways through which the device driver communicates with the tape drive. No particular port addresses are reserved for this purpose. While many addresses are available, other non-standard hardware may happen to select the same addresses, in which case conflicts occur and the system crashes. For the same reasons, drives may also have a selectable **interrupt vector**, which is a mechanism by which the tape unit exerts control over the computer.

All of these selections may be made through the backup software, or by changing DIP switches or jumpers on the tape drive's controller board. The vast majority of tape drive owners need never concern themselves with these technicalities. The manufacturer makes settings at the factory that work in almost all machines. Problems arise in machines set up in a local area network, or equipped with unusual hardware. If you have problems getting the tape drive working on a specially equipped machine, you'll need to check the documentation. It will tell you the current settings, and (ideally) you can compare them to records you've kept of the port address and interrupt vectors used by other equipment (again, ideally).

With a measure of good fortune, you may be able to reconfigure the tape drive just by trying a few new settings at random. There's no intrinsic need to understand what the settings mean. You just have to hit on settings not currently used by other equipment. Unfortunately, the drive manufacturer's support service may be of only limited help, since they can't know the configuration used by unusual equipment installed in your machine. In the worst case, you may find it necessary to seek help from a dealer or consultant.

Tape Formatting

The final step in installation is formatting tapes. Formatting is required only for some tape formats. The format is a *single-pass* operation; the concepts of low-level and high-level formatting do not apply as they do to hard disk formatting. However, some machines make a second, verification pass over the newly formatted tape. Because the DOS FORMAT command is not used, there are no standard commands or procedures for initiating the formatting; the software for each tape unit has its own command interface (although some imitate DOS). You'll have to consult the documentation to get going. Some manufacturers sell preformatted tapes for their drives.

Cartridge Quality

Once formatted, keep an eye on your cartridges for damage to the tape. In spite of having few moving parts, cartridges can malfunction in many ways. So much data is packed into a small space that tiny inaccuracies make tapes unreadable. Many problems revolve around the tensioning of the tape. When the tape fails to maintain perfectly constant tension, it may begin to move laterally against the read/write head, or vertically, bouncing towards and away from the head. The lateral motion moves tracks away from the head gap. The bouncing motion moves the tape away from the head. When carried to extremes, either motion can move a track on the tape too far from the head for the head to do its work.

Inconstant tape tension leads to other problems. It can cause sections of the tape to stretch slightly. Particularly for preformatted tapes, the stretched sections can throw the read/write electronics out of sync. Poor tape tensioning also leads to minute instantaneous speed variations, which have much the same effect as tape stretching. These inaccuracies were not so problematic in the early days of tape backup when tape moved relatively slowly, but now the tiniest speed fluctuations lead to errors. In fact, much of the expense in designing and manufacturing tape drives lies in the fancy electronics that deal with the constantly changing tape conditions.

Tape Flaking

As if the tensioning problems were not enough, tape can also go bad through flaking. All tape rattles slightly between the guides that direct it across the read/write head. When the motion is severe, the tape edges become " scalloped" or "coined." In the extreme case, the outer tracks may become unreadable. More often, tiny particles of oxide coating separate from the tape surface. The loss of the oxide may not be a great problem in itself, since error correction facilities can compensate for the data loss. Rather, the problem with flaking is that the flakes tend to scrape off against the read/write head, possibly contaminating it so that errors occur repeatedly. They may even build up to the point that the tape is held away from the head surface. Eventually the particles break free and are redeposited elsewhere on the tape, overwriting data after the drive electronics have certified it as being correct.

The Future of Tape Backup

Ironically, just as tape backup has overcome serious technical obstacles and evolved into a mass-market product, it is threatened with extinction. Most observers believe that sooner or later erasable optical disks will completely supplant tape backup units. Laser disks are an ideal backup medium, since they are inherently cheap, and they permit random access at high data transfer rates. The relatively slow average seek times of optical disk drives are no impediment when used for backups. It is easy to imagine an inexpensive *fixed* laser disk that would constantly back up the slightest changes made on hard disks. Tape could not do this practically. But tape manufacturers are fighting back. Tape units with capacities measured in *billions of bytes* have appeared (albeit at very high cost).

In any case, it will be well into the 1990s before erasable laser technology becomes cheap. The write-once laser drives now appearing carry a high price for both the units themselves and the disposable cartridges they use. While we're waiting for inexpensive laser technology, tape drives will continue to be the most reliable and convenient way to back up data.

Instituting a Backup System

In devising a backup system, you must learn to think clearly about the different kinds of information on the disk. Which data files change and which do not? You must decide what sorts of backups will accompany particular kinds of work, how often the backups are to be performed, and how the backup media are to be organized. When the backup scheme encompasses many computers, you must also determine *who* is to look after backups and how backup records are to be kept. This may sound a little excessive, particularly if you are planning for yourself alone. But without a schedule, backups are likely to be neglected. Buying backup hardware and software is only half the battle.

Deciding among Backup Options

We've mentioned four kinds of backup media: diskettes, high-capacity removable disks, a mirror-image second hard disk, and streaming tape. Each technology has its strengths and weaknesses:

- **Ease-of-use.** Tapes, magneto-optical disks, WORM drives, and removable hard disks are easiest, with diskette backups far behind.
- **Flexibility.** Diskette backups may be best of all, since you have such a broad choice of backup software, and since diskettes are completely portable between machines. Removable disks and mirror-image disks have the advantage that they can directly substitute for a badly damaged hard disk. Owing to its linearity, tape is the least flexible medium.
- **Price.** Diskette-based backups are very cheap. Streaming tape units have now dropped in price to the point where they cost about the same as a typical hard disk drive. Mirror-image hard disk systems require a second hard disk and a special controller card that costs several times as much as an ordinary one. So this option is considerably more expensive than a tape drive. Removable cartridge drives are still quite expensive, but can be very useful for purposes other than backups.

Removable Cartridge Drives

For small hard disks, removable high-capacity cartridges are the ideal backup medium. The backup may proceed unattended, any file is instantly accessible, the backup medium may substitute for the drive itself, and the cartridges may be transported to a safe location. But removable cartridge drives are very expensive, and it is hard to justify buying one for backups alone. Today, most cartridges hold 20 megabytes, and soon they will hold 30 or 40; backing up a very large hard disk may require several cartridges, and this defeats some of the advantages of the medium.

Magneto-optical, WORM, and Removable Cartridge Drives

Any kind of removable disk is an excellent backup medium. The backup may proceed unattended, any file is instantly accessible, the backup medium may substitute for the drive itself, and the cartridges may be transported to a safe location. But removable drives are very expensive, and it is hard to justify buying one for backups alone.

Second Hard Disks

These reservations also apply to the use of a second, ordinary hard disk for backups, employing XCOPY or a backup utility to copy over the entire directory tree. The situation is much the same, but you lose the automaticity. Vendors report that this approach is becoming quite common, since a bare drive is relatively inexpensive, and it can readily be connected to the existing controller. The same dangers also apply, but perhaps the degree of risk from theft or destruction is no greater than other risks businesses undertake.

Streaming Tape

Tape drives have dropped remarkably in price over the past few years. If prices continue to fall, perhaps tape backup will stop being a luxury and become standard equipment, just as hard disks have. As we've seen, tape backup can be made cheaper by buying interface cards for several computers and sharing one drive among them. This approach tends to undermine tape's advantage in ease-of-use. It discourages frequent incremental backups and won't allow automatic off-hours backups on all machines. This approach may also create a confusion of tape cartridges. But it is a cheap and reliable way of getting backups done in offices where individual users cannot be counted upon to make backups themselves.

Diskettes

Diskettes are the most inconvenient backup medium. Even when used with a high-speed utility, diskettes can be onerous when a large hard disk undergoes a global backup, and this inconvenience is liable to discourage people from making backups at all. Diskette backup is unsuitable for very-high-capacity disks. A 250-megabyte hard disk needs *one hundred and seventy-five* 1.44M diskettes (or, heaven forbid!, *seven hundred* 360K diskettes). And diskette backups require exceptional organization if multiple series of diskettes are to be kept in proper order.

But diskette backups can offer flexibility. Utilities that store files in DOS format make searching through backups easy. And the diskettes can be read by any machine, anywhere. The backups can double as a means of moving work between office and home.

Those who ordinarily access only a small portion of their hard disk's data may find that diskette backup is no less convenient than any other approach. If global backups are required infrequently, the disadvantages of diskettes in large backups become unimportant. Most people who own, say, a 1.44-mega-byte diskette drive would find that a daily incremental backup can be performed in hardly a minute without a disk change. For those with simple needs, spending hundreds of dollars on a tape backup system would be wasteful.

In the end, you must pay whatever it costs to get the backups made. But keep in mind that not everyone's backup requirements are equal. The *best* backup system is the one that meets *your* requirements most cheaply in terms of both money invested in hardware and time invested in its use. To make the right choice, you must first think clearly about how much you will be backing up, and how often. That is our next topic.

Backup Frequency

Backups must be multiple. If you use a single series of diskettes for all your backups, or a single tape cartridge, you take the risk that a disk crash *during* the backup will wipe out both the original files and the prior backup copy. You would lose everything. Besides, backup media can be defective, and multiple copies are a wise precaution, as we'll explain in a moment.

Many corporations maintain sufficient backups that they can financially "re-start" the company on any prior day of the preceeding month. This is an extreme case: these companies are using *serial global backups*. More generally, the MIS (management information systems) world maintains three generations of global backups, known as the grandfather, father, and son, respectively. As time passes, the son becomes the father, the father becomes the grandfather, and the grandfather media is rerecorded as the new son. Global backups are made weekly. A second series of global backups may be kept at one-month intervals, usually made at the end of the month. Hence the company keeps end-of-month backups for the three prior months, and end-of-week backups for the three prior weeks, with some overlap. Copies of the most recent weekly and monthly backups are kept off-site. In addition, many companies ware-house the data source documents for long periods.

Most backup schemes consist of periodic global backups followed by frequent incremental backups. The frequency of incremental backups may be proportional to the amount of work done on the machine. But the schedule for global backups should be strictly observed. If a global backup is scheduled for the first and third Mondays of each month, the backup should be made even if the computer has been used very little during the preceeding two-week period. This rigidity is justified because global backups are the *base point* for reconstructing data after total data loss.

Extra global backups are a good idea on certain occasions. It's a good idea to follow heavy editing of the directory tree with a global backup. You could spend hours rationalizing the subdirectory system and moving files, only to have your last global backup restore the prior state of affairs. Keep in mind that files *erased* since the last global backup will reappear. An extra global backup is also a good idea immediately before introducing potentially dangerous software to the disk, such as a public-domain disk utility. Bad software can do a lot of damage. Be equally careful if you are learning to program and plan to experiment with DOS disk-access functions (*don't* use the absolute sector write function on the hard disk; confine your experiments to diskettes).

Always keep at least two generations of global backups. In doing so, you'll always have the prior backup on hand. If you do need to make a global restoration and something has gone wrong with the most recent global backup, you have something to fall back on. A good plan is to move the prior global backup off-site to guard against catastrophes like fire and theft. You'll need two sets of diskettes or tape cartridges. Take the current backup to the off-site location, bring back the old one, and use it for the new backup.

Some backup software lets you exclude certain kinds of files from global backups, particularly program files, which are easily identified by the .EXE and .COM filename extensions. The rationale is that you already have backups of these files because you own the original distribution diskettes. Program files may take up several megabytes of disk space, so excluding them may save many disk changes in backups made to diskettes. But it's not a good idea to exclude files from any global backup. The great value in a global backup is that, after data restoration, work can begin again *immediately*. You may have to spend hours reinstalling software if it is excluded from the backups.

One kind of file virtually never requires backing up at any time. These are **.BAK** files automatically made by software. As backups of backups, they are redundant. There's no harm in recording the files if it does not inconvenience you. But if there are many, your should either delete them or see to it that they are excluded from incremental backups. Without doing so, incremental backups could be doubled in length. Find out how your backup software can be made to ignore files with .BAK filename extensions. Or use the DOS ATTRIB command to clear the files' archive bit. For all .BAK files in the current directory, enter:

```
ATTRIB *.BAK -A
```

Or, for the entire directory tree:

```
ATTRIB \*.BAK -A  /S
```

A global backup is a good opportunity to perform various disk maintenance tasks. Take a little extra time. Delete unnecessary files, including .BAK files. Run a utility that checks for bad sectors and damaged files (we'll discuss these in Chapter 9). Most important, take time to run a defragmentation utility so that your files will be compacted into as few cylinders as possible. All of these tasks need to be carried out about once a month on a moderately-to-heavily used disk.

The ideal order for these tasks is disputable. Ideally, the backup should be made of a disk cleared of unnecessary files and free of defects. In addition, having the disk defragmented beforehand helps the backup run faster. But house cleaning is a rather dangerous activity; files are often mistakenly destroyed when they are thought obsolete. And disk utilities have often been known to damage the disks they are supposed to protect. Hence, it can be argued that you should backup *before* doing housecleaning and running utilities. This is particularly true when you are running utility software for the first time.

While the frequency of global backups depends in part on how often incremental backups are made, the frequency of incremental backups is entirely a matter of judgement. It all depends on the value of your data, and on how great a risk you want to take. Backups are so widely neglected that it is tempting to go to the opposite extreme and say that no amount of backing-up is excessive. But hard disks are more reliable than is popularly believed. When a disk is brand new, more frequent backups are a good idea, since manufacturing problems will appear early on. But after a few months of good service, a drive is very likely to perform for several years without problems, just like a quality automobile. As a drive ages, more frequent backups become advisable.

Incremental backups ought to be made at least once a week (on machines used all week long). Twice a week would be wiser, and a daily incremental backup is a good idea when the work that goes into files is unreproducible (you can always reenter data into a spreadsheet, but an inspired sonnet may come your way only once). If you make daily incremental backups, they will probably need to be *overwritten* if you use diskette backups, unless very few files are changed. Otherwise scores of diskettes will be required, or you will be forced to make global backups more frequently.

Organizing Backup Media

Whether you make your backups on disk or tape, you must carefully label and organize the media. Failure to do so leads to all sorts of confusion. You'll lose track of which backups have become dated and should be overwritten. You won't know which disk or cartridge to insert for an *append* backup. You'll forget whether scheduled backups have been made. Worst of all, when catastrophe strikes and it's time to restore data to your hard disk, you may be unable to locate the most recent backups. This problem is particularly acute when you must sort out the newest versions of files from several incremental backups.

Alas, we don't like to make an already onerous task more complicated. But there are four steps to organizing your media, and each step leads to its own brand of confusion when it is omitted. The steps are:

Labeling. Each diskette or cartridge must be labeled using a simple code showing where it belongs in the backup system.

Record keeping. Each diskette or cartridge needs some kind of written record of what was recorded on it, and when.

Storage. Groups of diskettes, and sometimes cartridges, must be kept in their own marked containers, each with its own labels and records.

Rotation. Procedures and record keeping must be instituted to see that backups are performed on the proper media, and that crucial backups have been sent off-site.

Always keep global and incremental backups on separate media. If possible, use different colors of labels for the two kinds of backups. Mark the media clearly, indicating both the backup's generation and, if multiple diskettes or cartridges are involved, a sequence number. For example, you might have media marked "Global A" and "Global B" for a two-generation global backup, plus other media marked "Incremental." Perhaps labels for the two global backups could be respectively colored red and yellow, and blue labels could mark the incremental backups. This simple measure helps avoid mistakes.

Using diskettes, each series of labels should have a number from 1 upwards. Be sure to have more than enough diskettes to handle the worst case, and preformat them if your backup utility requires it. Some backup programs cannot format diskettes on the fly, and you may have to interrupt the backup if you run out of diskettes. *Never* make backups on unlabeled diskettes, thinking that you'll sort through them if they are ever needed. Restoring a disk properly can be hard enough without adding to the confusion.

When data is critical and irreplacable, you may want to keep a second backup. It's best to perform a second backup onto a second set of media, rather than copy the first backup. This approach avoids duplicating undetected errors made in the first backup. And a direct backup is often faster than a diskette-to-diskette copy, since the data source operates at hard-disk speed. Those who use tape drives, or who haven't a matching diskette drive, have no choice in this matter. Remember that backups made with proprietary diskette formats can't be copied by DOS. Keep in mind also that a second incremental backup can be made only if attribute bits were not turned off while making the first; so you'll need to configure your backup software properly.

Most backup programs keep some kind of catalog of each backup session. A few can create a catalog retroactively by scanning the backup media. Some catalogs are readable only by the backup program. You may be able to ask the program to display information from the file, but you can't read it directly or print it out. These files are often kept on the hard disk in the subdirectory in which the backup program resides; others write the catalog on the backup medium when the backup is finished. Catalogs can slow down backups as the hard disk's read/write heads constantly move between the catalog file and the files that are backed up.

Off-site Data Storage

Giant corporations are so reliant upon their computers that they plan for even the most extreme form of data loss: utter destruction of the entire computer system. In addition to shipping daily backups to an off-site location, they maintain stand-by hardware. While most of us can afford to live without a computer for a few days until the insurance company replaces it, recovering from total data loss is another matter. Yet many who make backups religiously leave the backups open to destruction by fire, flood, or thorough-going thieves.

This sort of catastrophic data loss is much less likely than data loss to a drive failure or user error. But it is a serious possibility. Many who would not *think* of leaving $10,000 of computer equipment uninsured leave several times that value in data completely at the mercy of the Fates. Computer theft is sharply on the rise, so you should be concerned about crime. Those with modest backup needs often find it easiest to keep a sole copy of crucial files on a single diskette or tape cartridge, never removing the media from the drive. The backups may be of no value to a thief, but he'll carry it away with the equipment nonetheless.

Keeping a backup off-site is the obvious countermeasure. How often the off-site backup needs renewing depends on just how precious the data is to you. What's most important is that you chose an off-site location that is easily accessible. Otherwise you'll only be encouraging resistance to your own backup system. While nothing feels quite so secure as a safe deposit box, actually rotating backup media through a bank vault can be a tremendous hassle. If the hard disk is in an office, its much simpler to just take a copy of the backups home.

The ideal off-site location is cool, dry, and stationary. But the ideal is not strictly necessary. You'll find that diskettes are a lot more rugged than they appear. *PC Magazine* once sponsored a study of diskette durability, subjecting diskettes to high humidity, corrosive gases, microwave ovens, thermal shock, x-ray machines, and airport security machines. They also exposed them to a variety of magnetic sources, including welding machines, fluorescent lights, color televisions, calculators, and the insides of telephones. Of all the tests, only rubbing a bar magnet directly on the diskettes led to loss of data (a magnet held two inches away had no effect).

Those who work at home and lack an obvious second location might want to consider keeping off-site backups in their cars. Experience has shown that diskettes weather extremes of temperature, humidity, and motion quite well. So long as they're kept out of direct sunlight or moisture, they should be all right. Although storing diskettes in an automobile breaks all the rules, it's a far sight safer than having no off-site backup at all.

One way of updating the off-site backup is to use the prior global backup of a disk. Recall that when you make a new global backup, you should never over-write the prior backup, since a hardware failure during the backup could cost you everything. When the new backup is complete, shift the prior backup to off-site storage, and at the same time return the prior off-site backup to the hard disk site so that it may be used for the next global backup. This approach requires three series of backup media.

This brings us to the end of our discussion of backups. We've gone on at such length because the topic is so very important. Talking with disk repair services, we've found that they constantly encounter hysterical people who have lost one or two years work, or whose small businesses may have been destroyed for want of a few backups. The question is, can *you* learn from the experience of others, or...

Surviving Hard Disk Disasters

When your best efforts fail and a file, or a whole disk full of files, fly off to Never Never Land, there's still hope of reclaiming your beloved data. Utility programs exist that can unerase files, reassemble accidentally formatted disks, and repair damaged directories, file allocation tables, boot records, bad sectors, and format markings. None of these utilities can do the job perfectly every time, and you should NEVER neglect backups simply because you have a shelf full of recovery tools. Adequate backups are your best defense against the data gremlins.

Two kinds of disasters threaten a disk. In one case, files are lost due to operator negligence, but the disk itself is undamaged. In the second case, the disk malfunctions and requires repairs; "repair" can mean anything from running the DOS CHKDSK program to sending the drive to the shop. In the latter case, "repair" often means "replacement." Of course, files are frequently lost in the second case, too. Sometimes, a very small defect can stop you from using the disk at all. You'll encounter one of the much feared DOS error messages:

DISK ERROR READING DRIVE C:

GENERAL FAILURE

ERROR READING...

WRITE FAULT

BAD SECTOR

SECTOR NOT FOUND

FILE ALLOCATION TABLE BAD

DISK ERROR READING FAT

DISK NOT READY

INVALID DRIVE SPECIFICATION

DATA ERROR

NON-SYSTEM DISK OR DISK ERROR

READ FAULT

BAD DATA

ABORT, RETRY, IGNORE?

You can do *much* to avert these disasters, and to recover from them when they occur, by investing a little money and time. To do this intelligently, you must understand the different ways in which a disk can fail; that is where we shall begin.

How Disks Fail

Equipment failures may be *mechanical* or *electronic*. Most of us tend to visualize any drive malfunction as a "crash" where the read/write heads dive-bomb into the disk surface. Some people exhibit a near-hysterical anxiety about head crashes, as if every disk is poised to self-destruct at any moment, and that few live for very long. In fact, head crashes account for only about one percent of the hard disk drives sent in for repairs. The hysteria is a measure not of the imminence of a head crash, but of the consequences when the disk has not been backed up. Drives fail in many other ways, and in some cases you can recover some or all of your data (if you are willing to hand over a lot of money to a special repair service—more on this later).

Mechanical Failures

Mechanical failures generally center on either the motor that turns the platters or the actuator that moves the read/write heads back and forth. The head actuator is by far the more complicated of the two, but until recently many problems developed in drive motors. Sometimes the motor would burn out, or, if it used a drive belt, the belt would break or become slack. More often, the bearings in the motor or the spindle that supports the platters would wear out.

Electronic Failures

Electronic failures occur in the circuitry on the disk drive or on the controller board. Simple components may burn out. Complicated ones may malfunction because of design flaws. Electronic failures damage data only when the drive is writing data. The damage tends to be local, but a long time may pass before you first discover an instance of the damage, and in that time the faulty components may work their mischief again and again. The worst outcome occurs when a directory or file allocation table is the victim of a faulty write operation. This silent error can destroy all of your data just as surely as an all-out head crash.

Soft Errors

Other problems arise from *soft errors*. These result from changes in the drive's magnetic medium, or in its mechanical alignment. In a soft error, the drive continues to function mechanically and electronically. But, for various reasons, it fails to read a given bit of information the first time it tries. It may succeed the second time, or perhaps the third. If an operation fails, the disk controller typically makes nine more attempts, each time waiting for the platter to spin around once more.

The designers of DOS did not choose to let the user know that there might be a problem with the disk, even if all nine attempts fail. When the disk controller reports that it was unable to complete a request, DOS tells it to try again, and once more still if the second request also ends in failure. Hence, *thirty* tries are made before DOS finally gives up and reports a disk "failure". If it prompts you with the "Abort, Retry, Ignore?" message, the answer "Retry" may send DOS back for 30 more tries. Sometimes, numerous tries end in a success. There should be no reassurance in this outcome. The data is almost certainly lost. Ironically, this is the first time the user is made aware that there's any problem.

Kinds of Failure

With this understanding, let's look at what can go wrong:

- **Magnetic fade.** Magnetic markings on the disk surface slowly fade. Files tend to be rewritten periodically, so they stay intact. But the format markings that define sectors are written only when the disk is given its low-level formatting. Similarly, boot records and some directory information are written only once. After some years, the disk controller may be unable to read some of the markings, or soft errors may increase to unacceptable levels.

- **Media degeneration.** The magnetic coating on the platters disintegrates very slowly. Recall that, even when a disk drive is new, some points on it's platters have relatively low *magnetic retentivity*, and they can barely act as magnetic domains. As the medium deteriorates, these points become ineffective, soft errors increase, and new bad sectors form.

- **Track misalignment.** The actuator that pushes and pulls the read/write heads across the platters may gradually pull out of alignment, especially on drives that use stepper motors. Depending on the nature of the misalignment, the heads will stray to the sides of tracks, varying as the temperature rises. More and more soft errors occur, and gradually the heads are pushed too far out of alignment to be able to read data at all.

- **Platter wobble.** With time, the bearings in the spindle that supports the platters begin to wear. A platter may begin to wobble very slightly. With each revolution, the wobble increases and then decreases the distance between the heads and the disk surface. Again, soft errors increase.

- **Controller malfunction.** Sometimes the electronic components on controller cards stray outside acceptable tolerances. The result is a slight misalignment of magnetic domains that throws off timing in read/write operations.

- **Electrical surge.** A strong voltage spike may find its way past your surge protector and the computer's built-in protection circuitry. It's possible, but unlikely, that this surge will propagate to the read/write head and damage the disks; however, it can damage the electronics, causing the drive to stop working.

- **Head crashes.** A head touches down on the disk surface. In the best case, only a tiny stretch of a track is affected, and the disk may be returned to service by reformatting it so that the affected areas are set aside from further use. In the worst case, a read/write head crashes on Cylinder 0, where DOS keeps the partition table, root directory, and file allocation tables. The medium may be damaged to the point that the disk cannot support the DOS area after the disk is reformatted. Or the read/write heads may be fatally damaged. Even when damage is slight, particles of the medium may break loose and fly around inside the disk drive casing, ready to cause another crash at any time.

- **Software error.** "Freeware," possibly written by an aspiring nine-year old, may run amok and erase files right and left. Even software from reputable firms may sometimes commit datacide. In the worst case, the software will inadvertently overwrite FAT sectors held in DOS buffers, and these will be written to both copies of the FAT kept on the disk. All data may be lost.

- **Operator error.** Besides accidentally erasing files or reformatting the disk, an inexperienced user can damage data by rebooting during a disk operation. The directory entries of individual files are not updated until the file is completely written. Directories themselves may be damaged. *Don't use Ctrl-Alt-Del as a panic button!*

Of course, sometimes components just blow out. The drive motor may burn out, or a capacitor may short-circuit. But more often a drive gradually descends into decrepitude. As it does so, soft errors occur with greater frequency. Unfortunately, this process is invisible until it is too late. DOS does not notify you until the drive fails 30 times in a row. When deterioration is widespread across the disk surface, performance may be compromised as many extra turns of the platters are inserted into read and write operations. This is particularly true when the problems lie upon the crucial DOS structures on Cylinder 0.

Recovering Erased Files

In Chapter 2 we explained how DOS organizes files by directories and file allocation tables. A file's directory listing contains its name, size, and other information, including the number of the first cluster of disk space it occupies. The file allocation table keeps track of each additional cluster the file occupies, each position in the table telling which cluster is next.

How DOS Erases Files

When DOS "erases" a file, it does two things. First, it changes the first character of the file's directory listing to the Greek *sigma* character. In subsequent directory searches, the character indicates to DOS that the directory slot is "empty" and open for insertion of a new file. Still, all information from the prior file remains intact except for the first character of the file's name, which is overwritten by the sigma character.

Second, DOS goes through the file allocation table and *deallocates* clusters given to the file. That is, it changes the markings that keep track of the file to markings that indicate that the clusters are free for use by other files. What DOS does not do is actually erase the information in the clusters occupied by the file. It would be easy enough to do this, but there is no point in it. (If very high security is desired, however, there *is* a point in it; some security software for the PC automatically scrubs parts of the disk that are freed by DOS.) When the clusters are required for another file, they can be allocated even with old information in them. The old information is destroyed only when a new file overwrites it.

Unerasing a Deleted File

Since a deleted file remains intact, it should be an easy job to recover it, and often it is. But sometimes problems arise. Losing the file's information in the FAT is pretty disastrous. After all, there are thousands of clusters on the disk, and the FAT is the only way of knowing which is linked to which. The *starting cluster* of the file is recorded in its directory entry, so we can always be sure where it is. But subsequent clusters may be anywhere on the disk. To recover a file, we not only have to find its clusters, we have to get them in the right order.

The Simplest Case

In the simplest case, a file occupies only one cluster. To unerase it, a utility has to find its entry in the directory, using the former file name and extension, minus the first character. It asks the person who erased the file to enter the deleted first character of the file name, and it replaces it. Then it looks up the *starting cluster* in the entry and goes to the FAT to reallocate the cluster to the file. That's all there is to it.

Multicluster Files

When the file stretches across several contiguous clusters, the utility has a bit more work to do, but not much. After restoring the directory entry, it goes to the FAT and reallocates as many successive clusters as are required to hold the file. It knows how many clusters are needed, because the file size is recorded in the directory. Figure 9-1 diagrams this scheme.

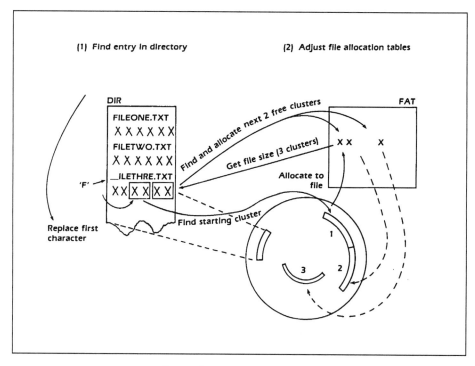

Figure 9-1. Automatic unerase

Actually, the unerase utility reallocates *successive* clusters only when it finds that those clusters are not currently in use by other files. If successive clusters are free, there's a good chance they belong to the erased file. Otherwise, odds are that the file is dispersed across the disk, making recovery much more diffi-cult, and perhaps impossible.

Dispersed Files

Unerase utilities deal with the latter case in two ways. They may go ahead and gather together as many nearby clusters as are required. This is "auto-matic recovery," and it's based on blind hope. Once the file is resurrected, you can look into it and see if the correct clusters were chosen. Alternatively, unerase utilities offer a "manual mode" in which cluster after cluster is shown on the screen, and the user strikes one key or another to include or reject the cluster in the rehabilitated file. There are some serious drawbacks to the latter approach. To understand them, lets first take a look at how files become fragmented.

The Origins of File Fragmentation

In Chapter 7 we learned about file fragmentation, and about defragmentation utilities that physically unify files so that they may be read with minimal head movement. Prior to DOS 3.0, when DOS needed to allocate a cluster to a file, it simply scanned the file allocation table from its beginning and allocated the first cluster it found. By doing so, the disk was filled from its outer edge inward.

This approach was ultimately abandoned because it promoted file fragmentation. Imagine that a small file is placed on Cylinder 1, and that many more follow. Then the file is erased, opening up a single cluster on Cylinder 1. Thereafter, a new file is copied to the disk, and it requires *two* clusters. DOS searches the FAT, finds the open cluster in Cylinder 1, and allocates it to the file. Then it goes on looking for a second cluster, and finds one farther inwards on the disk, perhaps in Cylinder 10. The new file is fragmented.

Ideally, DOS would scan the file allocation table for a free block of clusters large enough to fill the file. But that would be slow, and as the disk fills, it would become impossible. To do the job right, DOS would need to take on the role of a defragmenter. Some operating systems do this job, but DOS is not one of them.

An Improved Method

Nonetheless, later DOS versions introduced two measures that help overcome file defragmentation. First, as the disk fills, DOS keeps track of the position in the FAT from which it last allocated a cluster. When another cluster is required, it begins its search from that location in the FAT. This is to say that DOS allocates every cluster *once* before it goes back and *re*allocates clusters freed by file erasures. If the last allocated cluster was on Cylinder 600, DOS starts its next search for a free cluster at this same cylinder, rather than seek out freed clusters closer to the outer edge of the disk. Once every cluster on the disk has been allocated once, DOS reverts to its 2.x-style mode of allocating whatever cluster is closest to Cylinder 0. This state of affairs continues indefinitely thereafter—or at least until the machine is rebooted. But, for a while, it does quite a lot to discourage file fragmentation.

The second improvement is that now, when you load a file and later save it, the new version is also written to previously unused clusters. The clusters previously occupied by the file are freed. This measure avoids the fragmentation that occurs when a file slowly grows. For example, if you were to add a cluster's worth of data to a file every day for a month, the file would probably become fragmented into 30 parts. This fragmentation is overcome by repeatedly rewriting the entire file in a group of clusters large enough to contain it. Of course, this measure causes the disk's clusters to fill all the more quickly during the first pass across the disk. And after every cluster has been used once, you're right back to the situation of DOS allocating clusters as it finds them.

Manual File Recovery

Now, let's reconsider what goes on during a manual file recovery. This process is diagrammed in Figure 9-2. First, the clusters belonging to a file may be widely dispersed across the disk. This is most likely to happen when the disk is nearly full, or when the file is very large. If many files are subsequently deleted (say, in a general housecleaning), hundreds of open clusters may lie between the clusters given to a particular file. It's a long haul looking through all these clusters.

Cluster Order

Worse, the file's clusters may get out of order. When a file gradually grows over months and even years, DOS may allocate new clusters from any point on the disk. A file can begin on Cylinder 200, continue at Cylinder 400, then 300, then 100, then 500, and so on. This is often the case with very large files, and it makes them difficult to recover. Not only is it hard to find the clusters, but it may be impossible to put the reclaimed clusters into the proper order.

Inspecting the Clusters

This problem leads us to the greatest impediment of all to manual file recovery. Many data files cannot be visually inspected. Program files, in particular, appear as so much gobbledygook when they are displayed. If you accidentally erase a program file and then attempt to undelete it, you can only use automatic recovery. If the recovery is successful, the program will run. If it was not, you'll quickly know, because the machine will "hang" and you'll need to reboot to get going again (no harm is done).

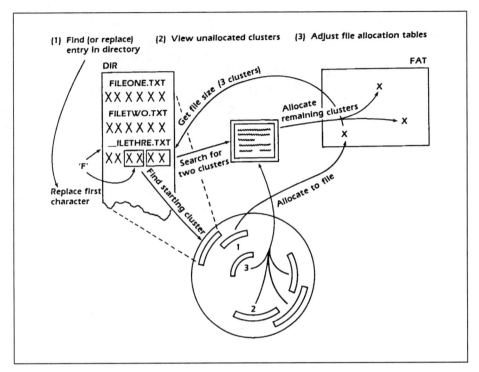

Figure 9-2. Manual unerase

Most data files, other than simple word processor files, are also difficult to reclaim manually. True, files for databases, spreadsheets, and outliners are likely to have intelligible English written amidst the gobbledygook, But figuring out the proper sequence for the clusters is often next to impossible. If one cluster is out of order, the software that uses the file will almost definitely freeze up—and that means that all of the data is as good as lost.

Other Problems

So far we've spoken about an erased file as if nothing had happened on the disk from the moment of its accidental erasure. Often, the person who deleted the file recognizes the error immediately and runs straight for the unerase utility. But sometimes hours or days may pass before it's realized that valuable data is missing. During that time, DOS may hand over to a new file the directory slot formerly occupied by the file. Or DOS may allocate to another file some (or all) of the erased file's clusters. When this happens, you've got Big Trouble on your hands.

Directory Entries

When the directory slot is taken over by another file, two crucial pieces of information are lost. The number of the starting cluster is gone. And the file size is no longer available to tell how many clusters are involved. But the file may still be recovered. It's done by searching every unallocated cluster on the disk.

Lost Clusters

When a file's former clusters have been given over to another file, the data is obliterated permanently. Still, it may be possible to *partially* recover the file. After all, its better to rewrite only *part* of the Great American Novel. But generally only text files are useful after a partial recovery. When a sector is missing from a database, the alignment of all the records is thrown off and the database program reads the surviving data improperly.

Incidentally, if you've erased a file and wonder what's happened to it, *don't* use file recovery utilities until you've tried an unerase program. In DOS, both the CHKDSK and RECOVER programs create temporary files that may overwrite the deallocated clusters of the files you wish to reclaim. Other utilities may do the same.

Multiple Erasures

When many files have been unerased, perhaps by using the DEL command with wildcard characters, problems are compounded. A utility attempts to recover them by repeating the procedure for recovering a single file. But if the files are fragmented, a cluster belonging to one erased file may easily be incorporated into another. Hence, a failure to correctly reclaim one file can cause a failure to reclaim a second. If you attempt to manually reassemble the files, sorting through the numerous deallocated clusters can be overwhelming.

Unerase Utilities

There is no standard design for unerase utilities. Each has its own way of doing things; some offer more features than others. Most provide two approaches to reclaiming a file: a "manual" method and an "automatic" method. The automatic method is preferred. You specify the file to be recovered and the software does the best job it can of it. When the results are not good enough, you may turn to the manual method in which you inspect the contents of the clusters to be included in the reconstituted file.

Automatic File Recovery

The automatic method works by locating the file's erased directory entry. It learns from it the size of the file (which tells the number of clusters it must find) and the location on the disk of the starting cluster. It then assembles the starting cluster and as many free clusters as it needs, taking the clusters closest to the starting cluster, moving inward toward the center of the disk (the direction in which DOS allocated clusters to a file when it was created or expanded).

When you start an unerase utility, you begin by telling it which drive and directory the erased file was located in. The utility then displays the names of all erased files for which the directory slots have not since been taken over by other files. It identifies these entries by a special character written where the first letter of the file name would be kept. If the file was named **ELEPHANT.TXT**, the utility will find and display the name with some other character in place of the initial "E," such as a question mark. Figure 9.3 shows a status report from the *Norton UnErase* program for an erased file named ?GLIB.EXE. Notice how the utility is able to judge the likelihood of a successful recovery; the chances are poor in this case because the file was erased long before recovery was attempted.

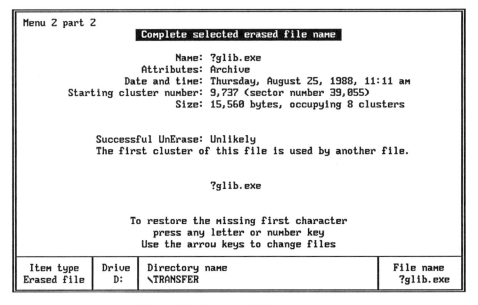

Figure 9-3. An erased file status report.

If you can find the file's listing, you select it and supply a first character for its name. Then recovery begins. If you can't find the file, and you're sure it was in the directory you specified, recovery will be more difficult since you must track down the first cluster of the file by instructing the utility to display one free cluster after another, examining each in turn. As mentioned above, that can be a tremendous amount of work. Besides, if the file's directory entry has been taken up by another file, you confront the possibility that some of the file's sectors may have been absorbed as well.

Most unerase utilities help you with this problem by offering a search facility. You specify a few words that you recall being near the start of the document and the utility then examines every free disk sector to see if it can find them. If you can locate the first cluster, you may then initiate an automatic file recovery. The unerase utility will provide a way of creating a new directory entry for the file. You'll need to specify a probable file length, and then may need to make adjustments to the length until the file is properly reconstituted.

Manual File Recovery

An automatic recovery always generates a file of the specified name and length, but the file may have picked up clusters that did not belong to it. If the file contents are bad, you'll know it right away when you try to use the file. In this case, you must continue the recovery by searching for the missing clusters manually—that is, by employing a search facility to view free clusters. A well-designed unerase utility does a good deal to help you with this process. With just a keystroke it displays cluster after cluster and provides a way of tracking and reordering clusters that belong to the file. Figure 9.4 shows the main menu for these facilities in the *Norton UnErase* program.

Yet even the best-designed utility makes a manual recovery chancy. The problem is not just in finding a file's clusters, but also in recognizing them when they are before your eyes. Clusters belonging to text files are the easiest to discern, but it may be difficult to decide whether a given cluster belongs to the erased file, or to some other long-abandoned document. Other kinds of files are far more difficult to track and reassemble. Spreadsheet and database files contain identifying words and phrases, but much of a cluster's content is numeric data that appears as sheer gobbledygook on the screen. Some clusters may be impossible to identify, and even when all can be rounded up, it may be prohibitively difficult to arrange them in the proper order.

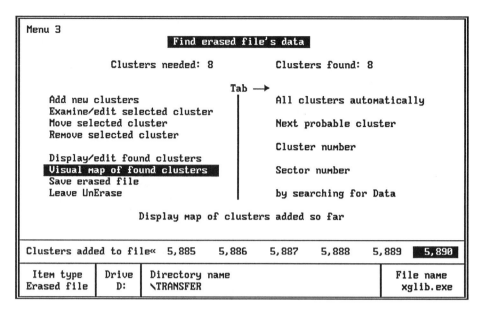

Figure 9-4. Norton UnErase main menu.

For these reasons, a manual recovery of an erased file is unlikely to succeed except for text files. Fortunately, files are seldom completely fragmented. Usually the clusters fall into a few blocks of contiguous sectors, and you need only locate the beginning of each block. But, still, considerable labor is required, and, if you are unlucky, the recovery may fail despite your efforts. It is far easier to make frequent backups than to struggle through this experience.

Unerasing Files in DOS 5.0

Starting with Version 5.0, DOS can undelete files. DOS can now work like more sophisticated utilities in that it has the option of modifying what happens when the ERASE, DEL, or DELETE commands are used. It does this by providing a way in which information about every deleted file can be set aside when the file is erased. To recover a deleted file, all DOS needs to do is consult this information to find out which clusters the file occupied. Of course, as is always the case, a complete recovery can't be made when one or more of those clusters has been appropriated by other files.

DOS 5.0 does not automatically set aside information about deleted files. Instead, this is done by the MIRROR command, which we'll be discussing a little later in this chapter. MIRROR is used to set up the disk so that data can be recovered easily should the disk be accidentally reformatted. To do this, it's generally best to execute the MIRROR command everytime the machine starts up by placing the command in AUTOEXEC.BAT. DOS is made to set aside information about deleted files by adding a /**T** switch (for "deletion-*tracking*") to this command, following it with the name of the drive it should serve. For example, the command:

```
MIRROR /TC
```

sets aside information about drive C. Multiple drives may be specified:

```
MIRROR /TC /TA
```

In the root directory of each disk specified, MIRROR sets up a file to hold information about deleted files. The file (called a "delete tracking file") is named **PCTRACKR.DEL**. This file cannot be allowed to expand in size indefinitely, lest it ultimately take over the entire disk. So, by default, MIRROR limits the file's size. For diskettes, the file ranges from 5K (25 entries) for 360K diskettes to three times this size for 1.44M diskettes. On hard disks, sizes range from 18K (101 entries) for 20M drives to 55K (303 entries) for drives holding 32M or more. You can set a different value by specifying the number of entries along with the /**T** switch. Just follow the switch with a dash and the number. For a 300-entry limit, you would type:

```
MIRROR /TC-300
```

When the file fills to its limit, information for new deletions replaces that of the oldest deletions.

The UNDELETE command restores a file. To restore the file **\RODENTS\MICE\MICKEY.DOC**, you simply enter:

```
UNDELETE C:\RODENTS\MICE\MICKEY.DOC
```

UNDELETE will search the file containing information about deletions for an entry for this file. If it doesn't find it, UNDELETE will proceed to search the directory **\RODENTS\MICE** for an empty directory slot that had previously been held by the file, and then will go on to do the best job it can of recovering the file. In the latter case, UNFORMAT automatically replaces the missing first character of the file with a pound sign (#).

Groups of files can be undeleted. For example, to restore all batch files in the MICE directory, you'd type:

```
UNDELETE C:\RODENTS\MICE\*.BAT
```

Or, to recover all files in the MICE directory:

```
UNDELETE  C:\RODENTS\MICE
```

If you want UNDELETE to recover only files found in the tracking file, add a **/DT** switch at the end of the command. Conversely, to have it undelete only files not listed in the tracking file, add **/DOS**. To find out what files are available for recovery, enter the command:

```
UNDELETE /LIST
```

If you follow the rules given in Chapter 6, you can avoid accidental erasures. And, if you make frequent backups, you can avoid unerasing files altogether. A good unerase utility is an essential part of any software library. When you purchase one, practice using it a little bit. You'll quickly learn the limitations of unerase utilities, and you'll be better prepared to deal with a crisis when it comes.

Recovering from Accidental Reformatting

The accidentally reformatted hard disk holds a special terror all its own: a few false keystrokes and every byte of data disappears. It's difficult to take precautions against this disaster, because its perpetrator, the DOS FORMAT program, is often required for formatting diskettes. Computer novices—who may have trouble getting *any* DOS command right the first time—can easily direct FORMAT to drive C: instead of drive A:. And even experienced users can make the Great Mistake in a moment of foggy-headedness.

Avoiding the Problem

In Chapter 6 we suggested several ways to avoid accidental reformatting. First, you should keep your low-level formatting program (if you have one) and the FDISK partitioning program away from the hard disk. Next, place FORMAT.COM in its own subdirectory and do not give automatic access through the PATH command. Consider renaming the program and calling it through a batch file that always directs it towards drive A. Or replace the program with a safer one, like the *Norton Safe Format* utility. If, after all this, you still worry that someone will break through your defenses, move FORMAT.COM off the hard disk, buy preformatted diskettes, and lock away the DOS diskettes.

How FORMAT Works

Since good advice is as often ignored as taken, you'd better know about "unformatting" hard disks. The very notion of unformatting a disk seems a logical impossibility. After all, "formatting" lays down sector markings on every track on the disk, and these overwrite any recorded data. But recall that there are *two* levels of formatting, and it is *low-level formatting* that defines sectors. The DOS FORMAT command performs only *high-level formatting* when applied to hard disks. Hence your hard disk data can be obliterated only if you inadvertently run a low-level formatting program. Many people buy disks that are preformatted at low level, and they don't own a low-level formatting program. But even those who do have such a program can easily avoid an accidental low-level formatting. Just keep the program off the hard disk and the diskette that holds it out of reach. After all, it makes no sense to store a low-level format program on the hard disk that it operates on—the program would erase itself when used.

Recall from Chapter 4 that a high-level format writes the DOS root directory and file allocation tables. When the **/S** option is used to make the disk bootable, the boot record and system files (IBMBIO.COM, IBMDOS.COM, and COMMAND.COM) are also written. That's all. Data previously recorded on the disk is untouched, including all subdirectory files. But the data is as good as lost, since without a root directory, there's no way to find the subdirectories, and without a file allocation table, there's no knowing which clusters are linked together to form files.

The "Snap Shot" Approach

There are two approaches to "unformatting" an accidentally reformatted hard disk. The first works by keeping a utility on the disk that takes a "snap shot" of the root directory, file allocation table, and other DOS information. The utility may be executed at any time, but usually it is called from AUTOEXEC.BAT, so that a snap shot is made automatically at least once a day when the computer is booted. It stores the information in a file, adding a unique sequence of characters (a "signature") to the beginning of the file. The file is listed in a directory like any other file so that it can be quickly found and updated. In addition, the utility that creates and updates the file sees to it that all clusters occupied by the file are contiguous.

If the disk is accidentally reformatted, a companion utility is started up from diskette. The directory entry telling where the data file begins has been lost, so the utility must scan the disk until it finds the unique signature at the start of the file. Since the file's clusters are contiguous, the utility has access to all data in the file, and it goes about replacing the root directory, FAT, and other structures. In essence, the disk has been "unformatted." But there may still be problems. Changes probably were made to files between the times the last snap shot was taken and the reformatting occurred. Parts of files may be lost, or nonsense may be inserted. New subdirectories, and all the files they contain, vanish without a trace. Still, compared to losing everything, these problems seem small, and they can later be remedied by an unerase utility. Updating the image file more than once a day can reduce the risk of corrupted files or subdirectories.

The Recovery Approach

When no image file has been created to hold copies of the root directory and file allocation table, an unformat program must go it alone. In essence, it takes on the role of a gargantuan unerase utility. It valiantly faces overwhelming odds, and you can't expect a perfect recovery of your data. The utility starts by searching for old subdirectories by seeking out sectors that contain the dot (.) and double-dot (..) entries. If the subdirectory is unfragmented, the program can find its way to the subdirectory's end and then scan it for the starting clusters of other subdirectories. With luck, the directory tree will completely re-emerge from the ashes. One problem, however, is that the names of subdirectories listed in the root directory have been obliterated when the root directory was erased by the format program. The unformat utility will substitute its own names for these directories, and later you can rename them.

Once the directory tree is re-established, the unformatting utility learns the starting clusters for each file listed in the subdirectories and begins the familiar "unerase" procedure for each file. The lengths of the files are known from the directory listings, so the utility can tell how many sectors to look for. Files located in the root directory can't be recovered, however, because their names, and pointers to their starting clusters, disappeared during the format operation. Normally this is not a problem since data files shouldn't be placed in the root directory. CONFIG.SYS and AUTOEXEC.BAT can easily be re-claimed with an unerase utility.

If the disk has been recently defragmented, practically everything can be re-covered. More typically, fragmentation makes it impossible for the utility to effectively unerase many of the files. Without a file allocation table to tell the program which sectors are incorporated in *other* files, thousands of sectors present themselves as possibly being part of any given file. It can be the most chilling nightmare ever to fill a computer screen. Rather than go this route, it's well worth the trouble to install the utility that maintains an image file.

Using an Unformatting Program

Let's look at what unformatting looks like, using the facilities provided in Version 5.0 of *The Norton Utilities*. You begin by inserting a line in AUTOEXEC.BAT that starts up the IMAGE program. This program creates a file named IMAGE.DAT in the root directory of your hard disk. The file is given read-only status so it can't be erased. Each time the machine is started up, IMAGE.DAT is updated in the blink of an eye. A second, backup copy of the file is automatically maintained. This is required because your file allo-cation table may be corrupted one day without your noticing it. When you boot the machine the next day, the corrupted version will overwrite the prior IMAGE.DAT file. You'll still have an older version of IMAGE.DAT to fall back upon.

After the worst happens, you run the UNFORMAT program. If an error mes-sage has told you exactly what has gone wrong, such as a bad boot record, you can instruct UNFORMAT to restore only part of the DOS information. Then UNFORMAT looks for the IMAGE.DAT file and, when it finds it, tells you the date the file was last updated. Then it restores the data. At this point, you're instructed to run the *Norton Disk Doctor* program to look for prob-lems on the disk. Its role is to correct problems created by changes made on the disk between the time IMAGE.DAT was updated and the disk failed or was reformatted.

When UNFORMAT fails to find an IMAGE.DAT file, it proceeds to scan direc-tories and recover files as best it can. As it works, UNFORMAT displays a screen like the one in Figure 9.5 to show its progress. Since the contents of the root directory have been irrevocably destroyed, subdirectories named in the root directory are renamed, using the names DIR0, DIR1, and so on. You can later rename these subdirectories using a utility like the *Rename* command in the *Norton Change Directory* program.

Unformatting in DOS 5.0

Starting with Version 5.0, DOS contains its own provisions for recovering from accidental formatting. Like other such utilities, it works through either a *snap shot* or *recovery* approach. As we mentioned earlier in our discussion of *unerasing* files, the MIRROR command creates a file named MIRROR.FIL to hold copies of the root directory and file allocation table. The file is listed in the root directory of the disk. As usual, this command should be placed in AUTOEXEC.BAT so that it is executed every time you start up the machine. To have MIRROR update the unformatting information for drive C (or to create the MIRROR.FIL file for the first time), you would type:

```
MIRROR C:
```

MIRROR normally keeps a second, older copy of the relevant information in a second file it names MIRROR.BAK. Each time MIRROR runs, it renames the format MIRROR.FIL as MIRROR.BAK. You can use either file when it's time to unformat a disk. The second file can be dispensed with by adding a **/1** switch to the end of the command:

```
MIRROR C:   /1
```

The UNFORMAT command is partner to MIRROR. When you enter the command:

```
UNFORMAT C:
```

UNFORMAT looks for the MIRROR.FIL file and uses it to reconstruct the disk. Before starting, it reports the time and date at which the file was last updated and gives you the option of halting the recovery if the file is too old. If you're not sure whether MIRROR.FIL ever existed, add the **/J** switch to the end of the command. In this case, UNFORMAT will report whether the file is present, but won't actually unformat the disk.

When no mirror file is found, or the file is too old, you can have UNFORMAT skip the file and try to recover data by scanning for subdirectories to piece together the disk as best it can. As it works, UNFORMAT reports how many subdirectories it has found. Add an **/L** switch to the command to make it also display the names of files it finds. Each time a fragmented file is discovered, UNFORMAT asks you whether to truncate the file so that you're left with the first part of it, or whether to delete the file altogether. Add a /P switch to the command to have the screen messages echoed to a printer.

Dangers

Prior to the DOS 5.0, the DOS FORMAT program always performs both low- and high-level formatting on diskettes, so your data really *is* lost forever if you mistakenly reformat a diskette. Some versions of FORMAT.COM supplied with clones perform both levels of formatting even on hard disks. There's no inherent need to do a low-level format on a diskette when it is reformatted, any more than there is for a hard disk. If you're not using DOS 5.0, you'll find that a utility like the *Norton Safe Format* program can limit diskette reformatting to high-level so that you can later apply recovery tools. A good formatting utility also provides a simple, clear user interface so that people are much less likely to make formatting mistakes in the first place.

In a world of widespread computer illiteracy, "unformat" utilities provide a welcome safeguard against Murphy's Law. But they should not be adopted in lieu of good management. The FORMAT program is dangerous even in the hands of experienced computer users. Care and training in its use should not be neglected just because a partial recovery can be made when mistakes occur. Above all, an "unformat" utility must not be allowed to encourage a false sense of security or to allay anxieties about insufficient backups. Frequent backups remain the most effective defense against *all* kinds of data damage—accidental formatting included.

Recovering Damaged DOS Structures

If you've read Chapter 2 closely, you'll understand that the worst place a disk can sustain damage is on the master boot record, directories, or file allocation tables. When the partition table in the master boot record is harmed, there's no way for the computer (the fixed-disk BIOS) to find its way to the beginning of the DOS partition (an "Invalid drive specification" message results). A damaged DOS boot record is less serious—it merely prevents you from booting from the hard disk, but you can still use it after booting from drive A. Damage to directories means the loss of file names and starting clusters, and possibly the loss of a chain of subdirectories. And damage to file allocation tables means that DOS can't find most of the clusters that make up a file.

What can you do? One solution is to keep an unformat utility on hand. When DOS structures on Cylinder 0 are damaged, you can treat the disk as if it had been reformatted. The recovery program will replace the damaged structures. The problem, of course, is that unformatting a disk is very disruptive. Why go through this ordeal when only one directory entry has been corrupted?

Disk Analysis Software

Before going to such extremes, try running a general purpose disk analysis and repair utility, such as the *Norton Disk Doctor* program. A program like this one is the first line of defense when something has obviously gone wrong with your disk, although the cause may not be apparent. It should be used when the computer will not boot properly, when the disk starts to behave erratically, or when data, including directory data, mysteriously disappears. You also can run *Disk Doctor* for frequent preventive maintenance, since it may avert incipient problems that have not yet done the disk any harm.

When *Disk Doctor* starts up, it lets you specify any number of drives to analyze, and it offers to make an *UnDo* file in which it records changes it makes. Should something go awry, you can later use this file to reverse the utility's alterations. As it analyzes the disk, *Disk Doctor* shows a screen like the one in Figure 9.5, telling you what disk structure it is currently looking at, and how much of the analysis is complete. It will verify the accuracy of the boot record and its partition table, and it will check for consistency between the file allocation table, directories, and files. *Disk Doctor* can also analyze the integrity of every disk sector, just like a low-level formatting program. But this feature is time-consuming and may be excluded if you choose.

Disk Editors

For the technically adept, a disk editor is the most versatile of all recovery tools. It is a kind of software than lets you look at any cluster on a disk. What gives a disk editor its power is that it incorporates a number of templates for presenting the data it finds. When a cluster holds part of a subdirectory file, you can specify that the data should be shown both in its raw form and as it would in a directory listing. Then you can edit any part of the listing to repair corrupted data. The same applies to file allocation tables or any other DOS structure.

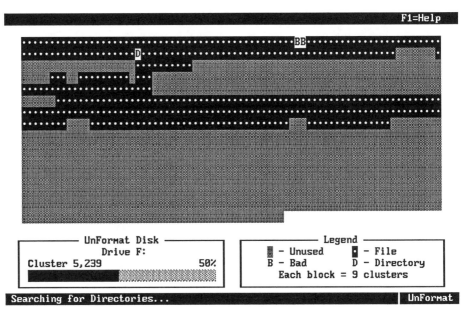

Figure 9-5. UNFORMAT in progress.

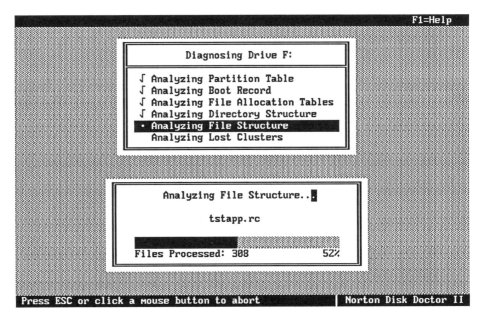

Figure 9-6. Analyzing a file structure.

Disk editors include a number of features to make editing easier. They can search through some or all of the disk for a specified string of characters, such as a file name. You can view two disk objects at once and compare them. You can overwrite parts of the disk to clear the data it contains, and can move data from one cluster to another. You can even move data to other disks. Throughout, an *UnDo* facility lets you reverse changes you've made and had second throughts about.

As you can see, disk editors are very invasive. If you don't know what you're doing, you can as easily damage data as save it. Normally, data recovery is best left to automatic utilities. But when absolutely crucial data must be recovered at all costs, and automatic utilities won't do the job, a disk editor is the only solution. There are some tasks that simply can't be performed automatically since there is no practical way to make the recovery program understand what needs to be done. For example, when a flaw appears in a file allocation table and a file is consequently damaged, you need to track down the missing clusters and relink them to the file in the proper order. Human guidance is required every step of the way.

Disk editors are also useful for unusual situations, as when you want to lift data off a disk that has gone bad and can't be rejuvenated. You can use an editor to alter ("patch") data inside files, or even character strings inside program files. And a disk editor can get at non-DOS parts of a disk to view unpartitioned disk space, or files in partitions that use a different operating system. Because disk editors are so invasive, they can also sometimes be used to circumvent hard disk security systems.

Recovering the Partition Table in DOS 5.0

DOS does not give this sort of access to a disk, but DOS 5.0 *can* repair a disk's partition table. The same command that stores information for unformatting a disk also saves the partition data. This is the MIRROR command, and it saves partition information only if it is followed by the **/PARTN** switch. Normally, the MIRROR command is placed in AUTOEXEC.BAT so that it executes every time the machine starts up. But the partition table needs to be saved only once, using the command:

```
MIRROR /PARTN
```

The partition data cannot be left on the hard disk because DOS wouldn't be able to find the disk if the partition table fails. For this reason, the MIRROR/ PARTN command writes the files containing the partition data (**PARTNSAV.FIL**) to a diskette. It prompts you to insert the diskette into drive A. The UNFORMAT command restores the partition table. Just place the diskette holding the partition data in drive A and type:

```
UNFORMAT /PARTN
```

File Recovery

When a file is damaged, the obvious solution is to replace it with a backup. There's no simple formula for repairing any kind of file, since each kind of software structures its files in its own way. Special recovery utilities are available to piece together files produced by certain popular programs like *Lotus 1-2-3* and *dBase.* But even when these utilities are successful, often all they can do is make the file readable so that the application program that created it can open it and retrieve what data remains. Data that has been destroyed cannot possibly be recovered—only a backup can fill that role.

The DOS RECOVER Program

There are also general-purpose file recovery programs. These are designed to piece together what remains of a file after one or more sectors go bad or are somehow damaged. DOS includes the RECOVER program for this purpose. Like most such utilities, RECOVER can operate on a single specified file, or it can scan the whole disk. It does not work very well in the latter role, and you'll only want to use it for individual files. This job is done simply by naming the file on the command line, as in **RECOVER MYFILE.DOC**. Wildcards are accepted in the file name.

When it is loaded without a file name, RECOVER automatically works on every file in the current directory. Whether a file is damaged or not, it renames it in the format **FILE0001.REC, FILE0002.REC,** and so on. When a file contains a bad sector, it is broken in two, with each part placed in its own file. The result is a complete mess. Many people think it's a good idea to delete RECOVER from a disk so that it can never be used. In fact, *The Norton Utilities* includes a program that undoes the mess created by a multi-file RECOVER command.

Alternate Utilities

The RECOVER command gives you no control over file recovery. You can either take it or leave it. Other utilities are more flexible. Most important, they do not break a damaged file into pieces, and do not rename it. Rather, they mark a bad cluster used by the file as being off-bounds and then insert a new cluster into the file as a replacement. Since a bad cluster may still occasionally be readable, many attempts are made to recapture the data and transfer it to the replacement cluster. When all data cannot be recovered, part of the new cluster is arbitrarily filled with a character, such as an asterisk. These characters do not interfere with text files. But many other kinds of data files may be rendered useless. When program files are recovered this way, they will crash. Hence, "file recovery" is not a sure thing, and owning a good recovery utility is no substitute for frequent backups.

Orphaned Clusters

Orphaned clusters are clusters that appear to be occupied by a file, but which are not linked to any file listed in a directory. In Chapter 2 we described how each position in the file allocation table gives the number of the next cluster in a file, and that cluster's corresponding position in the FAT gives the number of the next cluster still. Special codes are inserted in the table when the cluster is free, or when it is marked off-bounds because of media damage.

CHKDSK

When you run the DOS CHKDSK command, DOS traces every file through the FAT, keeping track of which clusters are occupied. Then it checks all remaining FAT positions to see that they are either free or discarded. When CHKDSK finds clusters that are marked as belonging to a file, but in fact do not, it announces "xx lost clusters in xx chains—convert to files?" If you answer "Yes," CHKDSK places the clusters into files in the root directory, using the names FILE0000.CHK, FILE0001.CHK, and so on. CHKDSK makes these files only when you add an /F switch to the end of the command; otherwise, CHKDSK merely reports the existence of any orphaned clusters.

How Orphaned Clusters Originate

Orphaned clusters are often linked into chains, where one orphaned cluster points to another, which points to another in turn. This is the case because orphaned clusters are nearly always parts of files that have fallen apart. Most originate when software is abruptly terminated while it is in the midst of file operations. Sometimes this happens because of a power outage, but more often it results when a novice user employs Ctrl-Alt-Del as a panic button. In file operations, DOS fills in FAT information last. If the machine is rebooted after a file has been written and before the FAT can be updated, clusters can be orphaned.

When CHKDSK retrieves orphaned clusters, it places them in files that have no date or time stamp. A directory listing gives a file size, but, in fact, DOS cannot know exactly where in the clusters the data ends, so the value is only approximate. Generally, the data you'll find in recovered clusters is useless. Often it comes from temporary work files set up by your software; these files are normally erased when the program terminates. After visually inspecting the files, you can delete them all by entering:

```
DEL FILE*.CHK
```

Using Orphaned Clusters

Occasionally you'll want to keep the orphaned clusters. It sometimes happens that a work file mysteriously disappears after it has been loaded and a power outage has suddenly occurred. The file will continue to be listed in the directory, but with a file size of 0 bytes. What has happened is that DOS has prepared to rewrite the entire file, and it has temporarily set the file size to 0 until it has finished writing it. In this situation, you can run CHKDSK and recover the orphaned clusters as best you can. Text data may be easily recovered this way, since you can rename the files CHKDSK creates and load them into a word processor. But when the file is full of binary gibberish, it may be impossible to reconstitute a usable file. Orphaned clusters may also be used to rebuild *cross-linked files*, our next topic.

Cross-linked Files

Sometimes an error creeps into the file allocation table and two files become *cross-linked*. Consider two files that each stretch across five clusters. The first might cover clusters 101 through 105, and the second, clusters 201-205. Now, say that somehow an error is made when the file allocation table is written (perhaps because of an electrical transient), and the third cluster of the first file is recorded as 203 instead of 103. When DOS reads the file, it will load sectors 101, 102, 203, 204, and 205. The chains of FAT entries that track the files have become *cross-linked,* and clusters 103 through 105 have become orphaned clusters. Figure 9-7 diagrams this phenomenon. Only the first file is damaged in this case. The FAT entries for the second file continue to point from clusters 201 to 205. Incidentally, there are rare occasions when a file becomes cross-linked to itself. In the worst case, the linkage forms a loop, and *total* confusion results.

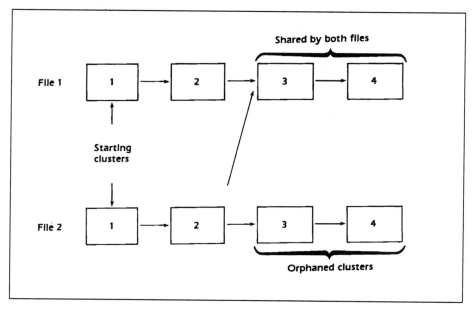

Figure 9-7. Cross-linked files

The DOS CHKDSK command can detect cross-linked files. But it cannot do anything about them. DOS has no way of knowing which file is damaged, since it has no knowledge of the contents of the files. Besides, repairing the damaged file entails finding the orphaned clusters that belong to it. When more than one string of orphaned clusters is found, DOS would not know which to reattach to the damaged file.

Fixing the Files

While DOS is helpless in this regard, you can sometimes solve the problem quite easily. First, you must inspect the two files to see which is damaged. If it is a data file, load it into the software that uses it and see that everything is all right. Often, when the file is damaged, the software will refuse to load it, or it will crash when it loads, and you'll have to reboot the machine. A cross-linked text file may suddenly change topics as it shifts into the contents of the second file; or the latter part of the file may be nothing but gobbledygook.

Once you've decided which file is the damaged one, you have several tasks. You must reclaim the orphaned clusters, perform surgery on the damaged file, and then reconnect the orphaned clusters to the end of the file. Generally, this process can only be performed for text files. Surgery on most other kinds of data files requires technical sophistication and an insider's knowledge of the file structure. Still, you can try using a disk editor or unerase program to view cluster contents and change cluster order until you hit on a combination that works.

Text Files

To recover a cross-linked text file, make copies of both files involved, and operate upon these copies. Erase the originals. This action makes each file independent of the other in the file allocation table. Load the damaged file into your word processor. The file may have been cross-linked to a file that contains characters that confuse your word processor. You may have to try a variety of editors before you find one that can load the text. Often, the simplest editors, such as *notepad* editors, are the most accepting. Then delete the unwanted part of the file. Next, run CHKDSK to organize the orphaned clusters into files, and look through the files using the DOS TYPE command. Finally, combine the two files using the COPY command. Say that the damaged file is named **GOODBYE.TXT**, and CHKDSK has named the orphaned clusters **FILE0003.CHK**. The files are combined by entering:

```
COPY GOODBYE.TXT+FILE0003.CHK GOODBYE.TXT
```

If you truncated **GOODBYE.TXT** just right, the original file will be exactly reconstituted. Otherwise, you may have to do a little surgery at the junction between the two files using your word processor. Figure 9-8 diagrams the procedure.

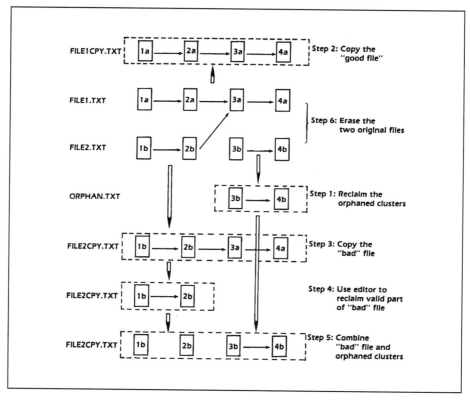

Figure 9-8. Recovering cross-linked files

Guarding against Hard Disk Disasters

There is a lot you can do to avoid hard disk disasters. Earlier in this chapter, we looked at utilities that keep an eye on soft error rates to warn you about incipient problems. We also saw how "unformat" programs regularly take a "snap shot" of crucial DOS information as a precaution against accidental reformatting. In Chapter 6, we discussed a number of techniques for protecting your files from inadvertent erasures and formattings. And in Chapter 7 we presented a number of optimization techniques that reduce the movement of the read/write heads, lengthening the disk's life.

These precautions guard against operator error and equipment failure. Alas, there is more to the demonology of hard disks. In this section, we'll look at some other important hazards, and what you can do about them.

Locating the Machine

You can do a lot to protect your hard disk just by situating the computer in an environment where it won't be knocked about. The machine should rest on a sturdy table or desk. The more massive the furniture, the better it can absorb shocks, rather than pass them on to the hard disk. Tables pose particular risks, since they are apt to sway when nudged. If the movement is towards an adjacent wall, a collision could send a shock wave back towards the machine. In this situation, always buttress the table firmly against the wall.

Vibrations

Never place impact printers on the same desk as the computer. In particular, daisy-wheel printers send out fearsome vibrations. Although these disturbances will not overwhelm a hard disk by themselves, they contribute to the general seismic climate, and they help to push both hard disk drives and diskette drives out of alignment.

Ventilation

Position the machine in a way that avoids heat buildup, which is the foremost cause of erratic hard disk failures. Avoid pushing the machine flush against a wall, or blocking the rear ventilating fans. And try not to place the machine in the outflow of the room heating system. If the machine must be used in a sweltering environment, consider implementing some of the heat-reduction techniques discussed below.

Sideways Installation

Be especially careful about standing the machine upright on its side using one of the special floor stands designed to support it. This approach is wonderful for freeing desk space, but it leaves the machine out of the line of sight, making it easy to kick or bump. Perhaps the worst danger is a heavy office chair careening into a free-standing system unit. Be aware that some hard disk drives are not designed to operate on their sides (or even upside down). It's a good idea to check with the manufacturer.

Educating Others

Finally, the most important measure of all is to thoroughly educate the people who will be around the computer about the damage caused by physical shocks. While the system manager's usual problem is getting people to *not* be afraid of computers, here is an exception. When a desk or table supports a computer, one should not sit on it, lollying one's legs, one should not drop piles of books onto it, and one should not shove aside the machine to make room for something else. Offices that fail to instruct every new employee in these matters can lose $1,000 of hardware (and $100,000 of data!) in a fraction of a second.

Power-Line Protection

Power-line disturbances create their greatest damage when they occur as the disk writes to the DOS system area on Cylinder 0. DOS cannot deal with a damaged root directory, and that means that all your data is stranded. Voltage spikes that barge through a disk drive's protective circuitry may spray magnetism down at the disk surface, damaging format markings as well as data. Again, DOS can not recover from the resulting error.

There are three levels of protection against power-line interruptions. At the lowest level, you may add a power-line filter that "clamps" high speed, high voltage transients. This service is performed by the familiar **surge protectors** with which most machines are equipped. Contrary to what many will tell you, not all are the same. Surge protectors have two tasks—to "grab" a spike, and to diffuse it. The best designs combine devices called *metal-oxide varistors* and *avalanche diodes* to respond to spikes within billionths of a second, and a *gas discharge tube* to diffuse the excess power. When you buy one, be sure that it is U.L. (Underwriter's Laboratory) tested, and that its specifications allow for a clamping level of at least 50 to 100 joules; ideally it will meet the IEEE 587 standard. (Sorry to throw technical terminology at you about this, but there's no simple explanation.)

The next level of protection comes through **voltage regulators** and **line protectors**. Besides intercepting voltage spikes, these constantly filter and regulate power to provide optimal, "noise-free" electricity to your machine. They are much more expensive than surge protectors, and you must take care to buy one large enough to meet your present and future needs. This entails adding up the total wattage of all your components, or simply buying one with as great a capacity as your computer's power supply. Ratings are often given in *amps*, which may be multiplied by the usual 110V line current to get the equivalent wattage (for example, 2.0 amps times 110 volts = 220 watts). Add at least 10 percent extra capacity for the startup ("inrush") current.

Finally, the ultimate in power-line protection is afforded by a **standby power supply** (SPS) or an **uninterrupted power supply** (UPS). In addition to voltage regulation, these provide battery backup that takes over when power is lost. Standby units quickly switch over to battery power—they have less than 15 milliseconds to do so—while the more expensive UPS units always supply power through the batteries (which are constantly recharged). This equipment costs several hundred dollars. The backup power lasts from about five minutes to a few hours, depending on the supply and your system's power requirements. Five minutes may not sound very long, but it's plenty of time to save your work and turn off the machine. Most come with an alarm that rings when the power goes off.

Guarding against Theft

An all-too-common way of losing all one's data is by having the computer stolen. Used diskettes or tape cartridges are not usually a thief's target, so your backups ought to be safe. But a tape backup unit will surely disappear along with the computer, and if the cartridge holding the recent backups is inside the unit...

Several companies manufacture devices that can make it very difficult to steal a PC without doing considerable damage to it. One strategy is to insert adhesive mats between the computer and the desk it rests on, and between the monitor and the top of the computer case. These can cling to the equipment with 6,000 pounds of force. Similar devices are made to hold down printers. Also, some computer furniture has been designed so that you can easily lock away the machine and peripherals.

The next line of defense is to stop someone from opening the computer's case and stealing a hard disk drive. It is, after all, a lot easier to leave a guarded building with a drive than to exit carrying a whole computer. There are products that make it impossible to take the cover off a computer without the proper key. Many machines already have a lock, of course, although it's been reported that you can get into some using a crowbar and a lot of brawn. To stop people from booting the system, there are also devices that lock into the front of a diskette drive. Finally, some drives are specially designed for daily removal. When you're done with work, you can lock it away. Perhaps more importantly, you can transport the drive to another computer and start up work just as you left it.

Vandalism

Don't overlook the possibility of the *intentional* destruction of data. A disgruntled employee (or ex-employee) may take revenge in a big way. Little knowledge is required to enter **FORMAT C:**. And your *unformat* program will offer little protection if the perpetrator knows enough to erase the utility's special "snap shot" file before firing up the format program. Even if you have an elaborate security system in place, it may be possible for a well-informed employee to run a low-level format program from drive A to decimate every sector on the hard disk. A person inclined to commit these crimes may be all the more encouraged by the knowledge that it will be next to impossible to prove that he or she is the one who has done it.

If this calamity ever happens to you, you can be sure that your first thought will be, "The backups! where are the backups?" There's much to be said for locking away backups—at least the monthly global backup that we discussed in Chapter 8. Locking away both low- and high-level formatting programs can also be a good idea.

Viruses, Worms, and Trojan Horses

If you're the only person having access to a machine, you may feel that vandalism is of no concern. But no treatment of hard disk disasters is complete without a discussion of viruses, worms, Trojan horses, and other instances of pathological programming. These are bits of code inserted into software which, at an appointed moment, attack your hard disk and destroy every file in sight. Such programs are created by adolescents, or adults with adolescent minds, whose peculiar brand of moral imbecility leaves them incapable of feeling guilty about destroying something so abstract as thousands and thousands of hours of labor.

Worms are generally found in mainframe computers that are never turned off. The software migrates around the system like a worm, hiding itself here and there. *Trojan horses*, on the other hand, are nested inside an applications program, where they may sit quietly for months until, one day, something activates the destructive code. Trojan horses are a threat to many people because they may be placed inside public domain software.

Computer viruses are a much greater concern. A computer virus is a kind of program that sneaks into your machine by hiding in software you introduce by diskette or modem. They also may enter through a local area network. At best, viruses make mischief by displaying unwanted messages on the screen; at worst, they may destroy data on your hard disk and diskettes. Viruses are one example of a genre of software created for no purpose other than vandalism. They are called "viruses" because in some ways they act just like biological viruses. They are small fragments of code that have no life until they invade other software. They hide themselves within healthy programs and may lie dormant for long periods until suddenly they awaken and start doing harm. And they go through periods of replication in which copies of the virus spread elsewhere in the system, making it difficult to eradicate them completely.

Vaccine Programs

In response to the viral menace, a new genre of software called vaccine programs have been developed. They have two functions: to detect and to remove viruses. Often, they're far better at the former. Actually, the word "vaccine" is not entirely appropriate. Computers have no immune system that may be bolstered, and most of these programs cannot identify and attack viruses at the moment they enter the machine or are replicated. Rather, they recognize individual viruses, or evidence of viral damage, and report the viral presence to you by providing a list of suspect files. You can prevent further spread of the infection by removing infected files swiftly. Sometimes you can have the vaccine program try to "sterilize" your hard disk by tracking down and removing every instance of a virus.

Vaccine programs work in many ways. To be effective, they must be run frequently, usually at startup from the computer's AUTOEXEC.BAT file. They'll maintain information about your program files and DOS files so that changes can be detected. The most obvious sign of infection is an alteration of a program's length, which may be checked easily and quickly. But only shell viruses can be detected this way. Invasive viruses are found by looking for fragments of their code within the program's own code. (More and more, software authors are including antiviral self-analysis within the application programs they write.) Vaccine programs also operate by closely monitoring all parts of DOS, and by surveying supposedly "bad" disk sectors for hidden code. They may watch out for inexplicable shrinkage of available system memory—another sign of viral proliferation. Finally, vaccine programs may watch for certain characteristic "signals" given off by viruses when they interfere with the operating system.

Viruses become ever more sophisticated, not by some form of natural muta-
tion, but because the sociopaths who create them constantly release new ones.
In response, vaccine programs undergo constant change. Owners of these
programs must constantly upgrade to new versions to renew their protection.
Updates may include signatures from the most recently introduced viruses. A
signature is used as a sort of mug shot to track down the virus in your files.

Repairs

If it is faulty, most computer equipment fails within the first 90 days. Thereafter, you're likely to have several years of carefree service before decrepitude
slowly sets in. As they gain experience, manufacturers are making equipment
more and more reliable. Unfortunately, two trends work in the opposite direction. The technology changes so rapidly that experience quickly becomes obsolete. And the cut-throat competition at the low-end of the computer market
has tempted many manufacturers to create products that are not nearly as
good as they might be. It often pays to buy quality. Repairs tend to be very
expensive, and a single trip to the shop may cost you much more than you
saved by bargain-hunting. When a mechanical failure damages your data, the
cost may be far greater still.

Before turning to the ins and outs of repair services, let's look at what you can
do on your own.

Dealing with Sporadic Failure

Sporadic failures are the most exasperating of all hard disk problems. Suddenly the computer "locks up"—the screen freezes, the keyboard refuses all
keystrokes (even Ctrl-Alt-Del), and diskette drives go on spinning. Sometimes,
turning off the machine and then starting it up immediately sets everything
right; then you can pick up the pieces and continue your work. Other times,
the machine will not run again until some hours later. In either case, you can
expect the machine to crash again, perhaps in an hour, perhaps in a month.

Erratic failures are especially vexing because you can not be sure what part of
the machine caused the crash. When your system suffers a complete hard disk
failure, you need only disconnect the drive, reconfigure the machine, and
reboot to see if the machine works fine without it. But when the problem is
erratic, you have no way of knowing whether the faulty component has been
removed from the machine, or whether the next failure just hasn't arrived yet.

Such occurences are a surprise in a *digital* computer, where things tend to work either completely or not at all. There are two very common culprits—heat and power insufficiency—and you should consider whether they are responsible for your problems before seeking professional help.

Overheating

Heat is everybody's business. Like the oil in an automobile, it is one of the very few aspects of a complicated device that anyone can easily comprehend and look after. Every time you add another expansion board or disk drive to your machine, you should make a mental note that you have changed the heat load in the machine. Months later, when your machine abruptly crashes on a mid-August afternoon, one of the first questions you should ask is, "Too hot at last?"

Heat interferes with hard disk drives when some parts expand more than others, throwing off the alignment between disk and read/write heads. No permanent damage is done to the drive, although data may be destroyed if the heads are writing when the drive fails. Turning off the machine and waiting for a half hour or so is usually enough to return the machine to working order—for a while. But if high temperatures regularly occur, you'll need to add some cooling to the machine. We explained how to do this in Chapter 4. Remember that you should not leave slot openings in the back of the machine. When you fail to replace a plate after removing a card from a slot, you are undermining the machine's cooling system.

Insufficient Power

Another cause of sporadic failures is insufficient power. This topic was also covered in Chapter 4, so we won't dwell on it here. However, we want to reiterate that a *barely sufficient* power supply may become *insufficient* in hot weather. Higher temperatures raise the resistance of all electrical circuits, so slightly more power is required to run the machine. Power insufficiency is generally only a problem on early IBM PCs, which have a meager 63.5 watt supply. When sporadic system crashes may be attributable to *either* the power supply or an overheated disk, diagnosis is difficult. If you remove the drive to see if the machine works all right without it, you're also unburdening the power supply. Try running the machine with the cover off, directing the flow of a small room fan into the cabinet. If the machine doesn't crash, you'll know that added cooling will probably solve your problems.

Getting the Drive Started

When the drive has suffered a mechanical crisis of some kind, it often will refuse to respond to DOS. An "Invalid Drive Specification" error message may result. Sometimes you can get it going one last time by turning the drive in various orientations. There's value in this, since you may need to make last-minute backups, and you may be able to park the heads before sending it to a repair service.

Open the machine and carefully remove the drive, leaving the cables connected (or remove the drive and reattach the cables). Place a book or magazine on top of the power supply and place the drive on it. Absolutely do not let any part of the drive electronics touch any part of the machine, or any conducting surface. Next, place the DOS diskette in drive A and boot from it. Then try for a directory reading from drive C. No good? Keep trying, holding the drive in various orientations. Be ready with your backup software for the moment the drive comes through. Be very careful of vibrations once you get it going.

Facing the Music

Many people respond to erratic hard disk failures by pretending that they have not occured. It is *so* much easier to hope that the machine crashed because of an errant cosmic ray than to acknowledge that you have a serious problem on your hands, one that could take up a lot of your time and energy. There's no joy in the prospect of running the computer off of diskettes while the hard disk is away at the repair shop. But it's best to address the problem while you still have some choice in the matter. Pay special attention to backups until the drive is repaired.

Kinds of Repairs

Although head crashes are widely feared, they actually occur very rarely. Disk repair services report that only about one percent of their business comes from repairing crashed heads. In fact, they more frequently receive drives that have been intentionally opened by curious users! This is good news. When your drive will run no more, most likely it has failed in a way that can be repaired without loss of data.

After all our talk about spinning cylinders and flying heads, it may surprise you to hear that most drive failures are electronic. One of the chips or other components mounted on the outside of the drive gives up the ghost. This means that the drive can be repaired without opening it up. If you've kept an eye on the disk, testing it periodically for incipient problems, it's unlikely that the faulty components damaged much data prior to failure.

When the drive mechanics have failed, repair is more serious. The repair service must be equipped with a *clean room*. The drive is meticulously cleaned before it is passed into the room, and employees dress with face masks and caps. Various parts may be replaced, including a platter scratched by a serious head crash. Repair services report that it's not always easy to get replacement parts for drives, and that often they are stripped from "rejects." They tend to consider some of the cheaper drives as "throw away" drives. It makes more sense to buy a new one than to repair it.

When you take a drive in for repair, the service may ask whether you want the data on the drive saved or not. If so, they'll do their best to keep it intact. For them, "saving data" means that they won't reformat the drive, which means that they won't be able to test it very thoroughly. The usual 90-day warranty on repairs may be waived when data is "saved." Incidentally, when the servo markings on the platters of voice-coil drives have been damaged, they can usually be remedied only by the manufacturer.

Because most repairs are electrical and do not require opening the drive, the average repair takes only about half an hour. The base price for the repair usually runs from $80 to $100. To this basic fee, a charge may be added for every megabyte of drive capacity—typically $1. This may seem like a soak-the-rich scheme, but it actually reflects the time required to reformat and test the drive.

Deciding on a Repair Service

Services that specialize in hard disk drive repair have sprung up in large metropolitan areas. If one of these shops is near you, take your drive straight to it. The base charge may be a little higher than at a general-purpose repair service, but it's more likely that the repairs will be made without cost overruns. General repair shops often must forward damaged drives to one of these services in any case, since they haven't a clean room (or the expertise) to do the job themselves. They'll bill you generously for this delay.

You can find out about specialty repair services in your phone directory—if such a service is located nearby. Otherwise, you'll need to hunt around. Ads often appear in computer magazines. Try asking around an electronic bulletin board, or contact a local user's group. Of course, if the drive is under warranty, you won't have any choice about where it goes for repair. You may have no say about saving the data in this case. Rather than blindly return the drive to the vendor, find out where it is going and see if you can't save time by sending it directly to the manufacturer or repair service.

If you can't drive to the service, try to send the drive through the gentlest form of conveyance you can find. Be sure to repack it in its original container (you *did* set it aside like we advised, didn't you?). And try to park the heads before shipment. Drives that won't work in any other respect will sometimes obey the SHIPDISK program.

Afterword

If you've stayed with us from cover to cover, congratulations! You're now in a position to understand just about anything you'll encounter concerning hard disks. In the introduction to this book, we explained that your hard disk is the control center of your machine. You may have found this claim a bit hyperbolic, but by now you ought to understand why it is so—or why it *should* be so.

We hope you'll put what we've taught you to work. The first priority is a backup system. Then get the tree organized and do a thorough housecleaning. Install some productivity tools for zipping around the disk and automating tasks that you've performed hundreds (even thousands) of times by hand. Then turn your attention to optimzing disk performance. At the very least, install a defragmentation utility and take a serious look at caching. Finally, get into the habit of running a disk diagnostic tool periodically. If you'll follow the most important rules we've taught you about disk backup and maintenance, you are almost certain to avoid a catastrophic loss of data, and you'll probably never lose more than an hour's work (even when others are doing their best to lose it for you).

We'd like to propose that you set an immodest goal for yourself: that you strive to increase the speed of the average disk access in your machine by 500 percent. By this, we mean the time it takes to load a program or file, to make a backup, or to copy or move around files, measuring even from the first keystroke you make to initiate it, to the moment the disk drive stops blinking. You certainly have the knowledge to do this now, and in many cases a 1,000 percent improvement is in store. Make it a game. You can only win.

Glossary

8086 A microprocessor chip similar to the 8088 microprocessor used in IBM PCs, XTs, and compatibles. It accesses memory two bytes at a time, as compared to one byte at a time in an 8088 chip.

8088 The microprocessor chip used in IBM PCs, XTs, and compatibles. The 8088 is a 16-bit chip, meaning that it performs its calculations two bytes at a time. But it access memory only one byte at a time.

80286 The microprocessor chip used in IBM ATs and some PS/2 models. It is a 16-bit chip, which means that it processes data two bytes at a time; it also accesses memory two bytes at a time.

80386 The microprocessor chip used in the IBM PS/2 model 80 and other advanced machines, including many AT-style clones. The 80386 is a 32-bit chip, meaning that it accesses memory and performs calculations four bytes at a time. The 80386 chip is fast becoming the industry standard.

80386 SX A less-expensive version of the 80386 microprocessor. It differs from the 80386 chip chiefly in that it accesses memory only two bytes at a time, although it still processes data four bytes at a time.

80486 The most recent microprocessor chip, used only in the fastest machines. Like the 80386 chip, it is a 32-bit microprocessor, accessing memory and performing calculations four bytes at a time.

* A *global file name character* representing any number of file name characters. In the DOS command, **COPY AB*.TXT A:**, the asterisk matches any number of characters following **AB**; thus, the files **ABCDE.TXT**, **ABWXYZ.TXT**, and **AB.TXT** would all be copied.

? A *global file name character* replacing a single character in a file name. In the DOS command, **COPY AB?DEFGH.TXT A:**, the question mark matches any character in the third position in the file name. The files **ABCDEFGH.TXT**, **ABXDEFGH.TXT**, and **AB3DEFGH.TXT** would all be copied.

accelerator board An *expansion board* that substitutes a faster microprocessor in place of the one that comes with the machine.

active directory The directory to which DOS directs its activities when no other directory is specified in DOS commands.

actuator The device that moves a disk drive's read/write heads across the platter surfaces.

adapter See *expansion board.*

APPEND A DOS command that configures DOS to automatically search for data files (and sometimes program files) in specified directories when the files do not appear in the current directory.

application program Software that processes data—word processors, data bases, spreadsheet programs, accounting packages, and so on. Application programs contrast with *utility programs,* such as file "unerase" programs or file backup programs, which are used to manage the computer rather than to attain some final purpose.

archive attribute A *file attribute* that, when set, indicates that a file has been changed and should be copied when backup software is next run. The backup software turns off the attribute after it makes the backup. DOS turns the attribute back on if the file is changed again.

archive bit The bit in a file's attribute byte that sets the *archive attribute.*

archiving The storage of seldom-accessed data on diskettes or magnetic tape. Archiving makes space available on a hard disk for new data.

ASCII character A character taken from the *ASCII character set*, which includes all alphabetic characters, numerals and punctuation marks, and special characters that have meaning only to the computer. Each character has its own code number, from 0 to 127. (*ASCII* stands for *American Standard Code for Information Interchange.*)

ASCII file See *text file.*

ASSIGN A DOS command that assigns a different drive specifier to a disk drive.

ATTRIB A DOS command that reads and sets file attributes (that is, it makes changes in a file's *attribute byte*).

attribute See *file attribute.*

attribute byte A byte of information that is held in the directory entry of every file. The byte keeps track of various *file attributes*, such as whether the file is *read-only*, whether it has been changed since it was last backed up, and so on.

AUTOEXEC.BAT A file automatically read by DOS when the machine is switched on. It may contain any number of DOS commands which are automatically executed at startup. The file is optional.

automatic data compression A technique in which data is automatically compressed and decompressed as files are written and read from disk.

automatic head parking The automatic movement of a hard disk's read/write heads to a *landing strip* when the machine is turned off. Once positioned this way, the heads cannot damage the disk's surface if the machine is jolted.

average latency The average time required for any byte of data to rotate to a read/write head—one half rotation of a platter.

average seek time The average time, measured in milliseconds, required for a disk drive's read/write heads to move from one track to another across the disk surface. A measure of disk-drive performance.

background backup A backup of the files on a hard disk that proceeds automatically *in the background* (invisibly) while the computer is used for other purposes.

background printing The process of sending output to a printer "in the background" while using the computer for some other task.

backup program Software that scans a hard disk for altered or new data files and makes copies of them on diskettes or tape cartridges.

backups Extra copies of data files made for safekeeping.

bad sector A disk sector that cannot reliably hold data because of a flaw on the disk surface or damaged format markings.

bad track table A label affixed to the casing of a hard disk drive indicating tracks that are flawed and cannot hold data. The information is entered into the low-level formatting program before it divides tracks into sectors.

bare drive A disk drive sold without a controller card.

.BAT A file name extension given to *batch files*. When a file with a .BAT extension is named on the DOS command line as if it were a program to run, DOS recognizes the extension and proceeds to execute each line of the file as if it were a DOS command.

batch file A file containing a series of DOS commands that are executed in sequence when the file is "run" as if it were a program. All batch files have a *.BAT* file name extension.

bay An opening in the computer cabinet that holds disk drives.

Bernoulli Box A removable-cartridge, semi-floppy disk drive made by Iomega Corporation.

Bernoulli principle A principle of physics which states that as the velocity of a fluid increases, its pressure drops. This principle is used in airplanes as well as Iomega's Bernoulli Box disk drive.

bezel A plastic panel that covers an unoccupied part of a drive *bay*.

bit One of the eight on/off settings that constitute a *byte* of data. Sometimes a bit will act as an indicator flag. For example, every file has in its directory entry a byte in which particular bits are set to *on* or *off* depending on whether the file is *read-only, hidden*, and so on.

BIOS The *Basic Input-Output System.* Part of the computer's operating system that is built into the machine, rather than read from a disk drive at startup.

blank An aluminum disk that is coated or plated to make a hard disk platter.

block In tape backup, a "block" is a number of sectors written in succession and followed by various identifiers and error-correction codes.

board See *expansion board.*

booting The process of starting up the machine. It means *"to pull up by the boot straps,"* and consists of a series of operations in which the computer reads in the main operating system file **COMMAND.COM** from drive A or drive C, and then reads the contents of the **CONFIG.SYS** and **AUTOEXEC.BAT** files to configure the machine, load device drivers, and carry out predefined DOS commands.

boot record A disk sector filled with information used to boot the computer. It is created when the disk is formatted.

boot security The ability of *security software* to circumvent a break-in made by restarting the computer with a boot diskette in drive A (thus preventing the security software on drive C from automatically loading).

bpi Bits per inch. A measure of data density along a track.

Break See *Ctrl-Break.*

bubble memory A relatively slow type of memory chip that continues to hold data after power is removed.

buffer A temporary holding area in memory for data. See also *DOS buffers.*

bug A fault in software or hardware that causes it to malfunction.

bus The system of circuitry that ties together different parts of the computer, including the expansion slots.

byte The basic unit of computer memory. One byte holds one character of data (one letter of the alphabet).

caching A process in which frequently accessed data is kept on hand, rather than constantly being reread from the place where it is stored. See also *disk caching*.

card See *expansion board*.

CD-I "Compact Disk—Interactive." A special optical disk standard devised by Sony and Philips, which combines program code, data, photographic stills, moving video, and sound on a compact disk.

CD ROM "Compact Disk Read-Only Memory." A compact disk that holds reference materials, such as a dictionary or business statistics.

central processing unit The *microprocessor* chip that does most of the work in a computer.

certification utility Utility software that certifies that a tape or disk cartridge is free of flaws.

CGA See *Color Graphics Adapter*.

CHDIR A DOS command that changes the *current directory*, that is, the directory to which DOS directs its operations *by default* when no directory is expressly named in a DOS command.

check box Check boxes are small squares drawn inside the *dialog boxes* that some software uses to communicate with the user. When a check box is "checked" (contains an "X"), the feature associated with the box (such as "print page numbers") is enabled. The box is checked and unchecked through a mouse or the keyboard.

child directory A subdirectory within a directory. In \PLANTS\TREES \WILLOWS, TREES is a child directory of PLANTS, and WILLOWS is a child directory of TREES.

chip See *integrated circuit*.

CHKDSK A DOS utility that looks for errors on disks. It detects errors in directories and in the allocation of disk space, but does not sense imperfections on the disk surface or failing low-level formatting.

clean room A dust-free repair facility in which hard disk drives can be opened for servicing.

clicking In using a mouse, one is said to *click* the mouse on an object appearing on the screen when one moves the mouse cursor over that object and then presses and releases a mouse button.

clock speed See *processor speed.*

cluster The basic unit of allocation of disk space. A cluster is a collection of contiguous disk *sectors*, usually four sectors on hard disks, often one or two on diskettes. When DOS needs more disk space for a file, it takes it one cluster at a time, not one sector at a time.

CMOS chip The battery-powered memory chip that holds the clock setting and system configuration information. It is found in all PCs except PC- or XT-style machines.

coated media Hard disk platters coated with a reddish iron-oxide medium upon which data is recorded.

Color Graphics Adapter The earliest IBM graphics video adapter. It can display no more than 16 colors at once operating in low resolution, or 2 colors in medium resolution.

.COM A file name *extension* that appears only on *program files.*

command A series of words or symbols typed in at the DOS prompt (such as **A:**) that tells DOS what to do next (to load a program, copy a file, etc.).

COMMAND.COM The main DOS program. It is loaded automatically when the machine starts up. COMMAND.COM normally remains in memory the entire time the machine is in operation. Sometimes part is overwritten by applications programs, and this *transient part* of COMMAND.COM must be reloaded from disk when an application terminates.

command line The area to the right of the *DOS prompt* where you type in commands to tell DOS what to do next.

command line parameter A word, number, or symbol typed in a DOS command to specify how the command should work. For example, many DOS commands require parameters to specify which file a command should operate on. In the expression **COPY MYFILE.TXT A:**, the **COPY** command has two parameters, the first of which names the file that is to be copied (**MYFILE.TXT**), and the second of which indicates the destination of the copy, in this case drive A.

communications The process of sending data between two computers.

compression See *file compression.*

conditional test A situation in which if a condition is met (for example, "there has been an error") one set of instructions are followed, whereas if the condition has not been met ("there has *not* been an error") a different set of instructions are followed.

CONFIG.SYS A file automatically read by DOS when the computer is booted. It contains information for configuring the computer, such as the names of *device drivers* to load, the number of *DOS buffers* to create, and so on. The file is optional.

configuration The process of tailoring hardware or software so that it operates properly with all other hardware and software that is being used at the same time.

configuration file A file that holds information that hardware or software uses to configure itself when it starts up.

console The combination of keyboard and screen.

control cable The wider of two cables that connect a hard disk drive to a controller card in most machines.

control character A character typed at the keyboard to send a command to software running in the computer. Control characters are generated by pressing Ctl key plus one other key.

controller The electronics that control a hard disk drive and intermediate the passage of data between the drive and the computer.

controller card See *disk controller card.*

conventional memory Memory used by DOS, consisting of up to 640K (kilobytes). All machines have conventional memory, and so it is often referred to simply as "memory."

copy protection A system for discouraging software piracy by making it impossible to copy a program. Most copy-protection schemes work by specially modifying the diskettes on which the software is distributed, or by modifying a hard disk when the copy-protected software is installed.

coprocessor An *integrated circuit* chip that works in tandem with the computer's main *microprocessor.* The best known coprocessors are *math coprocessors,* which perform certain kinds of mathematical calculations more quickly, and with greater accuracy, than the microprocessor can.

CPU See *central processing unit.*

CPU speed See *processor speed.*

crash Any malfunction that brings work to a halt. A *hard disk crash* or *head crash* may entail physical damage to a disk drive. A *system crash,* on the other hand, usually is caused by a software malfunction, and it can ordinarily be remedied by rebooting the machine.

CRC See *cyclic redundancy check.*

cross-linked files Two files that have been "crossed" such that both share the final portion of one of the files. This problem is caused by an error in the *file allocation table* of the disk holding the files.

Ctrl-Break A keystroke combination that causes DOS to terminate a program. It should be used only when a program cannot terminate normally.

current directory The directory on the *current drive* to which DOS directs its activities when no directory is specified in DOS commands. For example, when the current directory is **C:\DOS**, the command **DIR** would give a directory listing for the **DOS** directory on drive C, whereas the command **DIR C:\UTIL** would list a directory other than the current directory—the **UTIL** directory. The current directory is set through the **CHDIR** command.

current drive The drive to which DOS directs its activities when no other drive is specified in DOS commands. When the DOS prompt is **A>**, drive A is the current drive. In this case, the command **DIR** would give a directory listing for drive A, since no drive is specified in the command.

cylinder Hard disk drives have multiple platters, with parallel concentric circular *tracks* on each side. A read/write head is associated with each side of each platter, all heads moving in parallel. The group of all tracks at a given head position forms a *cylinder*. The concept is useful because all sectors in a cylinder can be read or written to without moving the read/write heads; the more sectors in a cylinder, the more potentially efficient the disk drive.

cylinder 0 The outermost cylinder on a disk. It holds the root directory, file allocation tables, and other critical DOS structures.

cylinder density The number of *sectors* in a cylinder on a hard disk drive. That is, the number of sectors that can be read without moving the drive's read/write heads.

data cable The narrower of two cables that are used to connect a hard disk drive to a controller card in most machines.

data decryption See *data encryption.*

data density The density at which data is recorded along a track, usually expressed as "bits per inch."

data encryption The transformation of data into a form that can't be read by anyone who doesn't know a special "key." Both encryption and decryption (the restoration of encrypted data to its original form) may be performed by hardware or software.

data file A file containing data (as opposed to a *program file*, which contains *code*). All files that are not program files are actually data files. Usually, the term "data file" refers to files that you create for your own purposes (such as a letter or spreadsheet), rather than data files the program creates for its own purposes (such as a *configuration file* the program uses to store data by which it configures itself).

data transfer rate The rate at which data is transferred between a disk drive and system memory.

DC600A The standard quarter-inch tape cartridge.

deallocated cluster A *cluster* of disk space that was once occupied by a file but is now free.

dedicated servo surface In multiplatter voice-coil drives, a dedicated servo surface is a whole platter side given over to *servo data* that is used to fine-position the read/write heads.

DEBUG A DOS program used to examine what is happening in the computer's microprocessor or memory. DEBUG can also modify files, and so it is sometimes used for repairing software.

decryption See *data encryption.*

default directory The directory in a *directory tree* to which DOS directs its actions by *default* unless some other directory is specified. When a disk has no directory tree, its *root directory* (the only directory it has) is the default directory.

default drive The disk drive to which DOS directs its actions when no other drive is specifically named by means of a *drive specifier* (such as **A:**). The DOS prompt normally indicates the default drive; when it is **A>**, drive A is the default drive. In this case, the command **DIR** causes DOS to give a directory listing from drive A, since no other drive has been indicated in the command. On the other hand, the command **DIR B:** would give a directory listing from drive B even while drive A remains the default drive.

defragmentation See *file defragmentation.*

defragmenter Utility software for defragmenting files. See *file defragmentation.*

DEVICE A DOS command (placed in the CONFIG.SYS file) that makes DOS load a device driver into memory when the machine is booted.

device driver A memory-resident program that lets the computer control an unusual device, such as a plotter or expanded memory board. Device drivers are loaded into memory by DOS *DEVICE* commands.

dialog box A small window opened on the screen by software to convey messages about what is happening in the software, or to ask you for information the software needs to do its work. For example, when you print a document, a dialog box may open to ask how to set page margins, page numbering, and so on. Similarly, if an error occurs during printing, a dialog box may open to tell you about it.

dip switch A miniature switch found on circuit boards that is used to configure hardware.

direct memory access (DMA) Electronic circuitry that transfers data between computer memory and a peripheral, such as a disk drive, without passing the data through the microprocessor chip. DMA allows computers to operate more quickly.

directory A collection of information about a group of files on a disk. Directories tell the names of the files, their sizes, and the times and dates they were created or last modified. Directories also keep track of each file's starting location on the disk.

directory entry The 32-byte record, held in a directory, that tells a file's name, size, time and date, starting cluster, and other pertinent information.

directory listing The display of information about some or all files in a directory.

directory path The sequence of directories that leads from the root directory in a directory tree to a particular subdirectory. For example, the directory path **\MAMMALS\AQUATIC\DOLPHINS** tells that the **DOLPHINS** subdirectory is listed in the **AQUATIC** subdirectory, which is listed in the **MAMMALS** subdirectory, which is listed in the root directory (the initial backslash stands for the root directory). The complete directory path to a file named **FLIPPER** in the **DOLPHINS** subdirectory would be **\MAMMALS\AQUATIC \DOLPHINS\FLIPPER**. A directory path may also include a leading *drive specifier*, such as **C:**. When the directory tree is located on drive C:, the complete path would be **C:\MAMMALS\AQUATIC\DOLPHINS\FLIPPER**.

directory tree A hierarchy of directories that begins with a *root directory* that contains a number of *level-1 subdirectories*, each of which may contain *level-2 subdirectories*, and so on.

disk caching A process in which recently accessed or frequently accessed disk sectors are kept in memory so that they can be quickly retrieved when software requires them again. The apparent speed of a hard disk can be tripled by this measure.

disk controller Electronics that mediate the transfer of data between disk drives and the computer's memory.

disk read The act of reading one or more sectors of data from a disk.

disk sector See *sector.*

disk write The act of writing one or more sectors of data to a disk.

diskette A removable disk contained in either a "floppy" $5\frac{1}{4}$-inch sleeve or a $3\frac{1}{2}$-inch rigid casing.

distribution diskettes The "original" diskettes upon which software is sold.

DMA See *direct memory access.*

DMA channel A data path that conveys data directly between a peripheral and memory, without passing through the computer's microprocessor. A computer may have several DMA channels.

DOS buffers Small holding areas in system memory through which data passes on its way to and from disk drives.

DOS command line The line on the screen at which a *DOS prompt* (such as **A>** or **C>**) appears. It is called a *command line* because it is the place where DOS commands are typed in.

DOS error message A message displayed by DOS when an error has occurred while trying to execute a DOS command. Occasionally a DOS error message appears when application software has tried to use DOS and run into trouble.

DOS path See *directory path.*

DOS prompt The symbol DOS writes on the screen to indicate that it is waiting for a command. The normal DOS prompt tells the *current drive*: **A>, B>, C>** and so on. The DOS **PROMPT** command can alter the form of the prompt.

DOS shell A program that extends the capabilities of DOS and makes it easier to use.

drive See *disk drive.*

drive geometry The specifications that define a disk drive's capacity: the number of *platters* it holds, the number of *tracks* on each side of each platter, and the number of *sectors* in each track.

drive specifier A symbol used in DOS commands to tell which disk drive to direct an operation to. For example, the symbols **A:**, **B:**, and **C:** are all drive specifiers.

DSS See *dedicated servo surface.*

DV-I A video compression technique that allows over an hour of moving video to be stored on a compact disk.

dynamic linking A technique in advanced operating systems in which parts of a program are constantly swapped in and out of memory as they are required.

EGA See *Enhanced Graphics Adapter.*

embedded servo data Magnetic markings embedded between tracks on disk drives that use voice-coil actuators. The markings allow the actuator to fine-tune the position of the read/write heads.

EMS The "extended memory specification." See *extended memory.*

encoding The system by which data is laid down on the disk surface as a pattern of "ons" and "offs."

encryption See *data encryption.*

Enhanced Graphics Adapter A video adapter that includes the capability of the *Monochrome Display Adapter* and the *Color Graphics Adapter*, and adds several advanced modes.

environment A list of information about the computer's configuration that is maintained by DOS and made available to all programs. The SET command can add information to the environment and its current contents can be viewed by typing **SET**.

errorlevel code A code transmitted to DOS when a program terminates. It tells whether the program was able to do its work successfully. Batch files can intercept errorlevel codes and use them to decide what to do next.

error message A message displayed by DOS or a program to inform you that you have done something wrong, or that something has gone wrong with the computer hardware, the software in operation, or the data with which the software is working. The DOS manual includes a listing of error messages, as does the documentation accompanying many programs.

.EXE A file name *extension* that appears only on *program files*.

expanded memory A way of adding additional memory beyond 640K to any kind of IBM microcomputer. Software must be tailored to use expanded memory.

expansion board A circuit board that may be inserted in one of a computer's *slots*. Expansion boards are used to add memory, input/output ports, modems, and many other kinds of hardware.

expansion slot An oblong socket inside a computer. A circuit board can be plugged into an expansion slot to expand the machine's capabilities. Most computers have several slots.

extended boot record A *boot record* that begins each volume of an extended DOS partition. The machine uses these records for identifying and managing the partitions, not for actual booting.

extended memory Memory beyond the one megabyte that can be accessed by all IBM PCs. PC ATs and PS/2s can have extended memory; PC XTs cannot. Most software running under DOS cannot use extended memory.

extended partition In DOS 3.3 and later versions, a hard disk may have two partitions that serve DOS—an ordinary, bootable partition (called the *primary partition*) and an *extended partition*, which may contain any number of *volumes* of up to 32 megabytes each.

extension See *file name extension*.

external command A DOS command that is performed by software held in a file separate from the main COMMAND.COM program that is kept in memory at all times. An external command can't be used unless the required file is in the current directory, or is accessed by a directory path or a PATH command.

external drive A disk or tape drive mounted in a separate cabinet with its own power supply and fan.

FASTOPEN A DOS command that initiates a time-saving feature in which DOS keeps track of the placement of files it has already opened once.

FAT See *file allocation table.*

FCB See *file control block.*

FCBS A seldom-used DOS command that increases the number of *file control blocks* available to programs.

FDISK The standard DOS utility for *partitioning* hard disks.

file A collection of information given an identifying name and stored on disk. A file may hold pages of text, the numbers in a spreadsheet, the instructions that form a *program* like a word processor, and many other kinds of information as well.

file allocation table A table of numbers kept on every floppy or hard disk that keeps track of the contents of every disk sector. Chains of numbers in this table report the sequences of sectors that make up individual files.

file attribute One of several markings kept in the directory entry of every file that defines special characteristics of the file, such as that it is a *read-only* file.

file compression The reduction of files to a smaller size so that they will take up less disk space. File compression utilities may link into DOS to automatically compress files as they are written and automatically uncompress them as they are read.

file control block A small block of memory initialized by DOS when it opens a file. File control blocks are now obsolete and are only found in old PC software.

file defragmentation A process in which utility software rearranges the placement of files on disk. A file that is dispersed over the disk surface takes longer to read or write, since the disk drive's *read/write heads* must make more motions to reach the file's sectors. Defragmentation software rearranges the sectors into consecutive sectors in adjacent tracks.

file locking In networks, the temporary denial of access to a file to anyone other than the person currently working on it. Locking prevents people from undoing each other's work.

file name A word of from one to eight characters assigned to a file when it is created. A *file name extension* of up to three characters may optionally be appended to the file name, with a period separating them (as in **MYFILE.TXT**).

file name extension A tag added to the end of a file name, and separated from the file name by a period. For example, **.TXT** is the extension in **MYFILE.TXT**. Extensions are used to classify files. Some extensions always have the same meaning. For example, the extensions **.EXE** and **.COM** indicate program files (files containing software), and **.BAT** indicates a *batch file*. Other extensions are defined by application software, or by the person who creates the file. Thus a word processor might always append **.DOC** to a file name, or a user might assign **.DOC** to files to mark them as documents.

file recovery Techniques for repairing and reassembling files that have been damaged by failures in hardware (such as bad disk sectors) or in software (such as files that have become fused with others).

file server A hard disk drive that runs under special software to "serve" shared files to computers on a *local area network*.

filter A program through which the output of some DOS commands are altered. For example, the SORT filter sorts the output of commands like DIR.

FIND A DOS command that searches files for a specified line of text.

fixed disk Another name for a hard disk. See *hard disk drive.*

flaw density A measure of the number of flaws on the platters in a hard disk drive.

floppy disk See *diskette.*

FORMAT.COM The DOS format program that performs both low- and high-level formatting on diskettes but only high-level formatting on hard disks.

formatting For disks, formatting is the process of writing magnetic lines on the disk surface to define tracks and sectors, and the installation of structures used by DOS to keep track of files, such as the *root directory* and the *file allocation table*. Formatting may optionally add files to the disk that allow the disk to be used for *booting* the computer.

formatted capacity A disk's capacity in bytes after it has been formatted. The formatted capacity is usually several percent less than its unformatted capacity because disk space is lost between sectors.

fragmentation The dispersal of disk sectors belonging to one file to non-adjacent positions on the disk. Fragmented files take longer to read and write because more motions of the disk drive's read/write heads are required.

freeware Software that is shared with others free of change.

full track buffering A kind of *disk caching* in which an entire disk track is read whenever only part of it is required. Statistically, other sectors from the track are likely to be required next, and so they will already be in memory, thus avoiding redundant mechanical activity. Full track buffering may be handled either by specially designed hardware, or by disk caching software. It is most efficient on very fast hard disks.

geometry See *drive geometry*.

gigabyte One billion bytes (a thousand megabytes).

global backup A backup of every file on a hard disk, whether it has been changed since the last backup or not.

global file name character Two special characters—the asterisk (*) and question mark (?)—that may be inserted in file names within DOS commands to designate a group of files.

graphical user interface A way of presenting information on the screen in which a program is operated by a system of *icons, pull-down menus, windows*, and *dialog boxes*. Graphical user interfaces work best with, and sometimes require, a mouse.

graphics mode See *video mode.*

GUI See *graphical user interface.*

guide rails Plastic strips attached to the sides of some hard disk drives so they may be mounted in a drive bay.

hard disk card A miniaturized hard disk built into a controller card and installed in one of a computer's slots.

hard disk crash Any mechanical failure of a hard disk drive. The term "crash" comes from *head crash,* in which the disk drive's read/write heads slam into the disk surface, destroying data and perhaps themselves. Most hard disk disasters result not from a mechanical "crash," but from damage to DOS structures that keep track of data, including *directories* and *file allocation tables.*

hard error An error that occurs because of a continuing hardware failure. Compare to *soft error.*

hardware configuration The job of setting up hardware so that it can work with DOS and software without conflicting with other hardware. Hardware configuration is performed by setting switches on the hardware, by running special configuration software, and by installing *device driver* software to control the hardware.

hardware installation The process of physically inserting, connecting, or cabling hardware to the computer.

head See *read/write head.*

head actuator The device that moves read/write heads across a disk drive's platters. Drives use a stepper-motor actuator or a voice-coil actuator.

head crash A kind of hard disk failure in which the drive's read/write heads slam into the disk surface. Usually data is destroyed, a problem that at best may be confined to only a file or two, and at worst may wreck directories and other DOS structures so that massive amounts of data are made inaccessible.

head parking A procedure in which a disk drive's read/write heads are moved to an unused track so that they won't damage data in the event of a head crash or other failure.

head seek The motion of a disk drive's read/write heads from one disk track to another.

head seek test A rigorous test that checks the accuracy of head seek operations.

hexadecimal number A number counted in base-16, a system that uses the letters A–F as well as the numerals 0–9. The numbers are counted 0, 1, 2, 3, 4, 5, 6, 7, 8, 9, A, B, C, D, E, F, 10, 11, and so on. These numbers are sometimes employed in configuring memory expansion cards.

hidden attribute A *file attribute* that, when set, causes a file to be omitted from directory listings.

hidden file A file for which the *hidden attribute* is set, such that it is omitted from directory listings. DOS leaves two hidden files in the root directory of every disk. Others may be created by software, although generally they are not.

high-level format The part of disk formatting in which structures required by DOS are written on the disk, including the boot record, root directory, and file allocation tables.

history file A file created by utility software to keep track of earlier use of the software. For example, many backup programs keep history files describing earlier backup sessions.

hot key A keystroke combination that brings a *memory-resident program* into action.

IBMBIO.COM and **IBMDOS.COM** Two files kept in the root directory of every *boot disk* that DOS requires to start up the computer. These are *hidden files* not shown in a directory listing.

incremental backup A backup of all files that have been changed since the last backup was made.

installation The process of physically moving and connecting hardware or software to a computer. Hardware installation consists of inserting expansion boards into slots and connecting cables. Software installation usually entails copying files to a hard disk. In addition, *configuration* may be required to tailor the hardware or software to your system.

installation program A utility program shipped with many application programs that transfers files from the *distribution diskettes* to a hard disk in your machine. It may also help you *configure* the software at the same time so that it matches your printer, video display, and so on. The program is usually named INSTALL and is started up by entering **INSTALL**.

integrated circuit An electronic component containing many thousands of miniturized circuits. Often called a "chip."

interface A protocol, embodied in the electronics of the disk controller and disk electronics, that intermediates the exchange of data between the drive and computer.

interface card An *expansion board* that connects a computer to an external device, such as a *modem, plotter,* or *local area network.*

interleave factor The number of sectors that pass beneath a disk drive's read/write heads before the "next" numbered sector arrives. For example, when the interleave factor is 3:1, a sector is read, two pass by, and then the next is read. Ideally, the sectors are numbered so that sectors with successive numbers arrive at the read/write heads just in time for the computer to access them.

internal command A DOS command that resides in the main COMMAND.COM file that is always in memory, such that the command is always available for your use.

internal drive A disk or tape drive mounted inside one of a computer's disk drive bays (or a hard disk card, which is installed in one of the computer's slots).

inter-record gaps In tape backup, sections of wasted tape that occur when the disk cannot supply data as quickly as the tape drive can write it.

interrupt A brief interruption of the computer's activity so that an urgent task can be performed. For example, a modem may interrupt the computer every time it receives a character of data from a telephone line, requesting that the character be stored in the computer's memory. Interrupts constantly occur in a computer, but happen so quickly that they generally go unnoticed by the user.

interrupt vector A computer may use up to 256 *interrupts*, and, loosely speaking, the number of each interrupt, from 0 to 255, is the *interrupt vector*. (The vector is actually a memory address associated with this number). When configuring hardware, you may be called upon to specify an unused interrupt vector that the hardware can employ to interrupt the machine.

JOIN A DOS command that can link a directory on one drive into a directory tree on another drive.

jumper A primitive kind of switch found on the surface of some expansion boards. The jumper is a tiny box that connects pins protruding from the board. You may need to change jumpers to configure a board to your system.

KB See *kilobyte*.

keyboard macro A sequence of keystrokes that is recorded and then associated with a single keystroke, such that the whole sequence is sent to the computer when the single keystroke is typed.

keyboard macro file A file holding a set of keyboard macro assignments. Loading a different file customizes the keyboard layout for a different purpose.

key disk A diskette that must reside in a diskette drive for a program to run, even if the program is installed on a hard disk. Key disks are sometimes shipped with copy-protected software.

kilobyte 1024 bytes. The prefix "kilo" means "one thousand," so this term is an approximation. If you have 10 kilobytes of disk space available (10K), you have 10,240 bytes, not 10,000.

kit All components required to install a hard disk in an IBM PC or compatible: drive, controller card, cables, and various attachments.

label In a *batch file*, a word that marks a position in the file. Labels begin with a colon, as in **:BEGIN** or **:END**. GOTO statements in the file can cause control to jump to the point in the file marked by the label.

LAN See *local area network*.

landing strip A track on a hard disk, usually the innermost, to which the drive's read/write heads are retracted when the machine is turned off. No data is recorded on this track.

laser disk See *optical disk.*

level-1 subdirectory A subdirectory immediately "above" the root directory of a directory tree, and thus one that is listed in the root directory. Level-1 subdirectories hold level-2 subdirectories in turn, and so on.

listing See *directory listing.*

loading The process of moving data from disk to system memory. A program is "loaded" into memory and then run. Similarly, data is loaded from disk into memory when a file is "loaded."

local area network A system in which two or more microcomputers are linked together to share files and peripherals such as printers.

logical drive A disk drive regarded from the point of view of a DOS prompt. A single hard disk may be partitioned into two or more *logical drives* named **C>**, **D>**, and so on. Conversely, special software can combine the space on two *physical* hard disk drives so that they appear as one *logical* drive.

low-level formatting Formatting that lays down markings on a blank disk surface to define disk sectors. The root directory and other structures are created by *high-level formatting.*

magnetic domain A tiny segment of a track just large enough to hold one of the magnetic flux reversals that encode data on a disk surface.

magneto-optical recording An erasable laser-disk recording technique that uses a laser beam to heat pits on the disk surface to the point that a magnet can make flux changes.

master boot record A sector of data used during booting by hard disks. It contains essential information about the disk and tells the starting location of the various *partitions.*

M See *megabyte.*

mean time between failure A statistical measure of the average time a device will run before it breaks down and requires repair. MTBF is usually measured in tens of thousands of hours.

medium The magnetic coating or plating that covers a disk or tape.

MHz See *megaHertz*.

megabyte One million bytes.

megaHertz A million cycles per second. A 12-megaHertz computer uses an internal electronic clock that pulses 12 million times a second. The pulse sets the tempo at which the microprocessor and other components operate.

memory allocation The process of deciding which programs will be used, and how they will be used, so that they can all fit into memory at once. Besides application programs, memory can hold *device drivers, memory-resident programs, and operating environments* like a *DOS shell.* Some of these programs, such as *RAM disks* and *disk caching* programs, can take up large amounts of memory to hold data. Besides deciding *which* programs to load, you may also need to decide in *which kind of memory* a program is to reside: conventional, extended, or expanded.

memory-resident program A program that stays in memory after it terminates. When started up, most memory-resident programs display a message saying that they have been loaded and then they quit immediately. Thereafter, the program can usually be "awakened" by pressing a special key combination (the *hot key*). These "pop-up programs" include a wide variety of calendars, calculators, notepads, and other utilities. Memory-resident programs are also know as *TSRs*, or *terminate-and-stay-resident* programs.

menu bar A menu whose options are displayed (usually) along the top line of the screen. Each menu selection opens downward into a vertical submenu called a *pull-down menu.* A pull-down menu is activated by clicking a mouse over a menu bar selection, or by entering a code from the keyboard—often the first letter of the menu selection's name.

menu program Utility software that makes a computer easier to use by letting you run programs and use basic DOS commands simply by making menu selections.

MFM See *modified frequency modulation encoding.*

MicroChannel The *bus design* (the system used to interconnect expansion boards with the computer's main circuitry) employed in most PS/2 machines. The MicroChannel bus has potential performance advantages over earlier designs.

microprocessor The main integrated circuit chip that does most of the computer's work. A number of microprocessor models operate in IBM PCs, including the 8086, 8088, 80286, 80386, and 80486. A microprocessor is also called a *central processing unit* or *CPU.*

millisecond One-thousandth of a second.

MKDIR "Make Directory"—the DOS command that creates a new subdirectory.

modified frequency modulation encoding The method of encoding data on the disk surface that is most widely used today. The coding of a bit of data varies by the coding of the previous bit.

monitor See *video monitor.*

Monochrome Display Adapter An early, text-only video system that has no color capability.

MORE A word used in some DOS commands, such as **DIR** and **TYPE**, that causes the command to display only a screenful of information at a time, waiting until you strike a key before showing the next.

mother board The computer's main circuit board. Usually the mother board has a number of *slots* into which *expansion boards* may be inserted.

ms A *millisecond*—one thousandth of a second.

MTBF See *mean time between failure.*

multifunction board An *expansion board* that provides more than one service, such as adding both additional memory and additional ports to a machine.

multitasking A system in which two or more programs can run at the same time in a computer. The computer switches back and forth between the programs many times a second, creating the illusion that each is completely in charge of the machine. Multitasking allows a user to perform several tasks at once, or, in *multiuser systems*, allows several people to use the same computer at once.

multiuser system A computer system in which multiple keyboards and video displays are connected to one machine. All users may work in the same program at once, or the machine may use *multitasking* to allow individual users to run different programs at the same time.

network See *local area network.*

nonvolatile RAM disk A RAM disk powered by a battery supply so that it continues to hold its data during a power outage.

off-hours backup A backup that is performed automatically while the computer is not in use. A *tape backup unit* is normally required.

operating environment An extention to DOS, such as *Windows* or *DesqView*, that makes DOS easier to use, allows you to run several programs at once, and makes more memory available. Programs specially written to work with particular operating environments may take on features of the environment, including a *graphical user interface* and the ability to transfer data directly to other programs.

operating system The basic software that runs the machine, such as DOS or OS/2. A primitive part of the operating system called the BIOS is built into the machine. Part of the operating system is always kept in memory. Other parts are utility programs that are loaded as they are needed.

optical disk A disk that encodes data as a series of reflective pits that are read (and sometimes written) by a laser beam.

orphaned clusters A *cluster* (group of disk sectors) that has been accidentally cut off from the file it was associated with. The disk's *file allocation table* (the mechanism by which a disk tracks files from cluster to cluster) considers the cluster to still be in use, and so the disk space cannot be allocated to another file.

OS/2 An advanced operating system intended to replace DOS, at least in powerful PCs. Unlike DOS, OS/2 can run several programs at once. It offers a number of advanced features, including a *graphical user interface* called the *Presentation Manager*.

overlay Part of a program that is kept on disk until it is required; it is then read into memory *on top of* some other part of the program (which may itself later be read back into memory at the same place). In this way, scarce memory is conserved by having a program share one section of memory between several parts of the program.

overlay file A file that contains a program *overlay*. Overlay files must be in reach of the program that uses them or the program will not be able to operate properly.

overrun A kind of data loss. *Overruns* occur during data communication when data arrives more quickly than the receiving electronics or software can process it.

overwrite To write new data on top of older data, destroying the older data.

parameter A word, number, or symbol that is typed after a command to further specify how the command should function. For example, many DOS commands require parameters to specify which file a command should operate on. In the expression **COPY MYFILE.TXT A:**, the **COPY** command has two parameters, the first of which names the file that is to be copied (**MYFILE.TXT**), and the second of which indicates the destination of the copy, in this case drive A.

parent directory The directory that holds another directory. In **\PLANTS \TREES\WILLOWS**, **TREES** is a parent directory of **WILLOWS**, **PLANTS** is a parent directory of **TREES**, and the root directory is the parent directory of **PLANTS**.

parity bit In *serial communications*, a *parity bit* may be added to the end of every byte of data that is transmitted. When the byte arrives at the receiving station, the parity bit is tested to see if an error was introduced into the data as it was transmitted.

partition A section of a hard disk's total capacity that is accessed under a single drive specifier. For example, a hard disk may be divided into three partitions named **C:**, **D:**, and **E:**. Some partitions may be devoted to operating systems other than DOS and cannot be accessed by DOS.

partitioning The process of dividing a hard disk's capacity into *partitions.* Partitioning is performed by the DOS **FDISK** program after *low-level formatting* and before *high-level formatting.*

partition table A table kept in a hard disk's *master boot record* that keeps track of how many partitions the disk has and where each begins.

PATH A DOS command that configures DOS to automatically search for a program file in specified directories when the file is not found in the current directory.

perpendicular recording A recording technique in which magnetic domains are created perpendicular to—rather than parallel to—the disk surface, making possible much higher data densities.

physical drive A term used in opposition to *logical drive.* A single hard disk may be partitioned into two or more *logical drives* named **C**, **D**, and so on. Conversely, special software can combine the space on two *physical* hard disk drives so that they appear as one *logical* drive, **C**.

plated media Hard disk platters plated with a metal film upon which data is recorded.

platter Hard disks have multiple disks turning in parallel. Each disk is referred to as a *platter.*

port A point of connection between a computer and other electrical devices, such as printers, modems, mice, scientific instruments, and so on. A port is an electrical circuit that presents a socket, usually at the back of the machine, to which a device is connected. There are a number of different kinds of ports, including *serial ports, parallel ports, mouse ports,* and *game ports,* some of which may be built into the computer, and some added through *expansion boards.*

port address A number used by software to access a peripheral device, such as a disk drive or printer. Port addresses range from 0 to 65535. Occasionally hardware must be configured so that it uses port addresses that do not conflict with those used by other hardware. These *software* ports are not to be confused with *hardware* ports, such as *serial ports* or *parallel ports*, which are addressed by DOS using names like LPT1 or COM1.

POST See *Power-On Self Test.*

Power-On Self Test Build-in software that the computer runs when it is turned on to test that the machine is functioning properly.

power supply A metal box, found inside most computers, which converts line current into the voltages required by the computer.

Presentation Manager The graphical, icon- and window-based software interface offered with the OS/2 operating system. Programs must be specially designed to operate in the Presentation Manager.

primary partition In DOS 3.3, a hard disk may have two partitions that serve DOS—a *primary partition*, which is an ordinary, bootable partition, and an *extended partition*, which may contain any number of *volumes* of up to 32 megabytes each.

processor See *central processing unit.*

processor speed The speed, measured in *megaHertz (MHz*—millions of cycles per second), that a microprocessor performs its simplest instructions. Every cycle is referred to as a *clock*. Complicated instructions, such as multiplications, may take many clocks, so there is no simple correlation between processor speed and the number of instructions a processor can perform per second.

program file A file that holds a program, whether an application program like a word processor, a utility program, or DOS files like COMMAND.COM. Generally speaking, program files have **.EXE** or **.COM** file name extensions. However, auxiliary files containing other parts of the program may have different extensions, and you must take care that they are in reach of the main program file.

prompt See *DOS prompt.*

PROMPT A DOS command that changes the form and content of the DOS prompt.

proprietary format In backups, a format in which data and error-correction codes are compressed on diskettes, sometimes without using ordinary DOS sectors. The format is entirely the creation of the backup utility's manufacturer.

PS/2 *Personal System/2.* One of IBM's second generation of personal computers, featuring built-in video systems and ports. Most PS/2 machines use a *MicroChannel bus*, which allows more advanced communications and control between the computer and expansion boards placed in its slots. These PS/2 machines cannot share expansion boards with non-PS/2 computers.

pull-down menu A kind of *menu* that descends from the top of the screen to reveal its selections. This name is given because these menus work most quickly when "pulled down" by a mouse.

QIC Committee An industry association that sets hardware and (increasingly) software standards for tape backup units.

RAM See *random-access memory.*

RAM disk A "phantom disk drive" for which a section of memory is set aside to hold data, just as if it were a number of disk sectors. To DOS, a RAM disk looks like, and functions like, an actual disk drive. RAM disks are also called *virtual disks.*

random-access file A data file in which all data elements are the same length. Software can calculate the location of any element and read it directly, without tracing it from the start of the file. Compare this organization to that of *sequential files* in which data elements have different lengths, with special characters between them. To find a particular element, software must read through each element *in sequence* from the beginning of the file.

random-access memory (RAM) A computer's electronic memory in which it stores programs and data. The three basic kinds of memory used by software—*conventional memory, extended memory,* and *expanded memory*—are all random-access memory. Random-access memory loses the information it holds when the computer is turned off. Compare it to *read-only memory,* which permanently holds special software, such as parts of the computer's operating system.

read-only attribute A marking in a file's directory entry that makes it a *read-only file*.

read-only file A file that can be read, but not written to, and thus not changed. In DOS, read-only files also cannot be deleted, although they can be renamed.

read-only memory (ROM) Memory that already has information written in it, information that is not erased when the computer is turned off. ROM chips built into the machine hold important parts of the operating system.

read operation In disk drives, the act of reading one or more sectors of data from a disk.

read/write head In disk drives, the armature that moves across the disk surface to read or write data. Most disks have a read/write head on each side. The heads move between disk tracks. Data is read as the sectors along the tracks rotate beneath the heads.

real-time clock A battery-powered clock that keeps the time and data in a computer even when the machine is turned off. A read-time clock is different from the *system clock*, which is a timer created by operating system software, one that exists only when the machine is turned on.

record In files, a *record* is one instance of a collection of related data. Database files typically contain many records, each holding, for example, the name, age, and height of an individual. All records in a file are the same length so that the computer can calculate the position of any record in a file and access the record directly.

record locking An operating system facility used in networked computers. When one computer accesses a particular record in a database file, all other computers are barred from accessing the record until the first computer relinquishes it. This feature prevents two or more computers from trying to change the same data at the same moment.

RECOVER A DOS command that recovers the fragments of a damaged file.

removable cartridge drive A hard disk drive in which the platters are contained in a cartridge that may be removed and replaced with another. Some removable cartridge drives include the head actuator in the cartridge.

restocking fee A fee charged by mail-order vendors when goods are returned for reasons that aren't the vendor's fault.

retensioning utility A software utility that runs a tape cartridge through a drive to equalize the tension throughout the cartridge.

RLL See *run-length limited encoding.*

RMA number "Return Merchandise Authorization"—A number given to you by a vendor when you arrange to ship a drive for repairs.

RMDIR A DOS command that removes a subdirectory from a directory tree. There is also an abbreviated form of the command, RD.

ROM See *read-only memory.*

ROM BIOS See *BIOS.*

root directory A disk's main directory. All disks have a root directory, even disks that do not have a *directory tree.* What some call "the directory" on a diskette is the same thing as the root directory. Root directories have a fixed size, so they can hold only so many files. The size varies by disk type.

run-length limited encoding A data encoding method in which patterns in the data are translated into codes that can be written more densely on the disk surface. The technique can increase data densities by 50 to 100 percent over conventional encoding methods.

sector A tiny area on the surface of a disk that normally holds 512 bytes of data. Every sector is surrounded by markings laid down during formatting. These give the sector an identifying address and other information that enables the disk drive to read and write the data. The 512-byte sector size is a convention used on all IBM microcomputers; in special circumstances small or larger sectors may be employed.

sector caching A procedure in which frequently read (or recently read) disk sectors are stored in memory in anticipation that they will be required again. By keeping them on hand, time-consuming disk accesses are avoided.

sector size The number of bytes in a sector—normally 512 bytes in DOS, but alterable by special utility software.

security shell Special software that restricts the access of computer users to particular directories or files, particular programs, and particular DOS commands. A *security shell* inserts itself between DOS and the computer user. Using a system of passwords and authorizations, It intercepts all incoming commands, evaluates them, and restricts user access accordingly.

seek time See *average seek time.*

sequential file A data file in which variable-length data elements are laid end to end with demarcating characters between. To find a particular element, software must read through each element *in sequence* from the beginning of the file. Compare this organization to that of *random-access files,* in which all data elements have the same length, and so software can calculate the location of a particular element. Text files are the most common kind of sequential file.

servo data Magnetic markings written on disk platters, They guide the read/write heads in drives that use voice-coil actuators.

settling time The time required for read/write heads to stop vibrating once they have been moved to a new track.

shell See *DOS shell.*

SHIPDISK A short utility program shipped with many hard disks (usually on an accompanying floppy). When run, it *parks* the disk drive's read/write heads over an area of the disk that goes unused. Should a severe jolt slam the heads into the disk surface, no data is lost. The program should always be run before relocating the computer. Most recently made disks do not require a SHIPDISK program, however, since they automatically park their heads when the machine is turned off.

shock rating A rating (expressed in Gs) of how much shock a disk drive can sustain without damage.

simultaneous backup Backups automatically written to a second hard disk whenever data is written to a first hard disk.

slot See *expansion slot.*

soft error An error occuring in disk drives or other computer hardware that is not attributable to permanent hardware damage, and thus is not likely to happen again soon. Soft errors may occur because of power surges, cosmic rays, vibrations, and other physical factors.

software installation Generally, the transfer of program files from the diskettes they are distributed upon to a hard disk. Subdirectories of a particular name in a particular directory tree position may need to be created to receive the files. Often an INSTALL program accompanies the software to perform this task. For machines lacking a hard disk, *software installation* may consist of combining required files from several distribution diskettes onto one diskette used to load the program.

SORT A DOS *filter* that can sort the lines of a file. It may be applied to directory listings.

source disk In a **COPY** or **DISKCOPY** operation, the *source disk* is the disk from which files are copied.

spindle The post upon which a disk drive's platters are mounted.

spooling The process of sending output to a printer "in the background" while using the computer for some other task.

ST506/412 The standard five-megabyte per second interface used by most hard disk drives in IBM PCs.

stack A place in the computer's memory where the microprocessor can momentarily store information.

standby power supply A backup power supply that very quickly switches into operation during a power outage.

starting cluster The first *cluster* (group of disk sectors) occupied by a file on a hard disk or floppy diskette. Every file's starting cluster is recorded in its directory entry. The *file allocation table* keeps track of the remaining clusters belonging to the file.

stepper band A notched band that marks the track positions traveled by the read/write heads in drives that use a stepper-motor actuator.

stepper-motor actuator An assembly that moves read/write heads across platters by a sequence of small turns of a special kind of motor.

streaming In tape backup, a condition in which data is transferred from the hard disk as quickly as the tape drive can record it so that the drive does not start and stop or waste tape.

string A sequence of characters. "A gray cat" is a 10-byte string in which two of the characters are spaces.

subdirectory A directory listed in another directory. DOS maintains subdirectories as variable-length files.

subdirectory attribute A setting in a directory entry's attribute byte that marks the entry as representing a subdirectory file.

subdirectory file A file that holds a subdirectory. Unlike a disk's root directory, which is always located in the same place on a disk and has a fixed size, subdirectories may be positioned anywhere on a disk, just like files, and may be any length.

SUBST A DOS command that can assign a drive specifier to a subdirectory.

surge protector A device that provides minimal protection against voltage spikes and other transients in the power line that feeds the computer.

switch A symbol appended to a DOS command to make it act in a special way. In DOS, all switches consist of a slash character followed by a letter. For example, the format of directory listings is changed when the /W switch is appended to a **DIR** command.

SYS A DOS command that transfer the two hidden system files (used for booting the computer) to a particular position on a diskette so that it can be used for booting the machine.

system attribute A *file attribute* that marks a file as belonging to the operating system.

system clock A clock maintained by the computer's operating system. The clock is set automatically by the computer's *real-time clock*, if it has one, or else it is set when the user enters the time at startup. Because the clock is implemented by software, it does not operate when the computer is turned off.

system crash A general failure of the computer's operation. Usually the machine "freezes" and refuses to respond to input from keyboard or mouse. System crashes mostly result from software bugs rather than hardware problems.

system file A file that is part of the computer's operating system.

system integrator A computer consultant/vendor who tests available products and combines them into highly optimized systems.

tagging A technique in many DOS shells that lets you use the cursor to "tag" files in a directory listing. The files may then be copied, erased, and so on, as a group.

tape backup unit A special kind of tape recorder used for backing up data from a hard disk.

tape format The way in which data is laid out in tape backups. The various tape formats differ in the number of tracks on the tape, the kind of error checking performed, and in directory layout.

target disk The disk to which data is transferred from a *source disk.*

temporary file A file temporarily (and invisibly) created by a program for its own use.

text editor A simple word processor.

text file A file that holds nothing but text. A true text file contains no formatting codes or other specialized information, thus allowing it to be read by many kinds of software. These files are also called *ASCII files.*

text mode See *video mode.*

thin-file media See *plated media.*

TPI "Tracks per inch"—a measure of track density.

track A ring of disk sectors on a hard disk or floppy diskette. Both sides of a disk are formatted into scores of concentric tracks, each divided into (typically) 9 to 15 sectors.

track density The number of tracks that can be fit on a platter side.

track-to-track seek time The time required for read/write heads to move between adjacent tracks.

tree See *directory tree.*

tree diagram A diagram of a disk's directory tree. Tree diagrams are displayed by *DOS shells* and other utility software.

Trojan horse Destructive code hidden in programs by vandals. The code remains inoperative until a particular event occurs, whereupon it destroys as much data as it can, usually by erasing the hard disk.

TSR Stands for "terminate and stay resident." See *memory-resident program.*

TYPE A DOS command that displays files.

underrun In tape backup, underruns occur when data cannot be delivered from the hard disk as quickly as the tape drive can record it.

unerase program A program that attempts to recover one or more accidentally erased files. Such programs are not infallible, and they are often useless for recovering files erased long before the program is applied.

unformat program A program that attempts to recover as much data as possible after a disk has been inadvertently reformatted. These programs work best when they are installed on the disk *before* the accidental reformatting takes place.

unformatted capacity The total number of bytes of data that could fit onto a disk. The *formatted capacity* is lower because space is lost defining the boundaries between sectors.

uninterrupted power supply An electronic device connected between the computer and the wall socket. It sees to it that the computer continues to receive power when a power outage occurs.

utility program Software used to manage the computer and the data it stores, such as backup programs, DOS shells, data compression and encryption software, and so on. Utility programs contrast with *application programs* (such as word processors and databases) which perform the basic functions for which the computer is acquired.

VDISK A *RAM-disk* program that accompanies DOS.

video adapter A circuit board that fits into one of the computer's slots to run the video monitor. Video adapters match video standards, such as *CGA* or *EGA*, which determine graphics and color capability.

video mode A mode—usually one of several offered by a *video adapter*—that sets the way the video display operates. Video modes affect the screen resolution and the number of colors that may be shown at once. There are two basic kinds of modes, *graphics modes* and *text modes*. Graphics modes can display text, but text modes cannot display graphics (however, they can assemble special graphic characters into primitive figures). The screen is generally drawn more quickly in text modes.

video monitor The video display tube and its casing and controls.

video system A computer's video circuitry and video display. In combination, they determine what *video modes* the machine is capable of.

vaccine program Utility software that detects the presence of computer viruses. In some cases it may be able to remove the virus.

virtual disk See *RAM disk*.

virtual memory A technique used by some operating systems, including OS/2 but not DOS, in which it appears that more software and data is loaded into memory than there is memory available. This is done by constantly swapping parts of the programs and data between memory and disk storage.

virus A maliciously devised program that attaches itself to programs and travels from machine to machine as software is passed around. Once in a computer, a virus can spread to "infect" numerous files on hard disks and floppies. It may lie dormant for months before becoming active, whereupon it may destroy massive quantities of data.

voice-coil actuator A device that moves read/write heads across hard disk platters by pushing and pulling at a bar inserted through a coil.

voltage regulator An electronic device that monitors the flow of electricity on its way to the computer from a wall socket. It keeps fluctuating voltage perfectly constant.

volume Basically, everything contained on a disk. Hard disks, however, may be partitioned to hold two or more volumes, each with its own *drive specifier*, *directory tree*, and so on.

volume label An electronic label that may be added to a disk. It may be up to 11 characters long and is kept in the disk's root directory. Volume labels are useful for finding out which diskette currently resides in a diskette drive. It is added to the disk during formatting, and is displayed at the top of directory listings or by the **VOL** command.

volume label attribute A setting in the attribute byte of a directory entry. It specifies that the entry is to be interpreted as the disk's volume label. This attribute occurs only in a root directory.

Whitney technology An advanced suspension system for read/write heads.

wildcard characters Another name given to *global file name* characters.

Winchester drive An ordinary, nonremovable disk drive.

window A rectangular area of the screen devoted to a particular purpose. Many windows may be displayed at once, with, for example, a calculator in one, a directory listing in another, and a spreadsheet in a third. Windows may overlap in some software, and you can adjust their sizes.

Windows An *operating environment* that extends the capabilities of DOS by allowing several programs to be run at once, and by making more memory available to programs. Windows also provides a *graphical user interface* that makes DOS commands easier to use. Programs specially crafted to work with Windows can use all features of this interface, including icons, pull-down menus, multiple windows, and dialog boxes.

worm Maliciously devised software that spreads through a computer network, continuously replicating itself until the network is overwhelmed and stops functioning.

WORM drive A "write-once, read-many" optical disk drive. It uses cartridge disks on which any sector may be written upon only once, but that can be read back any number of times.

write operation In disk drives, the act of writing one or more sectors of data to a disk.

XCOPY An advanced version of the DOS COPY command that can copy groups of files from multiple subdirectories. It also can select files on the basis of their time, date, or archive attributes.

Y-connector A Y-shaped cable that divides a power supply cable into two cables so that two drives may be connected.

Index

A

accelerator boards, 277
activity indicator, cabling, 117
actuators, 26-29
    stepper-motor, 26-28
    voice-coil, 27-28
Advanced Diagnostics, 129
allocation units, 45
alternative storage technologies, 55-65
    Bernoulli technology, 57-58
    diskette drives, 55-56
    optical disks, 58-62, 64
    solid state storage, 62-63
analysis software, 380
APPEND command, 161-62
    optimizing, 396-97, 300, 301
archive attribute, 48
archive bit
    backups and, 319-20
    XCOPY command and, 325-26
archived files, 240-42
    DIR command for displaying, 226
archiving, on WORM drives, 59
ASCII compression, 254
ASCII standard, 12
ASK program (*The Norton Utilities*), 168-69
ASSIGN command, 172-73, 175
AT-style computers, inserting a drive in, 113
ATTRIB command, 251
    searching for files with, 188-89
attributes, 47-49
    archive, 48
    hidden, 48
    read-only, 48
    subdirectory, 48-49
    system, 48
    volume label, 48
audit trails, 204
AUTOEXEC.BAT file, 148, 209, 210
    creating, 144
    installating new software and, 243
average access time, 262
average seek times, 28, 269-71, 298, 300

B

BACKUP command, 313, 326-30
    dangers of, 329
    date and time with, 328
    diskette formatting and, 328
    format for, 327
    incremental backups with, 328
    logging the backup, 328
    speed of, 329
    syntax for, 326-37
    tracking diskettes with, 327
backups, 303-58
    archive bit and, 319-20
    attended versus unattended, 314-15
    aversion to, 305
    background, 315
    copy protection and, 317
    differential, 318-19
    diskette-based, 321-26
        COPY command, 321-22
        XCOPY command, 323-26
    with DOS BACKUP and RESTORE commands,
    326-30
        date and time, 328
        diskette formatting, 328
        format, 327
        incremental backups, 328
        logging the backup, 328
        performance, 329
        syntax, 326-27
        tracking diskettes, 327
    DOS shells and, 154
    DOS versus proprietary formats for, 312-13
    error checking and, 315-16
    errors in the backup media itself and, 314
    global, 318
    image versus file-by-file, 311-12
    incremental, 48, 318
    instituting a system for, 349-58
        deciding among backup options, 350-52
        frequency of backups, 352-55
        off-site data storage, 356-58
        organizing backup media, 355-56

local area networks (LANs) and, 316
off-hours, 315
pitfalls in, 316-17
practice, 313-14
processor speed and, 317
restoring data and, 313-14
risks to your data and, 303-7
serial, 320-21
software for, 307-8
   restore features, 313-14
space requirements for backup files, 72-73
speed versus flexibility of, 309-11
tape-based, 308, 337-49
   buying a tape drive, 344-46
   cartridges for, 348
   cartridge types for, 340
   file-by-file backups with, 343
   formatting tapes for, 348
   fundamentals of tape technology, 337-38
   future of, 349
   helical scan drives for, 341-42
   ideal, 343-44
   installation of a tape drive, 346-47
   misconceptions about, 339
   performance of tape drives, 342-43
   QIC-40 standard, 340-41
   streaming, 338-39
   tape flaking and, 348-49
   tape formats for, 338
   tape standards for, 339-40
   underruns, 339
temporary, 320
types of, 317-21
with utility software, 330-37
   data restoration, 335
   diskette requirements, 335
   error checking, 335-36
   error recovery, 336
   flexibility, 336-37
   operation, 332-35
   performance, 330-31
   proprietary formats, 331-32
on WORM drives, 59
bad sectors, 16
bad tracks, 94-95, 130-31
bad track table, 33, 94, 130-31
.BAK files, 72-73, 320
bank switching, 283
Basic Input-Output System. See BIOS
batch files
   changing directories with, 165
   interactive, 168-69
   for moving files, 184-86
   PATH command and, 160-61
   subdirectory for, 218
bays, installing a drive and, 111-12
Bernoulli technology, 86-88
   as alternative storage technology, 57-58
bezel (face plate), 98
BIOS (Basic Input-Output System), 33-34, 51
BIOS chip, replacing, 100, 125-27
bit-mapped displays, 74

booting, 51
   security systems and, 203
boot record, 51
   master, 52-53
buffers, 10
   DOS (sector buffers), 287-90, 299, 301
      disk caching and, 290
   full-track, 41-43
BUFFERS setting, 145-46, 288-90
bump detection, 29-30
buying a hard disk, 2-3
   accessories needed, 98-99
   capacity needed, 68-79
   checklist, 101-6
   choosing among types of disks, 80-92
      Bernoulli technology, 86-88
      card drives, 80-85
      external drives, 80
      high-capacity drives, 88-90
      power supplies, 90-91
      removable hard disks, 85-86
   quality of the drive, 94-97
   speed and, 92-94

C

cables, disconnecting, 109-10
cabling
   activity indicator, 117
   grounding cables, 118
   IDE and SCSI drives, 118
   MFM, RLL, and ESDI drives, 114-18
   power supplies, 124
caching, disk, 43, 289-93, 299, 301
   advanced disk cachers, 293
   DOS buffers and, 290
   FAT (file allocation table), 291
   IBMCACHE program, 292
   performance improvement, 291
   reading vs. writing data, 291-92
   sector selection, 290-91
   SMARTDRV.SYS program, 292-93
Calibrate program, 273-75
capacity of hard disks, 68-79
   assessing requirements for, 77-78
   of card drives, 81
   forecasting future needs and, 68-70
   formatted versus unformatted, 70-71
   hidden requirements and, 72-73
   newer applications that require more, 74-76
   nominal versus actual, 71-72
   ratio of RAM to, 1-2
cards, hard disks on, 80-85
   capacity of, 81
   compatibility of, 82
   drawbacks of, 85
   indicator lights for, 81
   installation of, 81-82
   installation problems, 84
   placement of, 83
   power requirements of, 82-83
   for PS/2 computers, 82

cartridges for removable hard disks, 85-86
cataloging
    directory tree, 223-24
    files, 237-39
catch in cover of computer, 110
CD-I standard, 62
CD ROMs, 58-62
CHDIR (or CD) command
    in batch files, 165
    dot (.) and double dot (..) symbols with, 165-66
    finding out the current directory with, 164
CHKDSK command, 384
clock pulse, 36
clusters, 45-46
    orphaned, 384-85
    starting, 47
CMOS memory, 126
coated media, 13-15
coercivity of magnetic media, 13
COMMAND.COM, 209-10, 52, 155
command stacks, 156-57
compression, 254-57
    backups and, 312-13
    decompression and, 256
    file, 76
    hardware-based, 257
    techniques of, 254-55
    utility programs for, 255-57
CONFIG.SYS file, 209-10
    BUFFERS command in, 145-46
    creating, 144
    device drivers in, 147-48
    file control blocks (FCBs) in, 247
    FILES command in, 146-47
    installating new software and, 243
    interactive commands in, 148
configuration programs, 127
configuring the system, 125-27, 143-48. See also
    AUTOEXEC.BAT file; CONFIG.SYS file
contiguity, loss of, 263-64
control cable, 114, 115
control codes, 231
controllers (controller cards), 10, 34-43
    adding as third or fourth hard disk drive and, 121
    for Bernoulli Boxes, 86
    data compression built into, 257
    error correction and, 37-38
    with full-track buffers, 41-43
    inserting, 110-11
    interfaces for, 38-41
    RLL, 276
cooling fans, 92, 124
COPY command, backups with, 321-22
copying files, 175-83
    current directory and, 176-77
    to a directory above, 178-79
    in DOS Shell program, 181-82
    in DOS shells, 153
    drive specifiers and, 177
    to the parent directory, 178
    to a subdirectory at the same level, 179-80
    target directory and, 177

with utility programs, 180
    in Windows 3.0, 182-83
copy-protected software, 244-45
copy protection, backups and, 317
CORE disk performance test, 270-71
crashes, computer, power supply and, 122
crashes, head, 15-18
    designs resistent to, 17
credit card, payment by, 104
cross-linked files, 385-87
CSC, encoding and, 35-37
Ctrl-Break key combination, 235, 236
    disabling, 204
Ctrl-PrtSc (or Ctrl-P), 237
Curie Point, 60
cyclic redundancy code (CRC), 37
cylinder density, 20
    optimization of, 262-63, 270, 298, 300
cylinders, 19-20

D

data cable, 114, 115
data compression. See compression
data densities of high-capacity drives, 89
data transfer rate, 21-22
date of files, 47
DEBUG program, 100, 129
decompression, 256
dedicated servo surface (DSS), 28
defragmentation, 265-69, 298, 300
    software for, 265-68
    without utility software, 268-69
deleting
    directories, 247-48
    files. See recovery of erased files
density
    cylinder. See cylinder density
    of sectors, 18-19
DES (data encryption standard), 204
desktop publishing, 74
device drivers, 147-48
    in root directory, 210
    for tape drives, 346-47
Diagnostics Diskette, 127
DIR command, 224-28
    finding out the current directory with, 165
    scanning parallel subdirectories with, 226-27
    searching for files with, 189-90
    sorting directory listings with, 227-29
    switches for, 225-26
direct memory access (DMA), 10
    backups and, 309
    tape drives and, 347
directories, 46-50. See also directory trees; organizing a
hard disk
    attribute bytes in, 47-49
    changing, 165-67
    deleting, 247-48
    dot and double-dot entries in, 49
    erased files in, 49-50
    global (combined), 153
    size of files in, 47

sorting, 153
  disk optimization and, 294
starting cluster of files in, 47
time and date of files in, 47
directory trees, 149. *See also* DOS shells; organizing a
hard disk
  broad and shallow, 211-14
  diagrams of, 220-24
  DOS commands that temporarily modify, 172-75
    ASSIGN command, 172-73, 175
    JOIN command, 174-75
    SUBST command, 173-75
  in DOS shells, 151-52
  moving through, 162-71
    changing directories, 165-67
    copying files. *See* copying files
    DOS prompt display and, 162-64
    with keyboard macros, 169-71
    with menu programs. *See* menu programs
    moving files. *See* moving files
    simple menus for, 167-68
  optimization and reducing levels of, 294-95
  paths and, 158-61
disasters, recovering from, 359-98
  accidental reformatting, 374-79
    avoiding the problem, 374-75
    recovery approach, 376-79
    "snap shot" approach, 375-76
  damaged DOS structures, 379-83
    disk analysis software, 380
    disk editors, 380-82
    partition table, recovering the, 382-83
  equipment failures, 360-63
  guarding against disasters, 388-98
    location of the computer, 389-90
    power-line protection, 390-91
    repairs, 394-98
    sporadic failures, 394-97
    theft, 391
    vandalism, 392-94
  recovery of damaged files, 383-88
    cross-linked files, 385-87
    orphaned clusters, 384-85
    RECOVER program, 383-84
  recovery of erased files, 363-74
    automatic, 370-71
    in DOS 5.0, 372-74
    fragmentation and, 366-67
    how DOS erases files, 363-64
    manual, 367, 371-72
    unerase utilities, 369-74
    unerasing, 364-65
disk caching. *See* caching, disk
DISKCOPY command, 78
disk editors, 380-82
diskette drives
  as alternative storage technology, 55-56
  backups and, 79
  high-density, 56-57
  AT incompatibility problems, 79
  number needed, 78-79
  power failures and, 122
  for XTs, high-capacity, 79

diskettes
  as backup medium, 351
  crashes not a problem with, 56
  hard disks compared to, 8-9
  high-density and double-density, 13-14
  3 1/2-inch, 56
displays, bit-mapped, 74
DMA (direct memory access), 10
  backups and, 309
  tape drives and, 347
documentation, 127
  hard disk, 101
DOS, 11, 20
  cataloging files in, 237-39
  files in. *See* files
  optimization and, 286-98
    buffers, 287-90, 299, 301
    directory tree organization, 293, 299, 301
    disk caching, 289-93, 299, 301
    FASTOPEN command, 297-98, 300, 301
    file layout, 296, 300, 301
    PATH and APPEND commands, 296-97, 300, 301
    reducing levels of directory trees, 294-95
    sorting directories, 294
    subdirectory layout, 295-96, 299, 301
    subdirectory size, 294
  space requirements for, 72
DOS 5.0. *See also* DOS
  DIR command switches in, 225-26
  high-level formatting in, 142
  macros in, 170-71
  recovering the partition table in, 382-83
  searching for files in, 189-90
  unerasing files in, 372-74
DOS buffers, 10
DOS commands in DOS shells, 155
DOSKEY program, 157
  macros in, 170-71
DOS prompt display, 162-64
DOS Shell program, copying files in, 181-82
DOS Shell program (DOS 4.0 and later)
  file attributes in, 252-53
  mass file erasures in, 248
  moving files in, 186
  running programs in, 196
  searching for files in, 190
  sorting directory listings in, 228-29
  viewing files in, 232-33
DOS shells, 150-57
  backups in, 154
  capabilities of, 151
  choosing among, 157
  combined directories in, 153
  command stacks in, 156-57
  copying files in, 153
  copying files with, 180
  directory displays in, 152
  directory trees in, 151-52
  DOS access in, 155
  erasing files in, 155
  file searches in, 152
  memory requirements of, 155-56

moving files in, 154
passwords in, 203
printouts from, 153
reloader for, 156
running programs in, 195-98
sorting directories in, 153
tagging files in, 154
viewing and editing files in, 155
dot (.) and double dot (..) symbols, 49, 165-66
drive geometry. *See* geometry of the drive
drives, 7
drive select setting, 116
drive specifiers
copying files and, 177
in FDISK program, 137-38
low-level formatting and, 130
DV-I, 62
dynamic linking, 93
dynamic link libraries (DLLs), 93

E

edge connector, 114
encoding, controllers and, 35-37
encryption, 204-5
erased files, 49-50
recovering. *See* recovery of erased files
erasing files in DOS shells, 155
error checking
in backup software, 315-16
backup utilities and, 335
with COPY command, 322
error correction code (ECC), 37-38
error detection, 37
error messages, DOS, 359-60
ESDI drives and controllers, 34, 39, 300
cabling, 114, 115
.EXE files, 75
expanded memory, RAM disks in, 282-83, 285-86
extended boot record, 134
extended partition, 133, 136-37
external drives, 80

F

failures, drive, 94-97
fans, cooling, 92, 124
FASTOPEN command, 262, 297-98, 300, 301
FAT (file allocation table), 50-51, 291
size of, 50
structure of, 50
FDISK program, 54, 133, 135-40
creating a first partition with, 135-36
creating multiple extended partitions with, 136-37
deleting a partition with, 138-39
drive specifier in, 137-38
getting partition information in, 140
menus, 135
fields, 44
File Allocation Table (FAT), 50-51, 291
file attributes, setting, 251-53
file-by-file backups, 311-12
file-by-file restoration, 313-14

file compression, 76. *See* compression
file control blocks (FCBs), 45, 247
file handles, 45
File Manager (Microsoft Windows), 182-83
file names
coding, 238
subdirectory names should not be the same as, 216
file recovery. *See* recovery of erased files
files, 43-55
archiving, 240-42
attribute bytes of, 47-49
backing up. *See* Backups
cataloging, 237-39
clusters and, 45-46
copying, in DOS shells, 153
defragmentation of, 265-69, 298, 300
erased, 49-50
erasing, in DOS shells, 155
fragmentation of, 263-64
listing, with TREE command, 222-23
mass deletion of, 245-51
with advanced erasure utilities, 250
in DOS 4.0/5.0 Shell, 248
DOS safeguards against, 245
"junkyard" subdirectories, 250-51
typing errors and, 246-47
wildcards and, 245-46
in Windows 3.0, 249
moving, 183-88
batch file for, 184-86
in DOS 4.0/5.0 Shell, 154, 186
in Windows 3.0, 187
optimizing layout of, 296, 300, 301
recovery of erased files. *See* recovery of erased files
searching for, in DOS shells, 152
sequential and random access, 44
size of, 47
staring cluster of, 47
systems, 52
tagging, in DOS shells, 154
temporary
RAM disks for, 281
space requirements for, 73
time and date of, 47
viewing and editing, in DOS shells, 155, 229-33
FILES command, 146-47
file searches. *See* searching for files
FIND command, 192-93
finding files. *See* searching for files
Flash EEPROM, 63
flux changes, 12
FM encoding, 36
FORMAT command, 52, 141, 219-20, 379-42
formatting, 128-43
accidental reformatting. *See* disasters, recovering from, accidental reformatting
diskettes, 14
high-level, 52, 141-43
low-level, 13, 99, 128-33, 375
bad tracks and, 130-31
drive specifier and, 130
geometry of the drive and, 131
interleave and, 132

ROM code and, 129-30
 testing and, 133
 utility programs for, 99, 128-29
fragmentation, 263-64
 recovery of erased files and, 366-67
frequency modulation (FM) encoding, 36
full-track buffers, 41-43
future of technology, 64

G

geometries, disk, 33
geometries of drives, 125-26
geometry of the drive, low-level formatting and, 131
global directory, 153
graphics, digitized, 74-75
grounding cables, 118
guide rails, 113

H

Hardcard, 80
hard disks
 benefits of, 2
 diskettes compared to, 8-9
 early, 1
 future of technology, 64
hard errors, 17
hard-sectored disks, 18
head actuators. *See* actuators
head crashes, 15-18
heads. *See* read/write heads
heat load, 91-92
hidden attribute, 48
hidden files, DIR command for displaying, 225-26
high-capacity drives, 88-90, 100
 cost per megabyte, 88-89
 data densities of, 89
 manufacturers' performance claims for, 90
 1,024-track limit of, 89-90
 track densities of, 89
high-density diskette drives, 56-57
high-level formatting, 52, 141-43, 375
 cylinder 0 problem and, 143
 in DOS 5.0, 142
 volume label and, 143
host adapter, 35

I

IBMBIO.COM, 52
IBMCACHE program, 292
IBMDOS.COM, 52
IDE drives, 35, 40-41
 cabling, 118
image backups, 311, 313-14
IMAGE program (*The Norton Utilities*), 377
image restore, 313-14
indexing, searching for file contents by, 194-95
indicator lights, 81
installation of a hard disk, 107-28
 activity indicator, 117
 adding a second drive, 119-21, 130

adding a third hard drive, 121
 of Bernoulli Boxes, 87
 cabling IDE and SCSI drives, 118
 cabling MFM, RLL and ESDI drives, 114-18
 card drives, 81-82
 connecting the cables, 118
 drive select setting, 116
 external drives, 119
 grounding cables, 118
 inserting a drive, 109-13
  AT-style computers, 113
  bays and, 111-12
  disconnecting cables in back, 109-10
  inserting the controller card, 110-11
  PS/2 computers, 113
  removing the cover of the computer, 109-10
  XT-style computers, 112-13
 mopping up after, 127-28
 optimization and, 108
 power supplies and, 121-25
 power supply connections, 116
 reconfiguring the systemn and, 125-27
 self-reliance in, 107-8
 terminator resistor pack and, 118-20
 warranty violations and, 108
installation of power supplies, 123-24
installation of software, 242-45
Intel, 62
interfaces, 38-41
 device-level and system-level interfaces, 38
 ESDI, 39
 SCSI, 39-40
 ST506, 38-39
interleave, 21-24
 for Bernoulli Boxes, 87-88
 full-track buffers and, 41-42
 low-level formatting and, 132
 optimization of, 132, 271-75, 298, 300
 of preformatted drives, 99
 too-low, 271-72
IO.SYS, 52

J

JOIN command, 174-75

K

Kerr Effect, 60
keyboard macros, moving about directories with, 169-71
key disks, 175, 245

L

LASTDRIVE command, 286
latency, average, 29
line protectors, 390
loading programs. *See* running programs
locaation of the computer, 389-90
local area networks (LANs), backups and, 316-17
logical drives, 133
logical drive tables, 134

Lotus Magellan, 194
low-level formatting, 13, 99, 128-33, 375
    bad tracks and, 130-31
    drive specifier and, 130
    geometry of the drive and, 131
    interleave and, 132
    ROM code and, 129-30
    testing and, 133
    utility program for, 128-29

M

macros, moving about directories with, 169-71
magnetic domains, 12
magnetic media, 11, 13-14
    coated versus plated, 14-15
magneto-optical drives, 59, 61
mail-order vendors, 102-3
manufacturers of hard drives, 97
master boot record, 52-53
Mean Time Between Failure (MTBF), 95-96
media descriptor byte, 51
memory
    CMOS, 126
    DOS shells' requirements for, 155-56
    virtual, 76
memory-resident utilities, 75
    data compression, 254
menu programs, 199-205
    accessing commands in, 200-1
    advanced features of, 199-200
    crating menus in, 201
    limitations of, 201
    usage tracking with, 201-2
metacharacters, 194
MFM drives, 21
    cabling, 114, 115
MFM encoding, 36
MIRROR command, 372-73, 378-79, 382
MKDIR command, 49
modified frequency modulation (MFM) encoding, 36
motherboards, replacement of, 278
motor, 9
mounting rails, 98
MOVE command in DOS shells, 154
moving files, 183-88
    batch file for, 184-86
    in DOS 4.0/5.0 Shell, 186
    in Windows 3.0, 187
MS-DOS. *See* DOS
MSDOS.SYS, 52
MTBF (Mean Time Between Failure), 95-96
multitasking in Windows 3.0, 198

N

NeXT computers, 59
noise of hard drives, 96-97, 122-23
Norton Backup, The, 332-35
Norton Commander, The
    copying files and, 180-81
    running programs in, 195
    searching for files with, 191

Norton Disk Doctor, 380
Norton Utilities, The
    ASK program in, 168-69
    Calibrate program, 273-75
    disk caching program in, 293
    encryption program in, 205
    FI (File Info) program in, 239
    NCD (*Norton Change Directory*) program in, 166-67
    Safe Format program, 220
    searching for files with, 191, 194
    Speed Disk program, 266-67
    UnErase program, 370-72
    unformatting program, 377-78

O

opening a hard disk, 7-8
operating system, space requirements for, 72
optical disks, 58-62, 64. *See also* CD ROMs
optimization, 259-302
    choosing methods of, 298-302
        cost effectiveness, 300-1
        recommendations, 302
        tradeoffs, 298-300
    controller-level, 275-86
        data transfer rate, 276
        processor speed, 276-78, 299, 301
        RAM disks, 280-86, 299, 301
        track buffers, 278-79, 299, 301
    disk-level, 262-75
        average seek time, 269-71, 298, 300
        cylinder density, 262-63, 270, 298, 300
        fragmentation and defragmentation, 263-69, 298
        interleave setting, 271-75, 298, 300
    DOS-level, 286-98
        buffers, 287-90, 299, 301
        directory tree organization, 293, 299, 301
        disk caching, 289-93, 299, 301
        FASTOPEN command, 297-98, 300, 301
        file layout, 296, 300, 301
        PATH and APPEND commands, 296-97, 300, 301
        reducing levels of directory trees, 294-95
        sorting directories, 294
        subdirectory layout, 295-96, 299, 301
        subdirectory size, 294
    15 determinants of performance and, 260-62
    installing a drive yourself and, 108
organizing a hard disk, 207-57, 293, 299, 301
    directory trees, viewing and cataloging, 220-24
    managing disk space, 242-57
        data compression, 254-57
        file attributes, setting, 251-53
        installing new software, 242-45
        mass file deletions, 245-51
    rules for designing the directory tree, 209-20
        batch files, subdirectory for, 218
        broad and shallow directory tree, 211-14
        building as much of the tree as possible before transferring files, 214
        dangerous files, where to put, 219-20
        DOS files, subdirectory for, 217-18

file names should not be the same as
        subdirectory names, 216
    many small subdirectories, 215
    project-based organization, 212-14
    root directory reserved for subdirectory listings,
        209-10
    short directory names, 215-16
    transferring to disk only the program files you
        need, 218-19
    utility programs, subdirectory for, 216-17
    viewing and printing directory listings, 224-29
    viewing and printing files, 229-37
        with PRINT command, 234-37
        TYPE command, 230-33
orphaned clusters, 384-85
OS/2, 76
    average seek time and, 270
overheating, 124, 395
overlays, 281

P

parking, head, 30-33
partitioning, 52-55, 133-41. *See also* FDISK program
    32-megabyte limit, 54
    advanced schemes for, 55
    primary and extended partitions and, 133-34
    rationale for, 53-54
    utility programs for, 140-41
partitions, large, 100-1
partition table, 52
    recovering the, 382-83
passwords, 202-3
PATH command, 159-61
    optimizing, 396-97, 300
paths, 158
payment, 104-5
performance test, 270-71
perpendicular recording, 15
PKZIP program, 254
plated media, 13-15
plates, slot, 125
platters, 9
Plus Development Corporation, 80
port addresses, tape drives and, 347
power, insufficient, 395
power-line protection, 390-91
power requirements of card drives, 82-83
power supplies, 98-99
    cabling, 124
    choosing, 123
    connecting, 116
    installation of, 123-24
    insufficient, 122
    noisy, 122
    quality of, 123
    quiet, 123
    ratings of, 91
    replacing, 91, 121-25
    short circuits and, 123
    sporadic power failures and, 122
primary partition, 133, 135-36

PRINT command, 234-37
    /D switch, 235
printing directory tree listings, 223
processor, 10
processor speed
    backups and, 317
    increasing, 276-78, 299, 301
programs. *See* software; utility programs
PROMPT command, 162-64
PS/2 computers
    adding a sceond drive to, 121
    bays in, 112
    card drives for, 82
    inserting a drive in, 113
    low-level formatting program built in, 129

Q

QIC-40 standard, 340-41

R

RAMDISK program, 284-86
RAM disks, 62-63, 280-86, 299, 301
    drawbacks of, 282
    in expanded memory, 282-83, 285-86
    in extended memory, 282
    non-volatile, 280
    positioning, 284
    for program files, 281-82
    programs for setting up, 284-85
    for read-only files, 281
    for reference files, 281
    speed of, 280
    for temporary files, 281
    VDISK or RAMDISK programs for, 284-86
random access files, 44
read errors, recoverable and non-recoverable, 38
read-only attribute, 48
read/write heads, 8-10, 24-34
    actuators, 26-29
    bump detection, 29-30
    crashes, 15-18
    design of, 26
    gap in, 24-25
    parking, 30-33
    settling time of, 28-29
    write precompensation and, 25
reconfiguring the system, 125-27
records, 44
recovering from disasters. *See* disasters, recovering
    from
RECOVER program, 383-84
recovery of damaged files, 383-88
    cross-linked files, 385-87
    orphaned clusters, 384-85
    RECOVER program, 383-84
recovery of erased files, 363-74
    automatic, 370-71
    in DOS 5.0, 372-74
    fragmentation and, 366-67
    how DOS erases files, 363-64

manual, 367, 371-72
unerase utilities, 369-74
unerasing, 364-65
Reference Diskette, 127
reformatting accidental. *See* disasters, recovering from, accidental reformatting
removable hard disks, 85-86
repairs, 394-98
restocking fee, 105
RESTORE command, 329
dangers of, 329
restoring data, 313-14
retentivity of magnetic media, 13
ribbon cables, 98, 114
RLL controllers and drives, 276, 300
cabling, 114, 115, 118
RLL encoding, 36-37
RMA number (returned merchandise authorization), 105
RMDIR command, 248
ROM chip, formatting program on a, 129-30
root directory
device drivers and utility programs in, problems with, 210
reserved for subdirectory listings, 209-10
running programs, 195-98
in DOS 4.0/5.0 Shell, 196
utility programs for, 195-96
in Windows 3.0, 197-98

S

SCSI drives and controllers, 35, 39-40
cabling, 118
SCSI host adapter, 35, 40
Seagate Technologies, 38
searching for files, 188-95
by content, 191-95
advanced search utilities, 193-94
FIND command, 192-93
by indexing, 194-95
time needed for, 194
with DIR command, 224-25
directory tree structure and, 211
in DOS 4.0/5.0 Shell, 190
in DOS 5.0, 189-90
by name, 188-91
with utility programs, 191
in Windows 3.0, 191
sectors, 8, 18
bad, 16
density of, 18-19
numbering of, 33
size of, 19
tracks without, 43
sector translation, 34
security systems, 202-5
seek errors, 38
seek times
average, 28, 269-71, 298, 300
track-to-track, 29
sequential files, 44
servo data, 28

settling time, 28-29
SETUP program, 127
SHARE command, 136
shock rating, 96
short circuits, 123
sides in a drive, 33
16 byte architecture, 54
slot plates, 125
slots, 46
SMARTDRV.SYS program, 292-93
soft errors, 17-18
soft-sectored disks, 18
software
capacity requirements and, 74-76
proliferation of, 75
SORT.EXE, 228
sorting directories, 227-29
disk optimization and, 294
speed, 259-60. *See also* optimization
buying a hard disk and, 92-94
file compression and, 257
RAM disk, 280
Speed Disk program, 266-67
spindle, 9
sputtering, 14-15
ST506/412 standard, 38-39
standby power supply (SPS), 391
starting cluster, 47
startup current, 90
stepper-motor actuators, 26-28
straight-through cables, 116
streaming, 338-39
stretch-surface recording, 17
string compression, 255
subdirectories. *See also* directories; directory trees; organizing a hard disk
DIR command for displaying, 226
for DOS files, 217-18
DOS shells and, 152
fragmentation of, 264
"junkyard," 250-51
names of, 215-16
optimizing layout of, 295-96, 299, 301
optimizing size of, 294
project-based, 212-13
subdirectory attribute, 48-49
SUBST command, 173-75
surge protectors, 390
SYS command, 52
system attribute, 48
system files, 52
DIR command for displaying, 225-26
system library, 127
systems integrators, 103

T

tagging files
in DOS shells, 154
tape backups, 308, 337-49
buying a tape drive, 344-46
cartridges for, 348
cartridge types for, 340

file-by-file backups with, 343
formatting tapes for, 348
fundamentals of tape technology, 337-38
future of, 349
helical scan drives for, 341-42
ideal, 343-44
installation of a tape drive, 346-47
misconceptions about, 339
performance of tape drives, 342-43
QIC-40 standard, 340-41
streaming, 338-39
tape flaking and, 348-49
tape formats for, 338
tape standards for, 339-40
underruns, 339
technical support, 103-4
temporary files
    RAM disks for, 281
    space requirements for, 73
terminator resistor pack, 118-20
tests, disk performance, 270-71
theft, guarding against, 391
thin-film media, 15
time of files, 47
toolkits, 111
track buffers, 278-79, 299, 301
    full, 41-43
    media for, 350-51
track densities
    of high-capacity drives, 89
tracks, 8
    numbering of, 33
    without sectors, 43
track-to-track seek times, 29
TREE command, 221-24
Trojan horses, 392
TYPE command, 230-33
    control codes and, 231
    limitations of, 230-31

U

UNDELETE command, 373-74
unerase utilities, 369-74
unerasing deleted files, 364-65
UNFORMAT command, 142, 378-79
uninterrupted power supply (UPS), 391
usage tracking, 201-2
utility diskettes, 128, 239
utility programs, 75. *See also* DOS shells
    cataloging files with, 239
    for changing directories, 166-67
    compression, 255-57
    in root directory, 210
    for running programs, 195-96
    for searching files by content, 193-94
    setting file attributes with, 251-52
    for sorting directories, 294
    subdirectory for, 216-17
    for viewing files, 232

V

vaccine programs, 393-94
vandalism, 392-94
VDISK program, 284-86
vendors, choosing, 102-6
ventilation, 92, 124-25, 389, 395
viewing files, 229-33
    with DOS Shell program (DOS 4.0 and later),
        232-33
    with TYPE command, 230-33
    with utility programs, 232
    in Windows 3.0, 233
virtual disks. *See* RAM disks
virtual memory, 76, 93
viruses, 392-94
voice-coil actuators, 27-28
voltage regulators, 390
volume label, 143
volume label attribute, 48

W

warranties, 104-5
warranty violations, installing a drive and, 108
Winchester drives, 8
Windows 3.0, 76, 94
    copying files in, 182-83
    file attributes in, 253
    file deletions in, 249
    moving files in, 187
    running programs in, 197-98
    sorting directory listings in, 229
    viewing files in, 233
WORM drives, 58-60
worms, 392
write precompensation, 25, 126

X

XCOPY command, 184
    backups with, 323-26
XT-style computers
    adding a second drive to, 120
    inserting a drive in, 112-13
    power supplies of, 91

Z

zzq
    defragmentation fragmentation, 366-67
ZZQ
    repeated sentences, 98
zzq
    there is no info on printing directory listings,
        224-29
ZZQ
    /X switch to a BUFFERS command undocumented
        in DOS 5.0, 145